In Christ

E. Stanley Jones

ABINGDON
Nashville

IN CHRIST

A Festival Book

Festival edition published February 1980

ISBN 0-687-18786-9

Printed in the United States of America

IN CHRIST—THE GOSPEL ACCORDING TO PAUL

From the glory and the gladness,
    From His secret place;
From the rapture of His Presence
    From the radiance of His Face—

Christ, the Son of God hath sent me
    Through the midnight lands;
Mine the mighty ordination
    Of the pierced Hands.

Mine the message grand and glorious
    Strange unsealed surprise—
That the goal is God's Beloved,
    Christ in Paradise.

Hear me, weary men and women,
    Sinners dead in sin;
I am come from heaven to tell you
    Of the love within;

Not alone of God's great pathway
    Leading up to heaven;
Not alone how you may enter
    Stainless and forgiven—

Not alone of rest and gladness
    Tears and sighing fled—
Not alone of life eternal
    Breathed into the dead—

But I tell you I have seen Him,
    God's beloved Son,
From His lips have learnt the mystery:
    He and His are one.

There, as knit into the body
    Every joint and limb,
We, His ransomed, His beloved,
    We are one with Him.
All in marvelous completeness
    Added to the Lord,
There to be His crown of glory,
    His supreme reward.
Wondrous prize of our high calling!
    Speed we on to this,

Past the cities of the angels
  Farther into bliss;
    On into the depths eternal
  Of the love and song,
Where in God the Father's glory
  Christ has waited long;

There to find that none beside Him
  God's delight can be—
Not beside Him, Nay, but in Him,
  O beloved, are we.

—Lois Buck
(Daughter of a missionary to India)

INTRODUCTION

Fifty-two years ago I knelt before a chair with a letter spread out before me—a letter from a mission board secretary, asking me to go to India. I knew that the answering of that letter might determine my life work. So I prayed: "Dear Lord, I'm willing to go anywhere, do anything, and be anything You want me to be, provided You show me where." The Inner Voice replied, "It's India." I arose from my knees and repeated those words to myself, "It's India." It was settled. I was called to be a missionary. Fifty-one years later I knelt in that same room before a chair, probably not the same one, and thanked God with a deep heartfelt thanks for the unfolding purpose of these glorious years as a missionary. Success or failure mattered little—being true to that call was the only thing that mattered.

If I was called to be a missionary, I was pushed into being an author—it was a very gentle push, but a push nevertheless. Dr. Diffendorfer, secretary of the mission board, said to me, "Why don't you write down what you have been saying to the American people, before you return to India?" I replied, "Give me a month off and I'll do it." So during the month of May, 1925, I wrote *The Christ of the Indian Road*, gave it to the publishers with an apology (which they deleted), and went back to India. I was surprised to find I was an author, for I had no intention of becoming one. I was pushed into it. Since then it has been the same push or pull that has led me to write another book. Some need has tugged at my inmost being demanding to be met, and a book has resulted. This twenty-third book is the result of a feeling of a need. The need is this:

Some concept that would reduce the whole of life to the utmost simplicity. If you have that, you're "in"; if you don't have it, you're "out." By "in" I mean "in life," and by "out," "out of life." I felt I had found that concept in the phrase "in Christ." If you are "in Christ" you're "in life"; if you are "out of Christ" you're "out of life." If that proposition be true, then it cuts down through all veneer, all seeming, all make-believe, all marginalisms, all halfwayisms—through everything—and brings us to the ultimate essence of things: If you are "in Christ" you are in life; if you are "out of Christ" you're out of life, here and now, and hereafter.

Obviously, this concept goes deeper than being interested in religion, for you may be interested in religion and not be "in Christ." You may be in the church and not be "in Christ"; in orthodoxy, and not in Him; in the new birth and not "in Christ," for the new birth may be in the past and only faintly operative now; you may be in conversion and not "in Christ," for the conversion may have ceased to convert to Him.

The phrase "in Christ" is the ultimate phrase in the Christian faith, for it locates us in a Person—the Divine Person—and it locates us in Him here and now. It brings us to the ultimate relationship—"in." Obviously this "in" brings us nearer than "near Christ," "following Christ," "believing in Christ," or even "committed to Christ." You cannot go further or deeper than "in."

What would be involved in becoming "in Christ"? Some are "in self"—they are determined by self-interest primarily—it is the driving force of their lives. To get and to get on for self is the compelling motive. Some are "in the herd." Before they act, they look around—they don't act; they only react to what the herd does. The roots of their motives are in "What will people think?" Making self or the herd our God is sin, the chief sin.

To be "in Christ" means to pull up the roots of one's very life from the soil of sin and self and herd and plant them "in Christ." He becomes the source of our life, the source of our thinking, our feeling, our acting, our being.

This obviously involves self-surrender. Not merely the surrender of our sins, our bad habits, our wrong thinking, and our wrong motives, but of the very self behind all these. All of these are symptoms; the unsurrendered self is the disease. So the phrase "in Christ" is not only the ultimate concept, but it demands the ultimate act—self-surrender. The only thing we own is just ourselves. We don't own our money, our property, not even the house we live in, for we will leave it all behind. The only thing we will take out with us is just ourselves. It is the only thing we own. That one thing we own—the self—is deliberately handed back to the Giver in an act of supreme self-surrender with words something like these: "I can't handle this self of mine. Take me as I am and make me as I ought to be. I give myself and my sins and my problems to Thee; but myself first and foremost. I've been 'in myself'; now I am 'in Thee.' " We lose ourselves and to our astonishment find ourselves. We live when we live "in Him."

INTRODUCTION

One would expect that this ultimate concept in Christianity, "in Christ," leading to the ultimate human response, self-surrender, would be deeply embedded in the New Testament. Is it? It is far more deeply embedded in the New Testament than many things upon which we have built whole denominations—the new birth, conversion, baptism of the Holy Spirit, justification by faith, baptism by water, apostolic succession, presbyters, bishops, forms of church government, inner light, absence of forms.

The phrase "in Christ" or its equivalent is found 172 times in the New Testament. It is found in every book except the Synoptic Gospels (Matthew, Mark, Luke) and the Epistles of James, Jude, and II and III John. Why the phrase "in Christ" is not used in these places in the New Testament we shall take up later.

Paul, the greatest interpreter of Christianity, fastens upon the phrase "in Christ" and uses it in his epistles ninety-seven times—more than all the rest put together. With deep insight he saw that this was the ultimate phrase, dividing all humanity into two classes, "in Christ" and "out of Christ"; so that his world was not divided by B.C. and A.D., but into I.C. and O.C.—"In Christ," and "Outside Christ." Those "in Christ" have life, those "outside Christ" have death.

This is the ultimate division. Each person is placed, not arbitrarily, but by the facts, on one side or the other of that line—"in Christ" or "outside Christ." This is a division that divides—the only division that divides. It reduces life to simplicity. Every thought, every aspiration, every act, every reaction, all one's possessions, all one's relationships are either "in Christ" or "outside Christ." If they are "in Christ" they have eternal life; if "outside Christ" they have eternal death. This is the thesis of this book. To the exposition of this thesis we now turn.

Like all my books for the cultivation of the inner and outer life, this book is divided into readings of a page a day which will take approximately five minutes to read. This book can also be used by groups on a weekly study basis. At the same time it is a book that can be read straight through, for a single theme runs through the whole: What happens to life and living when you are "in Christ" and what happens when you are "out"?

INTRODUCTION

The angel said to the writer of the Book of Revelation: "Write what you see." This I have tried to do; I've written what I see in Scripture and what I see at work in life. They are the same.

A non-Christian chairman of one of my meetings in India commented at the close of my address: "If what the speaker has said isn't true, it doesn't matter; but if it is true, then nothing else matters." If the thesis of this book isn't true, then it doesn't matter—forget it; but if it is true, then nothing else matters—you can't forget it.

E. STANLEY JONES

CONTENTS

WHO IS THIS "CHRIST"?

This book is an invitation to live life in Christ as the only way to live. But before we issue that invitation and before the thoughtful reader can accept it, we must explore what we mean by "Christ." I came near saying "we must define," but to define is to confine, and when we are dealing with the Eternal God manifested in the flesh, which I conceive Him to be, we can only explore—our definitions are departure points, eternally open to eternal explanations.

We begin with Jesus, not with Christ, for you cannot say Christ until you have first said Jesus—the Incarnate One. For Jesus puts His own character content into Christ. The Jewish people had the idea of a conquering Christ, the Messiah, conquering by force. The "Amplified New Testament" when it uses the word "Christ" amplifies it into "Christ, the Messiah," but this isn't amplification—it is minification, for it puts Christ back into a Jewish messianic mold. That mold has been broken; it was too small.

Other molds have proved too small. One by one they have been broken. Christ, the Teacher, the Greatest of all Teachers? Yes, but more, for a teacher imparts knowledge—He imparts Life. The Greatest of Characters, the Best of Men, the Highest Example? Yes, but more, for we are not to imitate Him in life, we are to receive Him as Life. Someone pin-pointed in history, our Guide and Inspiration: Yes, and more, for we cannot live on a remembrance, we must live on a realization. A Martyr to the cause of the Kingdom of God? Yes, and more, for His death seems to have all the signs of a cosmic struggle with a cosmic result—the redemption of the race. Who then is He? He is the Word become flesh, God become man, the Eternal manifesting Himself in time, God simplified, God approachable, God lovable.

O Christ, while we cannot define Thee precisely, we can know Thee intimately. And to know Thee is to know Life, to know release and redemption. We thank Thee. Amen.

AFFIRMATION FOR THE DAY: *"This is eternal life, that they know thee, the only true God, and Jesus Christ whom thou hast sent."*

IS CHRIST COSMIC?

A refugee from North Korea to South Korea, an elder of the Presbyterian Church and an artist, has produced a very remarkable picture of Christ—remarkable in detail and conception. It has to be seen to be believed. In a space of three feet by four feet of canvas he has written by hand the whole of the New Testament in minute letters in English. There are approximately 185,000 words, with about a thousand words in a line. Out of these words arises the full length figure of Christ. The figure is produced by inking some words more heavily than the others. Out of the words arises the Word. Out of the gospels arises the Gospel. He Himself is the good news.

Around the figure of Christ are twenty-seven little angels, all looking toward Him, some with folded hands in adoration. These twenty-seven little angels represent the twenty-seven books of the New Testament. They are all looking at Him, bringing out the fact that the whole New Testament brings out the Person of Christ—it all· looks at Him, the Center.

This fits in with Paul's description of the Christian faith:

> Great indeed . . .is the mystery of our religion:
> He was manifested in the flesh,
> vindicated in the Spirit,
>   seen by angels,
> preached among the nations, believed on in the world,
>   taken up in glory. (I Tim. 3:16).

Note "our religion: He . . . ." One would have thought Paul would write "our religion: It . . . ." Our religion is not an "it"—a system of thought, worship, ritual, institutions—these are built up around the Person of Christ and may be more or less Christian. Our religion is "He." We may get caught in the system of thought, worship, ritual, and institutions and never get to a saving contact with the personal Christ. If so, we are this side of salvation. For salvation is in Christ, and not in the system built up around Him.

O Christ, we pant to get beyond forms to the Form, to go from the good to the Good. We who are personal cannot rest this side of the Personal. So take us by the hand and lead us to Thyself. Amen.

AFFIRMATION FOR THE DAY: *The words of Scripture take me beyond the words to the Word—the Word Made Flesh.*

"THE MYSTERY OF OUR RELIGION: HE"

We saw yesterday that a Korean, right out of paganism,
grasped with Paul the great "mystery of our religion: He"—a
vivid illustration of how our Christian faith is enriched by its
outreach.

Jesus emphasized His own centrality in Scripture: "You
search the scriptures, because you think that in them you have
eternal life; and it is they that bear witness to me" (John 5:39).
You think you find eternal life in the words, but out of the words
comes the Word—they "bear witness to me." Eternal life is in
Him. He points this out with "yet you refuse to come to me that
you may have life" (vs. 40). The business of the Scriptures is to
take us by the hand and take us beyond the words to the Word.
The Scriptures are not the revelation of God—that would be the
Word become printer's ink. The Scriptures are the inspired
record of the Revelation—the Revelation is seen in the face of
Jesus Christ, the Word become flesh. Every day I go to these
words and say to them: "Hast thou seen Him Whom my soul
loveth?" These words take me by the hand and lead me beyond
the words to Him Who is the Word.

The opening sentence of the book of Revelation says: "The
revelation of Jesus Christ, which God gave him" (1:1). This is
interesting and important. For in the rest of the Scriptures Jesus
is revealing God, showing us in concrete, human terms what
God is like: "He who has seen me has seen the Father." What a
revelation of God we find in Him! There can be nothing higher,
and there can be nothing other—this is it! Here, however, the
roles are reversed: God reveals Jesus! That is a fulfillment of the
law laid down by Jesus: "Whoever would save his life will lose it;
and whoever loses his life . . . he will save it." Jesus lost His life
in revealing the Father and found it again in the Father's
revealing Him. And the Father is revealing Jesus—He is
growing upon us, amazingly.

O Father, Thou art revealing Thy Son to us. He is growing
upon us so amazingly that we can scarcely keep up with Thy
revelation. He breaks out everywhere—from every bush,
every star, every happening—everywhere. Amen.

AFFIRMATION FOR THE DAY: *To see Jesus is to see what God and man
and life are like.*

IS CHRIST THE AUTHOR OF CREATION?

We saw yesterday that the revelation was reciprocal. Jesus reveals God, and God reveals Jesus. Jesus is growing upon the human race. He is proving to be so much greater than we thought. In that revelation "which God gave him" are the words saying that Jesus is the first and last—"the Alpha and the Omega." How first is that first, and how last is that last? Is He the "Alpha," the Christ of the beginning, and the "Omega," the Christ of the final word?

We see that that "beginning" stretches back further than we had thought—back beyond the historical account of two thousand years ago, back to creation, and beyond. Some strange passages like these take our breath: "All things were made through him [Christ], and without him was not anything made that was made" (John 1:3). And this: "but in these last days he has spoken to us by a Son, whom he appointed the heir of all things, through whom also he created the world" (Heb. 1:2). And this: "He is the image of the invisible God, the first-born of all creation; for in him all things were created in heaven and on earth, visible and invisible . . . all things were created through him and for him" (Col. 1:15-16). What do these passages, in which it is said unequivocably that God created the world through Christ, mean? The usual idea is that God created the world, and that Jesus appeared two thousand years ago to reveal God and to redeem us. Here it says that God created the world through Christ—without Him was nothing made that was made. Does this mean that the touch of Christ is upon all creation? That everything is made in its inner structure to work in His way? That if it works in His way it works well and harmoniously, and if it works some other way it works its own ruin? Is everything destined by its very nature to be in Him?

O Christ, we begin to see the revelation that God is making of Thee. We begin to see Thy footprints everywhere—in the Scriptures, in nature, in us. We are afire to see more, for what we see transforms. Amen.

AFFIRMATION FOR THE DAY: *If I am destined to be in Him, then I shall accept that destiny and work it out.*

THE CHRISTIAN WAY IS THE WAY

We ended yesterday with the question: "Is everything destined by its very nature to be in Him? Is everything made "by Him and for. Him"? Is that destiny written not in the inscrutable will of God, but written into our nerves, our tissues, our blood, our organs, our very souls, our relationships? Are we destined, by our make-up, to be Christian, to be in Him? Is He the "ground" of our being, the homeland of our souls? When we find Him, do we find ourselves? When we lose Him, do we lose ourselves?

These questions, boiled down to one—Is He our life?—are the most important questions, barring none, that can be asked of life and destiny. If they can be answered in the affirmative, then it is all over but the shouting. You cannot live against life and get away with it. Life will have the last word, regardless of whoever has the first or the intermediate words. You cannot buck the nature of the universe and not get hurt, for "the stars in their courses will fight against Sisera."

It was this interpretation which I presented in my book *The Way*. If I had one thing and only one thing to leave as a life contribution, I would unhesitatingly choose this: The Christian way is the Way, and that Way is written not merely in the Bible, but into the structure of reality—in us and in our relationships.

The fact is that the Christian way is called "The Way": "Saul . . . if he found any belonging to the Way . . ." (Acts 9:1-2); "but when some were stubborn and disbelieved, speaking evil of the Way . . ." (19:9); "About that time there arose no little stir concerning the Way . . ." (19:23). The Christian way is the Way—the Way to do everything; not merely "the way of salvation," but "the Way," full stop.

O my Father, we are beginning to see the wonder of the Way. As it dawns upon us, may we decide to be on the Way with both feet and with the consent of all our beings. If this is true, then nothing else matters. Amen.

AFFIRMATION FOR THE DAY: *I shall be upon the Way with both feet and full consent.*

THE DEMANDS OF HUMAN NATURE
AND THE CHRISTIAN OFFER

We saw yesterday that the Christian way is the Way—the way to do everything—to think, to act, to feel, to be in every single situation. This is for God and man and for man in his individual and social attitudes, acts, and relationships. There are just two things in life—the Way and not-the-Way. If God should act against the Way He wouldn't be God; He would be something less and something other. And if man acts against the Way he is something less than man and something other.

Are these statements of an over-enthusiastic Christian propagandist or simply an interpretation of what life itself says? Is life rendering a verdict, and is that verdict a Christian verdict? For over half a century I have lived amid world currents of thought and life in East and West, and the deepest conviction of my life is that the Christian way is proving itself to be the Way. I watch with breathless interest the unfolding of a drama on the stage of the world, and that drama has one theme: By putting the Christian way under the test of life to see which way life approves, the Christian way is turning out to be the Way. No more important statement has come from psychiatry than the statement of M. Boss, head of the International Analytical Association and professor of psychotherapy in the University of Zurich, when I asked him, "You seem to have put your Christian faith and your psychiatry together; how did you do it?" He replied, "When I began my work as a psychiatrist I had difficulty, for I began as a Freudian, but the demands of human nature drove me back to the Christian position." What human nature demanded for its fulfillment, the Christian faith offered. Suppose the basic demands of human nature and the Christian faith were at cross purposes. Then we would be in trouble—deep trouble, life trouble.

O Father God, by trial and error we are coming out to the way to live, and that way is turning out to be the Way—the Way revealed in Thy Son. We are not in trouble—we are in triumph. We sing with quiet hallelujahs. Amen.

AFFIRMATION FOR THE DAY: *If I take any way except the Way, it will turn out to be a dead end.*

THE FACE EMERGING FROM THE FACTS?

We saw that the figure of Christ in the Korean picture arose out of the pages of the New Testament—the words revealed the Word, the Word made flesh. He is the pivot around which the whole New Testament revolves. Must we now go further, is life compelling us to say that that same Figure arises out of the facts of life, apart from the New Testament? Does life reveal Life? Just as the watermark in paper is not stamped on but is wrought into the texture of the paper, a part of it, is the name of Jesus not stamped on us by human propaganda, but wrought within us by divine purpose? Are our faith and our fate the same? Is this Scripture true: "whom . . . he also predestined to be conformed to the image of his Son"? (Rom. 8:29). Are we predestined to be conformed to the image of His Son? And is that predestination not something imposed on life, but rather something that is being exposed out of life itself? Is a Face emerging out of the facts of life, and is that Face the "one Dear Face, that far from vanishing, rather grows and becomes my universe that feels and knows"?

A Freudian psychiatrist was driven to that conclusion, and the same thing happened to a Hindu philosopher: "My study of history shows me that there is a moral pivot in the world and the best life of both East and West is more and more revolving around that moral pivot. That moral pivot is the person of Jesus Christ."

"History is turning out to be His-story." Where men and nations depart from Him they decay. When they obey Him they develop. Whether or not we agree with the first part of the statement of Henry Higgins Lane, professor of zoology at the University of Kansas, we must agree with the second, "Evolution is God's method of operation in the realm of nature; Christianity is God's plan of operation in the spiritual world." That "One Dear Face" is beginning to emerge from the scientifically sifted facts of nature.

O God, we are like little children going to school, beginning to spell out by slow processes a name written into the nature of things, and that name is turning out to be "J-e-s-u-s." To that name every knee shall bow. Amen.

AFFIRMATION FOR THE DAY:
> *"Jesus! the Name that charms our fears,*
> *That bids our sorrows cease."*

GRAVEN ON HIS HANDS?

We saw last week that being in Christ is bigger than we supposed. Instead of being within the sphere of influence of a historical figure, who faintly and indirectly operate on us as any other historical figure, perhaps a little more vividly and vitally, we are beginning to see that to be in Him is to be in ultimate reality. To be in Him is to have the roots of our being in reality. To be in Him is to have the sum total of reality behind us, sustaining us and giving us cosmic backing.

Isaiah 49:16 says: "Behold, I have graven you on the palms of my hands." We are not chalked on God's hands, nor painted on; we are graven. If we were chalked or painted on His hands, He could wash His hands of us. If we are graven on His hands, however, as a sculptor engraves a name in granite, then we are literally on His hands forever. The name of Jesus is not chalked or painted on the facts of history or nature; it is graven—ineffaceably graven into the nature of reality. As one writer puts it: "The Name of Jesus is not written on history—it is plowed into it."

To be in Christ is to live life according to the grain of the universe, not against it. In the San Francisco airport is this sign: "As you slide down the banister of life, may all the splinters be turned the other way." Well, if you slide down the banister of life without Christ, then all the splinters are turned the wrong way. You get hurt. You cannot revolt against Him without revolting against yourself. "He who spits against the wind spits in his own face." We often think that the alternative is: To be His, or to be my own? If you are not His, however, you are not your own. If you lose Life, you lose life. You are like the child who beats his head against the wall to punish his mother—and finds it is a losing game.

To be in Christ is to be in life, to be out of Christ is to be out of life. He is Life. All else is anti-life.

O Jesus Christ, I see that to choose Thee is to choose life, to refuse Thee is to refuse life. So I choose Thee, not with a portion of my being but with all there is of me—now and forever. I am committed. Amen.

AFFIRMATION FOR THE DAY: *If I want to live, this is the Way. I can live some other way and get hurt.*

"THAT WHICH HAS BEEN MADE WAS LIFE IN HIM"

We are beginning to see that to be in Him is to be in something. That something is turning out to be Something, and the Something is turning out to be Everything.

The writer of the Fourth Gospel put it: "In him was life, and the life was the light of men" (John 1:4). In him was life—outside Him was not-life, decay, death. Is that a religious platitude, or is it just plain fact? The plain fact is that all life is a commentary on it. Life works that way. In Him life experiences Life, out of Him life experiences death.

The marginal reading of the above verse is even more striking: "That which has been made was life in him." "That which has been made"—all created things, man and material, when put into Him by decision and dedication become life in Him. Existence turns to life when it is put into Him by surrender. If you put yourself, your talents, your time, and your material goods into Him by dedication, then immediately they become alive—so alive that they become life itself. I have seen dead personalities turn into living personalities the moment they are put in Him. They glow, they shine, they scintillate—they exude life. Vice versa, I have seen radiant persons in Him step out of Him and in a moment they were rotting persons—decay had set in. Any talent that isn't used for Him is "buried in the earth" and begins to decay.

I spoke to a group of young people who were volunteering for service abroad. They were radiant, but one girl was miserable. She confessed her dilemma: "How can I sacrifice my music to serve people abroad?" Like the rich young ruler, she went away sorrowful. She had already sacrificed her music—the music within her had died. When she took her talent and herself out of Him and put them into herself, immediately both the self and the talent died. She became a discord trying to be musical. That which had been made became death out of Him.

O Christ, Thou art life and if I turn my back on Thee I turn my back on life. I embrace pleasure and find pain. I grasp the lurid colors of the sunset and instead I grasp the dark. Give me sense—just plain sense. Amen.

AFFIRMATION FOR THE DAY: *To live in Christ is just plain sense. To try to live some other way is plain nonsense.*

IN AND OUT OF CHRIST—TWO WORLDS

We saw yesterday that in and out of Christ represent two worlds—the world of heaven and the world of hell, the world of creation and the world of decay, the world of life and the world of death.

Take, for example, the disciples: As long as they stayed in Christ, obeyed His will, caught His ways, and showed His spirit they were happy, constructive, and creative. The moment they stepped out of Him even in thought and attitude they became unhappy, destructive, and noncreative. They departed from His spirit and began to quarrel over first places—immediately they were unhappy, destructive, and fruitless. They forbade other disciples to cast out demons because "they followed not us," and immediately faces, life, and work were clouded. They asked for permission to call down fire from heaven to consume Samaritans, and lo, relationships with themselves and others were as black as midnight. Later other disciples preached the gospel of love and redemption to those same Samaritans and lo, "there was much joy in that city."

Peter, walking with Jesus and catching His spirit, was an exuberant, creative man; but Peter, succumbing to the hard pressure, denied he had ever known Him. Result? "He went out and wept bitterly." Judas was the trusted treasurer of the most significant movement of the world, but Judas stepping out of that trust into treachery "went and hanged himself." A prominent pastor of a great city church was creative, helping innumerable people into new life through his preaching and especially his personal counseling. He stepped out of that great church, turned his back on his lovely wife and children, and disappeared with a young woman. He reappeared months later as a seller of cemetery lots in a distant city. When his landlady unlocked his apartment in his absence she found nine empty vodka bottles. In Christ he was constructive and creative; out of Christ, selling cemetery lots (suggestive!) and taking refuge from himself in vodka!

O God, our Father, we cannot break Thy laws without breaking the laws of our own being. We cannot go away from Thee without going away from ourselves. Help us this day to come back to Thee and ourselves. Amen.

AFFIRMATION FOR THE DAY: *If I run away from God I run away from all that is in God and am left with all that is in myself—emptiness.*

THE CENTER IS SELF, THE MARGIN IS DISORDER

Everything which is transferred from the kingdom of self to the kingdom of God has life in it—eternal life. It has security in it—eternal security. Everything transferred from the kingdom of God to the kingdom of self has death in it—eternal death.

Yesterday we saw a pastor dramatically step from life to death, but here is a pastor's wife who, though less dramatically, just as certainly stepped from life to death by stepping out of Christ into herself. She pulled me aside into the pastor's study and said: "Most of my life I've tried to charm people myself. I've been the center of all I've done. Now everyone has found me out. Everything has tumbled around me. Even my little boy has found me out, and I've lost my influence with him." Her self taken out of Christ and made the center became insecure—automatically.

This losing of God and self amid religious surroundings is depicted:

Cry aloud, spare not
....
declare to my people their transgression
....
Yet they seek me daily,
   and delight to know my ways,
....
   they delight to draw near to God.
"Why have we fasted, and thou seest it not?
   Why have we humbled ourselves, and thou takest no knowledge of
   it?"
Behold, in the day of your fast you seek your own pleasure
   and oppress all your workers.
Behold, you fast only to quarrel and fight. (Isa. 58:1-4)

Here a very religious people had inwardly stepped out of God into themselves—"You seek your own pleasure." Therefore the heavens were brass, and religion turned into a vast futility. The futility turned to fight. Out of sorts with God, they became out of sorts with themselves and others—"You fast only to quarrel and fight." The center was self and the circumference disorder.

O Blessed Father, life is very hard and very easy—hard if we step out of Thee and easy if we stay with Thee. "The way of the transgressor is hard"—on him and on others. Amen.

AFFIRMATION FOR THE DAY: *His yoke is easy and His burden is light, for they fit me as a glove fits the hand.*

WHO ALONE HAS IMMORTALITY?

We are considering the passage: "That which has been made was life in Him"—the created thing has only existence until it is placed in Christ by surrender. Then it has life, eternal life.

This is far-reaching in its consequences. All coming to Jesus has the feeling of a home-coming upon it. All going away from Him has the sense of sadness upon it; sadness, for the life forces out of Him begin to decay and crumble. We say of a man who steps out of Christ, "That man is going to pieces." He literally is going to pieces. Life has no inner cement to hold it together, so he is disintegrating. Suppose this process of disintegration continued beyond the borders of this life as we seek it taking place here, would the personality finally snuff itself out, be unfit to survive? John 3:16 says: "God so loved the world that he gave his only Son that whoever believes in him should not perish but have eternal life." Do those who continuously and persistently live outside of, apart from, and against Life "perish"? Do they "perish" by their own attitudes and actions?

In I Timothy we read of "the blessed and only Sovereign, the King of kings and Lord of lords, who alone has immortality" (6:15-16). Does Jesus Christ alone have immortality? It says so. Then do we have immortality only as we surrender our mortal selves and become in Him, who alone has immortality? The Scriptures and the processes of decay when we are out of Him both say yes.

Would grace follow that man through this life and beyond the borders of this life, and if he finally rejected that grace and the light flickered and went out, would there be a teardrop on the cheek of grace and a sigh: "You would not"? That would fit into the character of God as seen in the face of Jesus, and it would fit into the observed processes taking place now. Apart from Him life disintegrates, and if kept up long enough, would "perish."

O God, Thy grace is following us, following us, wooing us to Life. Help us yield to that blessed wooing and embrace Life, for suppose we live and miss Life? Then it is better that we should not have been born. Help us. Amen.

AFFIRMATION FOR THE DAY: *It would be better I had not been born, if I am not reborn.*

LIFE AND LIFE ABUNDANTLY

We have looked at the tragic results of being out of Christ, and now we will turn to the triumphant results of being "in Christ." There are both sides, and if we listen only to one side we become half persons, listening only to the half facts. In Europe the joyous smaller bells ring out the quarter hours while the deep-toned solemn bells sound out the hours. Life holds both the joyous silver bells and the deep-toned serious and solemn bells. In Jesus the joyous predominate—the solemn are an undertone, the joyous, the overtone. The Christian faith proclaims life—only its absence is death. "I have come that you might have life and have it more abundantly."

Life is ours the very moment our life is put by surrender in Christ. The moment the little boy transferred the ownership of the five loaves and two fishes from himself to Jesus, those loaves and fishes were under the law of multiplication—under the law of life. Anything in his hands has life. It has security for time and eternity. The business of a silk manufacturer was ruined by the coming in of rayon and nylon. When I saw him he was running the elevator in a Y.M.C.A., and doing it joyously, a happy, integrated man. He had given a pipe organ worth fifty thousand dollars to his church. It was the only thing he saved—the thing he gave! He delighted to go to the church and play the organ, and he delighted to run the elevator. Out of the wreck of outer fortune he saved two things: his soul and his organ. He gave them both to Christ, and then they were secure—eternally secure. I touched that man for just a few moments at the close of a meeting, but his victory has become a part of my victory. He had life, and he passed it on to me. He wiped his hands on his apron, for he had been on kitchen duty when I saw him, but when I took his hand, I knew that I held the hand of a real king—the greatest of them all.

O Father God, I know one bank that will not break—the bank of Thy hands. I can never become bankrupt when I and my possessions are there. I am grateful that they are there. Now there is no fear. Amen.

AFFIRMATION FOR THE DAY: *I am in Jesus, therefore the joyous will be the overtone, the solemn, the undertone.*

ONE RELATED—ANOTHER UNRELATED

Yesterday we saw the triumph of the silk manufacturer. He triumphed because he was in Christ. Here is a similar story with a different ending because this man is out of Christ. In Osaka, Japan, a wealthy man gave a check to build a new city hall. The next day the stock market broke, and he was left penniless. Friends urged that he call back the gift. "No," he replied, "since a promise is made it must be kept." Then he went out and shot himself. The endings of these two men were different because their beginnings were different. One began from the basis of being in Christ and worked out from that to victory—every real thing intact. The other began from the basis of a stoical self—"a promise must be kept"—noble, but this side of life, hence he went down in death.

The leading Christian layman of India holds the finance portfolio of the Railway Board, which manages all the railways of India. His elder brother brought him to one of my meetings in Madras in 1924, where he was converted. "As I sat in the tram car going home Christ sat beside me and I knew we belonged to each other." From that moment he knew he was in Christ. Working out from that basis his life has been a continuing miracle. He will probably take over the Sat Tal Ashram if and when I should drop out. If I had combed India I could not have found a better man. His brother, who insisted on his going to that decisive meeting, is a very brilliant professor doing research in "pure mathematics." When I asked him what "pure mathematics" meant he replied: "Mathematics unrelated to anything." He has spent his life researching in pure, unrelated abstractions. His life has become as empty as his research; he is a half-man, touching nothing and nobody. He is in himself. His brother, starting with being in Christ, is alive to his fingertips and touching all India. Both equally able, with equal opportunities, but one is fruitful, the other futile.

O Jesus, my Lord, if I withhold from Thee I withhold from me. If I withhold I impoverish myself—and others. I would give to Thee with both hands my all. It is little, but thou hast it. I am at peace. Amen.

AFFIRMATION FOR THE DAY: *If my life and possessions are related to the Eternal they will be eternal.*

THE CRUCIFIED REFLECTED ON THE WALL

We have begun to see that being in Christ is being in reality. When you put yourself in Him by surrender and trust and obedience you do not put yourself into a segment of life—an isolated movement going back to Jesus of Nazareth. You put yourself into Life itself; for He is the outcropping of that which is underlying the universe, underlying reality.

We were shown in Japan a mirror which had been used in the days when Christians were persecuted in Japan, when it was death to be a Christian. When we let the sunlight fall on this mirror the reflection upon the ceiling was Jesus hanging on the cross in a circle of light, very distinct and plain. The people sat and worshiped in their houses with the crucifix before them. If anyone not known to be a Christian came in the mirror was quietly taken out of the sun's rays and the Crucifix disappeared.

We were also shown a crucifix which had been used by the government in those days of persecution. It was placed on the ground, and everybody had to tread on the face of the Crucified. The non-Christians did not hesitate to tread on His face; the real Christians refused and were killed. The face of Jesus was worn down and marred by people's treading on it.

Through the ages the face of Jesus has been trodden on by persecution, by neglect, by the misrepresentation of His own followers, by hate and rejection—trodden on till "His face is mared more than any man." Yet the light of God falls on the facts of life like the sun upon that mirror, and before our astonished gaze the Crucified is before us upon the walls of destiny. The discoveries of science, the uncovering of the nature and needs of man through psychology—the sheer needs of life fall upon the mirror of nature, and the Crucified is upon the walls of this and every age.

O Jesus, it was said of Thee, "He could not be hid." Again Thou canst not be hid. Thou art shining forth from the depths of life, for Thou art Life. Help me this day to open my life to Life. Amen.

AFFIRMATION FOR THE DAY: *I will see the cross in everything I see today, for it is there—an open secret.*

THE INESCAPABLE CHRIST

We saw yesterday that Jesus was coming back again—coming back out of sheer necessity. I stood in the Mosque of Saint Sophia in Constantinople, formerly a Christian cathedral. All the Christian symbols had been wiped out and replaced by verses from the Koran. As I stood at the back and looked at the dome over what had been the Christian altar, I held my breath. There was the figure of the ascending Christ plainly seen coming back through the daubs of the centuries. They couldn't wipe Him out. That is true everywhere. Sheer necessity cries out for Him.

He shines through the prejudices and the philosophical thinking of India. In an extreme nationalist paper of India this appeared: "Calvary, where another great man of the East suffered martyrdom for the sins of the world, has today its counterpart in Yervada [the jail where Gandhi was kept] where our Mahatma suffers martyrdom for the thraldom of the world. Just as Calvary stood for the world's sinners, so Yervada stands for the world's downtrodden." A Hindu chairman said, "The problems of the day arise through the lack of the Spirit of Jesus in the affairs of men." A Japanese Cabinet Minister said: "How can you account for the immense increase of labor unrest since the war? It is Christianity at work among the people; the working man is testing Christ's preaching of larger life and freedom." An outstanding philosopher of India said: "We had high ideas of God before Jesus came. But Jesus is the highest expression of God we have seen. He is conquering us through the sheer force of His own person against our wills." Another Hindu, speaking on "The Inescapable Christ," said: "We have not been able to escape Him. There was a time when our hearts were bitter and sore against Him, but He is melting them by His sheer winsomeness. Jesus is slowly but surely entering all men in India—yea, all men." The light of God is falling on the mirror of our needs, and the Crucified is encircled before us.

O Jesus, Thou art the inescapable. Thou art conquering us, and we want to be conquered, for when we are conquered by Thee we are free. Then our hearts are open to Thy conquest—freedom. Take us, make us. Amen.

AFFIRMATION FOR THE DAY: *If I escape Him I escape from salvation.*

"THIS IS MY MEAT AND DRINK"

A Hindu sadhu, "a holy man," pulled out a New Testament from his saffron robe and said, "This is my meat and drink."

Is humanity more and more pulling from the folds of its heart the New Testament out of sheer necessity? Are our deep down needs taking us by the hand and leading us to Him? Yes, increasingly so.

> Jesus shut within a Book
> Is hardly worth a passing look;
> Jesus shut within a creed
> Is a fruitless Lord indeed.
> But Jesus in the hearts of men
> Shows His tenderness again.
> —Gordon Grooms

"Jesus in the hearts of men?" Yes, He is there in need—increasingly there as the fulfillment of a need. What is man's greatest need? I have one unhesitating answer: Redemption!

This verse in Romans, the beginning letter of Paul, expresses that need: "They are justified by his grace as a gift, through the redemption which is in Christ Jesus" (3:24). "Redemption which is in Christ Jesus." "What is redemption?" asked a modern girl wistfully. Literally it means "to buy back"—picture a man, woman, or child about to be sold into slavery; then someone comes along, pays the ransom price, and sets the slave free. Someone objects that the situation of the slave market is gone, therefore the idea of redemption is gone with it. Is it? Outer slaveries are going, but inner slaveries are increasing. We speak of being "tied up," "tied in knots," "all balled up," "mixed up," "confused"—revealing a bondage, an inner slavery far worse than the outer slavery ever was or could be. An outer slave could be free inwardly—he could escape within—but one who is in bondage within has no escape. To try to escape into the without only increases his inner tangles. He is caught. He needs redemption. And Jesus is the only open door.

O Jesus, my Lord, wilt Thou redeem me from my bondage? It is my deepest need. Without that central, inner freedom, I'm in bondage to everything—myself, my surroundings, my life. Free me. Amen.

AFFIRMATION FOR THE DAY: *I am a ransomed sinner—let every moment show my gratitude.*

THE DOOR?

Yesterday we dealt with our need of redemption. By "our" was meant not some men, but all men, with no exception anywhere. We ended by saying that Jesus is the only open door. Are both of those statements harsh and dogmatic, or do the facts say the same thing?

Jesus seemed dogmatic and exclusive in these words—words that made me wince, until I saw He spoke the naked truth: "Truly, truly, I say to you, he who does not enter the sheepfold by the door but climbs in by another way, that man is a thief and a robber. . . .I am the door; if any one enters by me, he will be saved, and will go in and out and find pasture" (John 10:1, 9).

"Climbs in by another way" depicts man trying to climb into the fold "by another way." That is the attempt to be saved by your own effort, by your own climbing—it is self-salvation. As I have said elsewhere, there are only two ways to try to find God. One is to try to find God by climbing the ladder rung by rung, to be able to meet God at the topmost rung of worthiness. You do this by your good deeds, by your disciplines, by your meditations, by attendance to duty. This is the egocentric attempt at salvation. The other way is God-centric salvation, where God comes down the ladder to us by Incarnation and meets us, not at the topmost rung of the ladder of worthiness, but at the bottom-most rung as sinners. "I came not to call the righteous, but sinners," said Jesus. At the bottom-most rung we are humble enough to receive salvation as the gift of God. We do not attain salvation—the ego-centric attempt; we obtain salvation—the God-centric offer. To climb up another way is to reject God's coming to us in favor of our coming to God. In other words, we make ourselves God and thus become thieves and robbers—robbing from God and ourselves.

O God, we reject Thy redemption of us in favor of our redemption of ourselves, and we end not in salvation, but in futile, tense striving, increasing the bondage we are supposed to cure. Forgive us. Amen.

AFFIRMATION FOR THE DAY: *Self-redemption is self-deception—God alone can redeem.*

"THE TWILIGHT OF THE GURUS"

Yesterday we said that to try to climb up some other way into salvation was to become a thief and a robber—robbing God and ourselves, and others of what we might have been. Those who attempt to climb up some other way never arrive. They strive but do not arrive. They are wistful, but never become witnesses.

"But," objects someone, "you come from India, the land of realization of God. What about those who have come up 'some other way'? Haven't they 'realized'?" Well, they may be there, but traveling over India for over half a century, I haven't found them. I've invited them to my Round Table Conferences, the finest and best. They are always on the way—I never have seen one who had arrived. One such holy man, famed for his "realization," said to a friend when asked whether he had realized himself as God, replied, "No, I'm a sinner." Another who has disciples all over the world to whom he sends touched-up photographs of himself with halos around his head is in fact a chair-ridden semi-invalid. He has a ceremony of washing his feet in milk, which his disciples drink in a sort of communion. A friend who has stayed in his Ashram and who is very sympathetic said: "He knows and I know he is a fraud. But I love him." When I held a Round Table Conference among them at his Ashram they revealed by their statements that they were all on the way—none had arrived. This sympathetic friend, having visited all the famous Ashrams of India with a Hindu doctor, came back to our Ashram at Sat Tal and said: "It's the twilight of the Gurus. They have let their devotees down. They haven't got what it takes." The other way, in East and West, is turning out to be the way to emptiness and futility. There is a door out of emptiness and futility, and that door is Jesus—the only Door I know.

O Jesus, my Lord, in Thee I see the open door to the Father, to my redemption from sin and evil, and the door into my highest realization of Life. I fly to that door with open arms. Receive me. Amen.

AFFIRMATION FOR THE DAY: *Soul of mine, there is no other way—it is this or nothing.*

ARE THOSE OUTSIDE LOST?

We are considering the open door—into salvation, into life. If Jesus is the Door, and the only door, what about those who died before Jesus came and those who lived after He came, but never have heard of Him—are they lost? I am grateful I do not have to decide that matter, for only God our Father is good enough and wise enough to decide it. It is my business to preach the gospel and leave judgment to God.

The Scriptures do give us guidance here, however. Paul says that those who have lived under the law will be judged by the law; those who have lived apart from the law have the law written within them—in their consciences, in their higher ideals—and they will be judged by the light they have had. Each will be judged according to his light. Now it says of Jesus: "The true light that enlightens every man was coming into the world"—the ex-carnate light of Christ is the light in conscience and in higher ideals in every man. If men live according to their light, then they have been unconsciously living according to "the light which lighteth every man coming into the world"—the light of Christ. If they have, they will be saved by Christ whether they knew Him or not. You and I have the light of Christ, and the bigger question is whether we will be saved, for of him to whom much has been given much will be required.

If the Scriptures say that Jesus is the Door, what does life say? The same thing? Yes. The only alternative for the modern man is Christ or nothing. There seem to be no other alternatives. Life eliminates the alternatives, and we are being more and more shut up to Him. If He isn't the Way there is no way. "Believe It or Not" had the picture of a stone stairway into a house. At the head of the stairway was a blank stone wall. It led nowhere. Life without Christ leads to a blank stone wall—leads nowhere.

O Jesus Christ, when I put my finger upon the latch by faith and surrender, the Door opens—opens to everything. I know You are the Open Door into redemption, freedom, everything. I am entering. Amen.

AFFIRMATION FOR THE DAY: *Listen my soul: Every road leading away from Jesus is a dead end road.*

"GOD WILL 'BOP' ME"

The fundamental and decisive difference that makes Jesus the door is in this statement of fact: "I lay down my life for the sheep." The cross makes the difference. Trying to get to God and salvation by self-striving presumes that the door to God is open from the side of man. The fact is that it isn't. It is shut by the fact of our sin—every man's sin. "For all have sinned and come short of the glory of God." The door is not open from our side at all. It is open only from God's side.

It is only open from His side provided He makes atonement for our sins by "bearing in His own body our sins upon a tree"—by becoming "sin for us."

A man in India had a dream in which Kali, a Hindu goddess, said to him, "Unless you sacrifice your son to me I'll destroy your whole family." He did just that and was brought up before an Indian court for murder. He was given two years, a light sentence, for he did it for religious motives. Kali demanded blood from her devotees. Those who try to win favor with God by offering their good deeds or by their devotions and sacrifices are worshiping a refined version of Kali as God. "I'd better go to church, or God will bop me," said a young man and said it seriously, offering churchgoing as a sacrifice to God. God demands atonement.

In Jesus God is offering atonement, not demanding it. "I lay down my life—I don't demand yours." The door is opened from God's side, not ours. A nail-pierced hand opens it. We are saved by God's grace, not by our good works. A Hindu said: "The difference between Christianity and Hinduism is this: We have to climb the ladder of austerity to get to Brahma. He doesn't lift his finger to help us. In Christianity God comes to the bottom-most rung at cost, the cost of a cross, to help us to the topmost rung. The difference is decisive." It is.

My Father, I can love and give myself absolutely to a God like Thee. Thou hast given Thy heart, so I give mine. Thou didst give all, so I give all. And now Thy "all" is open to my taking. I do take. Amen.

AFFIRMATION FOR THE DAY: *I do not advance toward God—I advance in willingness—willingness to accept His advance.*

SALVATION THROUGH CHRIST OR IN CHRIST?

We are considering the verse: "I am the door; if any one enters by me, he will be saved, and will go in and out and find pasture."

Through Jesus the Door we get into Him—He is the door to Himself. That raises the question, Is salvation through Jesus or in Jesus? The usual answer is through Jesus. If the "through" doesn't lead to the "in," however, it stops this side of salvation, for salvation is in Jesus. The "through" opens the possibility of salvation, but the "in" gives the actuality of salvation.

This is the central weakness of organized Christianity—it preaches salvation through Christ, but not salvation in Christ. The churches are filled with people who believe they are saved through Christ. That salvation is looked for in heaven—they will be saved in heaven through Christ. The salvation is in the past—through the cross, and it will be realized in the future in heaven. The present is but faintly redeemed, or not at all. Salvation is not now in Christ. It is in the past as a potentiality, or it is in the future as an actuality. But salvation that is not present is not salvation—it is only a hope. If you ask the average church member if he is saved he will probably answer, "I hope so." He is depending on salvation through Christ and not on salvation in Christ.

The Cross is the Door through which we can enter into Christ. Surrender and faith are the responses through which we do actually enter and become in Christ. Only when we are actually in Christ are we saved. He saves those whom He has.

O Jesus, my Lord, if Thou dost save only those whom Thou hast, it is of supreme importance that Thou shouldst have me—the whole me, for if I leave anything outside Thee it is outside salvation. Thou hast me. Amen.

AFFIRMATION FOR THE DAY: *Salvation through Christ is outside me, salvation in Christ is inside me.*

"LIVING ON THE MENU INSTEAD OF THE MEAT"

Yesterday we saw that salvation is in Christ and not merely through Christ. Someone asked a theologian when he was saved, and he replied: "At Calvary." This is a half-truth. Potentially he was saved at Calvary; actually he was saved if and when he surrendered to Jesus and by faith accepted that redemption which was purchased for him at Calvary, and thus became in Christ. If he stopped this side of being in Christ he stopped this side of salvation.

Jesus said to His disciples, "Receive the Holy Spirit." The Holy Spirit was theirs potentially, but actually the Holy Spirit was not theirs until by surrender and faith they received the Holy Spirit at Pentecost, when "they were all filled with the Holy Spirit." Potentiality had become possession. Without that possession they would have lived on a promise, and it is possible to have a promise in your hand and be empty. "The house of Jacob shall possess their own possessions." It is possible to have possessions as a possibility, but the possessions are only possessions when you possess them.

The lepers who at the word of Jesus were told to go show themselves to the priest to get a certificate of health started with health as a potentiality. "As they went they were healed." On the way the potentiality became possession. They were in health only when they were healed.

The dimness, the faintness, the dullness, the uncertainty of modern churchmen comes from believing in a salvation that is through Christ and not in Christ. They are living on the menu instead of the meat.

O Jesus, Thou art my home. I cannot live on the promise of a home—I must live in a home. I cannot live on a heaven hereafter, I must live in heaven now. I must have heaven as a state, if I'm to have heaven as a place. I have Thee—my heaven. Amen.

AFFIRMATION FOR THE DAY: *The menu is what I read, the meat is what I receive. I'm on the receiving end.*

IN CHRIST THERE IS FREEDOM "INDEED"?

This being in Christ seems to some to be in bondage—you are not in yourself, and you are not in the world if you are in Christ. This is our basic fear—the fear of losing our freedom. Surrender means a surrender of our freedom.

I spoke to a very influential group in Washington, made up of diplomats, several generals, and the Secretary of Defense. I spoke on surrender as the key to the Christian faith. The Secretary for Defense arose at the close and said: "I appreciated everything the speaker said, but I inwardly balked at that word 'surrender.' I deal with a group of people among whom the word would not be very popular or acceptable." I assured him that we surrender to God, but we don't surrender to anything else. Low at His feet we stand straight before everything else. Moreover, His will is our freedom. Bound to Him we walk the earth free. When we are most His, we are most our own. "That changes the picture," he replied thoughtfully.

Many in our churches have a wrong mental picture of what surrender to Christ means. A psychiatrist, brought up in a strait-laced missionary home where pigtails and long black stockings were signs of conformity and piety, reacted against it and was afraid of the power of Christ in a mental institution where people were in desperate bondage to themselves. She confused being in Christ with being in a system. Jesus was crucified because He wouldn't conform to a system. He said, "If the Son makes you free, you will be free indeed." In Christ there is freedom "indeed."

O my Lord and Savior, Thou dost bind me to Thy heart and set me free at the same moment—free to love, to live, to grow, to enjoy with joy unspeakable and full of glory. I open my arms to Thy bondage, for my heart wants freedom. Amen.

AFFIRMATION FOR THE DAY: *If I don't surrender to God I will surrender to things.*

THE NEED TO BELONG

In the passage we have been considering there is the sentence: "I am the door, if any one enters by me, he will be saved, and will go in and out and find pasture."

Four things are there: "enters by me"—a sense of belonging; "will go in"—will find security; "and out"—adventure; "and find pasture"—satisfaction. Four things are promised: belonging, security, adventure, and satisfaction. Basically we need those four things.

Psychologists say that all human nature has three basic needs: the need to belong; the need for significance; and the need for reasonable security. Here Jesus added a fourth—the need for satisfaction. We shall make our own four needs.

The first need is the need to belong. The delinquent child turns delinquent because he has no sense of belonging. Ninety-five per cent of delinquent children come from broken homes—they don't belong. The central sickness of the world is that

> your iniquities have made a separation
>   between you and your God,
> and your sins have hid his face from you.
> (Isa. 59:2)

The sickness of the world is homesickness—homesickness for God. There is a sense of orphanage, of estrangement, of being lost.

That first need is met when you are in Christ—you belong. You belong not to the marginal or ephemeral, but to reality—ultimate reality.

The second need is security—"will go in." You have the security of a fold—in Christ—of which almighty love is the keeper. Compared to this all other securities are insecure. This is "a kingdom that cannot be shaken"—the Unshakable Kingdom.

Dear Father, in the fold of Thy Son we belong and are secure. We are in, and the "in" has ultimate meaning. The security has ultimate security. We are now at home. Fears and tensions drop away. Finding Thee we have found all. Amen.

AFFIRMATION FOR THE DAY: *My business is to belong to Christ.*

SECURITY AND ADVENTURE

We saw yesterday that the four basic needs of all human nature, as amended, are the need to belong, to have security, to have adventure, to have satisfaction. We have looked at two; we must now look at the other two.

We looked at security. Ask the man feverishly piling up money at any cost why he is doing it and he will reply, "I want security, for myself and my loved ones." Strangely enough the head-hunters of Borneo say the same thing in answer to the question, "Why do you hunt heads?" The reply: "for security." The spirit of the man whose head is severed enters the skull of the dead man and becomes the servant of the man who conquered him. The more heads one has the more security one has. I stood under a cluster of twenty-one dried-skulls and preached the gospel to the head-hunters. The security of securities—of the Western man and of spirits in skulls—is vulnerable. But in Jesus security is secure—eternally.

He "will go in"—to find security, "and out"—to find adventure. It is not enough to be secure; we can be so secure that life turns dull and tame and full of boredom. We need adventure as well as security. Being in Christ provides for both—provides for security and adventure—"in" and "out." Does the Christian faith provide for adventure? It does—and how! To be a Christian is the most adventuresome thing in the world. You are exploring life—yes, Life. The limits of exploring the physical universe are fixed, but the limits of exploring Life are unfixed; they are limitless. In Jesus there is a surprise around every corner. Life is popping with novelty.

O Jesus, Thou art alive and Thou art making me alive—alive to beauty, to laughter, to wonders within and without. I rejoice with joy unspeakable and full of glory. I am free to live, free to enjoy, free to adventure. I thank Thee. Amen.

AFFIRMATION FOR THE DAY: *Christ is my adventure—I'm exploring the eternal in Him.*

"IT'S EMPTY"

We are considering security and adventure. Some have security and no adventure. I saw a couple on board ship who simply lived from meal to meal, their faces bovine. They were retired on plenty—and nothing. They sat in the living room staring. Finally the man got up, went to the mantle, lifted a vase, came back, and reported to his wife, "It's empty." It was momentous news—an empty vase! The couple were more empty than the vase. They had security with boredom—no adventure. They had expanding girths and narrowing horizons.

On the other hand, many have adventure and no security. They are always adventuring into adventure, but they have no base for inner security. In climbing Everest the climbers had to establish a base of supplies to which they could return after an adventure. Without the "base" they would have perished.

In Jesus we have both security and adventure. We go in and are secure. If the earth should drop from beneath us we would still be secure with a habitation of God, eternal in the heavens. Because we go in, we can go out—go out into adventure. With our base established and firm, we are no longer afraid of this thing called life. "He who would love life"—some fear life, some distrust life, some retreat out of life, some hate life—and some love it! In Christ we love life because we love Life. We can say to death: "O death, where is thy sting?" We can also say to life: "O life, where is thy sting?" Its very stings become our stimulus—they push us forward into the arms of Life. It's fun to be a Christian—and to me it's getting funnier all the time!

O Jesus, Thou dost redeem us from boredom and staleness and ennui. Thou dost put a tingle in our blood and dost make our brain cells dance to the rhythm of things. We bless Thee for life, and for life more abundant. Amen.

AFFIRMATION FOR THE DAY: *With one point of the compass on Jesus, I let the other point sweep as far as it will—into truth and adventure.*

WE FIND SATISFACTION

We are studying security and adventure. They are the alternate beats of the Christian heart. Without security, adventure is precarious—often fatal; without adventure, security is poverty-stricken, often fatal. With both, life is alive—gloriously so.

There is another element which if absent makes security and adventure both precarious—satisfaction. They "will go in and out and find pasture"—find satisfaction. If our security doesn't feed us—meet our deepest needs; and if our adventure doesn't feed us—meet our deepest needs, then we decay, perish from inner malnutrition. That is the trouble with mere money security—it leaves us with outer security, but with a sense of inner insecurity, of emptiness. Adventure without inner security is an adventure in futility. Halford Luccock tells of a grandchild on a merry-go-round who begged for another go at it each time it came to a standstill. When the grandfather's patience and money were exhausted the child got off reluctantly and said with a sigh, "I'd like to live on a merry-go-round all the time." But with all the going, the child got nowhere; he went round in circles.

I sat in a railway station at dawn and overheard a group of young married people who apparently had been "living it up" the night before. Their tempers were on edge and one woman said bitterly to her husband, "I've had enough of this." They had adventure, but when they returned to their base of life it was nothing but bitterness and disillusionment.

In Jesus we find pasture—our basic needs are satisfied.

O Jesus, my Redeemer, Thou dost redeem us from our illusions. In Thee there are no kickbacks, no hang-overs. There is more solid joy in Thee to the square inch than to the square mile outside of Thee. Am I grateful? Read my heart. Amen.

AFFIRMATION FOR THE DAY: *Life for me is not going around in circles—it is driving toward goals.*

"INTO THE HANDS OF OUR INIQUITIES"

We are considering the "in Christ" passages in Romans. We have seen that there is redemption in Christ. He buys us back from sin and death and redeems us to life and adventure. This verse vividly depicts what happens: "For the wages of sin is death, but the free gift of God is eternal life in Christ Jesus our Lord" (Rom. 6:23).

"For the wages of sin is death"—God doesn't give you "death"—sin itself gives you death. The payoff is in the person. The young man who said he had better go to church or God would "bop" him was wrong. If he didn't go to church he would "bop" himself—he would decay, inevitably. The wages of sin *is* death—not will be hereafter, but *is* death here and now. Just as when the spirit of a man leaves his body decay sets in at once, so when Jesus, Who is life, is absent from the person, decay sets in at once. Death takes over.

Isaiah, with deep penetration, saw this:

> for Thou hast hid Thy face from us,
> and hast delivered us into the hand of our iniquities.
> (64:7)

We would have thought he would have said, "into the hand of our enemies," but no, he saw that "into the hands of our iniquities" was the real punishment. I said in a high school address: "The Hindus have a saying: 'As a calf will find its mother among a thousand cows so your sins will find you out among a thousand rebirths.' The Christian Scripture expresses the same idea: 'Be sure your sins will find you out.' You are not punished so much for your sin as you are punished by your sin. Sin and its punishment are the same."

O God, our Father, we do not break Thy laws, we break ourselves upon them. They break us. The payoff is in us. It is our "wages," what we earn when we serve sin. Dear God, redeem us from ourselves, for we are our chief punishment. Amen.

AFFIRMATION FOR THE DAY: *I do not ask for exemption from the operation of God's laws, for if I do, I ask for exemption from salvation.*

"THE FREE GIFT OF GOD"

We saw yesterday: "For the wages of sin is death, but the free gift of God is eternal life in Christ Jesus our Lord." We saw that "the wages of sin is death"—not will be death when we die—the second death—but it is death now—death to the real person, death to his person and his possibilities, death to all God's plans for him, death to the inheritance of good he might have passed on to others, death to his influence—it is death here and now. On the other side, however, "the free gift of God is eternal life in Christ Jesus our Lord." Note that it is *in* Christ Jesus and not merely through Him. If it is merely through Him then it is in Him, not in me. If it is in Christ Jesus, then if I put myself in Him, by surrender and faith, it is in me, for I am in Him.

Note again "the free gift of God is eternal life"—not will be after death but is now. Those who are in Christ have eternal life, here and now, for in Him there is nothing but eternal life. The moment I put myself into Him I *have* eternal life whether I feel like it or not. Just as when two people stand up and pledge themselves to each other in marriage and are pronounced man and wife, then all the privileges and responsibilities are theirs the moment they put themselves in the marriage relationship, whether or not they feel like it.

You don't have to be good enough or worthy of eternal life. It is the free gift of God. But it is not a free gift of God apart from being in Christ Jesus. The moment you are in Him you are worthy, for you are in worthiness. The soiled clothes might say, "I'm not worthy to be put into those suds—I'm unclean." But being in the suds is the cleanness, is the worthiness.

O blessed Redeemer, Thou art my goodness, my worthiness, my all. In Thee I have Perfect Everything. Thy free gift creates the free-gift spirit in me. Take my all as my free gift—and all I expect to be. In Thy name. Amen.

AFFIRMATION FOR THE DAY: *The free gift of God will invoke within me a free response—the response of my all.*

"CONSIDER YOURSELVES DEAD TO SIN"

We turn to another "in Christ" passage in Romans: "So you also must consider yourselves dead to sin and alive to God in Christ Jesus" (6:11).

We take another step, "consider yourselves dead to sin." This is a breathtaking step. Is that all we do—"consider ourselves dead to sin"? Does it mean a mere change of mind—"consider"?

Whole systems of thought and philosophy are built up on this assumption: Change your mind, "consider," and it is done. "As [a man] thinketh in his heart, so is he" is the golden text of modern thought movements. These thought movements are a reaction against the negative thinking of much that passes as Christianity. As such these movements redress and balance. They are a redress, not a remedy. They are a shot in the arm and give you a momentary lift, but they are not a remedy for the deep-down disease. One of the adherents to a thought movement listened to our Morning of the Open Heart in one of our Ashrams as people told their needs. She sent up a note: "We shouldn't be blaming ourselves for all our faults. We should think positively." She squirmed at the diagnosis and wanted to pass over our needs to an affirmation of wholeness. She wanted to take immediate refuge in sentimentalism instead of in salvation. An M.A. in psychology took refuge in one of these thought movements: "At first for a few days I rode on air. They told me to say, 'I am perfect,' and I did and for a few days I felt so. Then the realities closed in. I wasn't perfect, nor were they. It was all a verbalism. Sadly I had to give up this unreality." What was the matter with all this?

O Jesus Christ, my Lord and Savior, save me from mental short cuts that leave me in the quagmire of disillusionment. I want something that lifts me up and keeps me up. I want Thee and only Thee, for Thou art life and only life. Amen.

AFFIRMATION FOR THE DAY: *I will not affirm my affirmities—I affirm His. Then and then only am I safe.*

SEEKING OUR PERFECTION

We ended yesterday with the question, "What was the matter with all this?" Why do these thought movements lift people up and then let them down? The answer is simple: When you say, "I am perfect" you are in yourself—I am perfect. It makes you the center of your salvation, makes you, to all intents and purposes, God. It is self-salvation by self-assertion: "I am perfect." Anything that leaves you at the center is off-center. The universe won't back our being God, so the facts close in and disillusionment results.

The "consider" passage is quite different: "So you also must consider yourselves dead to sin and alive to God in Christ Jesus." Note the "in Christ Jesus"—not in yourself, but in Him. When you are in Christ Jesus by surrender, faith, and obedience, then you have a right to consider yourself dead to sin and alive to God. You actually are as long as you stay in Christ Jesus. The moment you step out of Him into yourself and begin to assert your perfection, then you are not perfect, for any self that is centered in itself, however religious that self may be, is an inherently imperfect self by its very self-preoccupation.

Being in Christ, the Perfect One, however, you partake of His perfection by association, by assimilation. You are dead to sin to the degree you are alive to God. That is the positive element—alive to God. As long as I am alive to God—alive to His suggestions, His urges, His leadings, His love—I am by that very expulsive fact dead to sin. The higher expels the lower. I don't fight sin. I expel it by preoccupation with the Higher. Looking at Him I am spoiled for anything else.

O God, the God I see in the face of Jesus Christ my Lord, I look to Thee and I am forever dissatisfied with anything other than Thee. Sin loses its charm, and its beauty is only ugliness. It is so simple—and so profound. I thank Thee. Amen.

AFFIRMATION FOR THE DAY: *I am dead to sin when I am alive to Him.*

"NOW NO CONDEMNATION"

We now go on to a very important verse—a pivotal verse in victorious living: "There is therefore now no condemnation for those who are in Christ Jesus" (Rom. 8:1).

Perhaps the most important thing that can happen to a human being is to have the sense of condemnation lifted from the inner life. As long as a sense of condemnation rests upon the soul the shadow of that condemnation darkens the whole of life. To tell a man to buck up and be happy while this condemnation is there is like telling him to be joyous while a cancer is eating at his vitals. The lifting of that condemnation is the greatest contribution of the Christian faith.

This lifting of the condemnation is not a legal lifting—you stand robed in the imputed righteousness of Jesus. That would be verbal, not vital. The condemnation as condemnation must go. A half-protruding cannon ball is still embedded in the stone wall of a church in Bergen, Norway, a relic of the Napoleonic War of 1812. Many have the ball of condemnation still stuck in their souls, reminding of guilt and sin. A Japanese pastor told me that before he was converted he used to go out at daybreak and stand on a castle wall on a hill, the highest point he could find, and call to God, before anyone else got His ear, and cry for pardon and reconciliation. That lone figure calling for pardon and reconciliation is man. A young Dutchman came to India seeking inner peace. He sat for fifteen days and nights on the top of a mountain, fasting, looking at the peaks opposite with eternal snows upon them. He vaguely hoped that in his meditation the white purity of those virgin snows would enter into him and release him from condemnation. But nature worship left him as cold as those snows. He had a New Testament with him, and when he opened it after the fast he saw, "There is therefore now no condemnation for those who are in Christ Jesus."

O Jesus, I open this book and I see from its pages Thy face. Thy face shows forgiveness in Thine eyes. I read it there, and I rejoice with freedom and release. Now my happy heart sings its way down the waiting years. I am grateful. Amen.

AFFIRMATION FOR THE DAY: *Since He accepts me, I can and do accept myself. My self-rejection is gone—gone in His acceptance of me.*

"CONVERTED AND NOTHING HAPPENED"

The Dutch youth mentioned yesterday had sought for God through Indian philosophy and its assertion of our oneness, amounting to identity, with Brahma and through meditation on nature. Both came to zero, however, but he looked into the face of Jesus, and it came out yes!

Back of the huge figure of Buddha at Nara, Japan, stand two figures, the recording secretaries of the universe. One records what he sees and the other records what he hears. Nothing escapes them, and it is all written down against us. There is no forgiveness; everything has to be paid for to the last jot and tittle. No voice can or does come such as, "There is therefore now no condemnation for those who are in Buddha." In Jesus and only in Jesus does that voice come. It comes, not by doing penance nor by priestly absolution, which have no power to lift the condemnation. A convert from Protestantism to Roman Catholicism heard of "Mary's" going about and witnessing to her conversion, and she said in surprise, "Why I have been converted and nothing happened." No, for she went from a system to a system, but didn't get to the Savior.

This story is beautiful. A little boy stole five dollars from his father, and his conscience troubled him so he made up his mind to tell him, but he was afraid. When he finally did tell him, the father was furious at first. Then he softened and took the boy up in his lap and told of his stealing thirteen dozen eggs from his mother and selling them. The little boy put his arms around his father's neck and said, "Dad, we are partners together, aren't we? We are both thieves." A beautiful story, but this side of the necessities. They were partners in condemnation. They needed to be partners in forgiveness—forgiveness for each other and from God.

This forgiveness is not achieved; it is received. It is the gift of God.

O Divine Redeemer, only Thy divine voice can reach to the depths of my need and lift the burden of guilt and condemnation. "Who but God can forgive sins?" asked the bystanders. Yes, who? But Thou art God—God intimate, approachable, lovable. I come to Thee. Amen.

AFFIRMATION FOR THE DAY: *Formerly partner with all men in condemnation, I am now a partner with Him in reconciliation.*

"STANDING IN THE SMILE OF GOD"

We are considering how condemnation is lifted. Admiral Sato commanded the Japanese submarine fleet at Pearl Harbor. He told me that he really believed that the Emperor was divine and ardently indoctrinated the cadets in this belief. I asked him what happened to him when the emperor announced that he was not divine? His reply was: "My world turned upside down. I had been 'purged' by the Occupation, my rank as admiral taken away, my income cut off, and I was forced to work on a farm to gain a livelihood though I was not used to such work. And now my faith was gone. I felt stripped of everything—orphaned, estranged, alone. I thought of suicide. I became bad-tempered, lashing out at everybody and everything. A church member asked me why I was so bad tempered, why I didn't come to church and find a faith? I replied, 'I have no time for such things.' " Then he saw the Christian faith at work in a peasant family, bringing peace and joy amid poverty. He broke down and wept at the sight of it. He was led to peace by this verse: "He makes his sun rise on the evil and on the good." "Well," he said to himself, "I can't get in as 'good' but I can get in as 'evil.' " And he did. He was baptized at Easter—befitting, for it was the resurrection of dead hopes, a dead soul. I asked him whether that vacuum within had been filled? He smiled and put up his three fingers: "Jesus is Lord," our salutation in many parts of the world.

Nothing could have brought him out of that despair and gloom except the lifting of that dead weight of inner condemnation by reconciliation with God—nothing, absolutely nothing.

A banker's little boy stood by his desk. The little fellow was standing in a shaft of light falling on the floor, and he said, "Daddy, I'm standing in the smile of God." The banker said wistfully, "I wish I could stand in the smile of God." We all wish just that!

O Jesus, Thou art God's smile. And when we stand in Thee we stand in God's smile. Some still feel they are standing in God's frown. Help us to move over from frown to smile. Help us to do it now. It is Thy invitation to the evil and the good. Amen.

AFFIRMATION FOR THE DAY: *Out of Him my world is upside down, in Him it is right side up.*

JOYLESS SINNING

If "there is . . . now no condemnation for those who are in Christ Jesus," why do so many inside the church still go around bowed under inner condemnation?

For one reason, it is taught in some Christian circles that to acknowledge this inner condemnation is a sign of Christian humility. One leading churchman said, "The people outside the churches are unforgiven sinners and the people inside are forgiven sinners." Then they are both sinners and, as such, under condemnation. That kind of Christianity fits this description: "Just enough religion, not to keep one from sinning, but enough to take the joy out of it." So the ordinary church member goes on with joyless sinning. He calls it humility, but it is really a humiliation of the Redeemer, for if He doesn't save us from sin He doesn't save us from anything—including hell, for sin is hell begun.

In the communion ritual of The Methodist Church, after the prayers of confession and acceptance of forgiveness, and the partaking of the communion, there is this prayer, "God have mercy on us, Christ have mercy on us, Christ have mercy on us." As if nothing had happened! We go away still crying for mercy, our piety a guilt-ridden piety. Where is the note of the authentic evangelical movement?

> Long my imprisoned spirit lay,
>   Fast bound in sin and nature's night;
> Thine eye diffused a quickening ray,
>   I woke, the dungeon flamed with light:
> My chains fell off, my heart was free,
> I rose, went forth, and followed Thee.
>
> No condemnation now I dread.

A layman in Norway, a follower of the gloriously converted layman, Haug, was turned away on a rainy night from a farmhouse. As he went away he said, "It's wonderful to have the peace of God in the heart at this time of night." The farmer couldn't sleep, got up, ran after him, brought him back, and was converted.

O God, a guilt-ridden piety has no power to convert others. Give us the authentic note of "there is now no condemnation," and help us to shout it from the housetops. Amen.

AFFIRMATION FOR THE DAY: *There is therefore no condemnation in me for I am in Him.*

"A NEW CREMATION?"

Before we leave "There is . . . now no condemnation" we must note the emphasis on "for those who are in Christ Jesus." The reason we are still under inner condemnation is that we stop this side of "in Christ Jesus." We get as far as "in a belief," "in a church," "in His service," "in the ministry"—but not "in Christ Jesus." We hope to get to "in Christ Jesus" someday. This verse says there is *now*—it is in the here and now. But we have lived so long in nonexpectancy of deliverance from condemnation that we have taken for granted that this is all there is. A Negro guitarist in Atlanta sang rather pathetically, "Been down so long that 'down' don't bother me." Defeat is our climate.

I listened to someone quote, "If any man be in Christ he is a new creation," and I thought he said, "a new cremation." Well, this is not so bad. There must be a cremation of the old idea of the acceptance of condemnation as the normal Christian attitude. Out of the ashes of the cremation of that old idea will come a new creation. "When the burnt offering began the song of the Lord began." Joy will come out of the death of that idea and attitude. Someone has described Christian joy as the flag raised over the castle when the king is in residence. The heart will sing, and sing only when Christ the King is in residence.

What about those who have no king in residence—man himself is king. How do they put back the song into the songless heart? They are driven to a strange and desperate attempt—an attempt to get rid of condemnation by saying there is nothing about which to be condemned. There is no sin; sin is an outworn conception; and hence there is no condemnation. You are saved by denial.

O Christ, my Redeemer, they try to pull the rug out from under thee as Savior by denying that there is anything to be saved from. I can hear Thee say again, "Father forgive them; for they know not what they do." They really don't know. Amen.

AFFIRMATION FOR THE DAY: *The King is in residence—my flag is up and I sing within the Castle of my heart.*

"INSIGHT THERAPY—TO NO AVAIL"

We finished yesterday in calling attention to those who try to get rid of condemnation by saying there is no guilt, hence no condemnation.

Before seven thousand members of the American Psychological Association in a recent meeting, Albert Ellis said: "No human being should be blamed for anything he does. Therapists must rid their patients of every vestige of their blaming themselves, others, or fate, or the universe. . . . The more sinful and guilty a person tends to feel the less chance there is that he will be a happy, healthy, or law-abiding citizen." If there is no God and no moral universe, then there is no alternative except this one of trying to wipe out condemnation by trying to wipe out guilt.

That method is a dead failure—as psychiatrists themselves witness more and more. In that same Conference O. Hobart Mowrer, psychologist of the University of Illinois, said:

Our mental hospitals are full of patients who have had insight therapy—to no avail. . . . I see no alternative but to turn again to the old, painful but also promising possibility that man is pre-eminently a social being, or in theological phrase, a child of God. Future treatment of the emotionally ill will, like Alcoholics Anonymous, take guilt, confession, and expiation seriously and will invoke programs of action rather than mere gropings for insight.

That is the turning point of the road of psychology from futility to fruitfulness. It is a turning back to the Christian faith which teaches forgiveness and the wiping out of condemnation from the conscious and the subconscious. Without that cleansing of the subconscious this verse is descriptive:

> The wicked are like the tossing sea;
> for it cannot rest,
> and its waters toss up mire and dirt. (Isa. 57:20)

O Jesus, without Thy forgiveness and the wiping out of condemnation, our subconscious tosses up mire and dirt. We are filled with nameless dreads. But if Thou, the Son, dost make us free, then we are free indeed. I thank Thee. Amen.

AFFIRMATION FOR THE DAY: *"Who forgiveth all the iniquities, who healeth all thy diseases"—forgiveness and healing are intertwined.*

GODS BEING REPAIRED

We have been thinking of how to get rid of inner condemnation. A Harvard professor said that mankind is looking for two things—a song to sing and a creed to believe. The two cannot be separated. The song cannot be sung unless you have an adequate creed, and by adequate creed we mean a creed that provides for the lifting of the inner condemnation which in turn will allow the song to be sung. The heart full of condemnation refuses to sing—cannot sing, simply cannot.

Many have an adequate creed, but they do not appropriate that creed adequately. They do not believe that all condemnation can be lifted from the soul here and now. A young man in Japan wanted an education, but his father didn't want to give him an education. He said the son could carry on his business without it. The son married an educated girl who made him feel inferior. He became full of inferiority and self-condemnation and committed suicide with a Bible in his arms.

Many are like that young Japanese man. They are committing sudden or slow spiritual suicide—deteriorating through inner conflicts and condemnations, at the same time hugging a faith which they hug but do not appropriate. They press these promises of deliverance upon their hearts, but do not open their hearts to them.

Their creed is like the Japanese figure of the Goddess of Mercy with scaffolding around it, undergoing repairs. The goddess herself needed repairs. How could she mend broken hearts? Jesus, the same yesterday, today, and forever, needs no repairs of His inner or outer life and can repair the inner and outer life by making it free of condemnation.

O Jesus, I offer to Thee all that bows me in condemnation. Wash me, cleanse me, from all sense of guilt and condemnation, so I can stand before Thee, myself, and the world every whit whole. Only then can I be a man. Amen.

AFFIRMATION FOR THE DAY: *In Jesus I have a creed to believe and therefore a song to sing.*

A PARTIAL VICTORY AND FREEDOM

Just how does Jesus rid us of condemnation? By forgiveness, thus lifting the condemnation? If that were all His cure would be a dealing with symptoms, not with the disease. Quacks treat symptoms; doctors treat diseases. Condemnation is a symptom; sin is the disease. So to rid us of the symptom—condemnation—He must rid us of the disease—sin. How?

The next verse tells: "There is therefore now no condemnation for those who are in Christ Jesus. For the law of the Spirit of life in Christ Jesus has set me free from the law of sin and death" (Rom. 8:1-2). Note the "for"—the condemnation is banished, for the power of sin is broken in the life. When the sin goes the condemnation goes. Can the sin really go?

Some commentators balk or hesitate to say so. In the early days of the British occupation of India, it was proposed to send Bibles to India. A member of the House of Lords objected, "It is dangerous to send the Bible to India with its ideas of freedom and democracy, without the safeguard of a commentary." Commentaries made the Bible safe! A commentary on this passage says: "If Paul means here 'has already entirely freed me' he is speaking in the eschatological terms . . . and really means 'has already as good as freed me'—i.e., the thing is so certain and so imminent that it is fair to think of it as having already happened. More probably . . . he means to say that the possession by the Spirit has broken the power of sin and death, so that the man in Christ finds himself actually enjoying a partial victory and freedom." Toned down, eschatologically, it reads "as good as freed me"—future; "a *partial* victory and freedom"—present.

O Jesus, my Lord, I can't live on "as good as freed me," or on a "partial victory and freedom"—I want full victory and full freedom now. Thou art not "as good as" a Savior, or a partial Savior—Thou art Savior—Savior from the law of sin and death. Amen.

AFFIRMATION FOR THE DAY: *In Jesus sin and death have met their match. I'm in Him, so they have met their match in me.*

FREEDOM FROM THE LAW OF SIN AND DEATH

If Paul had preached a future deliverance from the law of sin and death or a partial deliverance now, we would never have heard of him again. Neither message would have met our need—a need to be delivered from sin and death now.

When the slaves in the Bahamas were freed the decree said: "When the sun rises above the horizon on August 1, 1838, you are free." A wave of jubilation swept those slaves. Some climbed to the highest mountain to see the sun rise first. If, however, the decree had said "Sometime in the future you will be free," or "We are granting partial freedom now," that would not have been good news. In both cases there would have been a paralysis at the heart of the announcement.

The only good news is freedom from the law of sin and death now. Paul announced it and thrilled the world—and still does, for it works. But how?

The passage connects sin and death—they are Siamese twins. Where you have sin you have death. To change the figure, they are the two sides of the same coin. This is so constant and regular that Paul called it a law. It is not a chance connection, a might happen or a might not happen; it always happens—sin and death are one. The chief illusion of man is, "I can have one, without the other." Every man on this planet has tried that and has had the same result—death, death to freedom, to peace, to usefulness, to the inner life. There have been no exceptions, and there can be no exceptions. Yet we keep on trying to prove ourselves the exception. This is the great illusion. A universal law is a universal law. That law is self-executing: death follows sin.

O Lord, my Master, I thank Thee for this law. I know what to depend on. But I'm grateful that there is another law—the law of the Spirit of Life in Christ Jesus. Help me to take advantage of that higher law and rise into freedom. Amen.

AFFIRMATION FOR THE DAY: *I will suffer no illusions: sin and death are inseparable and they will be inseparable in me.*

TWO LAWS

We ended yesterday on the note that sin and death were inseparably connected, so much so that it is no chance connection, but a law. If we are caught in this cause-and-effect law, how do we get out?

This passage points the way: "For the law of the Spirit of life in Christ Jesus has made me free from the law of sin and death." There is the introduction of a higher law—the law of the Spirit of life in Christ Jesus. This makes me free from the lower law—the law of sin and death. Just as the law of the elasticity of air and of muscular strength makes it possible for the bird to overcome the law of gravitation and thus fly, so when we take advantage of the law of the Spirit of life in Christ Jesus we overcome the law of sin and death. Except with this difference: the law of gravitation seems the universal law and the law of muscular strength seems the exceptional, the occasional. The law of the Spirit of life in Christ Jesus is the universal and all-powerful law, and the law of sin and death is the unnatural intrusion and has nothing back of it except decay and death. One has God behind it; the other has only man's sinful, and hence decaying, will behind it.

If we do not take advantage of the higher law every moment, the lower law sets in automatically. In a plane you do not struggle and try and get tense in order to fly—you simply surrender to the plane when shut in, let go and relax and trust and the plane does the rest. So you find release from the law of sin and death by surrendering to this law of the Spirit of life in Christ Jesus, by relaxing and receiving and trusting. He does the rest. I say "He," for it is not an "it," a law—it is a Person to Whom we trust our all. That Person is God available.

O Spirit of life in Christ Jesus—the Holy Spirit—come and bring release and victory over every clinging vestige of sin and death. For I would be free—free to be myself in Thee, free to be the best person I can be by this law of grace. Amen.

AFFIRMATION FOR THE DAY: *The law of the Spirit of life in Christ Jesus will be fully operative in me, therefore freedom is mine.*

"HE BREAKS THE POWER OF CANCELLED SIN"

We must emphasize the *freedom* from the law of sin and
death. We emphasized yesterday that we gain this freedom by
surrendering to the law of the Spirit of life in Christ Jesus. We
are free from the lower law by the operation of a higher law. We
are not free from sin by someone's waving a wand of forgiveness
over us and saying we are free. We are free from the law of sin
and death because we are literally free—"He breaks the power
of cancelled sin." The sin is cancelled in forgiveness and its
power is broken by the introduction of "the Spirit of life in Christ
Jesus." To forgive sin and not give power over the recurrence of
sins forgiven would be a moral danger. It would invite to further
sinning.

A Roman Catholic seeker at an evangelical altar of prayer said:
"I've asked for forgiveness all my life, but this is different. My
sins are all gone." Forgiveness was not condoning sin, but
cancelling sin by forgiveness and power. The sins are actually
gone as condemnation and as present fact. They are gone! He
forgives and gives—forgives the past and gives power for the
present and the future.

A woman went to a hospital to see a boy of fourteen who had
only a short time to live. She was called early one morning, for
he was sinking. She whispered to him: "God loves you, Jesus
loves you. He died to save you and to take you to heaven." The
boy replied, "Please say it again." Then his last words were
"Please thank Him for me." His sins were not only forgiven,
they were gone, buried in the love of God.

You are free from the law of sin and death because you are free
from sin and from sinning. Not that a momentary sin may not
recur for which forgiveness is immediately received, but the
habit of sin is broken.

**O Jesus, we look into Thy face and life is forever spoiled—we
can never try any other way to live life. This is it—and forever!
Our old songs are now discords, our old ways, ways of
destruction. Now we are on the Way! Amen.**

AFFIRMATION FOR THE DAY: *All my sins are gone except the memory,
and the memory is being erased or redeemed.*

"NO FEARS, JUST FAITH"

We ended yesterday by saying that one might fall into a momentary sin and yet remain in Christ. In that case, when we fall into sin we fall on our knees and get back immediately. The relation between you and Christ is not broken by sin, only clouded for the moment, for the basic intention is not to remain in the sin, but to get back into His arms "which are stretched out still." Out of that momentary sin we rescue a good—a new watchfulness, a new prayerfulness, a new love for such a Savior.

A woman writes: "There have been only momentary flashes in my life when my mind hasn't been walled in by fears, by conflicts, and by anxieties. Last night with your hands upon my head, kneeling down in Asbury Chapel, there was a feeling of strength, yet tender, and the hurting of a lifetime seemed to go away like magic. I went home walking on air and have felt beautiful all day—no fears, just faith that my life will work itself out all right and that my mistakes and sins are forgiven." She was free—free from the law of sin and death.

A Christian girl had a fiancé who was an alcoholic. She found him dead drunk on the streets of Richmond, Virginia. She took out a handkerchief with her initials on it and put it over his face. When he was taken up, this handkerchief was put into his pocket. When he had slept off his drunk, he put his hand into his pocket and found the handkerchief. Seeing the initials, he went to a group, confessed everything, and was converted. He and the girl were married. Someone asked the woman, "What did you see in that man?" She replied, "I saw the grace of God and what it could do for him." Forgiveness and the law of the Spirit of life in Christ Jesus made him free from the law of sin and death.

O my Lord, Thy forgiveness is Thy enablement—Thy enablement to walk free from the tyranny of cancelled sin. Whom the Son makes free is free indeed. We are free indeed. Read the gratitude of our hearts! Amen.

AFFIRMATION FOR THE DAY: *I am not perfect, but I am a very imperfect follower of a very perfect Savior—I'm on the Way!*

"IN ACCORDANCE WITH IMMUTABLE LAWS"

We said yesterday that "the law of the Spirit of life in Christ Jesus has set me free from the law of sin and death." It sounds like a contradiction—"the law of the Spirit of life"—what can be freer than "the Spirit of life" and what can be more regular and dependable than "the law"?

Is this Spirit of life in Christ Jesus as regular and dependable as an immutable law? It was E. D. Starbuck, the psychologist, who in modern times emphasized this statement of Paul's that the spiritual life is ruled by law. He said, "There is no event in the spiritual life which does not occur in accordance with immutable laws." He found "as great orderliness and sequence among the facts of emotion" as does the physicist in his laboratory.

This is what we would expect if the God of nature and the God of grace are the one and the same God. The God who works in nature by law and order would certainly not work in grace by whim, notion, and fancy. The laws of nature are dependable because God's mind is dependable.

So God is not like a potentate of ancient times, out of whom you could wangle benefits if you knew how to get on his good side by flattery and proper approach. He is constant and consistent. You do not have to overcome God's reluctance; you have to lay hold on His highest willingness. You lay hold on His highest willingness by surrender and faith and obedience. That sounds as though you get what you want by giving what you have! Precisely! You exchange your all for His all, and you find, to your surprise, that it is the best bargain this universe offers. The finite creature offers his all to the Infinite Creator and receives back all that he needs and can handle. There is no bargain like it!

O God, my Father, I bank on Thy constant consistency. I know Thou art love and Thou canst not violate Thine own nature. Thou canst not do an unloving thing. I bank on that with my very life, and I'm grateful it works. Amen.

AFFIRMATION FOR THE DAY: *A man spoke to God through an echoing barn, "I want more of You," and got back the reply, "I want more of you."*

THE FIRST LIE

We saw yesterday that the spiritual life is subject to law exactly as the physical life is. We cannot break physical laws and not get hurt, nor can we break spiritual laws and not get hurt. Paul here connects sin and death and he calls the connection between the two "the law." Are they always connected? Does death follow sin inevitably?

Perhaps not outwardly, but inwardly, yes. Something dies in a person the moment he sins. The greatest illusion, barring none, is that man can sin and get away with it. That was the first lie uttered in our world. Satan uttered that first lie in the Garden of Eden: "You will not die"—there is no connection between your disobedience and death. It was the first and it is the latest great lie that has ever been uttered—it is whispered into the ears of those dallying with temptation: "You will not die." That lie has been disproved in every single case from the first one to the last one with no exception. Yet each person who tries to be the exception fails. The payoff is automatic—it is registered in the very person. Something dies in the person. "I was a ninny to do it," said a cultured woman, all shot to pieces inwardly. A man with ten million dollars brooded amid his millions over the face of a betrayal and an illegitimate child. His millions could not buy off his inner unhappiness. "I did just what any man in my position would have done," said a man who was fighting an unequal fight with his conscience. It was in vain. His countenance reflected the unhappiness of his soul.

The moment sin enters, death enters too—as substance and shadow, inseparable. It is the death of inner peace, of influence, of power to help others, of self-respect, and of your relation with God.

O God, we've listened to this lie, and we haven't been the exception. Help us never to try it again. Give us the grace of intelligent discrimination. Help us to learn our lessons, for we do not break these laws; we break ourselves on them. Amen.

AFFIRMATION FOR THE DAY: *I shall surely die—something dies within me the moment I sin.*

"IN ALL THESE THINGS"

We have been thinking about the dependableness of being in Christ. It is not a hit-or-miss affair, coming and going with passing emotions; it is as dependable as the law of gravitation—and more! The law of gravitation is created by the Creator, a created thing, but when you depend on being in Christ you are dependent on the Creator Himself, on His character as revealed in Christ. Remain in Christ and you are as secure as security, as constant as constancy. The sum total of reality is behind you.

This is seen in this amazing passage:

Who shall separate us from the love of Christ? Shall tribulation, or distress, or persecution, or famine, or nakedness, or peril, or sword? . . . No, in all these things we are more than conquerors through him who loved us. For I am sure that neither death, nor life, nor angels, nor principalities, nor things present, nor things to come, nor powers, nor height, nor depth, nor anything else in all creation, will be able to separate us from the love of God in Christ Jesus our Lord." (Rom. 8:35-39)

This passage is remarkable in that it shows the essential difference between Christianity and all other faiths. The difference is to be found in that little word "in"—"No, *in* all these things. . . ." The Hebrew word is "*out of* all these things"; the Buddhist word is "*apart from* all these things"; the Hindu word, "*above* all these things"; the Mohammedan word, "*beyond* all these things"—in heaven; the materialist's word, "*by* all these things"; the Christian word, "*in* all these things. . . ." The center of the Christian faith is the Incarnation—"the Word became flesh." The Word became incarnate, not supercarnate, nor subcarnate, nor excarnate, but incarnate. The victory was wrought out "in." That "in" is the most important word in history.

O God, our Father, Thou didst not sit on a cloud and attempt to redeem us by picking us up with celestial tongs, lest Thou dirty Thy hands with this messy business of our sins. Thou didst lift us from within. I thank Thee. Amen.

AFFIRMATION FOR THE DAY: *If I work out my destiny it must be "in"—no other way.*

THE STEPS DOWN AND UP

We saw yesterday that "*in* all these things" we are to be more than conquerors. If the word had been "ex," or "sub," or "super," instead of "in," then the power of our faith would have been turned away from human problems. Not their solution, but escape from them—above, beneath, around, apart from, not *in*—would have been our interest. Any other word, except "in" is fatal. If religion cannot solve the problems of life as is, then it has no place in life. It is opium.

I have lived all my life amid religions which, when they came to this business of life now, have tried to rise above it, have tried to step apart from it, have feigned indifference to it, have steeled themselves against it, have done everything except face it and solve it—"in." That little word "in" has been the rock over which they have stumbled to their doom—usually gradual doom, but doom nevertheless. There is no way to solve life itself except from within.

Jesus did just that. He entered life—became incarnate. The steps in that incarnation are seven, according to Phil. 2:5-8:

Have this mind among yourselves, which you have in Christ Jesus, who though he was in the form of God, did not count equality with God a thing to be grasped [gave up the ultimate position and ultimate security—step number one], but emptied himself [emptied Himself of everything but love—step number two], taking the form of a servant [from Creator to creature, and a serving creature—step number three], being born in the likeness of men [not a verbal identification—a real one—step number four]. And being found in human form he humbled himself [became man and then lower than proud man—step number five] and became obedient unto death [the ultimate identification—with our death—step number six], even death on a cross [the identification lowest down—step number seven].

O Jesus, I marvel with a deep down marvel at Thy "in." How deeply in Thou didst come we will never know. We shall explore it forever. What we see sets our hearts atingle to know the wonder of it—to know it fully. I thank Thee for what I see. Amen.

AFFIRMATION FOR THE DAY: *Jesus "stooped to save"—how wonderful that stooping was I shall explore forever!*

THE DIVINE EXCHANGE

We have seen the seven steps of God's descent in man. He gave up His position as God, gave up His person as a member of the Trinity, became a servant instead of Creator, became a man, became a humiliated man, became identified with our death, and the ultimate identification—with our sin. From God to sinner—by identification—that is identification all-out. He couldn't go lower down than that. "In" became "in"—there was no further "in" to go! He hit bottom.

Having hit bottom He then began to go up—the seven steps up:

Therefore God has highly exalted him [the Humbled became the Exalted] and bestowed on him the name which is above every name [the highest Name in the universe—Savior!], that at the name of Jesus every knee should bow [ultimate acknowledgment as ultimate Authority], in heaven [ultimate in heaven] and on earth [ultimate where He wrought out the victory—on earth] . . . and every tongue confess that Jesus Christ is Lord, to the glory of God the Father" [universal confession as Lord—"every tongue"]. (Phil. 2:9-11)

His identification with us was complete—from being holy God to being sinful man. The Incarnation could not be more "in"—it was an ultimate in. Now if we identify ourselves with Him by surrender, at the cross, then we go up with Him and are identified with Him on His throne—we share His glory and His power. He was identified with us that we might be identified with Him. He shared what was in man that we might share what is in Christ. That is what can be called "the divine exchange"—He came down that we might go up. Salvation is not then a mere transferring us from earth to heaven, but a transference from what we are to what He is—it is to be in Him.

O Christ, my Redeemer, I am catching little glimpses of the purpose of my redemption. I am speechless with awe and glory. I'm being transformed from being in me to being in Him, and nothing can be more wonderful than being in Him. I'm grateful. Amen.

AFFIRMATION FOR THE DAY: *If I will be exploring forever the wonder of His stooping, I shall also be exploring forever the wonder of my ascent "in Him."*

"I HAVE OVERCOME THE WORLD"

We pondered last week over the phrase: "No, in all these things we are more than conquerors through him who loved us." The emphasis was "in all these things"—in the midst of "things," hard things, easy things, exasperating things, material things, spiritual things, impossible things—yes, in all these things we are conquerors.

I can conquer "in" because He has conquered "in." Everything I meet He has already met. When temptation, sin, difficulty, opposition, misunderstanding, criticism, fear, resentment, inferiority, pride, loneliness—yes, anything comes upon me to bully me, I ask that thing to bend its neck. When it does so, I exclaim with joy: "There I told you so—there is the footprint of the Son of God upon your neck. He has conquered you. I'm in Him and I conquer in His conquering." Everything I face is a defeated foe—I'm dealing with the already conquered. I do not have to conquer by struggling, trying—I simply take my stand by surrender to Him and am therefore in Him. Everything there is in Him is in me—in me by appropriation and receptivity—no trying, just trusting; no agonizing, only appropriation; no resistance, just receptivity.

Jesus said: "I have said this to you, that in me you may have peace. In the world you have tribulation; but be of good cheer, I have overcome the world" (John 16:33). "In me" you have peace. You have peace not by trying this mental discipline or that exercise, this program or that plan—you have peace by simply being "in me." The Christian life is not a struggle; it is a surrender—a surrender to Him, and therefore to everything in Him. Fully surrendered then I'm strong in His strength, pure in His purity, loving in His love, victorious in His victory. The father said to the elder son, "All I have is thine," and in a new way Jesus says, "All I have is thine"—thine for the asking and appropriation.

O my Lord and my God, I have naught to do but remain in Thee and then take—take with both hands all I need for myself and for others. I'm rich—in Thee. I'm adequate—in Thee. I'm nothing and have everything. I'm nobody and somebody—in Thee. Amen.

AFFIRMATION FOR THE DAY: *He was identified with my weakness. I am identified with His strength.*

"MY RESPONSE TO HIS ABILITY"

We meditated yesterday on "in the world . . . tribulation," "in me . . . peace." In the world we have peace amid tribulation, for the deeper "in" is being "in me." Being in the world is a surface "in," but being in Him is a depth "in." It is a depth "in" and an eternal "in." Being in Him we are in everything that is in Him. Being in Him we are in everything good, everything joyous, everything creative, everything healthy, everything I need for time and eternity. I am in His Everything.

The business of my life, and the only business of my life, is to abide in Him. All else follows. That is life reduced to its utmost simplicity and to its utmost vitality. There life is lived in Life. There is nothing, and there can be nothing in life greater than Life.

A saint has been defined as "one who tries a little harder." Another definition was given by someone who saw the light shining through the figure of a saint in a stained-glass window: "A saint is one who lets the light through." The first definition is unsatisfactory; it depicts a tense, anxiously striving person living by "by." The second definition depicts a person who is passive—just letting the light through. The saint is not one who lives "by" his own struggles or "through," but "in." He lives "in," and therefore in appropriation, in assimilation, in co-operation.

A motto on the Sat Tal Ashram wall gives it: "Not my responsibility, but my response to His ability." I live in response to His grace, His love, His resources, His purity, His power, His Everything. The alternate heartbeats of the Christian life are receptivity and response, receptivity and response—I take and I give. As I take from Infinity, I can give infinitely.

O Jesus, my Lord, I have found how to live. I live by Life. I've found where to live. I live in Life. What else do I need? Nothing, absolutely nothing—except more of your Everything. I take to satiation—to hunger for more. Amen.

AFFIRMATION FOR THE DAY: *Today I shall not struggle and try, but surrender and trust.*

"I FACE A DEFEATED·FOE"

We pause another day on: "in me you may have peace. In the world you have tribulation; but be of good cheer, I have overcome the world."

Being in Him we are in One who not merely *will* overcome the world, but *has* overcome it. That means that He has met everything which we have to face—the world of the mind, the world of the emotions, the world of the will. Not once did He cave in. If He overcame that inner world He overcame the outer world—the world of relationships, of misunderstanding, of hate, of misrepresentation of murder. He overcame the world of group relationships—the world of small-mindedness, of bickering and jealousy, of denial and betrayal. He faced everything, and He overcame everything.

No matter where I turn in this business called life I face a defeated foe. I do not have to defeat the foe. I simply remain in Him Who has defeated the foe, and I accept His victory as my own. This wipes out all sense of inferiority as I begin. I'm on top in His "on-topness." It saves me from a sense of pride, for I know that apart from Him I can do nothing; in Him I can do everything. I find myself a surprise to myself. I find myself doing things I can't do, undertaking things I dare not undertake, and undergoing tests I have no right or possibility to undergo. I am calm when I ought to be agitated. I am joyous when there is nothing to be joyous about. I thrill to this business of living energized by life. I am surprised at Goethe, at seventy-five, saying of his life, "It has been nothing but pain and burden," and at Luther, when he had grown old, confessing, "I am utterly weary of life."

O Jesus, my Lord, how can I say that while I am in Thee? In myself—yes. In the world—yes. But in Thee—no! I can only dance and sing and praise. If not on account of, then always in spite of. In Thee I overcome in Thy overcoming. Glory! Amen.

AFFIRMATION FOR THE DAY: *I am in love with life, for I am in love with Thee.*

FACING THE WORST FIRST

We come now to an astonishing passage following the passage we have been studying, "No, in all these things we are more than conquerors through him who loved us." The passage is this, "For I am sure that neither death, nor life, nor angels, nor principalities, nor things present, nor things to come, nor powers, nor height, nor depth, nor anything else in all creation, will be able to separate us from the love of God in Christ Jesus our Lord" (Rom. 8:37-39). Here Paul exhausts all the categories of possibility of separating us from "the love of God in Christ Jesus our Lord." Nothing is left out. To try to expound it is to attempt to paint the lily and to retouch the colors of the sunset.

One can try to tell the untellable and to express the inexpressible. Here goes! In four pairs of opposites Paul sweeps the horizon of any possibility of separating us from the love of God in Christ Jesus.

First, death and life—he takes death first, for people usually think of death as the greatest power to separate. It is called "the great divide"—dividing everything and everybody. This is characteristic of the Christian faith—it presents the worst first. Someone has said: "Raise any issue in its most difficult aspect first. Solve it there, and then you can more easily solve it all down the line." So death, the great divider, is faced first. This method of presenting the worst first is not mere chance in this instance—it is a revelation of the Christian method and strategy. The world's method and strategy is to present everything bargain-counter-foremost. The central confrontation of Christianity is a cross—*In hoc signo*—by this sign—you conquer. It confronts us with the worst—God's cross and ours. The sheer audacity of it!

O God, our Father, we are astonished at Thy audacity— putting the cross before us straight off and asking us for acceptance—acceptance as the central thing in Thee and in us. We love Thee for putting the worst first. All else is glory. Amen.

AFFIRMATION FOR THE DAY: *Today I shall conquer the worst, and then it will be easy to mow down the lesser things.*

THE ONE PLACE THE DEVIL CANNOT ENTER

We are considering the Christian method of putting the worst first. This reverses all our advertising: "No down payment," "Easy terms," "Cash for the asking," followed, of course, by wearisome down payments, harder and harder terms, and cash demanded, long and loud.

Is the Christian faith right in facing death first? Yes, for if anything gets into the love of God in Christ Jesus our Lord, even to separate from that love, it is immediately changed by that love. The love of Christ is the one and only thing which the devil cannot get into, for if he got into it he would cease to be the devil. The devil can get into our doctrines and become orthodox, and then make us fight over orthodoxy. He can get into the church and make us proud, exclusive, and egotistical in our church loyalties. He can get into preaching and make the preacher a better preacher to cover up moral delinquency. "I never preached better in my life," said a minister who had been living in adultery. The devil can get into the sacred precincts of the home and turn everything into bickering and struggle for ascendency, even though the home is religious. He can get into patriotism and turn it into "the first refuge of the scoundrel." He can get into our good works and twist them into egotistical display. He can get into everything, literally everything, except one thing—the love of Christ. If he got into the love of Christ he wouldn't be the devil. He would be transformed.

If death, the devil's twin—"sin and death" always go together—if death should get into the love of Christ to separate us, then death would no longer be death—it would be life. The love of Christ has transformed death at the cross into life. Calvary became Easter morning. So death can't separate from the love of Christ, for death in attempting it would be separated from itself and become life.

"O love of God, so pure and changeless"—yet while changeless, it changes everything. O blessed Refuge, O blessed Redemption. If I stay in Thee, O Love of God, nothing can touch me without being transformed. In Christ I am out of reach of everything else. Glory be! Amen.

AFFIRMATION FOR THE DAY: *Nothing can get into the love of Christ without being transformed, so I shall remain in that love today.*

DEATH BECOMES LIFE

Is this enthusiastic exaggeration to say that death when it got into the love of Christ would become life? No, it is sober fact. Death got into a missionary home in Foochow, China; father and mother were killed in the Vegetarian Riots. The four children escaped, met together, and decided on their revenge—they would get the best education possible and come back to China and serve those who had killed their parents. They did. Death didn't separate them from the love of Christ; death became life—a life of dedicated service. Alongside those two graves is another grave—that of the only daughter of a widow in Australia. This daughter was killed in the riots. The mother said, "I have no other daughters to give; I'll go myself." At sixty-two she sold everything, went to China, set up a school, and for twenty years served the people who killed her daughter. Death got into the love of God in Christ and became life—unwittingly so. Death got into a German missionary home in Purulia, India, and took an only daughter through leprosy. The parents said, "Now that death has taken our daughter by leprosy, we'll see what we can do for other lepers." They set up the greatest leper home in the world. Death became life—life to the daughter, life to the parents, life to thousands of lepers—life! "O death, where is thy victory? O death, where is thy sting?" Death getting into the love of Christ has no sting and has no victory. It is transformed into life.

Spiritual death which separates us from God, the source of our life, and which separates us from our highest selves and our greatest possibilities, is a calamity. But physical death to those who are in Christ is not a calamity but an opportunity. It is a part of redemption—the redemption of our bodies. It is a sowing—a sowing of a mortal body and the reaping of an immortal body; it is a sowing of a diseased, broken-down body and the reaping of a disease-free, death-free, decay-free body. So death cannot separate—it can only integrate.

O Jesus, Thou hast shown us that Thou art the Resurrection and the Life. Death brought Thee life. So begone my fear of death. I embrace it in His name and transform it by His grace and power. Death can only separate me from weakness. Amen.

AFFIRMATION FOR THE DAY: *Death is the anesthetic that puts me to sleep while God changes my mortal body to immortal.*

RUNNING AWAY FROM LIFE

We saw yesterday that death cannot separate us from the love of God in Christ Jesus. Can life separate us? Life can be a more effective separator than death. You can become afraid of life, step out of it, retreat into yourself, and disintegrate. If you become a self-preoccupied person you will be separated from the love of God in Christ Jesus our Lord. Life can separate you from that love, if life can induce you to attempt to live life in yourself.

This retreat from life into yourself can easily be accomplished. Fear of life and failure can induce you to do it. A Chinese student from Singapore at the University of Michigan in Ann Arbor began to get low marks in mathematics. Out of shame and a sense of inferiority he hid himself for four years in the attic of the Methodist church and lived there as a complete recluse. Fear and inferiority drove him in on himself and separated him from the love of God, the love of his fellow man, and the love of himself. When he came out at the end of four years, a wreck, he said: "You have to face up to truth—to reality. Four years ago I was a coward, but today I have learned to live again."

This student's retreat away from life was dramatic. But those who retreat out of life and responsibility in a covered, less dramatic way, are just as devastated inwardly as this Chinese student. In fact Carl Jung, the famous psychiatrist, said: "There is a difference between the psychology of Freud and myself. He finds the basis of neurosis in the past, in childhood. I find it in the present. I ask, what is the responsibility from which this patient is retreating? Why is he dodging out of life into illness?"

If we stay in the love of God in Christ we have learned to face up to life; we are afraid of nothing, for in Him we are adequate for anything. As long as we stay in Him, life cannot separate us.

O blessed, blessed Security. I am afraid of nothing that life can bring, for I am not afraid of life itself. I hide me in Life, then what can life do to me? I can not only bear everything that life brings, I can use it. I thank Thee. Amen.

AFFIRMATION FOR THE DAY: *I shall not hide in church towers or ivory towers. I shall run into Thy victory and be safe.*

EVERYTHING IN HIM LIVES

We meditated yesterday upon the fact that life cannot separate us "from the love of God in Christ Jesus our Lord." We said that when we stay in the love of Christ we have power to face up to life and its responsibilities. Therefore nothing in life can separate us. There is another consideration, however, and more far-reaching: If life gets into the love of Christ to separate us, then life itself is changed—changed from life to Life. This is no mere play on words—it is fact.

When a common noun is placed in Christ it passes at once into a proper noun. When Jesus says, "I am the Bread of Life," you have to spell both "Bread" and "Life" with a capital letter. Bread in Jesus is no longer bread, for it is bread in direct touch with the Author of bread—it is bread interfused with the life and love of Christ, and therefore Bread. Everything about it is heightened with new meaning, new purpose, new goal, new substance—it is Bread. It must be called "the Bread of the Presence." Bread outside Him is "the bread of the absence." It is just bread, keeping alive dead persons with dead purposes and dead goals.

If money is put in Christ, dedicated to Him and His purposes, it is money with a soul, with creativity at its center—it is Money. When money is put in Christ, then it is no longer subject to decay and death. It is put into the Creator God, and when it is it becomes alive with creative life and creative activity—it becomes Life.

If I stay in Christ, when life tries to get to me to separate me, it cannot reach me without itself being turned into Life. In which case it would not want to separate me—it would join me in Life in Him. So I have only one business in life—to stay in Life and then life can do nothing to separate me.

O Jesus, my Lord, I have the only security—the security of Life itself. Hidden in Thee, I laugh at the ragings of life around me. Standing in Thee I say to life, "Come on!" for I know life to get at me would have to become Life. Glory, glory, glory! Amen.

AFFIRMATION FOR THE DAY: *I have one business in life and that is to stay in union with Him.*

"GO DIRECTLY TO JESUS"

The next pair of opposites which cannot "separate us from the love of God in Christ Jesus" is: "nor angels nor principalities."

There are two possible interpretations of the meaning of angels and principalities. In the world of Paul the mystery religions, particularly Gnosticism, had built up between man and God a hierarchy of angels and principal powers as intermediaries. You could not get to God except through them. They were beneficent, but blocks on the climb to God—you had to go through them. Paul sweeps away these intermediaries when he says: "There is one mediator between God and men, the man Christ Jesus." We do not have to get to God—God comes to us in Christ. Jesus is a mediator only in the sense that He mediates God to us. When you take hold of Him you take hold of God. He is not a third person standing between us and God—He is God available. When we stay in Christ we stay in God. When I deepen the Christ-consciousness I deepen the God-consciousness. They do not rival or push each other out—they are One.

Men, even in Christianity, stop this side of getting in Christ and stay in themselves, in a system, in ritual, in rites and ceremonies, and feeling orphaned from God, set up intermediaries to intercede with God for them. Hence we find some Roman Catholics believe there is a hierarchy between man and God: the priest, behind the priest the church, behind the church the Virgin Mary, behind the Virgin Mary Christ, behind Christ—God! You cannot get to God except through these "angels" and principalities. They "separate us from the love of God in Christ Jesus." The remedy? Go directly to Jesus. He is the Door.

O Divine Redeemer, so close that all I have to do is step out of myself into Thee. In Thee I have no need of an intermediary. Thou art immediate, nothing between. So the intermediaries drop off—irrelevant. I thank Thee that in Thee I have reality. Amen.

AFFIRMATION FOR THE DAY: *I go through Jesus to everything good that this life or the next holds.*

NO "ANGELS" CAN SEPARATE YOU

Yesterday we saw that "neither angels nor principalities" could "separate us from the love of God in Christ Jesus our Lord." We mentioned that Jesus was imprisoned in the system of Roman Catholicism and that you couldn't get to Him except through that system. In more subtle ways this system of intermediaries is found within Protestantism too. When we stop at the church and give our loyalty and love to that and never get to the living Christ, then an angel and a principality is separating us "from the love of God in Christ Jesus." A good thing—an angel—is separating us from the Best. When we make the holding of orthodoxy the criterion of being a Christian, and make that the standard, we are stopping this side of being in Christ and have substituted for that being in orthodoxy. An "angel" has separated us. When we substitute faithfulness in churchgoing and church-support and recognize these things as the sign and standard of being a Christian, thereby making irrelevant being in Christ, we are being separated from the love of Christ by an "angel."

If we love husband, wife, or children more than we love Christ, an "angel"—a good thing—is separating us from the love of Christ. If a social set, a lodge, a service club, has our loyalty above Christ, then a good thing—an "angel"—is separating us from the love of Christ.

If, however, we remain in Christ, the ultimate best and the ultimate power, then all these "angels" and "principalities" are in their place—on the margin, held under the supreme loyalty to Christ. They cannot separate us from that love "for the love of Christ controls us"—and them. If sin cannot separate us, neither can the good things (which are often more dangerous than the bad) separate us. We are safe from the worst and from the half-goods when we are wholly and finally in Him.

O blessed Refuge, O blessed Security, I am safe and secure in the only security this universe knows—I am in Thee. Therefore all Thy security is in me. I inherit all that Thou, "the Heir of all things," hast inherited. I am rich in Thee. Amen.

AFFIRMATION FOR THE DAY: *No half-good nor any good shall separate me from Him—the Best!*

THINGS PRESENT NOR THINGS TO COME

We come now to another pair of opposites which "cannot separate us from the love of God in Christ Jesus our Lord": "Nor things present, nor things to come." This pair has perhaps the most devastating power of them all—it separates more people from the love of God in Christ than any other factor or factors in human living. "Things present" and "things to come" refer to things that happen in the stream called Time—present and future. "Things present" become so absorbing that they control us. They suck us dry by their demanding attention. The everyday things of life rob us of life. We become thing-possessed and happening-possessed instead of life-possessed. These things control us, we do not control them. "Things present" are on top of us; we are not on top of them.

Jesus put His finger on this danger when He said, "Take heed to yourselves lest your hearts be weighed down with dissipation and drunkenness and cares of this life" (Luke 21:34). He asked us to be watchful of ourselves at two points: at the place of dissipation and drunkenness—the sins of the flesh, and at the place of "the cares of this life"—the sins of the disposition. He said that they both weigh us down. Dissipation and drunkenness are attempts to lift the burdens of life—to forget them, to escape from them. Jesus saw, however, and life is increasingly seeing, that the more you try to escape from life the more burdensome life becomes. The more stimulants you take the more depressed you are. Sleeping pills, in the end, produce sleeplessness. It is all a losing game. You become "weighed down" by your very attempts to lift the weights of living. Pleasure-seeking is the great illusion. It is an illusion for it eludes. You grasp at the lurid colors of the sunset and find you've grasped the dark. You are "weighed down" with disappointment.

O Jesus, Thy realism punctures with a word our illusions. When we take Thy realism we live in a world of reality—with real pleasures, real joys, real life, and with no hang-overs. We grasp the sunset and find it a dawn. I thank Thee, thank Thee. Amen.

AFFIRMATION FOR THE DAY: *All the things intended to lift me depress me. He lifts me and keeps me lifted!*

"CARES OF THIS LIFE"

We finished yesterday on being "weighed down by dissipation and drunkenness"—the pursuit of pleasure through escapism. The other portion of the verse warns us against being "weighed down with . . . cares of this life." The first, through drunkenness and dissipation, attempts to escape from the cares of this life; the second, spurning the escape into dissipation and drunkenness, tries the method of handling the cares of this life by dutifulness and self-discipline. The persons involved may be religious, which holds them to duty—discipline. They are in their religious selves and not in Christ, and hence they are care-filled, weighed-down persons. They are tense, anxious, and strained. "Things present" are always present, absorbing time and attention and life.

Note: Jesus put this being weighed down with the cares of this life in the same category as dissipation and drunkenness. It is the sin of the conscientious.

What is the remedy for both of these? It is simple. In both cases there is a consciousness of being in yourself, hence of being in time. The remedy is to step out of yourself and out of time into Christ by self-surrender. Then when you are in Christ you are in eternal life. You are more conscious of eternal life than you are of temporal life. You have stepped out of a passing show into an Eternal Now. "Things present" are replaced by "The Thing Present." You don't run away from the things present— you relate them as subordinate to the eternal in Christ. They take their places on the margin of life; you have them in your control—they don't have you. You use them—they don't use you. You have separated them from the throne of your life by surrendering them to Christ, therefore they have no more power to separate you from Christ. In Him your values are straight—things are things. I submit not to things, but to Him.

O Jesus, Thou art my supreme value. I look into Thy face and I am no longer the servant of things. I am a servant of the Author of things. I can take little or much of things, for I have all of Thee. Blessed emancipation, glorious liberty! I thank Thee. Amen.

AFFIRMATION FOR THE DAY: *There are two ways to be rich—one in the abundance of your possessions and the other in the fewness of your wants.*

IN RELIGION, NOT IN CHRIST

We have looked at the power of things present to separate us from the love of God in Christ Jesus our Lord. We now look at the second, "things to come." The apprehensions about things to come turn into fears, and fears become all-pervasive as nameless anxiety. Those fears turned anxieties separate us from the love of Christ—and do so with religious people.

A very intelligent and religious woman told me of her minister husband's running off with the wife of a deacon. She married the deacon, and for a while they were happy—as happy as two people could be under those circumstances. But now she was filled with nameless fears, mostly fears of the future. The reason was simple. A religious woman she was "in religion," but not in Christ. Deep down she was really "in herself," and being "in herself" she felt insecure. She began to wonder what would happen to her when her physical attractiveness faded? Could she hold her new husband? Would she lose him as she lost the first? These are natural fears to one who is in herself, with nothing backing and sustaining her except herself and nothing within her except her decaying self. The remedy was simple: surrender to Christ. She did, and immediately her fears vanished—she was in eternal life now and hence secure. Time could do nothing to her. She belonged to Christ, and time and eternity belonged to Him, and hence to her.

I picked up my morning paper and under "Let's Explore Your Mind" the statement was made: "Once you hit forty, there's nothing to look forward to! Right or Wrong?" The published answer was: "Wrong. Each middle-ager is a pioneer in the new 'prime of life' assured by recent advances in medicine and technology." That is an earth-bound answer.

O Lord God, if science and technology are the answers to growing mental and physical decay, we are boosted in the beginning but caught in the end—caught by death. But in Thee we are deathless, therefore we are not bounded by time or bound by time. We are free in Thee. Amen.

AFFIRMATION FOR THE DAY: *The earth-bound answers to life don't answer—the Eternal must be in the answer.*

"I DON'T HAVE TO LIVE"

Yesterday we paused on the answer of psychology, that recent advances in science and technology make it possible for those past forty to be pioneers in "the new prime" of life. In other words, the "new prime of life" can be fifty, sixty, or even seventy. That is good. I've proved it to be true for myself. When I was seventy God said, "I'm going to give you the best ten years of your life—the next ten ahead." Those that have gone have literally been the best years of my life. I can bear the same load of work and responsibility as I did at forty-five, or fifty-five, and bear it with the same absence of fatigue and strain. Even so, suppose only science and technology were giving me this assurance instead of God. It would be a shot in the arm with a rude awakening from the effects. Without being in Christ, I would be in myself, therefore in mortality, and therefore in eventual decay and death. Science and technology can postpone, but cannot prevent decay and death. They only prolong the agony of eventual failure.

When you are in Christ, however, then nothing in "things to come" can separate you. Suppose I should die before the ten best years are completed; am I out on a limb? No, they will still be the best ten years of my life, for in Christ I have eternal life. In Him there is literally no death, only larger life, so I am safe. When I went out to India fifty-two years ago a chaplain on board ship said: "You don't drink? You can't live in India without drinking." My reply was simple: "Well, I don't have to live, I can die. A Christian has another alternative—he can die, and be better off. But if you're not a Christian you have to live or you're in for it!" There is nothing in things to come that can separate us. I don't know what the future holds, but I know Who holds the future. In Him there is life, Life, L-I-F-E—now and forever!

O Jesus, things to come are only things coming to Thee, for Thou art the heir of the ages. All things that live will come out at Thy feet. The rest will decay and perish. So we can sing and dance at the coming victory, for there is present victory—in Thee. I thank Thee, thank Thee. Amen.

AFFIRMATION FOR THE DAY: *If the Christian faith is "anticipated attainment," then I live in that anticipated attainment now.*

HOROSCOPES?

We pass to another pair of opposites which Paul says cannot separate us "from the love of God which is in Christ Jesus our Lord." It would seem at first sight that Paul had abandoned the plan of opposites and had inserted a single item—"nor powers." Phillips' translation keeps the opposites, however, combining the word "powers" with them: "neither a power from on high nor a power from below . . . has any power to separate us."

What is this power from on high which might separate us? When we look at the ancient world to see what power from on high had influenced it most, the answer is astrology. The stars decided the destiny of that ancient world, and still do in many parts of the world, including India, and strange to say, America. One of the things that strikes me as strange when I come back from the East where astrology has reigned and where they are gradually throwing it off as an outworn superstition, is finding the newspapers of America printing daily horoscopes, written according to the position of the stars for that day and given as a serious guide to conduct for its readers. This is Christian America! I thought we had passed from the stage of astrology, a pseudoscience, to astronomy, a real science. Perpetuation of this superstition by newspapers shows an incredible moral and spiritual shallowness. Believing that unconscious lumps of matter floating in space can determine the destiny of moral and spiritual beings capable of moral and spiritual choice, is materialism of the grossest kind. There is no essential difference between an ancient pagan bowing before a stone idol, asking for its guidance and blessing, and a modern pagan studying charts that depict the movements of lumps of matter in the sky to determine the guidance of his life. Nothing would paralyze a civilization quicker than for its citizens to abandon the responsibility of moral and spiritual choice in favor of letting the stars decide.

O Christ, forgive us when we abandon thee, the Light of the world, in favor of night lights that twinkle in the darkness. We have lost Thee and hence turn to these false lights that lead us into increasing folly and emptiness. Help us to look into thy face for guidance. Amen.

AFFIRMATION FOR THE DAY: *The only horoscope I'm interested in is my destiny in Christ—the rest is piffle.*

THE PARALYSIS OF LOOKING AT THE STARS

We are thinking about the "power from on high" which can separate us from the love of God in Christ Jesus. We fastened on astrology as that power which can separate us—and does. When people lose the guidance of God, they will turn to anything for guidance. Of all the things men turn to for guidance, astrology is the most devastating, for it means that moral considerations have been abandoned, and the position of the stars decides. Stars that have no consciousness, no moral sense, no intelligence, decide the destiny of conscious, moral, intelligent beings. Any nation or any individual who adopts that method of guidance will decay, has already decayed. Yet we are told that five million people in America decide their daily lives on the basis of astrology. The newspapers that publish these daily charts are contributing to this moral and intellectual decay.

I have seen the royal houseboat tied up to the bank of a river in Kashmir, India, because the astrologers had informed the Maharaja that the stars were not propitious for a continuance of the journey. The business of a state tied up till the stars gave them permission to move! An educated Hindu said to me, "I was about to take a train journey, but I found it was not a propitious hour to journey, but the next one would be; so I waited an hour, rushed to the station, but, alas, the train pulled out without me." It was a "propitious hour," but he missed his train! The train of human progress will pull out and leave the devotees of astrology behind as they study their charts for propitious hours and days to do this, that, and the other.

The stars, which the love of God has made, can separate us from that love if we make the stars our guide instead of letting the Creator revealed in Christ guide us. It is the sin of idolatry. It is paganism, pure and simple.

Dear Lord, forgive the sin of turning to the stars instead of to the Savior, the sin of turning to the work of Thy hands instead of to Thy Hands for guidance and direction. May this sin of idolatry be forgiven us. Save us from things that separate us from Thee. Amen.

AFFIRMATION FOR THE DAY: *Jesus is my Morning Star, ushering in my day—the day of God!*

SPIRITUALISM?

We have meditated on one of the pair of opposites which "separate us from the love of God in Christ Jesus"—"a power from on high." We now turn to the other: "nor a power from below." What would fit the description of "a power from below" which could separate us, except spiritualism? The ancient world looked on the abode of the dead as a shadowy world beneath us. Spiritualism turns to the world of the dead for guidance in life now. I do not affirm or deny the possibility of getting in touch with the dead and the dead's getting in touch with us. I simply do not know. I leave that open to scientific investigation. All I am interested in is the question of whether "a power from below" can and does separate us from the love of God in Christ, if we give our attention to it. The evidence is heavily on the side that it does separate from Christ those who are devoted to it, or dabble in it. So far as I can see and hear, not one new luminous word about human living has ever come through any medium, professional or amateur. Curious incidents and coincidents are cited as proving a connection with the departed, but no new luminous revelation beyond or in addition to what we find in Christ as revealed in the Scriptures. No new moral or spiritual insight has been revealed. It would imply that the moral and spiritual insight of the medium is the determining factor. It is earth-bound. If heaven were breaking through to us, it would be something more and different from the usual moral and spiritual piffle. The word of Isaiah is still valid: "And when they say to you, 'Consult the mediums and the wizards who chirp and mutter,' should not a people consult their God? Should they consult the dead on behalf of the living? To the teaching and to the testimony! Surely for this word which they speak there is no dawn" (8:19-20). The last phrase was true then and true now: "there is no dawn"—no opening light in it!

O Jesus, Thou art the light of this world and that world. Apart from Thee "there is no dawn," for Thou art the dawn. In Thee all our sunsets turn to sunrises and all our gloom into glow. When we walk in Thy light it is Light. We thank Thee. Amen.

AFFIRMATION FOR THE DAY: *In Jesus there is a perpetual dawn—leading to light and only light.*

PEERING BEHIND THE CURTAIN

We are considering the power to separate from the love of God in Christ Jesus our Lord when we give our time and attention and interest to astrology or spiritualism. The love of God in Christ Jesus is seen supremely in the cross. To take your eyes off the cross and put them on the stars or to spend your time in trying to peep beyond the veil of death is to substitute the purposely concealed for the purposely revealed. God revealed His heart at the cross. Nothing in heaven or on earth or under the earth can reveal anything deeper than, or different from the love of God when God in Christ died on the cross to redeem us. To get your eyes off that by putting them on the stars is to substitute the marginal and magical for the central and moral. To try to peep behind the veil is to substitute a peep show for the open vision we have as we gaze through the rent veil of His flesh into the redeeming heart of God.

Someone objects, "Didn't Moses and Elijah appear to Jesus from that other world?" Yes, they did. But what did they talk about? The account tells us: "And behold, two men talked with him, Moses and Elijah, who appeared in glory and spoke of his departure which he was to accomplish at Jerusalem" (Luke 9:30-31). Note: "they spoke of his departure which he was to accomplish at Jerusalem"—they spoke of the cross! Nothing bigger in that world or this than the cross!The focus of their attention was upon the cross.

To spend one's time and attention trying to peer into the secrets of the future takes our eyes off the redemptive act of God at the cross—separates us from that love. The adversary doesn't mind our being religious, in fact he would encourage it, provided he can get us on the marginal stars or the marginal knothole views of the next world instead of on the greatest thing that ever took place in this world, or any world, the cross.

O Father, Thou didst wrap Thy heart in flesh and blood and didst let it break on a cross for our redemption. To leave that in favor of marginal interests is to leave the fountain of living water and turn to broken cisterns that can hold no water. Save us. Amen.

AFFIRMATION FOR THE DAY: *If Moses and Elijah coming from that other world were interested in Jesus and His death, then that is where the focus of my attention will be.*

"NOR ANYTHING ELSE IN ALL CREATION"

With a final gesture Paul sweeps the horizon of possibilities and says: "nor anything else in all creation, will be able to separate us from the love of God in Christ Jesus our Lord." Note that: "nor anything else in all creation." If he has left out any possibility of separation after giving the pairs of opposites—death and life, angels and principalities, things present and things to come, a power from on high or a power from below—he now closes up all the gaps by saying "nor anything else in all creation."

While we marvel at Paul's faith and rhetoric, we have the lingering suspicion that it is faith, not fact, and it is rhetoric, not realism. These things do separate us from the love of God in Christ Jesus our Lord—and separate us every day. Then what is the secret of his being able to make this astounding assertion? He left out one thing—choice. As long as we choose to stay in the love of God in Christ Jesus nothing that Paul mentions can separate us. All these things which Paul mentions are on the outside of us. Nothing from without can separate us, but we can separate ourselves. We can choose to step outside the love of Christ, think thoughts other than His, show attitudes other than His, copy ways other than His, reveal a spirit other than His, and when we do then we are vulnerable to any or all of these things. They do separate us.

If we stay in the love of Christ, by surrender and faith and obedience, then nothing from without can touch us to separate us. Rufus Moseley, a modern saint, sums up his greatest life revelation in this, "God said to me, 'You have nothing to do in life except to live in union with Me.' " He was profoundly right. I do not have to do this, that, or the other—I have to live in union with Christ—all else follows. I do not have to succeed or fail—I have to live in union with Christ.

O Jesus, my Lord, life has found its utmost simplicity and its utmost profundity in Thee. I live in Thee and everything that is good lives in me. I have to ask for nothing, for I have all. I am rich beyond riches, I am free beyond freedom, alive beyond life. I thank Thee. Amen.

AFFIRMATION FOR THE DAY: *Nothing in all creation can separate me, for I have the Creator.*

A QUIETISM WHICH IS DYNAMISM

We ended yesterday by emphasizing that nothing from without can separate us from the love of God in Christ Jesus our Lord. But we can separate ourselves. We therefore have one business in life and only one business: to live inside the love of Christ, in union with Him.

"Isn't this quietism?" someone objects. Yes it is, but a quietism which is a dynamism. It is the same quietism which a plug has when it fits into a socket and remains there receptive and passive. That receptivity and that passivity transmits a mighty activity—the power of electricity. It is the same quietism of the great dams in the region of the Tennessee Valley Authority. The water of these rivers was free to run to the sea before they were dammed up, made to be still. The power of that stillness was harnessed to lifting the level of life for the whole of this section and turned it from a backward, paralyzed mountain section into the fastest growing section of America. The quietism turned into a quickening.

Inside Christ you transmit effortlessly; outside Christ you tear around in a fierce activity and wear out yourself and others around you. You may even become a "big wheel," but a wheel nevertheless which goes around in circles and gets nowhere, except into exhaustion. The quietism in Christ is the same kind of quietism which is at the center of a cyclone—a place of rest, but the place where the power of the cyclone resides. Paul put it thus: "But by the grace of God I am what I am, and his grace toward me was not in vain. On the contrary, I worked harder than any of them, though it was not I, but the grace of God which is with me" (I Cor. 15:10). You live in His grace, you live by His grace, you work by His grace, you are fruitful by His grace, you are everything in His grace.

O Christ, my Lord, I've found the true and only way to live—to live in Thee and in nothing but Thee. Here I am at home. Here is my native land. Here is my life. Here is my energy. I live with Thy life, love with Thy love, and work with Thy energy. Amen.

AFFIRMATION FOR THE DAY: *My heart is the center of creation, for the Creator is there creating.*

"HIS COMING WILL ONLY SERVE"

Before we leave this amazing passage which tells of the security—the perfect security—you find when you live within the circle of the love of God in Christ Jesus, we must emphasize the how of that security.

It is not a security where you are beyond temptation, or where you are exempt from trouble. It is deeper than that. The ancient legend tells of Antaeus who, when he was in touch with his mother Earth, was invincible, for in contact with her he possessed all her strength and resources. Only when he was lifted up and lost contact with his mother Earth could he be conquered. As long as you remain in Christ you possess all the strength, all the goodness, all the victory, all the love, of Christ. You are therefore invincible. But if you get out of Him—in thought, word, deed, or attitude—then you are weak and vulnerable.

As long as you stay in His love nothing can reach you, for in getting through that love to you everything is transformed. The love of Christ is the only thing the Adversary can't get into without ceasing to be the Adversary. Jesus said: "The ruler of this world is coming. He has no power over me; his coming will only serve." The devil actually served Jesus by putting Him on a cross, for He used that cross to redeem a race. Jesus lived in the love of God, and when the cross got to Him it was not calamity but opportunity—opportunity to redeem a race. Hate may try to get to you while you are in the love of Christ, but hate only does for you what it did for Stephen amid falling stones—it brought out a deathless prayer: "Lord, do not hold this sin against them." Hate "served" to bring out a deathless love. Lies, falling on Stephen before the council, turned into light: "And gazing at him, all who sat in the council saw that his face was like the face of an angel." Lies became light when they got into the love of Christ."

O Jesus, my Lord, when I remain in Thee, temptation is triumph, bitterness against me becomes blessedness within me, blows upon me only beat the glory out, misunderstanding becomes a deeper understanding of Thee. I am conqueror and more than a conqueror in Thy love. Amen.

AFFIRMATION FOR THE DAY: *Everything furthers those who follow Christ, if they learn how to use it.*

"SPEAKING THE TRUTH IN CHRIST"

We pass from the all-encompassing passage on security while remaining "in the love of God in Christ Jesus" and go to the next passage in Romans—a passage which tells of outgoingness while remaining in Christ: "I am speaking the truth in Christ. . . my conscience bears me witness in the Holy Spirit" (9:1). Someone has said: "In Christ don't wrestle; just nestle." There is a truth in nestling in Christ, but only a half-truth. The word "nestle" has the word "nest" in it, and a nest is not for comfort, but for creation—something hatches. In Christ something is always hatching, you are always creative. You now, having accepted the truth, begin to speak the truth.

There are three stages in speaking the truth: (1) You simply speak the truth—the bare truth. (2) You speak "the truth in love"—higher than bare truth. (3) You speak "the truth in Christ"—higher than bare truth and higher than speaking the truth in love.

You may speak the truth—the bare truth and be verbally correct, but it may be a lie for it may deceive. A lie is an attempt to deceive, and you can attempt to deceive while telling the truth, for you leave out here and you leave out there and the truth, being less than the whole truth, becomes a lie—an attempt to deceive. You may "speak the truth in love," but the love may be an Eros love—a possessive love and not an agape love—a self-giving love, a divine love. If you speak "the truth in Christ," however, then it is more than the bare truth, more than Eros love and more than agape love, for it is agape love with the content of Christ in that agape love—it is His kind of agape love. His agape love is summed up in the prayer: "Father, forgive them; they know not what they do." "Speaking the truth in Christ" is the highest speaking and the highest truth. It is the high watermark—nothing higher.

O Christ, my Lord, Thou art Truth, and to speak in Thee is to speak in truth. We become so truthful, so identified with it, that we become truth. Not "Truth," for Thou alone art Truth. But our truth echoes Thy Truth. Help me this day to speak the truth in Thee. Amen.

AFFIRMATION FOR THE DAY: *To be in Christ is to be related in love to everybody who is in Christ.*

CONSCIENCE NOT A SAFE GUIDE

We saw yesterday that it was not enough to speak the truth and to speak the truth in love; we must speak "the truth in Christ"—the highest speaking of the truth, for He is Truth. This needs a further statement to complete it: "my conscience bears me witness in the Holy Spirit." There must be a corroboration that we are speaking the truth in Christ—our consciences must bear witness and that witness of conscience must bear witness in the Holy Spirit.

Conscience by itself is not a safe guide. Conscience is the moral sense which approves or disapproves, but you put into the conscience the standards according to which it approves or disapproves. A Hindu's conscience is taught to approve of caste; my conscience is taught to disapprove—diametrically opposite standards are given to the conscience for approval or disapproval. Your conscience must be trained in Christ—not by the moral codes of many "in the churches." Often moral codes in the churches may reflect the social, economic, and racial attitudes of surrounding society.

Your conscience in Christ must be trained by the Holy Spirit. "He will take what is mine and declare it to you." The Holy Spirit is the interpreter, and the only safe interpreter, of the mind of Christ. A psychiatrist told a woman whose husband had set up a relation with his secretary: "You must accommodate yourself to the situation. You can supply his social and family needs like Martha, and the secretary can supply his spiritual and sexual needs like Mary." No wonder her moral nature was outraged by this pseudoscientific and pseudoreligious advice.

The Holy Spirit sensitizes our consciences in the school of Christ. He is the pattern after which our consciences are being patterned.

O Holy Spirit, when we are under Thy cleansing tutelage we are safe. Thou art the Divine Sculptor Who makes us after the ultimate likeness of God—Jesus. Take my conscience and cleanse it of false standards and make it a truly Christian conscience. Amen.

AFFIRMATION FOR THE DAY: *My conscience will be under the tutelage of the Holy Spirit this day.*

"ONE BODY IN CHRIST"

We come now to the next passage in Romans, telling of
another phase of the life in Christ: "so we, though many, are one
body in Christ, and individually members one of another"
(Rom. 12:5). We not only have to speak the truth in Christ, we
have to be related in life and thought and attitude to all others
who are in Christ. There is no such thing as being in Christ
unrelated to others who are in Christ. "To be is to be in
relation," and to be in Christ is to be related with everyone else
who is in Christ. There is no such thing as a Christian in isolation
or in insulation. You have to be in fellowship with all who are in
Christ, or you are thereby not in Christ.

Everybody who belongs to Christ belongs to everybody who
belongs to Christ. One may betray that relationship, but he
cannot deny it, for it is inherent. The inspired record puts it: "so
we . . . are one body in Christ." Not "ought to be," or "are
called to be," or "must recognize ourselves as such," but *are*
one body in Christ." You are in that body, and you can't get out
of that body without getting out of Christ. As long as you stay in
Christ you are in one body.

That doesn't mean that we are all to be in one church—my
church or your church—to be in the "one body." The text says:
"so we, though many, are one body in Christ." It provides for
the "many" and the "one." The New Testament knows of many
churches, but knows of one Church. The many churches were
branches of the one Church. They were the local expression of
the one universal Church. The modern idea of many churches,
separate, sovereign, independent, is unknown in the New
Testament. It is utterly foreign to the New Testament. Paul
cried out when separate denominationalism put up its head: "Is
Christ divided?" *If you are in Christ*, you are in one body.

O Christ, we divide Thee if we divide Thy body, for Thou art
the body and to be in Thee is to be in that "one body." Take
down the barriers in my heart, my prejudices and my fears,
and help me to clasp everyone who owns and names Thee Lord
as my brother. Amen.

AFFIRMATION FOR THE DAY: *Every cord that binds me to Christ also
binds me to my brother, and I can't break with one without
breaking with the other.*

ONE, ONLY AROUND CHRIST

We saw yesterday that the church is made up of "many" and yet is "one body in Christ." The many provides for diversity, and one body provides for unity—unity amid diversity.

That is the New Testament pattern: many, yet one—unity in diversity. That is not our pattern; we have the many but are not one. Each of the many looks on itself as the one—join me and then we will be one. That isn't often spoken, but it is usually the underlying thought. Yet it is sometimes expressed, as in a certain woman's will. She belonged to a very narrow group and her husband to another group, but they loved each other. In her will she asked that she not be buried alongside her husband, but in a different portion of the cemetery, for she said, "When Jesus comes I will be raised, but he won't, and I would hate to get up and leave him there, so bury me in another portion of the cemetery." When the husband saw the will he was broken-hearted. Denominationalism, as we now have it, divides people in life—and in death!

I say, "as we now have it"—but we needn't have it this way. In spite of all our divisions, Christians are the most united body on earth. They are united at the place of Christ. They are united in the deepest thing in life—life itself. They share a common life in Christ. They do not have to seek unity—they have it. I repeat: "Every one who belongs to Christ belongs to every one who belongs to Christ." We can get together around Christ, for that is the place where we are together. We are together there, not marginally, but centrally and inherently.

There are two other places where the attempt is made to make us one—around bishops and baptism. Accept our type of bishops, or accept our type of baptism, and we will be one. I respect any man's desire for a certain type of bishop and for a certain type of baptism, but to try to unite the Christian world around either one will result in division, not unity.

O Jesus, my Lord and Savior, Thou art our unity, for Thou alone art worthy to be the center of our unity. To be united around bishops or baptism, even if possible, would be an unworthy unity—around a man or a mode. Around Thee, the Divine, alone are we one. Amen.

AFFIRMATION FOR THE DAY: *In Christ I am inwardly unified and I am unified with my brother—a double unity.*

ORDINATION WITHOUT LAYING ON OF HANDS

We saw yesterday that the proposal to unite the Christians around a special type of bishop or a special type of baptism would result in division, not union. Neither bishops nor baptism can go back to Jesus for their starting point and for their authority.

It was said of Jesus: "Jesus himself did not baptize, but only his disciples." Why didn't Jesus baptize with water? He saved Himself to give the "one baptism"—the baptism of the Holy Spirit. "One Lord, one faith, one baptism"—what is that baptism? With water? The "one Lord" is the Lord Jesus; the "one faith" is the faith in the Lord Jesus; the "one baptism" is the baptism which the Lord Jesus gives. John said: "I came baptizing with water . . . this is he who baptizes with the Holy Spirit" (John 1:31, 33). Jesus said the same: "for John baptized with water, but before many days you shall be baptized with the Holy Spirit" (Acts 1:5). The fulfillment of that is this: "Being therefore exalted at the right hand of God, and having received from the Father the promise of the Holy Spirit, he has poured out this which you see and hear" (Acts 2:33). There He was giving the "one baptism"—the baptism with the Holy Spirit. So baptism with water cannot unite us, for it is not the "one baptism" which Jesus came to give—it is marginal—the baptism of the Spirit is central.

Nor could bishops unite us. Ordination of bishops by the laying on of hands in a line of succession does not go back to Jesus. There is no record that He laid hands on His disciples to ordain them. But He did ordain them: "Ye have not chosen me, but I have chosen you, and ordained you, that ye should go and bring forth fruit" (John 15:16, K.J.V.). They were "ordained" by the choice—He separated and commissioned them by that choice—not by any laying on of hands.

O Jesus, Thy choice is our ordination. All men can do is to recognize that choice, that ordination. They cannot give that ordination, for Thou art Lord, not they. Thy call is my separation. I yield to it and yield to it gladly and completely. Amen.

AFFIRMATION FOR THE DAY: *Thy choice is my consecration—I need and want no other.*

MANY ARE ONE BODY IN CHRIST

We have seen that no special mode of baptism and no special laying on of hands of bishops has any backing of Jesus. Neither of these can or does go back to Him for authority. If they begin, they must begin with the apostles. The gap between the apostles and Jesus in this matter is fixed. Therefore they can, in reference to bishops, talk only of "apostolic succession." I'm not interested in "apostolic succession," for the terminus of my faith is not the apostles, but Jesus Christ. Ours is not an apostolic church, but a Christian church. The apostles were men like ourselves, partly Christian, but no center of a faith. That faith can rest only in the Divine—the Divine Son of God. If our faith terminates in men, then it rests this side of the Divine and cannot be a Divine faith.

So our faith, and therefore our unity, are not in bishops, and not in baptism, but in Christ. The only place where we can be united is in Christ, for in Him we are one. We do not have to seek for unity; we have it in Him. All we have to do is to express what we already have. The Christians are the most united body on earth, and the most divided—united at the Center, and divided at the place of the "whats." Not what I believe, but Whom! If I say to any audience, "What do you believe?" they will automatically divide, no two believing exactly alike. But if I ask, "Whom do you trust?" then automatically they come together, one Name upon their lips—Christ.

So this verse is profoundly right: "so we, though many, are one body in Christ." We are not, and cannot be, one body in bishops, in baptism, in church government, but we are one body in Christ. Not we ought to be one body, but we are, inherently and intrinsically so.

O blessed Lord, we are grateful that we have a center of unity. We are grateful that that center is a divine center. Were it less than the Divine we could not rejoice in it. We do rejoice in our living unity in Thee. We thank Thee, thank Thee. Amen.

AFFIRMATION FOR THE DAY: *Not "what" but "Whom" shall be my emphasis.*

"THE CHURCH OF JESUS CHRIST IN _____"

We saw yesterday that "so we, though many, are one body in Christ." We emphasized the "one." Now we must emphasize the "many." This unity in Christ is not a unity of uniformity, but a unity of diversity. It provides for the many. It doesn't read "so we being one are one body in Christ." That would attempt unity only through uniformity, which would not be a living unity but a dead unity. Jesus prayed that "they may be one, even as we are One." How is God "One"? Undifferentiated Being? No. There is the Father, Son, and Holy Spirit, each with separate name, separate entity, separate function, and yet profoundly one. He prayed that we might have His type of unity—a unity in diversity.

The only type of unity in diversity that I know of is Federal Union. Federal Union puts together two apparently contradictory urges—the desire for union with the whole and the desire for local freedom. It puts together union and freedom and thus fulfills our very nature. Applied to the churches it would mean that we would have in America one church, "The Church of Jesus Christ in America." Dr. Kramer, a theologian, says that the only valid name for a church is "The Church of Christ in _____." We add "Jesus" to center it in the Incarnation and to distinguish it from local bodies which claim the name "Church of Christ." Under that "one body," that one church, we would provide for the many—many branches of the one Church—"The Lutheran Branch of the Church of Jesus Christ in America," and so on. In those local branches, there would be self-government, states' rights—union with freedom.

There will be one Church, many branches. Just as in a tree there is one trunk, but many branches all inhering in the one trunk, forming a symmetrical whole by the very diversity of the branches, so it must be with the Church.

O Christ, Thou art the trunk and we are the branches. We all inhere in Thee, draw one life from a common source. Then we manifest this one life in diverse forms. Help us to appreciate and love this diversity while being conscious of our oneness in Thee. Amen.

AFFIRMATION FOR THE DAY: *Let me be grateful for the diversity of the various branches which help make a symmetrical whole.*

PRIDE REDEEMED

We now move on to consider some other "in Christ" passages in Romans. The next is: "In Christ Jesus, then, I have reason to be proud of my work for God" (15:17). "Proud of my work for God." Is there a place for pride in a Christian? Pride is usually condemned as anathema, something to be cast out root and branch. Can pride be redeemed? Yes.

If pride is rooted in an unsurrendered ego, then of course it is sinful pride. It is a manifestation of self-centeredness, calling attention to itself. Pride can be constructive, however, and can help us to be at our best. Without any pride we become careless, slump, and deteriorate. "He has no pride" can be just as damning, as saying, "He is proud and vain." Pride, rightly rooted, can be an urge that keeps up our morale, a spur to achievement, a driving force. "Rightly rooted"—that is the real point. Rooted in egoism it is an ugly manifestation; rooted in Christ it can be a beautiful manifestation.

Our pride must be rooted up, surrendered when it has its roots in an unsurrendered self. It must be replanted in Christ. The pride must draw its sustenance from the humility of Christ. When it boasts, it makes its boast in the Lord. If you are boasting in Another, it is legitimate and right and befitting. At the heart of this righteous pride is a deep humility, for you know that everything you do you do by Grace—the Grace of Another. Pride is really converted into gratitude. Paul added: "For I will not venture to speak of anything except what Christ has wrought through me" (15:18). I am not the source—it is "through me," not "from me." That saves you from a false humility which is disguised pride and gives us a sense of self-respect and self-acceptance, because of gratitude for what He is doing. He uses me; therefore I cannot abuse myself. He lifts me; therefore I uplift Him.

O my Lord, Thy coming into me washes me from inferiority, from baseness, from a hangdog feeling and gives me a sense of divine self-respect and pride—righteous pride in what Thou art able to accomplish through me. I'm gratefully proud of Thy work in me. Amen.

AFFIRMATION FOR THE DAY: *My pride in Thee makes me humble.*

"THAT EXPLAINS IT"

We meditated yesterday on: "In Christ Jesus I have reason to be proud of my work for God." We saw that pride can be redeemed when it is pride of what He is doing in and through us. That pride, glorying in Another, becomes humility. You can be humble only when you are conscious of being great. This verse illustrates that: "Jesus, knowing that the Father had given all things into his hands, and that he had come from God and was going to God, rose from supper, laid aside his garments, and girded himself with a towel. Then he poured water into a basin and began to wash the disciples' feet" (John 13:3-5). Knowing that all things had been given into His hands—conscious of being great with an ultimate greatness—"all things into His hands"—He could afford to be humble. Real humility is not rooted in a sense of humiliation; it is rooted in a sense of being inwardly great in Him. The little person doesn't dare to be humble; it would give away his littleness. He has to act a part—a part of being great to compensate for his being small. The one who is truly great within doesn't have to act a part; he has nothing to keep up; he is great—great by the grace of God in Christ, therefore he can do the menial.

I once secured a sweeper's broom and cleaned the filthy toilet in a compartment in a train in India. Some Brahmins in the compartment, surprised, asked who I was? When I told them that I was a follower of Christ and that I had learned what I had just done from my stay with Mahatma Gandhi in his Ashram, one of them replied, "That explains it." In their eyes, that transformed it from being a degradation into being a sacrament, learned from Jesus and Gandhi. Jesus had cleansed the filth of my heart without being degraded, so in Him I could cleanse the filth of a toilet without being degraded. I was great by His grace, therefore I could afford to be small in this incident—out of gratitude.

O Divine Master, Thou Who dost stoop to wash my feet, my hands, my heart, by Thy very doing this Thou dost make my knees bend, my heart bend—dost make me prostrate at Thy feet—for I see greatness become lowly for my sake. Accept my gratitude. Amen.

AFFIRMATION FOR THE DAY: *The little man is afraid to bend lest he expose his littleness.*

"IN THE FULNESS OF THE BLESSING"

We pass on to another important "in Christ" passage in Romans: "and I know that when I come to you I shall come in the fulness of the blessing of Christ" (15:29). I shall come . . . in . . . Christ. In Christ there is blessing, and I shall come in the fulness of that blessing.

Here we find an amazing self-confidence: "I shall come"—not with a blessing from Christ, but "in the fulness of the blessing of Christ." He had an amazing self-confidence because he had an amazing self-surrender to Christ. The reason we have no self-confidence is because we have no Christ-confidence. We have no Christ-confidence because we have no self-surrender to Him. The unsurrendered self is always uncertain and hesitant—it has not made a complete surrender to Him; therefore it cannot have boldness to take from Him. When there is full surrender to Him there is full confidence that we will come "in the fulness of the blessing of Christ." Fully given, we can fully take. Paul was confident that he would be adequate for anything the situation in Rome demanded, and Rome was the nerve center of pagan power. In other words, Paul was saying, "I have enough and to spare to meet the worst." The secret was that full surrender meant full supply of the resources of Christ.

An Indian woman with radiant face emphasized that "we should be power conscious instead of problem conscious." Paul knew the secret of being power conscious. We can know it too. Then when we go to situations we will not be conscious of our emptiness, but conscious of His fullness. Then we won't be half-full vessels trying to run over. We will be fully committed, therefore fully communicative. The person who is fully in Christ is fully capable of anything he ought to do. As Moffatt puts it: "In Him who strengthens me, I am able for anything." I will come "in the fulness."

Spirit of God, Thou art supply. I can take from Thee, when wholly surrendered to Thee—I can take from Thee with both hands all I need for myself and others, anywhere and at any time. I am adequate in Thee. I overflow with confidence because I overflow with willingness. Amen.

AFFIRMATION FOR THE DAY:

> *"In the heart of man a cry,*
> *In the heart of God supply."*

FROM JOHN'S BAPTISM TO JESUS'

We note another "in Christ" passage: "Greet Prisca and Aquila, my fellow workers in Christ Jesus, who risked their necks for my life, to whom not only I but also all the churches of the Gentiles give thanks" (Rom. 16:3-4). Paul spelled the name of the wife of Aquila "Prisca," but Luke in Acts 18:2 spelled her name "Priscilla." Verbally they are not alike, vitally they are. So we do not look for verbal inspiration, but we can and do look for vital inspiration of the Scriptures.

He called them "my fellow workers in Christ Jesus." Luke revealed in Acts 18:2-3: "And he found a Jew named Aquila . . . with his wife Priscilla . . . and because he was of the same trade he stayed with them, and they worked, for by trade they were tentmakers." Aquila and Priscilla were refugees: "lately come from Italy . . . because Claudius had commanded all the Jews to leave Rome." They were refugees, but instead of going on charity, or relief, "they worked." Being in Christ gave them an inner self-respect—a self-reliance, a Christ-reliance. Perhaps there was no charity or relief in those pre-Christian days. In any case it made for toughened character. So toughened and strengthened were Aquila and Priscilla that they passed on their strength to the learned and eloquent Apollo, who "spoke and taught accurately the things concerning Jesus, though he knew only the baptism of John . . . but when Priscilla and Aquila heard him, they took him and expounded to him the way of God more accurately" (Acts 18:25-26). They probably took him from John's baptism—water baptism—to Jesus' baptism—the baptism of the Spirit.

Paul called them "my fellow workers in Christ Jesus." They were "fellow workers" where their work counted—they were making more effective workers by introducing them to the Holy Spirit. So Paul and Aquila and Priscilla were "fellow workers," working with their hands at the same trade and working "in the Spirit" in introducing others to the Spirit.

O Jesus, Thou dost include everyone in Thee who works by the Spirit. Blessed Lord, teach me to teach the teachers to know the Spirit of Truth Who will teach us all things. We know little or nothing if we don't know Him. Amen.

AFFIRMATION FOR THE DAY: *My work will be to introduce men to the working of the Holy Spirit.*

"APPROVED IN CHRIST"

We come now to four more "in Christ" passages, the last in Romans: "Greet Andronicus and Junias . . . they were in Christ before me" (16:7). Paul felt that the only thing that mattered was being in Christ, and the deepest regret was that he was not "in Christ" during those wasted years he spent out of Christ. The outstanding thing regarding Andronicus and Junias was that they were "in Christ before me." Anything in Christ is fruitful, anything out of Christ is futile.

Another passage: "Greet Ampliatus, my beloved in the Lord" (16:8). In a world where abnormality was prevalent and taken for granted, this phrase "my beloved in the Lord" was the most cleansing and consecrating phrase imaginable. It turned the sordid into the sacred, and made possible a deep, pure affection between those of the same sex.

Another: "Greet Apelles who is approved in Christ" (16:10). This set up a new standard of approval—"approved in Christ"—the highest standard possible. One may be approved in business circles, in professional circles, in social circles, in political circles, in intellectual circles, and the approval may be comparatively worthless, for the standards may be low. Only in one place approval is worthwhile and vital—"approved in Christ." Without being "approved in Christ" all other approvals are meaningless. Conscious of being "approved in Christ" you can face all the disapprovals of men with peace and assurance.

The last: "Greet Rufus, eminent in the Lord" (16:13). If "approved in the Lord" is the only approval that matters, so "eminent in the Lord" is the only eminence. We may be eminent in our estimation, in the estimation of others, but the real and only question is "Am I eminent in the Lord?" If not, my eminence has no permanence, a breath of questioning and it is gone. "In the Lord," it is permanent.

O blessed Lord, I want to be approved in Thee, and eminent in Thee. Wash me from all insincerity, all pride, and all make-believe, so I can have an approval in Thee and an eminence in Thee. Then nothing else matters. I walk the earth with my head up. Amen.

AFFIRMATION FOR THE DAY: *"Approved in Christ"—I look upon all other approvals or disapprovals as irrelevant.*

"IN CHRIST"—A THEOLOGICAL CONCEPT?

We have run through some astounding passages in Romans about the results of being in Christ. Before we can go on with any sense of certainty we must face this question: Is this being in Christ a theological concept, or is it a fact in life? If it is a theological concept, then we investigate it as we do any other verbal proposition and come to our intellectual conclusions. It may be intellectually satisfying, or it may not be. In any case life is not changed one way or the other. Suppose this being in Christ is not a figure of speech, however, but a fact; then we are up against a life decision and a choice: We are actually in Christ, or we are not—what are we going to do about it?

If Paul's emphasis on being in Christ is a theological concept imposed on the facts of life, it is one thing; but if it is something supported in reality—an experimental fact—then it is quite another thing. If it is a theological concept, it is out of harmony with the Christian faith. It would be the Word become word—a theology, a philosophy, a moralism. But the Christian faith is not the Word become word, it is the Word become flesh. That makes it different, radically different from all other faiths—all of them are the Word become word—they are good views. The gospel is not good views, but good news. This being in Christ cannot be a concept, but a condition. It is not a proposition—it is a position. We are actually in Christ. It is a world of its own, with its allegiance, its loyalties, its attitudes, its outlook, its very life. The person who steps into Christ becomes as different from the ordinary man as the ordinary man is different from the animal. It is not merely a change of location; it is a change of life. It is a world within a world—a world of freedom amid a world of bondage; it is heaven amid hell.

O Jesus, being in Thee is such bondage and such freedom; such exacting laws and such exulting liberty. When I am in Thee I walk the earth a conqueror, afraid of nothing, afraid of no one. My only fear is to step out of Thee. Keep me "in." Amen.

AFFIRMATION FOR THE DAY: *I pass from "in Christ" as a concept to an experience. I'm in Him, therefore in Everything in Him.*

IN HARMONY WITH, OR REVOLT AGAINST

We must linger another day on the thought that this being in Christ is not a theological figure of speech, but a fact—the most important fact in the universe, barring none. Being in Christ is as definite a thing spiritually as being in the United States of America is a definite thing geographically and spiritually. Being in the United States, really "in," brings you under its laws, its culture, its history, its outlook, its spirit. You can be in the United States geographically but not in it spiritually. You can be out of harmony with it, in inner revolt against it.

When I was a young Christian I went to a tent meeting and there was a great deal of uncontrolled emotion. The evangelist, under whom I was converted, saw me the next day and said, "Were you in the meeting last night?" I replied, "I was there, but I wasn't 'in' it." Physically I was there, but spiritually I was out of harmony.

Being in Christ is so real a condition that if you are not spiritually "in," you are not in Christ at all. If you have adopted tempers and attitudes out of harmony with Him, you are not in Him at all. You have stepped out.

I have seen people step in and out of Christ, and the difference was registered clearly on their faces. They were different persons. Some people are in themselves, tied up with themselves, bounded by themselves, choking with themselves; then I've seen those same people step out of themselves by surrender and in a moment they were in Christ, and they were entirely different beings. Nothing the same except their name. When you are in Christ you come under a new set of laws of life, new attitudes, new culture, new outlook, new spirit. You are a citizen of a new "country." You inherit the resources of Christ. Everything that belongs to Him belongs to you.

O Christ, my Lord, I step out of my poverty into Thy riches; out of my sin into Thy goodness; out of my sickness into Thy health, out of my nothingness into Thy allness. In Thee I am rich, good, well, and full beyond telling. I thank Thee. Amen.

AFFIRMATION FOR THE DAY:

> *In Christ I am alive,*
> *Out of Christ I'm dead—*
> *Enough said!*

"IN CHRIST"—PAUL'S PHRASE?

We paused at the end of last week to raise the question whether this being in Christ is a theological concept rather than a real state of being. We came to the conclusion that it is a real state of being—the only real state of being. Compared to this, all else is unreality. Here life is Life, being is Being, love is Love, joy is Joy.

A further question arises: Isn't this Pauline, rather than Christian—rooted in Paul rather than in Christ? It is true that Paul gives the chief emphasis to the idea of being in Christ, for he uses it 97 times out of 172 times. The phrase is found in all the other twenty-seven books of the New Testament except Matthew, Mark, Luke, Jude, James.

In Mark we find: "And he appointed twelve, to be with him" (3:14). It was with Him. That is as far as the Synoptics go, and that is about as far as present-day Christianity goes. To be with Him is the pattern, the norm. But a "with Him" Christianity is like an electric bulb's being with the socket but not in it, a seed being with the soil, but not in it, food being with you, but not in you. It's the "in" that counts.

In II John we find this: "Any one who goes ahead and does not abide in the doctrine of Christ does not have God; he who abides in the doctrine of Christ has both the Father and the Son" (vs. 9). Here "in Christ" has been shifted to abiding "in the doctrine of Christ"—a system built up around Him. If we have correct views about Him we have the Father and the Son. Christianity becomes correct belief about Christ instead of a surrender to Christ which puts you in Him. This is the Great Substitute—the "in" has become "about." Christianity becomes a theological system instead of a way of life—becomes good views, instead of good news.

O Savior, Thou art not satisfied with being with us and not in us, and we are not satisfied with being with Thee; we want to be in Thee. Love wants to be identified with the loved one. I want to be identified with Thee by surrender and obedience—I want to be in Thee. Amen.

AFFIRMATION FOR THE DAY: *All my "abouts" will become "ins"—this will be my progress in Christ.*

"IN CHRIST"—NOT IN THE EPISTLE
OF JAMES—WHY?

We are looking at some of the places in the New Testament where the phrase "in Christ" is not found. The Epistle of James is one. It is obvious why the phrase "in Christ" is not found in that Epistle. The emphasis there is on a moralism, an activism, good works: "Show me your faith apart from your works, and I by my works will show you my faith. . . . Was not Abraham our father justified by works, when he offered his son Isaac upon the altar?" (2:18, 21).

Luther, emphasizing justification by faith, called this Epistle of James "an Epistle of straw"—no wheat—because it emphasized justification by works. He was profoundly right, for in making justification by works your goal you emphasize the human endeavor—you are in yourself doing your good deed and not in Christ, living by His resources and doing good deeds because you are in Him and doing what He does, for you are partaking of His life.

The Epistle of James is the center of faith, unconsciously so, for the majority of Christians in our churches. In this Epistle the name of Jesus Christ is mentioned only twice: "James, a servant of God and of the Lord Jesus Christ," and "My brethren, show no partiality as you hold the faith of our Lord Jesus Christ, the Lord of Glory" (1:1, 2:1). Here he mentions that he is "a servant of the Lord Jesus Christ" and "the faith of our Lord Jesus Christ." He mentions Jesus Christ marginally, but his working faith is salvation by good deeds. That is an exact picture of much of modern Christianity: You are in yourself, doing good deeds and not in Christ, living by His resources and therefore doing good deeds as a manifestation of that life in Him.

One lives by flogging—flogging the will; the other lives by flowing—flowing of good deeds as the outcome of contact with the Source.

O Jesus, in myself I'm striving and tense and strained. In Thee I'm relaxed and receptive and releasing—releasing Thy Life to others. This is so divinely easy, so divinely natural, so divinely supernatural. I'm in Thee, and all Thou hast is mine—mine for the taking. Amen.

AFFIRMATION FOR THE DAY: *I shall live not by what I do, but what He has done for me and through me.*

"THE FAITH ONCE DELIVERED"

There is another Epistle in which there is no "in Christ" passage—the Epistle of Jude. This Epistle mentions Jesus Christ five times: "servant of Jesus Christ" (v. 1); "kept for Jesus Christ" (v. 1); "deny our only master and Lord, Jesus Christ" (v. 4); "mercy of our Lord Jesus Christ unto eternal life" (v. 21); "through Jesus Christ our Lord" (v. 25).

Here we have four different statements about Jesus: "servant of," "kept for," "deny," and "through Jesus Christ." None of them express "in Christ." There is "of," "for," and "through," but not "in." Why? A verse reveals the reason: "I found it necessary to write appealing to you to contend for the faith which was once for all delivered to the saints" (v. 3).

The faith was something "once for all delivered to the saints"—it was delivered in the past as a system of doctrine and belief and must be defended. The word used is stronger: "contend for the faith." This gives a slant to Christianity which has affected the ages and still affects them. Had the emphasis been on "in Christ," then Christianity would be something to be demonstrated. But the emphasis was on "of" and "through"— something outside us—a system of doctrine and belief handed down. This was not to be demonstrated, but defended. The appeal was verbal, not vital.

This is based on the conception of Christianity as the Word become word—a theology, a philosophy, a moralism. Christianity is the Word become flesh—the Idea become fact. Then the only way to be in line with that Word become flesh is for us to be a continuation of that Word become flesh in us. If we are in Christ, then we are not verbal defenders of that faith, but vital demonstrators. He Himself is His own defense. We show Him, and He defends Himself.

O Jesus, my Lord and Savior, when we lift Thee up by living Thy life, Thou dost appeal to men as the light appeals to the eye. Teach me this day in every thought I think, every word I utter, every deed I do, to lift Thee up. Thou art self-verifying. Amen.

AFFIRMATION FOR THE DAY: *Today I shall not try to defend the faith, but illustrate it.*

"I MUST CONTEND"—"I MUST COMMEND"—WHICH?

We pause another day on the emphasis of Jude on contending for the faith once delivered to the saints. This passage has a truth in it—the faith must be defended. All my life I've had to defend that faith before the non-Christian world. But how do you contend for that faith? Certainly not by contention! Christianity can no more be appreciated in a contention than sweet music can be appreciated in a dog fight.

To contend for the faith is to commend the Author of that faith to people. We lift Him up, and He does His own commending. To try to commend Jesus by verbal contention is like trying to organize a society for the protection of the sun because somebody is throwing mud at it. The sun doesn't need protection—it needs just to shine, and it does its own defending by what it is and does. Lift up Jesus by word and by life and He defends Himself. "And I, when I am lifted up from the earth, will draw all men to myself."

The difference between contending for the faith and commending the faith by lifting up Christ is the difference between unchristianity and Christianity. One is egocentric and the other is Christ-centric. One says, "I must contend"; the other says, "I must commend Him." One points to oneself as the defender of the faith; the other points to Him as the Faith itself. One tries to win an argument and the other tries to win the man. One creates combativeness, the other creates conversion. One tries to show off himself—his cleverness, his ability to down an opponent, the other shows off Jesus and His ability to save. One goes round in circles in argument, the other puts the others' feet upon the Way. The one has Christian words, but has lost the Word made flesh amid words. One is unchristian, the other Christian.

O God, Thou didst show Thyself not in words but in the Word—the Word made flesh. Help us not to depart from Thy method of revelation and take our own—a revelation of ourselves. Help us to point by word and deed and life and say, "Behold the Lamb of God." Amen.

AFFIRMATION FOR THE DAY: *Jesus defends Himself to the soul the way sunlight defends itself to the eye.*

"I COMMEND MY SAVIOR TO YOU"

There is a truth in the conception that Christianity is a faith "once for all delivered to the saints." The Incarnation has to be "once for all," and for all men. It could not be repeated. Every attempt to produce another Christ has ended in failure—and disaster to those who have followed the so-called "Christs." After a long line of prophets and teachers He sent His Son "last of all." So the Incarnation is "once for all."

Jesus provided for a continuing unfoldment of the meaning of that Incarnation. "I have yet many things to say to you, but you cannot bear them now. When the Spirit of truth comes, he will guide you into all the truth. . . . He will glorify me, for he will take what is mine and declare it to you" (John 16:12-14). Here Jesus provided for a fixed revelation—the Holy Spirit would continuously unfold the meaning of Jesus. So it was fixed and yet unfolding—static and dynamic.

The trouble with "the faith once for all delivered to the saints" interpreters is that they contend that their interpretation is "the faith once for all delivered to the saints." They confound the Incarnation with their interpretation of it. They have the Incarnation neatly tied up in a package of statements about it and they contend for the package. They feel they have caught the Word in a web of their words. But Jesus may have stepped out beyond the web of their words long ago. The Word is always bigger than our words. Paul calls Jesus the "unspeakable gift"—you can't speak Him completely. In the end you have to kneel in adoration at the Wonder of the Word.

You commend this Word to the astonished gaze as the Word unfolds before us and will forever unfold. We will never fathom its depths or reach its heights. It has a surprise in it eternally.

O Blessed Unfolding Lord! The Spirit of Truth is blessedly unfolding Thy glory. We stand lost in wonder, love, and praise. We will never outgrow Thee or catch up to Thee, and yet we are in Thee. Blessed assurance, blessed adventure! Amen.

AFFIRMATION FOR THE DAY: *Since my goal is a flying goal, I must grow to keep even.*

WITH HIM BUT NOT IN HIM

We have been noting the places in the New Testament in which "in Christ" is not found, and the reason for this omission. The three Synoptic Gospels—Matthew, Mark, and Luke—do not have the phrase for obvious reasons. They were at the stage of "Immanuel—God with us," but not "in us." The account says that Jesus chose twelve "to be with Him" (Mark 3:14). They were with Him, and not in Him. The "in Him" stage comes after the coming of the Holy Spirit at Pentecost. Up to then it was "with," and after that "in." The "with" had to end that the "in" might begin. He withdrew His presence and gave them His omnipresence.

The church as a whole is still in the stage of "with." Christ is with the members, inspiring, convicting, converting, and guiding, but He is not in them and they are not in Him. He comes and goes with changes of feeling. Sometimes there is what is called "the dark night of the soul," a condition which, I am persuaded, belongs largely to the "with" stage and seldom to the "in" stage. It lacks the sense of being a fountain of life bubbling up from within. It seems pushed from without rather than impelled from within. It is artificial rather than artesian. It has to be stirred by sermons, pushed by appeals, and reminded by reminders. It is not self-starting.

When the "in" stage comes, however, then the person isn't pushed; he pushes. He becomes the center of creative energy—from within. A man thoughtfully said to a minister, "You are an illustration of Christian dynamism." The man to whom he spoke was seventy-five! It was not just the bubbling of animal spirits, but a fountain of life that kept on flowing in spite of approaching age. When you are in Christ, then all that belongs to Him belongs to you—His energy, His buoyancy, His life, interfuses your life and makes it live and live abundantly.

O Savior Divine, I draw from Thee food for my thought, stimulus for my emotions, strength for my will, and Life for my life. All my springs are in Thee. I live by Life not my own, rejoice with joy not my own, and do things I can't do. Glory be! Amen.

AFFIRMATION FOR THE DAY: *Since I do all my living within, I shall cultivate the "in" side of my relationship with Him.*

"IN CHRIST" PASSAGES IN JOHN'S GOSPEL

We now turn to John's Gospel and, unlike the Synoptics, which do not mention being in Christ at all, we find the equivalent of being "in Christ" mentioned sixteen times. This is what we would expect, for John's Gospel, being written later, would reflect the general conception of being in Christ which took the place of being with Christ. The Christians found they were in Christ. They had moved from the "with" to the "in." John reflects that transition. This is important, for it shows that this being in Christ was not just Pauline—it was Christian. It was inherent. It was not invented by Paul and imposed on Christianity; it was something exposed out of its very nature.

John was saturated with it. The first passage: "In him was life, and the life was the light of men" (1:4). Nothing could be more penetrating and important than this: "In Him was life"—for nothing is more important in life than life. The alternative is not-life, or death, and that is exactly the alternative presented: in Christ you are in life; out of Christ you are in not-life, death. This is not arbitrarily imposed on life by the edict of God—it is just a fact. Those in Christ have life—have it now, and will have it hereafter; and those not in Christ do not have life—they do not have it now, and will not have it hereafter.

Nothing, absolutely nothing more important could be said than what I have just said—provided it is fact. If it is fiction, it doesn't matter. If it is fiction, it will prove to be an *ignis fatuus*, a false fire leading us into swamps of despair and disillusionment. If it is fact, however, it becomes the light of the world. Not to have it is to stumble into deepening gloom. To have it is to have a light which leads to the perfect day.

The more important thing is that this vast experiment we are making with this thing called life is working out just that way.

O Jesus, Lord and Master, something dies within us when we depart from Thee even in thought. Something lives within us when we step into Thee even in thought—we live! That awes us. That makes us yearn to be in Thee every moment so we can live every moment. Amen.

AFFIRMATION FOR THE DAY: *I am made by my very structural makeup to be in Christ. There I am at home.*

"IN HIM WAS LIFE"

We pondered yesterday on: "In him was life, and the life was the light of men." We saw that the moment this thing we call life is put in Him by surrender and obedience it begins to live. Begins to live in thought—the noncreative begin to be creative; in emotion—the noncaring begin to care; in will—the nonacting begin to act wherever human need presents itself. When you touch Him you begin to live—to live to your fingertips and beyond! The point is that just as a magnet magnetizes all it touches, so He makes living and life-giving all He touches. "The life was the light of men"—where that life comes it turns into light—light on this business of living, not for some men, but for men, universally.

The life of Jesus has literally become light for all men. George Bernard Shaw, whom no one would think of as being an avowed Christian, said: "After reviewing the world of human events for sixty years, I am prepared to say that I see no other way out of the world's misery except the way that Christ would take if He should undertake the work of a modern statesman." A little boy of twelve stood listening to the description of crime by a guide in the headquarters of the F.B.I. in Washington, and he spoke up and said to the whole crowd, "It's certain that these people never knew Jesus, or they wouldn't be doing this kind of thing." The guide came and put his arm around the boy and said, "Son, you said something." The great dramatist and the little boy both converge on one thing—the life of Jesus is the light of men. Wherever He comes there is light; wherever He is not there is darkness. There is no exception.

Thou Light of the World, may I take Thee as my light and only light. When I follow Thee I walk in light; when I don't follow Thee I stumble in darkness. In every situation Thou art light. May I take Thee into every situation in my total life. In His name. Amen.

AFFIRMATION FOR THE DAY: *I shall walk in the Light until I shall become light.*

"DRIFTING INTO HUMANISM"

We turn now to another "in Him" passage, and a very important one: "Now is the Son of man glorified, and in him God is glorified" (John 13:31). "In Him God is glorified." This is important, for this is unlike the Hindu system where you pick out the god you choose, your *ishtadeva,* your chosen deity, and let the rest go. In Him you do not let God go and concentrate on Jesus. When you concentrate on Jesus "God is glorified"—you find God when you find Jesus. The more you know of Jesus the more you know of God. Jesus doesn't rival or push out God. By actual experience, if Jesus is dimmed God is dimmed, and conversely, where Jesus is emphasized God is the more real. It is a strange phenomenon—but it is a fact.

A member of a Unitarian group came to me and said: "Won't you come to our national convention and help us get God back. We are drifting into humanism." That was strange—Unitarianism which concentrated on God was losing Him, and I who concentrated on Jesus had found God—and had found Him to the degree that I concentrated on Jesus. The fact is that apart from Jesus we know very little about God, and what we know is usually wrong. When you deepen the Christ-consciousness, you deepen the God-consciousness. I can't tell where one ends and the other begins in my experience.

Another amazing thing is this: God was glorified in Jesus at the moment when the cross began to loom before Him. "When he [Judas] had gone out, Jesus said, 'Now is the Son of man glorified, and in him God is glorified.' " The emphasis is on "now." God was glorified in Jesus as Jesus chose the cross. God approved of the cross and was glorified in it, for it was the revelation of the character of God as sacrificial love. There is no higher glory than that—none whatever.

O Father, I'm grateful that Your glory is not particularly in the stars or in the manifestations of Your might, but in Your self-giving at a Cross. Such a God can have my heart, and can have it without qualification, for at the cross I see the heart of my Father, and I'm satisfied. Amen.

AFFIRMATION FOR THE DAY: *The cross lights up the nature of God as love.*

IS GOD AS GOOD AS JESUS?

We examine some kindred passages in John: "Do you not believe that I am in the Father and the Father in me? . . . the Father who dwells in me does his works. Believe me that I am in the Father and the Father in me; or else believe me for the sake of the works themselves" (14:10-11). Here Jesus submitted the whole matter of His being in the Father and the Father's being in Him to a simple test: the works—the outcome.

He gave the same test regarding His disciples: "You will know them by their fruits." The outcome was the criterion. There is no higher test; the outcome in every case, in everything, is the criterion. You do not gather figs from thistles nor grapes from thorns. The manifestation is the revelation of the inner nature. The amazing thing is that He applied that test to Himself. "Is the manifestation of My life in deeds what you would expect God to do? As you look up through My deeds to God, what kind of God do you see? Is the kind of God you'd like to see in the universe the kind of God you are seeing through My deeds, My works?" No more searching test concerning both Jesus and God could be applied than that. How does Jesus come out? The amazing thing is that the doubt is not as to Jesus' character, but as to God's character. The question is not, Is Jesus as good as God? but rather, Is God as good as Jesus? If God is as good as Jesus, then He is a good God and trustable. Nothing higher can be said of God than to say that He is a Christ-like God. The highest adjective descriptive of God or man, in any language, is the adjective Christ-like.

So Jesus comes out of His own test with flying colors. The standard works for God and man are the "works" seen in Jesus. This is no snap judgment—it is the judgment of the testing ages. Nothing has ever been subjected to a greater scrutiny than the character and deeds of Jesus. And nothing has come out more clear and more final.

O blessed Redeemer, we thank Thee that the ages have sifted and have tested Thee, and Thou hast come out pure gold. I say "pure gold," but "pure gold" is impure alongside the white purity of Thy character. Thou dost judge our standards for Thou art standard. I thank Thee. Amen.

AFFIRMATION FOR THE DAY: *Jesus is an ultimate in character—for God and man.*

"WHATEVER YOU ASK IN MY NAME"

We pass now to a very illuminating passage: "Whatever you ask in my name, I will do it, that the Father may be glorified in the Son" (John 14:13). We saw that the Father was glorified in what Jesus did, and here it is said that the Father is glorified in the requests that Jesus answers. It is one thing to glorify the Father in what you do; it is another thing to glorify God in doing what others request you to do. In what you do there may be the pressure of your own will, but in granting the requests of others you are being pressured by other wills. To do the right things and to grant the right requests is a double achievement.

A young man writes that he is in a mental mix-up for he does a lot of things because people want him to do them. He fulfills their requests and their expectancy and is in an emotional and mental upheaval as a consequence. To respond rightly to the requests and expectations of others is a high test of character. Jesus said that the Father was glorified in what Jesus granted. He would never answer or refuse a request unless the Father too would have answered or refused that request. He and the Father were one in prayer requests.

Yet Jesus seems to leave the matter wide open: "Whatever you ask in my name." The important portion is "in my name." "In my name" would mean "in My spirit, in My character." It doesn't mean just repeating the name of Jesus at the end of the prayer, but putting into the request the very spirit and character of Jesus: "Pray the prayer that I would pray." If you do that, then God is glorified. Jesus prays for the highest and best things, and only the highest and best things for Himself. When He prays in us and we pray in His spirit and character we too will pray for only the highest and best. "Whatever you ask" is granted if it is highest and best. He refuses nothing that would be for our highest interest. All prayers in His name are answered.

O my Lord, what wonderful freedom to ask, and what a restriction! That means self-surrender in the asking so we will ask only Thy highest and best. When I surrender and obey I can command. I am grateful for this liberty and this law. In Thy name. Amen.

AFFIRMATION FOR THE DAY: *I obey the laws of prayer and find the liberties of power.*

"FROM THY THRONE . . . DISPENSE
PARDON AND GRACE"

In studying the verse: "Whatever you ask in my name, I will do it, that the Father may be glorified in the Son," we must note further: "ask . . . in my name" changes the basis on which prayers are answered. If anyone asks "in . . . my name," in my spirit, then he is heard and answered, no matter who he is. That broadens the basis of the possibilities in prayer. The usual thought is that if you lead a good life and are especially good, your prayers are answered. You are praying in your own name—in the name of your goodness. This reverses that—you are not heard at all according to your goodness—you are heard if you pray in His Name, in His Spirit, and for no other reason.

Therefore there are no "big names" in prayer—people who are heard because they have a special standing with God. They are heard just like anyone else because they pray according to the Spirit of Jesus—a privilege open to anyone.

The following prayer was used in a huge meeting to crown "Our Blessed Mother in heaven"—Mary:

Queen of the Most Holy Rosary, in these times of such brazen impiety manifest thy power with the signs of thine ancient victories, and from thy throne, whence thou dost dispense pardon and graces, mercifully regard the church of Thy Son, His Vicar on earth. . . . Do thou, who art the powerful vanquisher of heresies, hasten the hour of mercy.

Here Mary, who was hitherto prayed to in order that she might intercede with her Son, appears to be prayed to directly as though she is the source. She from her "throne" "dost dispense pardon and graces" and is asked to mercifully regard "the church of thy Son." She dispenses pardon and graces and protects the church of her Son, vanquishes heresies, and hastens the hour of mercy. This prayer is the heresy of heresies, another religion, not Christianity, but Mariology, another mediator, not Jesus the "one Mediator."

O Jesus, men do not reject Thee, they reduce Thee—reduce Thee by substituting this, that, and the other in Thy place. May I not be guilty; may I be single-minded in my devotion—"Jesus is Lord!" May my whole life say it. Amen.

AFFIRMATION FOR THE DAY: *A reduced Christ is the same as a rejected Christ.*

"IN ME . . . IN YOU"

Our next step in this exploration of being in Christ is an important one: we are not only in Christ, but He is in us. That sounds like a trite, commonplace platitude, but when looked at closely it is filled with significance—with significant significance.

Some of the passages where abiding in us is lifted up are these: "I am in my Father, and you in me, and I in you" (John 14:20). "Abide in me, and I in you" (15:4). "He who abides in me, and I in him, he it is that bears much fruit" (15:5). "I in them and Thou in me" (17:23).

I can understand why I should abide in Him, for He is divine. He is the center of authority and power and redemption. I was made by Him and for Him, so He is my home. To abide in Him is where I ought to be. But for Him to abide in me—that's different. Why should He? What does He get out of it? What? Except problems and heartaches? With some occasional satisfactions from our response and development in the new life. Then why should He do it and do it, not as occasional whim of wanting to drop in to see how we are getting along, but with a settled intention of abiding in us through thick and thin, abiding in us forever? The only answer seems to be that being love it is the nature of love to want to create and develop and to be with the loved one.

Evidently He wants to re-create and develop us into His own divine image, and He can do that only from within. He wants to create strong persons who can talk with Him face to face, can work with Him shoulder to shoulder, and can share the same life and outlook and dreams.

If the abiding were only in Him then we would be swamped in the Divine. Christ would be all, and we would be nothing.

O God, our Father, we thank Thee that Thou art our Creator and not our Supplanter. Thou dost create us and re-create us and Thou art glorified in our development and growth. I feel Thy expanding creation within me. In Thee I grow. Amen.

AFFIRMATION FOR THE DAY: *I am in Him—salvation and security; He is in me—creation and adventure.*

"MY CHURCH HAS WEAKENED ME"

This abiding in us sets the Christian faith off as unique, *a sui generis*. In the Vedanta philosophy you become the Divine, become Brahma—the personality is lost in the ocean of Being. In Islam Allah is over you and with you, but never in, except in a few mystics. In Buddhism God is a vast question mark. In Judaism He is "high and lifted up," or with His people. In the Christianity of Christ He is "in," and not a casual "in" but a creative "in."

He is there to heighten all our powers and to stimulate our minds, to kindle our emotions, to strengthen our wills, and to make the total personality effective, at its maximum best. Redemption is redemption from weakness as well as redemption from sin. "My church has weakened me," said a Latin American youth, "it tells me what to do, dictates everything I do." He could have added: "Everything I may read." The Church has oversight, but gives members no insight—no insight of their own. They are very obedient and very weak.

Being in Christ and His being in us is different. We are primarily in Him—"Jesus is Lord"—but He is also in us—He is Redeemer—Redeemer from sin and ineffectiveness and weakness. He is a strong man creating strong men around Him.

Note the double abiding as a condition of "much fruit": "He who abides in me, and I in him, he it is that bears much fruit." If you abide only in Him you do not bring forth much fruit—you are comparatively weak, depending on Him for everything with little initiative. You are pious, but not positive. On the other hand if He only abides in you then again you do not bring forth much fruit, for you are the center. You have not surrendered yourself to Him as Lord. You are finding all the answers in you. You are the center of reference, and when you are the center you become the center of weakness.

O Lord Jesus, my first abiding is in Thee. My first act is to surrender. Thou art Lord. I'm lost in Thee. Then Thou art able to be in me. I've lost everything and found everything. Thou dost make the surrendered self into the creative self. I thank Thee. Amen.

AFFIRMATION FOR THE DAY: *The answers are not in me but in Thee. I take Thee—and the answers!*

SUNDAY

Week 15

"THE SPACE MAKERS"

We continue our meditation on abiding in Him and He in us. Only where there is the mutual abiding is one's life fruitful. If we only abide in Him we are comparatively fruitless, and if He only abides in us again we are comparatively fruitless. When there is the double abiding, we trust as if the whole thing depends on Him and work as if the whole thing depends on us. We draw resources by abiding in Him, and we draw inspiration to use those resources by His abiding in us.

The Overstreets have a chapter in their book *The Mind Goes Forth* on "The Space Makers." They say that some people are "space makers"—they make room around themselves for others to grow. On the contrary some are "space-deny-ers"—around them you cannot grow. Like a great oak tree which overshadows the saplings, cutting off light and air and opportunity, so some people are benevolent tyrants. They suffocate and stunt those around them. Jesus was the Prince of Space Makers. It was said of Him that He would be "light for revelation to the Gentiles." The marginal reading is "a light to unveil the Gentiles." He unveils the possibilities in every man, even in those who were called "Gentile dogs." History has seen the fulfillment of that—the "Gentile dogs" have become the leaders of civilization. At the basis of that leadership is the stimulus of Jesus Christ. He makes the nobodies into somebodies, the down-and-outs into up-and-on-tops.

He has awakened interest in the despised. A blind beggar called out to Jesus to have mercy on him. The disciples told him to shut up. He was only a blind beggar. Jesus stopped and called him, and the disciples ran to him and said: "Arise, He calleth thee." They were not interested in him until Jesus was. Since that day we have followed his interest in the uninteresting— outcasts, lepers, blind, alcoholics, prostitutes, waif children— everybody. His interest awakens ours.

Jesus, Master, that Thou shouldst be in me is miracle of miracles. Only love could stand it. To be in me is to share intimately my inmost self which is often not beautiful. Love is a miracle, and Thy love is a continuing, creative miracle. Amen.

AFFIRMATION FOR THE DAY: *Out of gratitude for what grace has done for me, today I shall seek to create new worth in someone else who, like me, needs grace.*

115

"EAT WITH HIM AND HE WITH ME"

We are studying abiding in Him and He in us. The second saves the first from spiritual paternalism. I saw a carved wooden statue entitled "Paternalism." It was the figure of a tall man standing behind a shorter one. The face of the tall man was self-satisfied and smug. His hands were around the throat of the smaller man, whose tongue was out and his face in pain. "Paternalism" manages people in their supposed interests and feels righteous in doing so. The paternalistic point to the innumerable deeds of kindness they have done and are doing for the recipient. The central sin of the relationship is the sin of not allowing the recipient to grow and develop on his own. Therefore paternalism is sin—sin against another.

In Jesus the central redemption is redemption from the sin that hinders growth, plus the opening of opportunities for positive growth. Redemption is re-creation. Jesus said: "I am the light of the world," and then hastens to say, "You are the light of the world." He is not a light that would stand in lone grandeur and brilliance to be wondered at and admired. He is a light that creates light in us, so much so that He says, "You are the very light of the world." He glories in our glory, glad when we become the light of the world.

More amazing still is the passage: "Behold, I stand at the door and knock; if any one hears my voice and opens the door, I will come in to him and eat with him, and he with me" (Rev. 3:20). I will come in and eat with him—I will be guest and he will be host. Host to Christ—He depending on my bounty! That makes me at once very important, almost indispensable in that situation. Then He adds: "and he with me"—He becomes Host and I become guest. He adds it almost as an afterthought, but it is very important—in the end He is in charge. Jesus is Lord! But He became Lord through self-giving to the recipient.

O Jesus, my Lord, Thy Lordship is through Thy servantship. Thou dost go to the heights through the depths. Teach me the secret of Thy mastery. Teach me to bend so I can stand straight. Thy mastery is my freedom. I am grateful. Amen.

AFFIRMATION FOR THE DAY: *As I desire freedom to grow, so I will give freedom to grow to those around me.*

"TO SIT WITH ME ON MY THRONE"

We saw yesterday that Jesus becomes our guest and then our host—both! Suppose He had only become our Host, then we would become leaning personalities and hence lean personalities. He makes us feel important before He takes over as Host. He takes over free, up-standing people who can choose to make Him Host, hence Lord.

There is another passage which is more amazing still. It follows on the heels of this one which we have been considering: "He who conquers, I will grant him to sit with me on my throne, as I myself conquered and sat down with my Father on his throne" (Rev. 3:21). "I will grant him to sit with me on my throne"—He moves over and shares with us His universal authority and power. That is the final redemption from weakness and subservience—we share our Redeemer's power. The God Who created us and then redeemed us by coming to live among us now lives in us and then more amazing still, invites us to share His throne and to rule with Him. Nothing could be more self-giving than that—and self-finding. He tells us that the law of life is to lose your life in order to find it, and—wonder of wonders—He obeys that same law. And it works with Him, for we are at the feet of the God Who washed our feet! We bow before the throne which is shared with us. The God Who gives Himself finds Himself—finds Himself as ruler over our hearts—not merely ruler over our bodies and our wills, but our very hearts. We are in love with a God who loves like that.

Our God rules from a Cross. "And I, when I am lifted up from the earth, will draw all men to myself." When He was weakest He was strongest; when He was most helpless on a cross He was most powerful—the Magnet that draws all men unto Himself. The universe has at its head One who obeys His own laws and especially the deepest—finding life by losing it.

O God, we cannot thank Thee enough for the revelation of Thyself in Jesus. In Him Thou hast disclosed Thy heart— and what a heart! We look into it and see nothing but love. In my heart may there be nothing but love. In Jesus' Name. Amen.

AFFIRMATION FOR THE DAY: *At Thy invitation I share Thy throne, by my choice I share Thy Cross—more befitting!*

"I AM CRUCIFIED . . .I LIVE"

One of the passages which shows clearly the two-sided-ness—our being in Him and His being in us—is the passage: "I have been crucified with Christ; it is no longer I who live, but Christ who lives in me; and the life I now live in the flesh I live by faith in the Son of God who loved me and gave himself for me" (Gal. 2:20). The one side is: "I have been crucified with Christ"—I am so in Him that His crucifixion becomes mine—I die in His death. I lose my personality by a voluntary identification with Him at His lowest place—the cross. I literally die to myself. But in His rising from the dead I become alive too: "it is no longer I who live, but Christ who lives in me." I gave my all in His dying—died with Him—and He gives me His all in His rising—imparts to me His resurrection glory and power. He, the resurrected Lord, lives within me and lives within me in the power of that resurrection. Everything within me is resur-rected—my mind is made alive with the dynamic fact that the worst has been met and conquered and that I can do the same with Him within me. My emotions are kindled by His self-giving, conquering love; my will is aroused to act as He acted for He is acting in me; my whole being is alive with creation.

This alive life is a life lived "in the flesh." It does not await the sloughing off of the body before it begins. As Jesus is the Word become flesh, so I can be in Him the word of victory become "flesh." "The flesh" is a part of the victory, for the flesh partakes of that victory. The flesh is quickened into wholeness and integration and harmony. It is at its maximum best in Him, and, linked to His purposes, becomes alive with His life, vibrant with His vitality.

O Glorious Redeemer, Thou art redeeming me vitally, totally—mind, body, and spirit. Thou art becoming the Life of my life, the Joy of my joy, the Peace of my peace—my glorious Everything. In Thee I live eternally—now! I thank Thee. Amen.

AFFIRMATION FOR THE DAY: *When the Word becomes flesh in me, then my flesh becomes Word.*

"THE WATER I GIVE . . .
SHALL BECOME A SPRING"

We are emphasizing the fact that for us to be in Him is not enough. To be only in Him would make us a weak, absorbing, clinging, dependent, uncreative type of person. He must be in us if we are to be upstanding and creative with initiative and go. There is a passage which illustrates this: "but whoever drinks of the water that I shall give him will never thirst; the water that I shall give him will become in him a spring of water welling up to eternal life" (John 4:14). Note: "the water that I shall give him will become in him a spring"—the gift creates spontaneity. That is a miracle of giving! To give to people and not weaken them or make them dependent is difficult. Here what He gives from above becomes a spring from beneath. He gives and produces initiative in the recipient. That is not only grace, it is also a revelation of the intention of grace; it is to produce creative personalities. The end of creation is to produce creative persons.

That is more and deeper than the end of getting us to heaven. To get us to heaven would still find us recipients—still taking bliss, fellowship, love, and peace, but still *taking!* The end is not taking, but giving. That changes the nature of heaven. It must be a heaven of creation or it wouldn't be heaven. It must be a heaven, not of passivity, but of possibilities. A heaven with a creative God at the center receiving praise and adoration forever would be a God out of tune with Himself. This verse says: "a spring of water welling up to eternal life." This means not that we will well up till we come to eternal life and then drink eternally of eternal fountains without, but it means that we will well up eternally ourselves and from within. It means we will be continuously and eternally creative. That would be a worthwhile heaven worthy of creative beings.

O God, our Father, we tingle with excitement at the unfolding of Thy plan in creation. Thou art creating creators. And I am under the plan of Thy creation. It awes me, humbles me, and makes me stand up straight, eager, alert, Thine. In Jesus' name. Amen.

AFFIRMATION FOR THE DAY: *I am not a cistern; I'm a spring—a spring gathering resources from the eternal hills and flowing for the thirsty.*

"MAKE IT MY OWN . . . ME HIS OWN"

Another passage which teaches us that the redemptive purpose of God in Christ is to produce creative personalities is this one: "I press on to make it my own, because Christ Jesus has made me his own" (Phil. 3:12). "I . . .make it my own" because He "has made me his own"—"it my own . . . me His own." I master the "it," because He masters the "me." The "it" here was "attain the resurrection from the dead"—to have the final victory over the final enemy, death. I master the "it"—the worst "it," because I am mastered by the best Him. His mastery makes me masterful.

All the "its" of life belong to me, provided I belong to Him. I master the world around me, provided Jesus Christ masters the world within me. I am master because I am slave—slave to the rightful Master. I lose my life and I find it—lose it in utter subjection to Him and find it when everything is in utter subjection to me. Paul puts it in these words: "All belongs to you; Paul, Apollos, Cephas, the world, life, death, the present and the future—all belongs to you; and you belong to Christ, and Christ to God" (I Cor. 3:21-22 Moffatt). Here "all things belong to you" because "you belong to Christ." The "all" means all things—all great teachers—"Paul, Apollos, Cephas"; all great facts—"the world, life, death"; all time—"the present and the future." To be sure nothing is left out Paul sweeps his hands wide and says: "all belongs to you." You master everything in the world because Jesus Christ masters everything in you. The inner world masters the outer world. "Heal me at the heart and let the world come on."

So the purpose of this inner possession by Christ is to make us outer possessors of all things. He masters us to free us—free us creatively upon all things. We are being made into the image of the creative God.

O Jesus, my Redeemer, I see also in Thee that Thou art not merely redeeming me *from*—Thou art redeeming me *to*. Thou art redeeming me to creativity. When Thou art within me my touch upon life is creative—just like Thine. I am awed. Amen.

AFFIRMATION FOR THE DAY: *He has made me His own—the center; I will make it my own—the circumference.*

THE REDEEMED BECOME THE REDEEMING

This mutual abiding is seen in another passage. Of the Holy Spirit it is said: "I will pray the Father, and he will give you another Counselor, to be with you for ever, even the Spirit of truth . . . for he dwells with you, and will be in you" (John 14:16-17). Here the Holy Spirit is in you and yet He is a counselor. The word "counselor" is the paraclete—made up of two words: *para* = beside, and *kalein* = to call—the One Who is called alongside you, to counsel with you, giving wisdom and guidance. The older translation—"Comforter"—pieces out the meaning of the "Counselor," for Comforter is derived from *con* = with, and *fortis* = strength—One Who strengthens you by being with you. So He imparts not only counsel—verbal direction—He also imparts vital strength to all our faculties by being with us. His strength becomes our strength; His wisdom becomes our wisdom; His purity our purity; His creativity our creativity.

Yesterday I met a completely transformed woman. She and her husband had kept a gambling house with all the accoutrements in Louisiana for two and half years. She became an alcoholic to escape from herself—and her past. Now she is a radiant person, her home the center of youth, and her touch on life a creative touch. Conversion did it. The Holy Spirit is in her, but He is also beside her, counseling her, imparting His own strength and love and power, making her a person—a creative person. Her touch on life was destructive, now it is constructive. She is not absorbed into the Divine—she is absorbing the Divine into the human and making that human creative. Yet she knows where she belongs—at His feet. Being at His feet she stands straight before everything. She is being created, and she is creative. The redeemed become the redeeming.

My Lord and my Life, I thank Thee that Thou art making me a living soul and a life-giving spirit. The more Thou dost abide in me the more I want to abide in Thee. As Thou dost make me, the more I want to make Thee Lord! I thank Thee. Amen.

AFFIRMATION FOR THE DAY: *Have I passed from the "with" stage to the "in" stage? If not before, then now!*

"ABIDE IN ME, MY WORDS ABIDE IN YOU"

Perhaps the clearest metaphor of life in Christ is to be found in the Vine and the branches in John 15:1-11. Here the mutuality of our abiding in Him and of His abiding in us is most clearly seen.

I am the vine, you are the branches. He who abides in me, and I in him, he it is that bears much fruit, for apart from me you can do nothing. If a man does not abide in me, he is cast forth as a branch and withers; and the branches are gathered, thrown into the fire and burned. If you abide in me, and my words abide in you, ask whatever you will, and it shall be done for you. By this my Father is glorified, that you bear much fruit, and so prove to be my disciples (vss. 5-8).

The Vine-and-the-branches figure cannot be pushed beyond original intentions, but it does mean that the Vine and the branches share a common life—the life in the Vine is the same as the life in the branches. We share not merely the same intentions and the same purposes, but also the same life. That is breath-taking. It actually means that we live by the life of Another. "It is no longer I who live, but Christ who lives in me"—all my thoughts interfused with His thoughts, all my emotions interfused with His emotions, and all my acts with His acts. This is renewal by regeneration—everything reborn.

Does that mean that we are thereby divine? No, for there is this difference: the Vine sustains the branches—the branches do not sustain the Vine. It is true that the Vine cannot express itself except through the branches; so Christ has tied Himself to us as far as the expressions of His life and work are concerned in this world. Amazing limitation which Christ has imposed on Himself! No other hands but ours, no other feet but ours, no other tongue but ours! Amazing identification!

O Jesus, Thy incarnation in flesh and blood amazes me, but this continuous incarnation in our flesh and blood, limiting Thyself to us and our willingness to express that incarnation—this humbles me to the dust, and raises me to the highest heaven. Amen.

AFFIRMATION FOR THE DAY: *Abiding in Thee, Thy "words" become my direction and my delight!*

"FLATTER THAN A PANCAKE"

We saw yesterday that while Christ and we share a common life there is a difference—He sustains us, we do not sustain Him, except as He chooses to limit Himself to our co-operation. This is a chosen limitation.

Our limitation is inherent: "apart from me you can do nothing." So there is no divinity in and of ourselves. That is where the "divinity cults" have gone overboard—they have turned a voluntary relationship in which we share the Divine life, into an inherent divinity of our own. "You have all the answers within yourself" is the slogan. It is only a slogan, however, and gives you an initial lift as a reaction to the worm-of-the-dust attitude. But it centers you on you as the source, and anything that leaves you centered on yourself is off-center. There is nothing more pathetic than self-conscious mortals trying to convince themselves and others that they are divine. It produces the attitude of a spiritual self-strut instead of a spiritual self-surrender. It cuts across the deepest law of the universe: "Whoever would save his life will lose it; and whoever loses his life . . . will save it." All the cults that talk about self-realization, self-cultivation, self-development, all the answers in the self, cut across that law and are doomed to ultimate sterility and death. "I was on wings when I first heard this emphasis on our divinity," said a well-equipped woman, "but I soon became flatter than a pancake, for it centered me on me, and knowing me, I knew I was not divine and those who asserted most strenuously their divinity, revealed most clearly their earthiness."

Your significance is found in your relationship to Him and not to yourself—"apart from me you can do nothing"—and you *are* nothing—nothing except a bundle of problems. Every self-centered person—religious or otherwise—is a declining, decaying person.

O Jesus, Lord and Master, Thy word, "Apart from me you can do nothing," sounds the death knell of all our ego-strivings and dooms it all to sterility. I thank Thee for this word. It is purifying and redeeming. It puts Thee in Thy place and me in mine. I'm grateful. Amen.

AFFIRMATION FOR THE DAY: *I shall depend not on slogan shots in the arm, but I shall depend on Thy dependable day-by-day resources.*

THE GOAL OF SELF-PERFECTION

We come back to this relationship of self-surrender. The relationship of the Vine and the branches is not a relationship of equality—the branches are dependent on the Vine. "Every branch of mine" (vs. 2)—"of mine"—they belong to Him! That phrase from the Revised Standard Version clarifies the phrase found in the King James Version: "Every branch in me"—being "in me" means you are "mine." The relationship is primarily self-surrender to the Vine—to Jesus. Being in Him means you belong to Him. That saves you from the fallacies of self-realization, and gets your eyes on Jesus Christ, which brings Christ-realization, which brings as a by-product self-realization. You lose your life and you find it. It also saves you from striving after self-perfection. To strive after self-perfection makes you self-conscious.

I was talking to a young woman whose goal in life was self-perfection. She used everything and everybody for that end, and it crept into her conversation. Was the result perfection? The result was the opposite—she was a perfect nuisance to herself and everybody else. It disrupted her so that her engagement to a very noble young man had to be broken off. Had she surrendered herself to Christ and put the focus of her attention right—on Christ, fixing her eyes and attention and love on Him—she would have grown into His likeness, which would have been the goal. The goal is not my perfection, but my following with an all-out following the perfect Person. There "with unveiled face, beholding the glory of the Lord, [we] are being changed into his likeness from one degree of glory to another" (II Cor. 3:18).

We are "called to belong to Jesus Christ," and when we belong to Him we belong to His perfection, to His perfect everything. It is all ours—because we are all His.

O Jesus, my Lord, I am so grateful I belong to Thee and that everything Thou hast thereby belongs to me. It is so simple, so profound, so altogether sensible and right. I dance with joy over its simplicity, and then I'm at Thy feet over its profundity. I thank Thee. Amen.

AFFIRMATION FOR THE DAY: *I am not after self-conscious perfection, but after Christ-conscious perfect obedience.*

"SELF-SURRENDER ONCE AND FOR ALL—
AND CONTINUOUS"

We saw yesterday that the relationship between the Vine and the branches is the relationship of self-surrender—you abide in Him before He abides in you. But the moment you begin to abide in Him by self-surrender, that moment He begins to abide in you.

The term "self-surrender" needs to be supplemented if it is to express this relationship. Self-surrender is once and for all, like a good marriage. It doesn't have to be done over again each day—it is once and for all and forever. Yet while it is once and for all, it is continuous. You give your all once and for all, and yet there are little "alls" of self-surrender wrapped up in that big once-and-for-all surrender. These little "alls" have to be surrendered daily. So it is once and for all and yet continuous. The continuous part is expressed in these words: "Abide in me, and I in you" (John 15:4). So the relationship is surrender plus abiding. You don't plug into Jesus to get His light and power as needed and then plug out again. That is the attitude of many—they plug into Jesus once on Sunday and get their batteries recharged, and the rest of the week they are on their own. No, this is a continuous relationship—a life committal and a lifelong committal—you "abide" in Him. You are not in and out of Christ—you are "in" forever. You may cloud the relationship by a momentary slip, stumble, or even fall. But if you confess it immediately the relationship is unbroken. It was clouded, but not broken. The only way to break it is by continuous, deliberate, willful sinning.

To "abide" in Him is to surrender all you know and all you don't know. You give up all you know and if anything comes up you do not know, then that belongs to Him too. "His" is written across the known and unknown. There are no reservations in anything, at anytime, anywhere.

My Lord, Thou art Lord. Full stop. I have no ifs or buts left over—this is all, all the time, in all places. I'm bound to Thee unreservedly. And yet how free! I abide in Thee and yet I walk the earth free—free to the degree that I abide. Amen.

AFFIRMATION FOR THE DAY: *The once and for all surrender to Christ is not a matter of debate or question, but only the daily application to matters that arise.*

"NEUROSIS OF EMPTINESS"

This abiding in Christ or not abiding in Him is not a matter which you can take or leave and nothing much happens. Something does happen, in fact everything happens, for good or ill. If you abide in Him then everything He has is yours—His purity, His goodness, His victory, His peace, His joy, His everything is all yours. You can and do draw on the most important Fact of the universe—the fact of Christ.

If you do not abide in Him, then the direst of consequences follow. "Every branch . . . that bears no fruit, he takes away." "If a man does not abide in me, he is cast forth as a branch and withers, and the branches are gathered, thrown into the fire and burned" (John 15:2, 6). These sayings belong to lurid, verbal warnings without any basis of fact, or they belong to the facts themselves. These words are so close to fact that they are facts themselves. This removal of fruitless branches and their withering and their subsequent perishing into ashes are facts taking place before our very eyes. Every life cut off from Christ inwardly withers. This is not an arbitrary punishment imposed from without. It is the result of cutting oneself off from the root of his being—"the root of every man in Christ." We are made by Him and for Him, and when we are cut off from the source of our life the inevitable result is a withering; not a marginal withering of leaves leaving the tree intact, but a root withering, leaving nothing intact. This is what Dr. Boss, the head of the International Psychoanalytical Association, said, "Psychiatrists, who are not superficial, find that almost all of the vast neurotic misery can be called Neurosis of Emptiness or Dullness. People become ill when they cut themselves off from their real root, or innermost spring, that is, from God. They lose all real energy and all sense of life."

O Thou Who art the light that lighteth every man who comes into the world, when we are cut off from Thee we stumble in the darkness to our doom. Thou Who art the Life of our life, cut off from Thee we perish at the root. All our progress is progress toward decay and death. Save us. Amen.

AFFIRMATION FOR THE DAY: *"The root of every man is Christ"*—if I sever my relations with that Root by neglect, or deliberately, I am a withered branch automatically.

"WE LIGHT OUR OWN FUNERAL PYRE"

We are considering what happens when we do not abide in Christ. We are cut off from the source of our being—Christ—and when we are cut off from Him Who is life, then there is only one thing left: non-life, death. This passage describes that condition as withered, then ashes. Is that the destination of all life apart from Christ? There is only one Scriptural answer: Yes. That Scriptural answer is the answer that life is rendering now. All life separated from Christ is in the process of decay. We say of a person who doesn't know how to live: "He is going to pieces," and he is. He is tearing himself to pieces by his own inner conflicts. The life forces are breaking down. That happens when the life apart from Christ is lived in open blatant sin, or in secret self-centeredness. The joy, the peace, the hopes, the security, the wonder of living—everything begins to decay and the futile attempts by outer props to hold it together result in further inner dismay and hasten the process of deterioration and decay.

All coming to Jesus has the sense of a home-coming upon it, and all going away from Jesus has the sense of home-leaving—going into a far country, an alien land. Do all our sunsets turn to sunrises when we come to Him? Yes. That works with a mathematical precision—no exceptions: Come to Him and be glad; go from Him and be sad. The sadness is not a surface sadness—it is a deepdown sadness, for going from Him spells doom and the soul knows it.

"Withers" . . . "thrown into the fire and burned"—that is not rhetoric; it is reality. The soul perishes in the fires of its own impossible ways of life. God doesn't kindle that fire; we do. "Our God is a consuming fire"—to sin; we are a consuming fire to ourselves—on account of sin. We light our own funeral pyre.

O Jesus, Thou art Life, and when we are in Thee we live all over—body, mind, and spirit. When we are out of Thee we are death—death to ourselves, to our hopes, to everything we touch. Help me to live every moment in Thee and Thee alone. Amen.

AFFIRMATION FOR THE DAY: *The worm that dieth not and the fire that is not quenched I take within my bosom when I sin.*

SIN IS SELF-CONSUMING

We are considering the fact that all branches apart from Jesus wither and are gathered and burned. We once thought God threw people into the fires of hell. "Sinners in the Hands of an Angry God" was the title of a famous sermon of past generations. But something in the spirit of Jesus made us question this. The God revealed in Him was different. Does that mean that hell has been abolished? By no means. It means that we are putting the responsibility for hell where it belongs—on us. We said yesterday that we light our own funeral pyre. The punishment is inherent. Sin by its very nature is disintegrating. Sin and its punishment are one and the same thing. Does God punish sin? He doesn't have to, for He has made sin and its punishment one and the same thing. You don't have to punish the eye for having sand in it, the body for having a cancer, the soul for having evil in it. The word "evil" is the word "live" spelled backwards. It is an attempt to live life against itself, and it can't be done. Carlyle says: "Sin is, has been, and ever shall be the parent of misery." He could have added, "the parent of decay," for sin is disintegration.

"Where the carcass is, there the eagles are gathered together." Where there is the "carcass" of evil, there "the eagles," the forces that clean up the evil from the universe, are gathered together. Sin is self-consuming. It burns itself up. That is not something imposed on life by an angry God, that is something that is inherent in a moral universe. Sin is self-defeating and self-destroying. "He who spits against the wind spits in his own face." He who revolts against God revolts against himself, destroys himself, burns himself up in the fires of his own self-conflicts.

O God, Thy laws are our protection—our protection against self-destruction. They are the hedges set up so we will not fall to our doom. They are preventive grace. But we brush past Thy grace to our own destruction. Forgive us. Amen.

AFFIRMATION FOR THE DAY: *Iniquity is literally "missing the mark," so I miss the mark of life when I practice iniquity, hence I perish.*

"MY WORDS ABIDE IN YOU"

We come to another stage of His abiding in us and our abiding in Him: "If you abide in me, and my words abide in you, ask whatever you will, and it shall be done for you" (John 15:7). This is an amazing promise: "ask whatever you will, and it shall be done for you." This seems like unlimited request—"whatever" will be followed by unlimited answer—"it shall be done for you." There are two important provisions, however: "If you abide in me, and my words abide in you"—abide in Him, general surrender and obedience—"and my words abide in you"—specific surrender and obedience. There is a blanket and general surrender and obedience to Him, and then there is a specific surrender and obedience. Both must be cultivated.

In marriage there is a general surrender in the moment of marriage. Each belongs to the other, both belong to both. It is a giving which covers everything. If it is just left "general," however, and does not work out in the daily specific, then the "general" becomes sentimentality—the word of marriage become word instead of becoming flesh in little daily outer manifestations of tokens of love.

"My words abide in you"—this tells of a continuous study of these words and their application to daily and hourly obedience to them. A friend who has been brought up spiritually on "absolute honesty, absolute purity, absolute love, and absolute unselfishness" insists that there can be no blanket surrender, once and for all, but only specific surrender and specific obedience in the daily questions and issues that arise. There is a real truth in his insistence—obedience must be specific or it is not obedience at all—but it is only a half-truth, for if obedience is only in specific things it lacks that general once-and-for-all surrender and obedience.

O Jesus, I belong to Thee wholly and forever. That is settled, and settled forever. Teach me to manifest specifically in every moment, in every attitude, in every day, and in every way my specific love and loyalty to Thee. Thus dedication and deed will be one. Amen.

AFFIRMATION FOR THE DAY: *Generally and specifically I am His, and all that pertains to me is His.*

RELIGION OF LAW AND RELIGION OF GRACE

We are meditating on "If you abide in me, and my words abide in you, ask whatever you will, and it shall be done for you." We saw that it demanded the general—"abide in me"—and the specific—"my words abide in you"—both. If we love in general and not specifically then we become like the man who loved all mankind in general but hated everyone in particular. On the other hand, it is possible to love individuals and not love man.

One of the questions I hold regarding a program of absolute honesty, absolute purity, absolute unselfishness, and absolute love is this: it concentrates your attention on specific deeds and attitudes. It is life organized around the second commandment—"Thou shalt love thy neighbor as thyself"—instead of life organized around the first commandment—"Thou shalt love the Lord thy God." The primary concentration should be on surrender to and love of Jesus Christ as Lord. I say "Jesus Christ" instead of God, for apart from Jesus we know little or nothing about God, and what we know is usually wrong. When we go to God through Him we go to the real God and not a figment of our imagination, apart from Jesus. The primary concentration should be on the love of the Person, and then on these four absolutes as the result of and manifestation of that love. Otherwise obedience to the four absolutes may become a religion of law—a fourfold law—and obedience to law always produces strain, hence drain. It lacks a central resting in a final surrender and love for a Person—a fixed center, with the four absolutes as the result of that central loyalty and love. Without that center it becomes a religion of law instead of a religion of grace.

Only when we abide in Him—"If you abide in me"—are we able and willing to fulfill His words—"my words abide in you."

O Beloved Lord, I love Thy words, not because they are words, but because they are Thy words. Associated with Thee they become different, for Thou art different. Thou dost make everything different, including me. I thank Thee. Amen.

AFFIRMATION FOR THE DAY: *I am not whipped up by law, I am caught up by grace and live effortlessly and effectively.*

"MY WORDS ABIDE IN YOU"

We continue: "If you abide in me, and my words abide in you." The study of the words of Jesus must not leave us with our emphasis on the words—the words must lead us to the Word—"the Word made flesh." Neither must emphasis on the Word make us neglect the words. The words interpret the Word. Through them we see Him.

These words have become so important and so coherent that they are no longer mere words—they become the word—"You are already made clean by the word which I have spoken to you" (John 15:3). The words of Jesus were so consistent, so harmonious, so much a part of a whole, so luminous that they became the word. Not the Word—that is, the Person—the word—that is, the product of the Word. Most of us speak words, but some speak so consistently, so harmoniously, so much as a part of the whole, so luminously that their words become the word. When you think of them you think of a philosophy of life—their word.

Jesus spoke the word—a revelation of Himself. As the disciples listened to the word they were cleansed—"You are already made clean by the word which I have spoken to you." He cleansed their idea of God from a Jewish Jehovah to the universal Father; their ideas of religion from an obedience to a Law to a manifestation of Love; their ideas of man so that a man was no longer a man, but "a man for whom Christ died." He cleansed woman from a creature, obedient to and subordinate to man, to a person equal to and a partner of man. He cleansed prayer from being a means of getting the selfish desires of an unsurrendered self granted, to a surrender of the self and a desire for His desire. He cleansed everything.

O Lord Jesus, Thou didst cleanse everything Thou didst touch, and Thou didst touch everything. Now we walk into a world of thought, of motive, of action, and all is made clean through the word Thou hast spoken. We thank Thee. Amen.

AFFIRMATION FOR THE DAY: *Thy Word is cleansing me from untruth to Truth, from half-truths to whole truth, from my best to Thy best.*

"MADE CLEAN BY THE WORD"

We continue to meditate upon "You are already made clean by the word which I have spoken to you." He cleansed the universe of gods and goddesses of questionable character and gave us the one Christlike Heavenly Father. He cleansed the term "Christ" from being a conquering Jewish Messiah who would lead the Jews to supremacy, to a Messiah who would die for all men. He cleansed suffering from being a sign of God's wrath and made it an opportunity to manifest His love. He cleansed the grave from decay and made it Resurrection. He cleansed heaven from being a place of heavenly maidens— "horis"—into a place where men and women neither marry nor are given in marriage. He cleansed love from being Eros—possessive love—and made it into agape—a nonpossessive, sacrificial love. He cleansed the material earth from being an evil thing subject to doom and decay and made it into the scene of the coming kingdom of God on earth. He cleansed life itself as something to be avoided when He said: "I came that they may have life, and have it abundantly." He cleansed everything He touched, and He touched everything.

He said that they were "already made clean by the word" He had spoken to them. They were clean in a sense, and yet actually they were not. Their conscious minds were clean, but their subconscious minds were not clean—they quarreled over first places, wanted to call down fire on others, forsook Him and fled, and were behind closed doors for fear. Potentially they were clean in His cleanness, but actually they stepped out of Him into themselves so were full of self-assertions and consequent fears and conflicts.

O Jesus, my Lord, as long as I abide in Thee I am potentially and actually clean. As soon as I step out of Thee into my self-will I am not. Then keep me, O keep me, abiding in Thee, for apart from Thee I can do nothing except wrong. Amen.

AFFIRMATION FOR THE DAY: *The Holy Spirit is cleansing my subconscious at depths I am unable to control.*

SURRENDER IN GENERAL, OBEY IN PARTICULAR

We now come to the crux of our verse: "If you abide in me, and my words abide in you, ask whatever you will, and it shall be done for you." The crux is in the "if." The "if" covers two conditions—"abide in me, and my words abide in you." If you surrender to Him in general—"abide in me"—and if you obey Him in particular—"my words abide in you"—then the door is open to His Everything; ask whatever you will and it shall be done for you. This is the most limiting and yet the most unlimited conception of prayer ever propounded—limited to two conditions and limited to no conditions. He binds us and then frees us—frees us to ask anything! If you fulfill the first two conditions, then you will ask only what He would approve and will receive only what He knows is good for you—the best for you.

Does God answer all prayers? Some say He does, but the answer is, No! He cannot, by His very nature, answer prayers of those who do not abide in Him and in whom His words do not abide. They would pray apart from His spirit and whatever is apart from His spirit is apart from our good, for whatever is good in Him is good for us. His will is our weal-th and our wealth.

Here prayer is put on its highest level—every prayer prayed in the spirit of Jesus is answered. That cleanses prayer and consummates prayer. "Love God and do what you like," could be amended: "Love Jesus Christ and ask what you like," for you will ask the things He likes.

This cleanses prayer from all self-reference—"the answers are within you," for they are not; they are in Him. It cleanses prayer from all "much speaking," for you are not answered for your persistence, but by meeting these two conditions.

O Master of my heart, Thou hast opened the gates to Thy Everything. I am free to ask the highest, and the highest is free for the asking. I am rich beyond measure, for everything good for me is open to me. Prayer is possibility. Amen.

AFFIRMATION FOR THE DAY: *I do not want God to answer my prayers; I want my prayers to answer to God's will.*

"BEAR MUCH FRUIT, AND SO PROVE"

There is another slant to prayer in the next verse: "By this my Father is glorified, that you bear much fruit, and so prove to be my disciples" (John 15:8). Prayer is automatically answered if the granting of the prayer makes you more fruitful. The intention of God is to make you a fruitful person: "By this my Father is glorified, that you bear much fruit." The intention of the Creator God is to produce creator children. We are pleasing to Him when we are producing fruit, and we are most healthy in body, mind, and spirit when we are producing fruit. The end of a fruit-bearing tree is to produce fruit. It may have leaves, spreading branches, buds, and flowers, but if it has no fruit it has missed the purpose and end of its existence. Our Father is glorified, not when we attend church, unless the attending makes us fruitful; not when we read the Bible and pray, unless reading the Bible and praying make us fruitful; not when we do any other religious exercise, unless that religious exercise makes us fruitful.

I have been in homes for retired people—laymen, ministers, and Christian workers. Those who come in "to enjoy themselves" the balance of their days wither prematurely and become inane and empty. Only those who keep an interest outside themselves and engage in active service of others remain alive and vital and happy. Only the creative are alive. We are created by the Creator for creation, and when we don't fulfill our destiny we wither. The idea that travel will keep people alive, healthy, and happy is false—unless there is more than sight-seeing in the travel. Unless there is some creative reason for the travel other than being a spectator of things and persons, the travel will end in futility and ultimate unhappiness within. Where there is no creative purpose there is nothing but the creation of frustration.

O God, my Father, I am a child of Thy creative impulse. Put within me Thy same creative impulse. As I live in Thee I know Thy creative power will work in and through me. Together we will bear fruit—much fruit. Amen.

AFFIRMATION FOR THE DAY: *As a fruit tree is made to bear fruit, so I, the fruit of Thy love, am made to bear fruit.*

ABIDING IN LOVE

We go on to another step in abiding in Him: "As the Father has loved me, so have I loved you; abide in my love. If you keep my commandments, you will abide in my love, just as I have kept my Father's commandments and abide in His love" (John 15:9-10). Here abiding in Him emphasizes abiding in love. You are abiding in Christ to the degree that you abide in love.

This is an important step. This defines abiding in Him as abiding in love, and also defines fruitfulness as fruitfulness in love. This making love pre-eminent in abiding in Him runs true to the genius of the Christian faith. It makes love supreme in God—"God is love"—makes it supreme in our manifesting our loyalty to Him—"Thou shalt love the Lord thy God"—and makes it supreme in the fruit of the Spirit—"love, joy, peace." Love is first in God, in our loyalty to God, and in the "fruit" of our lives.

If we are not manifesting our abiding in Him by being a loving person, we are not abiding in Him. If our contacts with people are not love contacts, then we have no contact with Christ. It is a simple test, but very profound and important. Some hold that we are abiding in Christ if we have correct views about Christ—if we are orthodox; some hold that we are abiding in Christ if we have correct conduct—if we are orthoprax. Neither of these, though both are important, is the supreme test. The supreme test is: Do I manifest love in all the manifestations of my life? If not, then to the degree that I do not, I am not in Him. I am in something else.

Even this must be further qualified: it is not enough to be in love; we must be in a certain kind of love: "This is my commandment, that you love one another as I have loved you" (vs. 12).

O Jesus, my Lord, we have at last reached the summit—the summit of love and life. We are to love each other as Thou hast loved us. A Christlike love is love at its very highest. I am grateful that Thou hast brought me out at the Ultimate. I thank Thee. Amen.

AFFIRMATION FOR THE DAY: *I was made by Love, for love, and to love—I will fulfill my destiny.*

"AS I HAVE LOVED YOU"

We have seen that being in Christ is more than being in the Church, more than being in orthodoxy, more than being in orthopraxy, more than being in conversion or the new birth, though it may include any and all of these. To be in Christ is to be in love, and to be in love is to be in a particular type of love—a Christlike love.

"As I have loved you"—this is the word of love lifted from the word become word, to the word become flesh. Beyond that definition of love the human race will never progress, because beyond the life of Jesus the human race will never progress. The word "love" can never have a higher content than the life of Jesus. "As I have loved you" is the Absolute and the Ultimate in life and love.

This word of love came to its highest manifestation in the cross. "Greater love has no man than this, that a man lay down his life for his friends" (John 15:13). He might have added, "and for his enemies," for that is what the cross actually adds. He said "friends" in promise, and added "enemies" in performance. We give big promises and toned-down performance. He gave toned-down promise and toned-up performance. He always went beyond.

Note this contrast: I stood watching the sacrifice of goats to the goddess Kali. The goats' heads were thrust through a pronged stick and severed by one blow. A devotee crawled up and thrust his head through the pronged stick in order to be sacrificed to Kali. The priest took him by the hair of his head and threw him back. Again he crawled up, and again he was thrown back.

And this contrast: A Chinese Christian doctor's father had been killed by the head-hunters of Borneo. He is now serving those same head-hunters with love and devotion. Does it matter what you think of God?

O God, through Jesus we see in Thee love and only love. We see a quality of love in Thee that leaves us speechless—a love for enemies. "Greater love can no God have than this, that He lay down His life for His enemies." That leaves me at Thy feet. Amen.

AFFIRMATION FOR THE DAY: *"As I have loved you," shall be my standard and my example and my source of power."*

ORDINATION INHERENT

Connected with this passage on bearing fruit is this important one: "You did not choose me, but I chose you and appointed ["ordained," KJV] you that you should go and bear fruit and that your fruit should abide; so that whatever you ask the Father in my name He may give it to you" (John 15:16).

This raises an important question: Are there specially chosen people, who are ordained to bring forth fruit and who have limitless possibilities of answered prayer? If so, who are these ordained people? How are they ordained? This goes to the very root of our conception of Christian calling.

The usual conception is that this refers to people ordained by the laying on of hands—hands that are often supposed to convey special grace through a long line of succession reaching back to the apostles.

Contrary to this, I am persuaded that being in Christ in itself confers an ordination—an ordination that makes us fruitful and opens unlimited possibilities through prayer. Ordination is not something imposed; it is inherent in the very nature of the Christian faith and in the discipleship within that faith. Every person, male or female, who is in Christ is ordained. The ordination spoken of here is an ordination, not by the laying on of hands, for there is no mention of the laying on of hands, but an ordination by choice: "You have not chosen me, but I have chosen you, and ordained you" (KJV). The choice which set them apart was the ordination. It was vertical—from above, from the Divine, and not horizontal—from men. That is the only ordination the apostles ever received, so far as we have any record. Jesus never laid His hands on them to ordain them.

O Master, I thank Thee that Thou hast included all who are in Thee in Thy ordination. Being in Thee makes me partake of Thy call. Thy call becomes my call—I partake of Thy life and of Thy life work. I thank Thee. Amen.

AFFIRMATION FOR THE DAY: *I am a "chosen one," therefore ordained—let me act as a man of destiny.*

"HE WASN'T ORDAINED"

The Christian movement is essentially a lay movement. Jesus Himself was not "ordained" in the modern sense of having hands laid on Him in ordination. His ordination was a choice:

> The Spirit of the Lord is upon me,
> because he has anointed me to preach the good news to the poor.

By the fact of the coming of the Holy Spirit He was set aside to preach the good news. The coming of the Holy Spirit was the ordination—the choice.

A high churchman was asked in India if he would allow Jesus to preach in his pulpit if He should come, and the reply was: "No, I'm sorry I couldn't, for He wasn't ordained." He was right, if ordination is by laying on of hands; he was wrong if real ordination is the divine choice. A definition of ordination that would rule out the Founder of the faith shows how far we have wandered from that faith.

Jesus was not ordained by the laying on of hands, nor were His disciples. The laying on of hands is apostolic, but not Christian—it has its fountainhead in the apostles, not in Christ. Hence "apostolic succession" claims it is "apostolic"; it does not and cannot claim it is Christ-ian. But our faith terminates in Jesus Christ, not in His apostles. It is valid because it is in Him, not in them. If the claims of apostolic succession could be proved they would prove too much—they would prove that our faith terminates in men, not in the Divine Redeemer. I'm not interested in apostolic succession—only in Christian succession. To be in the apostles is not the issue; to be in Jesus Christ is—and the only issue. Everything else is irrelevant. The missing link in apostolic succession is the link between Christ and the apostles, for there is no link of laying on of His hands. That is fatal to the theory. It is stranded—this side of Christ.

O Lord Jesus, Thou art the Founder and the foundation of my faith. Give me touch with Thee and nothing else matters, for to belong to Thee is to belong to God and to the ages. I draw from Thee my all—*all else* is beside the point. I thank Thee. Amen.

AFFIRMATION FOR THE DAY: *I belong not to an apostolic faith, but to a Christian faith—let me live as one who glances at the apostles and gazes at Christ.*

THE CHRISTIAN FAITH
AN ESSENTIALLY LAY FAITH

The essential lay character of the Christian faith is further seen in the choosing of the seventy. Though the disciples were laymen they soon became possessive of the Christian movement. Individually they quarreled over first places; they told the man who cast out devils in the Name of Jesus to stop it "because he does not follow with us"; they wanted to call down fire from heaven to consume the Samaritans when they didn't receive Jesus and His disciples. Altogether they began to show an exclusive, possessive mentality—they were "special" in the kingdom.

Jesus had to correct this tendency in the direction of making His movement more essentially "lay." "After this" [the account of the quarreling, the forbidding of others to cast out devils, and the calling down of fire] "the Lord appointed seventy others, and sent them on ahead of him, two by two, into every town and place where he himself was about to come" (Luke 10:1). These seventy, of course, were laymen and yet they received exactly the same commission as the Twelve. The same important sentence is found in both: "He who hears you hears me," except that in the case of the seventy this is added: "and he who rejects you rejects me, and he who rejects me rejects him who sent me."

This is important, for it means that the direct authority of Jesus was behind the seventy—to receive them was to receive Him, to reject them was to reject Him. There was no going through the apostles to Jesus—no mediation—it was firsthand authority and equal authority. When they returned with joy saying the devils were subject to them in His name (the Twelve couldn't get them out!) Jesus "rejoiced in the Holy Spirit" and said: "I thank thee, Father . . . that thou hast hidden these things from the wise and understanding and revealed them to babes"—to the lay seventy. They were simple and effective.

O God, our Father, I too thank Thee that Thou hast revealed these things to the simple-hearted who seek only Thee and Thy glory. The highest is open to the lowest. The Kingdom belongs to the childlike. That opens the door to us all. I thank Thee. Amen.

AFFIRMATION FOR THE DAY: *May I be so identified with Christ that to reject or receive me is to reject or receive Him. That means, not pride, but surrender.*

"THE CHOSEN PEOPLE OF GOD"

The next step in lay emphasis was the fact that the Holy Spirit was not given to the Twelve alone, but to the 120, including the women. Had the Holy Spirit been given to the Twelve alone, that would have been decisive—there is an especially sacred group and an especially sacred calling. The fact that God's highest gift—the gift of the Holy Spirit—was given not to a prophet, priest, or pastor, but to a person as a person, was also decisive. There is no especially sacred group or especially sacred calling; there are only sacred persons. Those persons are the "chosen" and sent, and that includes everyone who is in Christ.

Interestingly enough the Greek word "laos," from which the word "laity" comes, means "the chosen people of God"—the laity were the chosen people of God. The word "kleros" from which the word "clergy" comes, meant exactly the same in the beginning. Bishop Westcott, an Anglican, said: "The only priests under the Gospel designated as such in the New Testament are the saints, the members of the Christian brotherhood." His concise formula: "All Christians are God's laity (laos) and all are God's clergy (kleros)." This was all changed in the Council of Nicea:

> The bishops did not allow this any more. Canons five and eighteen of the Council of Nicea define clearly, not the society of the church as a whole, but of the clerical order. The laity vanishes from the picture. The bishops in the Councils are collectively the organ of the Holy Spirit. As "spiritual" men they exercise their divine, disciplinary authority, and in their collectivity may judge all things, but be judged by none. (*A Theology of the Laity*, Kramer, p. 53.)

The opposition clergy-laity became practically synonymous with sacred-profane. There was a devaluation of the laity. Ignatius and Cyprian stated clearly: "The Church is constituted by the bishops and clergy." The laity were in the background.

O God, my Redeemer, we stand amazed at the twists we have given to Thy redemptive movement. We separate what Thou hast joined. Life is a whole, and Thou dost redeem it as a whole. We thank Thee. Amen.

AFFIRMATION FOR THE DAY: *I am a chosen person of God, for I choose God as my all and in all.*

A WEDGE BETWEEN THE SPIRITUAL
AND THE MATERIAL

We saw yesterday that the clergy became dominant and possessive and the laity receded. Gratian leaves no doubt that "the condition of the laity is a concession to human frailty." To be a layman was to have chosen a second-rate calling and the laity were second-rate people.

But to return to the New Testament. Here this was not true. When the question of distribution of food arose in the sixth chapter of Acts, the apostles called the main body of believers together and said: "It is not right that we should give up preaching the word of God to serve tables. Therefore, brethren, pick out from among you seven men of good repute, full of the Spirit and of wisdom, whom we may appoint to this duty. But we will devote ourselves to prayer and to the ministry of the word" (Acts 6:2-4). This has been usually looked upon as a spiritual and wise act and attitude. Actually, I believe it was a very wrong and disastrous move, though well intended.

They drove a wedge between the material and the spiritual. In Christianity the material and the spiritual are two sides of one reality. The apostles separated what God had joined in the Incarnation. There "the Word became flesh"; here the Word was to become word and the flesh was to become flesh. The spiritual was to be apart from the material, and the material was to be apart from the spiritual to the impoverishing of both—the spiritual was not to function in material terms and the material was not to function in spiritual terms. One was high and dry and the other low and secular. This division between the secular and the sacred persists today—a disastrous division. It destroys the essential nature of Christianity. It makes it like other religions where the Word becomes word instead of being true to itself where the Word becomes flesh. This makes the Christian faith less than and other than its true self.

O Jesus, we tear Thy seamless robe when we divide life into sacred and secular. Thou didst teach and heal and feed people in the name of the one Gospel. Help me this day to manifest Thee in *everything*. Amen.

AFFIRMATION FOR THE DAY: *All my barriers are down—life is one and that one life is His.*

141

THE SEVEN BECOME THE CENTER OF POWER

What happened when this division between the sacred and secular took place in the Acts? The so-called laymen took over in large measure the Christian movement. The Seven became the center of spiritual power. God seemed to tip His power in the direction of those who held the material and the spiritual together. It was Stephen, one of the Seven, who precipitated the revival in Jerusalem and brought on his own martyrdom— he was the first Christian martyr. It was Phillip, another member of the Seven, who first preached the gospel outside Jerusalem after Pentecost, winning the whole city of Samaria. "So there was much joy in that city." Then the apostles sent down Peter and John to regularize what they could not produce. They were the rear guard of an expanding movement, trying to keep up with it.

It was Philip who first preached the Gospel to an Ethiopian and who was the probable founder of the Ethiopian Church, the Coptic Church. He also founded the ministry of women, having "four unmarried daughters who did prophesy," the beginning of Christian spinsterhood!

It was the lay group who, scattered under the persecution of Stephen, went as far as Antioch, preaching the Lord Jesus. "And the strong hand of the Lord was with them and a great number that believed turned unto the Lord." It was out of the Antioch church, founded by these laymen, that Paul and Barnabas went on their great missionary journeys to Asia and Europe. Paul, belonging to the lay group, sent forth by the lay group, and representing the lay group, became the center of the Christian thrust into that non-Christian world. The Acts are called the Acts of the Apostles, but after the first few chapters the apostles drop out and the lay group take over. Th apostles still held an "authority," but the lay group had the initiative and the power. God was plainly lending His grace and power to those who made the spiritual and material one.

O Father, Thou art speaking still in the same terms. Thou art giving Thy power to those who manifest it in terms of life—spiritual and physical. Teach me this day to do every little and every big thing in a spiritual way. Amen.

AFFIRMATION FOR THE DAY: *I ask not for authority, but for power—and the power becomes the authority.*

THREE NAMES WHICH CANNOT BE USED

We have seen that everyone who is in Christ is one of the chosen and is ordained by that very choice. "As Thou hast sent Me into the world, even so have I sent them into the world" is the true apostolic succession, says Dr. Kramer. The ministry, he points out, is "a servantship." The real name was *dia konos*—"*dia*" = through, and "*konos*" = the dust; the figure of the camel driver who goes through the dust leading the camel while someone else sits on it. Jesus had just pointed out, according to Moffatt, that there were three names He could not trust them with: "Be ye not called 'Fathers' "—the "Fathers" were those who by reason of age were to be looked up to and obeyed. "Be ye not called 'Teachers' "—the "teachers" were those who knew and the rest were to listen and obey. "Be ye not called 'Leaders' "—the "leaders" were at the head of the procession; the rest were followers.

All three of these names represent attitudes, and all three names and attitudes represent self-assertion. Since it was self-assertion, these names could not be Christianized. These names and attitudes were to be renounced. There was only one name He could trust them with—servants, deacons. This attitude of servants was self-losing in the will of Another. The attitude is self-surrender. Only this attitude can be Christianized.

There is a place for ambitious men in Christianity. He who would be "great," let him be "the servant of all." He who would be "first," let him be "the slave of all." "Great" is to be the servant; "first" is to be the slave—a deeper self-giving brings a higher rising. The greatest of all is the Son of Man Who gives His life "a ransom for many." So this greatness is open to minister and layman alike, for it is the greatness of service, not of position or occupation. Greatness is open to both clergy and laity and on the same terms—both are to be "servants" or "slaves." If they are, then they rise according to the degree of self-giving.

O Father God, we thank Thee that Thou hast made service, and service alone, the badge of greatness. This makes greatness in reach of everybody, everywhere, in whatever occupation. And that greatness is beneficent greatness for it is service. Amen.

AFFIRMATION FOR THE DAY: *The word "service" will have a new content in it for me, for my surrender to Him will have a new content in it.*

"ALL CHRISTIANS ARE MINISTERS"

We meditate today upon a very decisive verse as to the status of laymen: "And he gave some, apostles; and some, prophets; and some, evangelists; and some, pastors and teachers; for the perfecting of the saints, for the work of the ministry, for the edifying of the body of Christ" (Eph. 4:11-12 KJV). The Revised Standard Version reads: "for the equipment of the saints, for the work of ministry"—not "the ministry," a separate specially ordained group, but for "the work of the ministry" (*diakonia*)—the work of "servantship." With the comma gone, then the whole passage reads, "for the perfecting of the saints for the work of servantship"—"the saints," who are the body of believers, become those who manifest "servantship." The whole body of believers become ministers, or servants, in this sense. As Dr. Kramer says: "All Christians are diakonia, ministers called to a ministry."

Some are called to the preaching ministry, but all are called to the ministry—all are called to servantship. An outstanding layman went to the altar as a young man to get a call to the ministry. While there he "got a call away from the preaching ministry to the ministry." His life has been a manifestation of servantship ever since.

This sense of laymen being "the chosen people of God" puts dignity and a sense of calling and mission into the ordinary occupation. The ordinary becomes the extraordinary, for it has extraordinary destiny in it. All life is lifted from the sordid to the sacred and becomes big with destiny. Anyone who is "in Christ" has within him a sense of royal dignity, a sense of being important in the scheme of things. The trivial becomes the tremendous; in the menial there is the ministry. The merchant now handles his ledgers with the same sense of sacredness as the preacher handles the Bible.

O God, our Father, we thank Thee that Thou hast cleansed all life and nothing right is to be called common or unclean. Every common meal becomes a sacrament. We thank Thee for this open opportunity. Amen.

AFFIRMATION FOR THE DAY: *I am called to the ministry, so I will "minister" to every one I meet—today.*

"WITH A SENSE OF COMMISSION"

We must now return to our verse: "Ye have not chosen me, but I have chosen you, and ordained you, that ye should go and bring forth fruit, and that your fruit should remain: that whatsoever ye shall ask of the Father in my name, He may give it you" (John 15:16 KJV).

This verse is my verse, given to me when I began my work as a missionary and evangelist. I have lived on that verse all these years. Just as I am about to speak to an audience I ask them to bow their heads in silent prayer. Invariably I repeat this verse to Christ, reminding Him that I am not there by my choice, but by His. Having put me there, it is up to Him to see me through, to give me all the grace and power I need to be effective in that hour, that that hour should "bear fruit." I straighten up with a sense of commission and backing, that all the Divine Resources I need are behind me.

I quoted that verse in a ministers' meeting, saying it was my verse. A Presbyterian minister came up and said, "But that's a Presbyterian verse—'Ye have not chosen me, but I have chosen you.' " We were both wrong—it was not "my verse" as a "minister," nor was it his verse as a Presbyterian. In both cases it would limit its scope to a class and a denomination. It belongs inherently to the Christian as such. Every Christian is chosen and ordained. Every Christian can stand with bowed head as he begins the daily task and can repeat that verse: "Ye have not chosen me, but I have chosen you, and ordained you, that ye should go and bring forth fruit." He can have a sense of divine backing and commission as he goes into any legitimate occupation. He is not in a second-rate calling, and hence he is no second-rate Christian. The full and unlimited power of Christ is behind him.

O Master, anyone in Thee is in Thy commission, Thy ordination, and is a disciple and an apostle. As such we can show apostolic authority and power to the limit of our obedience. Gratitude is the only word. I thank Thee. Amen.

AFFIRMATION FOR THE DAY: *I am a commissioned servant of the Kingdom—commissioned to represent the Kingdom and to serve all in Its name.*

"IF WE COULD GET ONE THING DONE"

We continue the meditation on the equal calling of everyone in Christ and the possible equal fruitfulness of that equal calling.

One of the most important things that happened in the post-war world was the announcement of the Emperor of Japan that he was not divine. That deflated the situation, brought Japan down to reality, and laid the foundation for her amazing recovery and progress. It marks her out as the eventual leader in the Eastern world. What lay back of this announcement?

Soon after the Occupation took over in Japan, a representative of the Occupation said to Dr. Vorhees, the head of the Omi Brotherhood: "If we could get one thing done our work would be over. If we could get the Emperor to say he is not divine, we could withdraw. But of course that can't be done." Dr. Vorhees, an American who, on marrying a titled Japanese lady took Japanese citizenship and stayed in Japan during the war, was appointed liaison officer between the Occupation and the Japanese Prime Minister, Prince Konoye. He replied: "Oh, yes, it can be done. The Prime Minister doesn't believe it, for he is a marine biologist. Leave it to us." Dr. Vorhees went to Prince Konoye and laid the matter before him, and he replied: "Yes, it can be done. You write out what you would like the Emperor to say." The Emperor, hearing of this, wanted to see Vorhees, but being a citizen he could not have an interview, so it was arranged that the Emperor would be walking in his garden and Vorhees would join him "by chance." It was decided that the statement should be given to a Court scribe who would put it into proper court language. It was a paragraph in the Emperor's broadcast to the nation on New Year's Day, 1946. It turned the Japanese world upside down—and set Japan right side up.

O Father, Thou dost match Thy servants against an hour of need. Thou didst match Vorhees against that hour of need. Thou didst begin a new era in the life of a great people, because a man was at Thy disposal. We thank Thee. Amen.

AFFIRMATION FOR THE DAY: *Let me be God's right-hand man, at hand for the little and the big.*

MATCHED AGAINST AN HOUR

We left off yesterday with the Emperor's announcement that he was not divine. Had that superstition lingered in the minds of the Japanese people it would have left a dangerous potentiality: "Yes, we've been defeated temporarily, but only temporarily, for you cannot defeat the Divine—we will come back and come back with revenge." The announcement of the Emperor was a national catharsis. It brought the situation back to reality and laid the foundation for Japan's recovery and progress. She is manufacturing more than she did before the war and is first in shipbuilding in the world.

But back of that announcement is this story: Mr. Hyde, inventor of Mentholatum, was a dedicated layman who lived in simplicity and dedicated millions to good causes. Among them he gave to Dr. Vorhees the right to manufacture Mentholatum in Japan and provided the machinery and the assembly lines. Vorhees supported the vast mission work which he carried on through the manufacture of Mentholatum. It kept him and his work going on through the war. When the war ceased and the opportunity opened for the Emperor to make the all-important announcement, Vorhees was there, matched against that opportunity. No Japanese could have touched it—it was too sacred. Only an American who was also a Japanese citizen could have touched it. God matched Vorhees against that hour.

Further, God matched Hyde against that hour too. Without Hyde and his dedicated money behind Vorhees, that amazingly important "fruit" could not have been brought forth. A dedicated layman changed the life and destiny of a nation. He was chosen and ordained to bring forth that fruit, because he was available and responsive to God's plan for his life. Anything can happen to and through a surrendered life.

O Master of my heart, may I be ready if Thou hast a situation against which you can match my life. May I be at hand, ready and prepared, for Thou dost use the "at hand" instrument. I thank Thee. Amen.

AFFIRMATION FOR THE DAY: *I am ready, make me prepared for the task that confronts me today.*

"PAUL WAS OUTSIDE IT"

To fix this idea of the laity as the chosen people of God, let us go back again to the early Scriptures for confirmation. Paul was undoubtedly the most influential man in the early development of Christianity, both as to the content of that faith and its spread. Paul was a layman; no apostolic hands were laid on him. If there was an "apostolic succession" then Paul was outside it. The idea that grace and authority were handed down through a line of tactual succession apart from the character of the persons concerned but inhering in the office was so foreign to Paul's gospel that Christ is immediately available to anybody, anywhere, by faith, that Paul never would have fitted into that "line." He would have broken the "link" out of sheer principle.

God broke the link when He chose Ananias, a layman, to lay his hands on Paul that he might receive his sight and be filled with the Holy Spirit. When Paul came into Damascus blinded, God said, "Ananias," and he replied, "Here am I, Lord"—I'm at your immediate disposal. When he heard what the errand was he trembled, for Paul was murdering Christians, but he trembled bravely and went. He laid his hands upon the head of the stricken Saul and said, "Brother Saul." When he called this murderer brother, it shook Paul to his depths and opened the gates to the Divine forgiveness through this human forgiveness. The greatest Christian of the centuries walked through the gates of eternal life—and it was a layman who opened the gates to the greatest lay minister of Christendom.

Moreover, it was a lay group—"prophets and teachers" but no apostles—who laid their hands on Paul and Barnabas and sent them forth on those great missionary journeys to Asia and Europe. Laymen ordained the greatest layman of the centuries—and the most effective.

O Jesus Christ, my Lord and Master, I thank Thee that Thou art not choosing priests or prophets or pastors or popes, but persons. Let me be that person—a person for whom Christ died. In Thy Name. Amen.

AFFIRMATION FOR THE DAY: *I am a person, therefore eligible for the highest God has for any man.*

A LAWYER WHO RECONCILES

This idea of "servanthood" and greatness coming through "servanthood" alone fits in with the character and genius of the Christian faith. The Son of Man becomes the greatest of all through laying down His life a ransom for many—that sets the pattern of greatness for God and man. Any attempt to find greatness through popes and prelates and ecclesiastical position and power is an alien type of power imported into the Christian faith. It is always corrupting, for it is alien to the faith it purports to lead. Jesus was specific at this point: "You know that the rulers of the Gentiles lord it over them, and their great men exercise authority over them. It shall not be so among you; but whoever would be great among you must be your servant" (Matt. 20:25-26). "It shall not be so among you"—and yet it has become "so" among us. Greatness is measured, more often than not, by ecclesiastical position instead of through "servanthood." Hence there is an inner—and an outer—struggle for position, place, and power, and the ministry, or "servanthood," both lay and clerical, is corrupted by this self-assertive struggle. It is all outside Christ instead of in Christ.

I was recently in a city filled with religious leaders, lay and clerical. The one whom I will remember most and longest was a lawyer—a lawyer who reconciles 40 percent of the people who come to him for a divorce. This Christian lawyer loves his work, for he prefers reconciliation to recompense. He loses money on reconciliations, but he gains in inner joy and outer stature. The servant of all becomes the greatest of all. He was pointed out to me as the outstanding Christian layman of that city. He fulfilled the law of greatness.

O Jesus, my Lord and Savior, Thou hast set a standard by which men everywhere rise and fall. If they fulfill it they rise, if they break it they fall. The sum total of reality silently decrees it. Thou hast interpreted reality to us. Amen.

AFFIRMATION FOR THE DAY: *I ask for no recompense—I ask only for reconciliation for myself and others.*

"SANCTIFIED IN CHRIST"

We have looked at the "in Christ" passages in Romans and then in the Gospel of John to see the connection between Paul and John in their emphasis on being in Him. This conception we have seen is not merely Pauline—it is Christian. It is not the emphasis of one man—it is the emphasis of the God-Man. To abide in the God-Man is to abide in God and man. It means to find God and ourselves. Being outside Him means to lose God and ourselves. .

We now return to Paul to see what he says about "in Christ" in I Corinthians. The first passage that meets our eye is "to those sanctified in Christ Jesus" (I Cor 1:2). This is an important passage in that it tells us where the sanctification lies—it lies not in ourselves, but in Christ Jesus. Sanctification comes through surrender to Jesus Christ, and remains as long as we continue in Christ Jesus. If I say, "I am sanctified," instead of saying, "I am sanctified in Christ Jesus," then I am calling attention to an experience instead of to the One Who brings the experience. It makes me experience-centered instead of Christ-centered—self-conscious instead of Christ-conscious. When I am self-conscious the experience fades; when I am Christ-conscious the experience remains and grows.

If we emphasize "the doctrine of sanctification," it remains a doctrine—often threadbare and verbal. But if we emphasize the fact of being "sanctified in Christ Jesus," the doctrine becomes a fact—vital and victorious.

As long as sanctification remains in Christ Jesus it is sanctification. When sanctification gets out of Him, it is "cranktification"—a bone of contention instead of the Word become flesh. The word "sanctification" and the experience become redeemed when they are "in Christ Jesus." Outside of Him they rot.

Lord Jesus, Thou dost redeem everything that is in Thee. Thou dost not bring redemption; Thou art redemption, and everything is redeemed and stays redeemed as long as it stays in Thee. I thank Thee for this simplicity, this profundity. Amen.

AFFIRMATION FOR THE DAY: *My "sanctification" may be barren in me, but it is blessed in Him.*

"THE GRACE . . . IN CHRIST JESUS"

The next important verse in I Corinthians reads: "I give thanks to God always for you because of the grace of God which was given to you in Christ Jesus" (1:4). "The grace of God which was given to you in Christ Jesus" is the grace of God given especially "in Christ Jesus." I say especially, and not exclusively. Yet I am tempted to say exclusively, for while God loves everybody He can manifest His grace only in terms which represent His character, and in no other place is the character of God seen except in the character of Jesus. "Grace and truth came by Jesus Christ."

If God gave His grace except in terms of Jesus Christ He would misrepresent His own character. In misrepresenting His own character He would misrepresent the nature of the moral universe. So His giving in terms of Jesus Christ is not arbitrary, but obligatory. He can't give in terms other than Jesus Christ and be God, for God is a Christlike God.

In Jesus Christ God can give with both hands. Outside Christ He gives just enough to let the recipient know He is there—just enough to spur him to seek the grace of God in Christ, where he receives fully and abundantly. If God should give fully and abundantly outside Christ, the recipient would be satisfied this side of Christ, which would be this side of reality, which would be harmful to the recipient.

"Grace and truth came by Jesus Christ"—note the "and truth." If grace came apart from Christ it would be other than truth. For it to be grace and truth it would have to come through Jesus Christ. If God gave grace through an idol it would make God into the image of the idol. An idol doesn't represent God, it misrepresents God. So grace and truth have to come through Jesus Christ and only through Jesus Christ.

O Jesus, I thank Thee that in Thee God is free—free to give with His whole heart and His whole resources. Therefore I can come to God in full confidence when I come in Thee. I am free to take, for Thou art free to give. Amen.

AFFIRMATION FOR THE DAY: *Grace outside of Jesus is legalistic; in Jesus, grace is life.*

"ENRICHED IN HIM"

We continue with another portion of the passage from yesterday: "that in every way you were enriched in him" (I Cor. 1:5). This passage is important. Does religious faith enrich or impoverish human personality? No more important question can be asked.

A religion which dictates what you should read and what you should listen to weakens you. The Moslem could reply, "Up to a certain point my religion strengthens me, but since it is a religion of rules instead of principles when I grow up to those rules and want to go beyond them, I am caught and cramped by the rules and hence weakened." The Hindu could reply, "My religion weakens me at the point where it tells me that this earthly life is *maya*, an illusion, hence it unfits me for continuous motivation for social and material change." The Buddhist could say, "My religion weakens me at the point of believing in life itself. It tries to get me beyond life into Nirvana, the state of the snuffed-out candle." The religion of Mysticism could say, "My religion weakens me in that it is a retreat—a retreat inward into mystical states, apart from the needs and problems of the world."

Only the real Christian faith, believed in fully and applied in its total implications could say, "In every way you are enriched in Him." And you are! I visited the Central Congo in Africa. I listened to people who less than a generation ago were just out of the Bush, now intelligently and ably discussing how to meet the demands of imminent independence. Had independence been given into their hands instead of into the hands of the politicians, the story of the Congo might have been different. These men and women were in every way enriched in Him. Their minds, their bodies, their emotions, their outlook, their motives—their total persons have been enriched in Him.

O Jesus, Lord, Savior, and Enricher, I thank Thee that when we are exposed to Thee we are enriched. Thou art to us what sunlight is to greenness and growth, what air is to the lungs—Thou art life, and life abundant. Amen.

AFFIRMATION FOR THE DAY: *I am an enriched person—enriched by the only riches in the universe—the riches of God.*

RECEPTIVITY AND RESPONSE

We are meditating on: "In every way we are enriched in Him." Note the "in every way." If that means anything it means that the life, here and hereafter, is enriched in Him. It does not mean, as some suppose, that the present life is to be impoverished in order for heaven to be gained. It means that everything Jesus touches He enriches. He is Life touching life and enriching it.

The New Testament teaches that "in him all things were created . . . all things were created through him and for him" (Col. 1:16). If all things were created by Christ and for Christ, then when we surrender a spoiled creation to Him He re-creates it, and in recreating it enriches it. He enriches the mind by cleansing away alien thinking, gives it single-pointedness and direction, and drives it toward great ends. The mind is enriched; the soul is enriched. It is cleansed from contradictions and conflicts, the wanting of mutually exclusive things, and is filled with a single loyalty and love. The body is enriched, for many of the diseases which afflict the body are passed on to it by sicknesses in mind and soul. Since the mind and soul are enriched, the body inherits that enrichment. The total personality is enriched. Since mind and soul and body are now one in purpose and loyalty, the total personality working as a well-oiled and smooth-running unit is a rhythmical and harmonious and impressive person. He gets things done, for he knows how to receive. An organism can expend only what it receives, so the person knowing the secret of active receptivity takes from Him and expends on others. He knows the secret of receptivity and response. Since he is rich in resources, he is rich in response and becomes rich in his very self in the process.

O Jesus, Thou art rich, for in Thee the divine fullness dwells and when we are in Thee and only in Thee, then all those riches are ours for the taking. We are rich in Thy riches and full in Thy fullness. Amen.

AFFIRMATION FOR THE DAY: *I am rich in inner unity and outer direction, and rich in power to hold to both.*

THE WHOLE PERSONALITY ENRICHED

I have spoken of being in the Central Congo and of the enrichment coming to the people through being in Christ. My African interpreter's wife has branded on her cheeks and forehead ugly tribal marks. Her parents wanted to marry her to a polygamous man. She ran away into the jungle and hid in a tree all night. Her sister had done the same thing and had been eaten by lions. When the interpreter wanted to marry her, the missionary who had raised him from a child objected because she was uneducated and jungly. The son born to them stood at the top of his class in Belgium in classes where French—to him a foreign language—was the medium of instruction. In America amid Negro students in Augusta, Georgia, where the medium of instruction was English, also a foreign language, he was chosen the valedictorian of his class. In Luluaburg, Congo, in a school amid Belgian students, he stood at the very top of his class. He is fluent in six languages. A white boy, irked at his brilliance, called him an "imbecile." The principal suspended the boy for three days. The African boy went to the Belgian boy and said, "You didn't mean that, did you?" When he said he didn't and was sorry, he took the white boy to the principal and said: "I forgive him, will you please forgive him?" The principal did and reinstated him.

The white parents of the boys in this school saw a new Africa in the person of this lad. His parents and he are being enriched in Christ.

When we are in Christ the whole personality is awakened. On this journey to the heart of the Belgian Congo I came through cannibal tribes, women wearing little but G strings, to a mission station. It was like going from pitch darkness to light, from the Stone Age to Enlightenment, from life unenriched and poverty-stricken to life rich and full.

O Jesus, Lord, we thank Thee that Thy touch upon life is life giving. Withered life begins to bloom and dead life begins to live. The bad become good and the good become better and the better become the best. We thank Thee. Amen.

AFFIRMATION FOR THE DAY: *"It yet remains to be seen what God can do with a surrendered life."*

AN AMAZING AWAKENING

We are meditating upon "in every way you were enriched in Him." I saw the most remarkable spiritual and moral awakening among primitive people imaginable—a Pentecost in an African setting—a real work of the Spirit. This place was virgin soil; the revival was in a new section and could not have been staged for my benefit; it was only two days old. Yet there were a thousand people out at 5:30 A.M., and the same number at 10 A.M., 3 P.M., and 7 P.M. The people had built a palm branch tabernacle; they sat on small logs for seats. Most of the women had no clothing above their waists. There were babies galore. Yet there was an astonishing decorum. They listened with eager attention to the message. Then the Africans took charge of the after-meeting. They called for those who would repent and seek Christ to come forward. The long bamboo altar was filled inside and out, and there were rows of seekers behind them. The seeking was not confined to those at the altar, however. The whole audience became a seeking unit. Workers moved around in the midst of the audience calling out: "Give up your sins—all of them." "Believe in Jesus." "Make a full surrender to Him." Everybody was praying audibly. It was the cry of a whole people for a long-lost heavenly Father. This would go on for half an hour; then the African leader would give them an opportunity to tell what they had found.

The chief stood up first and said that he now believed in Jesus, that before he thought only of cheating and deceiving the people, but now that was all gone. Another would tell of lying, adultery, and stealing. It was all gone. A chief's wife told of stealing the *"kasawas"* (a kind of tapioca) from the fields of the other women, another of deliverance from the power of the witch doctor and evil spirits. It was an amazing story of deliverance and redemption.

O God, our Father, we thank Thee for the possibility of change, of new birth, of new life. We are grateful that the worst can become the best, the weakest become the strongest. In Jesus' Name. Amen.

AFFIRMATION FOR THE DAY: *Since conversion is a possibility I shall be its chief illustration.*

CONFESSION!

We continue the story of men and women in the Central Congo being enriched in Christ. One man said, "I've ruined my life by drinking and adultery, and my marriage was on the rocks, but that's all gone, and I'm happy now." Another man said, "I'll never turn my heart toward dirty things again. Now I don't know anything in my heart but God." A woman said, "I was a thief, stole chickens, I was married three times, I worshiped idols, went to the witch doctor for the birth of a child. I've given it all up, and I'm thankful to God, morning, noon, and night." Another woman said, "I was bewitched, smoked, committed adultery. But now the very smell of cigarettes is bad to me." A man said, "I went to the witch doctor to get a charm so I could get animals, as I had a gun. He gave me the tail of an animal—he said that would help to have success in hunting. I now see it was no good. I've renounced it all." Another man said, "I acted like a crazy person. I had bad affairs with the witch doctor. I also discovered that the Kings of the Forest [a secret society] had an idol pit in the forest and had a man down in it shaking the head of the idol when questions were asked."

A man began to tell how good he was—how he had not done this or that—and all of a sudden from the side of the women there was a concerted, "Boo!"—which meant, "Bunk"! The man sat down abruptly. A witch doctor said, "I gave it all up. Now Jesus has come into my heart." A man said, "I gave up to 2,600 francs to see the face of an idol." A woman said, "We were in darkness, we didn't know any better. I've been going to the witch doctor. Now I believe in Jesus."

In front of the pulpit there was a pile of renounced idols, charms, and leopard skins used by the witch doctor, symbols of the cleansing taking place. There was a perfect stillness over the audience as each person told of his or her personal conversion. It was the most cleansing movement I have ever seen. They were "enriched in him."

O Jesus, Lord and Savior, I thank Thee for Thy cleansing power among the people emerging from barbarity, and among the cultured and refined but inwardly beaten and empty. Everywhere Thy touch is saving. I thank Thee. Amen.

AFFIRMATION FOR THE DAY: "A more equitable distribution of riches" is a socialistic slogan—God's distribution of the riches of grace is equitable and lavish.

IN EVERY WAY—ENRICHED

We have noted the phrase, "in every way you were enriched in him." We must pause to emphasize "in every way." We know that our souls are "enriched in him." As we expose our souls to Him miracles of changed souls take place. It works to the degree that that exposure to Him takes place. But will it work "in every way"? Does this enrichment turn out to be a total enrichment, enriching body and mind, social and economic relationships? The answer is yes. It is Life-touching, enriching the whole of life.

Take the mind. Forgive the personal illustration: I was toward the bottom of my class until I was converted. After conversion I said to myself, "This is no place for a Christian," and I moved toward the top. Here was a woman whose marriage was on the rocks, and she herself was empty and frustrated. She was converted and with conversion mentally awakened. At forty-five she decided she wanted an education, but would have to keep a full-time job to support herself. She entered the University and came out four years later with her degree *cum laude*. She was given a scholarship for an M.A. in Psychology and got all A's. She has organized a continuous prayer vigil going on through the 24 hours, throughout the 365 days a year in shifts of half an hour each. I have found people in Japan, India, and Africa who take half hours of the vigil, difficult in America. The continuous prayer goes on night and day. This came from a once-empty and frustrated life. "In every way you were enriched in him"— mentally, spiritually, in life output. An African woman converted in a hospital, walked home seventy-five miles by stages, and through her radiant witness for Christ established five congregations on the way, the mission sending teachers and preachers to take over behind her. She left a trail of light and joy behind her—"enriched in him."

O Father, how can we thank Thee enough that we need not be poor right next door to Thy available resources. They are all ours for the asking and receiving. So I walk from my poverty to Thy riches. In Jesus' name. Amen.

AFFIRMATION FOR THE DAY: *A red hen sat on an open barrel of grain and starved to death—save me from the nonreceptive mentality.*

"IN ME YOU ARE WELL AND WHOLE"

We are considering "in every way you were enriched in Him." "In every way" includes the body. I have often imagined a convention of bodies talking about the people who inhabit them. A body stands up and says: "Oh my, the man who lives in me doesn't know how to live. He ties me up into knots by his fears and worries and resentments. Then he blames me for getting out of sorts, and I'm dosed with all kinds of medicines that have nothing to do with my ailments. If he knew how to live I would have no ailments. My ailments are all rooted in his wrong attitudes and reactions. I wish he knew how to live. I'd be well." Another body stands up and says, "The man who lives in me is wonderful. He lives in Christ and hence knows how to live. He is harmonious and adjusted and happy. You should see how we get along. I would do anything for him—and do! I go beyond my own capacity for such a man—he's a joy to live with."

The body is made by Christ, for Christ, and lives as it lives in Him. Some time ago I was threatened with a serious ailment. In the midst of it the Lord said, "In Me you are well and whole." That phrase struck me—"In *Me*." Out of Him I was not well and whole, but in Him I found that I was well and whole and have continued to be as I have remained in Him. It is as simple and profound as that! Here was a woman who because of her impossible way of life became ill, and one after another had to have her appendix, her gall bladder, and other organs taken out. The doctor said, "What are you going to do when you run out of parts?" She was allergic to all sorts of things. Then she was converted and began to live in Christ. Her allergies dropped away, her body bounded back to health, and she has amazing vitality and health. The body is His home and is at home in Him.

O Christ, Thou dost heal our sicknesses, but more, Thou dost save us from getting sick. We throw off our sicknesses by Thy vitality within us. We live in Thy health, Thy joy—Thy everything! I thank Thee. Amen.

AFFIRMATION FOR THE DAY: *May I be so healthy in Christ that no disease germ can gain a lodging.*

WISDOM, RIGHTEOUSNESS, SANCTIFICATION, REDEMPTION

We pass on to another phase of being in every way enriched in Him. The next passage in I Corinthians, emphasizing the result of being in Christ, says: "He [God] is the source of your life in Christ Jesus, whom God made our wisdom, our righteousness and sanctification and redemption" (1:30). This passage adds a phase of our being enriched in Him and an important one. We are enriched culturally in Him.

Back of Greek culture lay the desire for wisdom, and back of the Jewish culture lay the desire for righteousness. Paul here said that in Christ we inherit both—He is "made our wisdom" and "our righteousness." The Greeks had missed wisdom, for the wisdom had turned into pride which destroyed itself. The philosophy of Greece philosophized and spun theories about everything while their civilization rested on slave labor. That slave labor destroyed their wise civilization. They were not wise enough to be just—to man as man.

The Jews wanted righteousness, but their righteousness became self-righteousness; the Pharisee was the end product. It destroyed itself because it became a legal righteousness, obeying laws, instead of a life righteousness, obeying principles.

Both of these failed, but in Christ these two things are fulfilled. In Him we become wise and we become righteous, for He is both, and both in a living blend. The wisest person in the world is the person who acts upon the principles and mind of Jesus. He is always wise in every situation. The most righteous person is the person who is righteous according to His righteousness—a righteousness of love to all.

O Father God, we thank Thee that in Jesus nothing is lost. In Him we gather up the fragments that remain—the fragments of many cultures. They are all ours in Him. What a heritage Thou dost give us. Amen.

AFFIRMATION FOR THE DAY: *Wisdom, righteousness, sanctification, redemption—all in Him and in me for I'm in Him.*

JESUS FULFILLS THE CULTURAL HERITAGE

We are looking at the enrichment that comes through Jesus—the cultural enrichment. When Jesus said, "I came not to destroy but to fulfill," He said something vastly important. Many think that the coming of Christianity to a people means that we wipe the slate clean of past culture and write on it an alien culture mediated through the West, making it mostly a Western culture. This is a serious mistake.

Jesus is the "Son of man," as if all mankind were in travail to bring forth such as He. He is "the desire of the nations"—those incoherent, often unconscious, desires expressed in various ways, come to completion in Him. When you see Him you see what you have been looking for, but haven't quite known what it was. It is a kind of home-coming to the homeland of your soul. Jesus is at home in every race, in every land. You have the feeling that He knows you and understands you and wants to give you the best which you have been unconsciously seeking.

If Jesus fulfills the highest in the Greek and the Jewish culture, He also fulfills the highest in Hindu culture. If the Greeks sought wisdom and the Jews righteousness, the Hindus have sought sanctification. If sanctification means "to be set apart," then the Hindus have sought that "set-apartness" very strenuously. The Brahmin tries to maintain a ceremonial and outer cleanness by not touching anything defiling. The ascetic goes apart from the world to merge himself into Brahma. All of these have failed. The sanctification of the Hindu has resulted in a physical apartness—an outer sanctification that covered an inner pride. The pride of being different—and superior. But it was a sanctification that was outer and empty—and is passing away.

Divine Father, Thou art turning our wisdom into foolishness, our righteousness into pretension, our sanctification into sanctimoniousness. We see in Jesus the real. The rest is unreal. We thank Thee. Amen.

AFFIRMATION FOR THE DAY: *No holier-than-thou attitudes today, for Jesus is holier than I am, and I am at His feet.*

REDEMPTION—OUR REAL NEED

We have studied how the nations have sought after wisdom, righteousness, and sanctification and have failed. Why have they failed? They failed because of a lack of the last thing mentioned which Jesus becomes to us, redemption. "In Christ Jesus, whom God made our . . . redemption." This redemption comes last. We would have thought it would be first. We would have thought so because we are Christian and have looked into the face of Jesus and know thereby that all our best and our worst needs redemption. The Greeks, the Jews, and the Hindus, however, have not looked into the face of Jesus and hence felt they had the answers in themselves. So they went out to establish a wisdom of their own, a righteousness of their own, and a sanctification of their own. It became in each case a self-wisdom, a self-righteousness, a self-sanctification. In each case it resulted in a self-pride which destroyed itself.

The Christian faith believes and starts from the starting point of redemption—we need redemption not only from our worst sins and corruption, but from our best—from our wisdom, our righteousness, and our sanctification. At the center of our wisdom, our righteousness, and our sanctification is the unsurrendered ego which keeps intruding into our wisdom and making it strutting egoism; into our righteousness, making it bad-smelling self-righteousness; into our sanctification, making it uninviting sanctimoniousness. "Lilies that fester smell worse than weeds"—virtues that have a basis of egoistic pride become bad-smelling vices. They need redemption, and the wonder of Jesus is that He came to redeem the Pharisee as well as the publican, the proud duchess as well as the prostitute. He is redemption—full stop—redemption to everything that needs it, and everything does need it, including our virtues.

O Redeemer, redeem our bad and make it good, our good and make it better, and our better and make it best, and our best and make it Thy best—for Thy best is ultimate. We cannot go beyond it, nor do we want to. Amen.

AFFIRMATION FOR THE DAY: *In the South Sea islands are flowers which when alone are evil-smelling, but mingled with the scents of other flowers are attractive—learn thy lesson, O, my soul.*

GOOD THINGS NEED REDEMPTION

We are noting that everything needs redemption—through and in Him. Until it is redeemed through Him it is suffering from an incurable malady—unsurrendered egocentricity. Wisdom that has an unsurrendered egocentricity at its heart is foolishness—the foolishness, for instance, on the part of psychiatry that knowledge, or insight, will cure you of mental and emotional sicknesses. It doesn't. Very often—too often—the psychiatrist himself suffers from the very maladies he attempts to cure. One of the basic sicknesses of the mentally and emotionally ill is that they have not loved or been loved. Insight into that will not cure them. They must actually love and receive love. The knowledge is moonlight, the giving and receiving of love is sunlight.

Paul puts it in unforgettable terms: " 'Knowledge' puffs up, but love builds up" (I Cor. 8:1). Knowledge puffs up because at its heart is an unsurrendered ego; love builds up because at its heart is a surrendered ego, surrendered by the very fact of loving others.

Righteousness that is obedience to law and regulation is self-attainment—and self-attainment means pride of attainment. Righteousness that is an attainment needs redemption—redemption from the self that attains. Until that self is redeemed it lays a contaminating hand on all its attainments. Self-righteousness is not righteous.

Sanctification which is attained by keeping aloof from outward contaminations, by the touch-not, taste-not, handle-not method, soon turns into an outwardism which declares, "O God, I thank Thee that I am not as other men." Jesus said such outwardism does not go away justified, let alone sanctified.

All three of these need redemption—redemption from the central sin, the sin of making the self central, naming the self God.

O Jesus Christ, my Redeemer, redeem me from my virtues that miss the mark and become iniquity. I bring to Thee my sins, yes, and also my so-called good. It isn't good enough. Not after I've seen Thy face. Amen.

AFFIRMATION FOR THE DAY: *My wisdom, righteousness, and sanctification apart from Christ are obnoxious—in Him, perfect.*

EVERYTHING REDEEMED!

The central thing in the Christian faith is the last thing mentioned—redemption. All the good things—wisdom, righteousness, sanctification—have to exhaust themselves and become bankrupt before they are ready for redemption. The good things have to be put under life and be tried and show themselves not good enough. Then redemption steps in and redeems all the exhausted good things. That happened on a world scale—Jesus redeemed the philosophies and moralities of the ancients, not by destroying the good in them, but fulfilling it in Himself. He made wisdom into Wisdom, righteousness into Righteousness, sanctification into Sanctification. When these things are surrendered to Him they are made into something higher and hence redeemed.

The word "redeemed" means literally "bought back"—the slave was redeemed when bought back from slavehood to manhood. All these virtues which have become enslaved and corrupted by our egoisms, which creep in and become the basis of those virtues, are redeemed by putting the love of Christ at the basis. We do these things for His sake, not for our sakes.

All our virtues need to be redeemed. Service can become domination by the service; self-respect can become pride; sex love can become sexuality; the social urge can become subservience to the herd; judgment can become mote picking; learning can become pedantic; love can become possessive; orderliness can become perfectionism; self-love can become selfishness. All these good things need to be redeemed by surrender to Jesus. Surrendered to Him, they are cleansed, consecrated, and given back to us. They are ours because they are His.

The fact of Jesus at the basis of our lives redeeming us from twisted good as well as from downright evil is the most important and precious fact in our universe. There is nothing like it.

O Jesus, Redeemer and Lord, how grateful I am for Thy redemption. Take my good and make the good into the best, and my bad into good. Redeem me all over—body, mind, spirit, and contacts, for I need redemption. Amen.

AFFIRMATION FOR THE DAY: *Redemption puts humility at the basis of all I do and say and am.*

"BABES IN CHRIST"

We come to another "in Christ" passage in I Corinthians: "But I, brethren, could not address you as spiritual men, but as men of the flesh, as babes in Christ" (3:1). And the reason he gives for calling them babes in Christ is that "one says, 'I belong to Paul,' and another, 'I belong to Apollos.' " This is a startling passage, for we usually use the phrase "babes in Christ" when we describe those who have just become Christians and are as yet not well-informed about the faith. I once said to Madame Chiang Kai-shek concerning the Generalissimo who was seated there, but was not supposed to know English, "Is your husband a real Christian?" She replied, "Yes, he reads his Bible daily and gets guidance from God, and we have an hour of prayer together from five to six o'clock every morning. But you must remember he is only a babe in Christ." Here she meant that he had not grown to maturity as a Christian.

Paul puts his finger on a special sign of being a babe in Christ. "I belong to Paul," and "I belong to Apollos." Centering one's allegiance around religious teachers instead of centering allegiance around Christ is a sign of being a babe in Christ. If that be true—and of course it is—then that makes a great many Christians, perhaps the majority, "babes in Christ." Barthians, Neo-orthodox (meaning allegiance to those who teach Neo-orthodoxy), Calvinists, Lutherans, Wesleyans, Campbellites, Mennonites, and so on all down the line—it includes those who, while not holding a personal name to the denomination, hold the teaching of a person or persons who founded the denomination. It renders immature those who center their faith in anything less or anything other than Jesus Christ Himself. This is not a label that Paul sticks on people—it is a fact. Christianity not centered in Jesus Christ, and in Him alone, is an immature Christianity and the product is "babes in Christ."

O Christ, we cannot be mature until we are Thine and Thine alone. Outside Thee everything is secondhand and hence unsatisfactory. Everything in Thee is firsthand, vital, and hence mature. I thank Thee. Amen.

AFFIRMATION FOR THE DAY: *If my spiritual life has grown up around persons instead of the Person, I am immature. I must shift my basis from them to Him.*

MONDAY

Week 22

"ATTACHED TO EXHAUSTIBLE EMPHASES"

We are studying the fact of "babes in Christ"—those who are in Christ, but never grow up in Him. The chief cause, Paul says, for such a state is that the faith of these babes in Christ is centered in men—good teachers and their interpretations. You soon exhaust their emphases and then you go round and round. on those teachings, and soon you are repeating phrases and slogans such as "sovereignty of God," "justification by faith," "New Testament church," "the warmed heart," "Pentecost," "apostolic succession," "historic episcopacy," "the sinfulness of man," "man's predicament," "adult baptism by immersion." These phrases and slogans become more and more emptied of content and become slogans where the adherents hold the line against all comers.

Every emphasis or slogan detached from the living Christ soon becomes sterile and empty and exhausted of meaning. Those who commit themselves to these persons or systems remain babes in Christ. They are attached to exhaustible emphases and systems and hence they become sterile. They never grow, or grow only as they transcend the systems and get to the Living Christ.

When your faith and loyalty and love are fastened on Jesus Christ centrally and fundamentally, they are fastened upon the inexhaustible. He never grows stale, trite, or empty of growing meaning. In Him you find an eternal unfoldment. The more you see the more you see there is to be seen. In Him there is a surprise around every corner. The Holy Spirit unfolds the unfolding revelation—He takes of the things of Christ and shows them unto us. It keeps one running to keep up with unfolding truth. The absolute in Him is always beckoning to our relativisms. We are under the law of an eternal change—a change "into His likeness from one degree of glory to another."

O Christ Jesus, Thou art behind me in history, but Thou art before me. What I see of Thee sets me on fire to see more of Thee. What I have of Thee makes me thirst to drink in the depths of Thee. In Thy name. Amen.

AFFIRMATION FOR THE DAY: *If I am centered upon anything less than Christ I am centered upon the exhaustible and will become exhausted pursuing the exhaustible.*

165

GAZING AT JESUS, GLANCING AT OTHERS

We have seen that to center your faith in a religious leader and his emphasis or in a religious system of thought and its emphasis is to produce "babes in Christ." None of us has the truth, only Jesus is the Truth. "I am the way, and the truth, and the life." What we hold is truths about the Truth.

Paul puts the religious leaders in their places: "For all belongs to you; Paul, Apollos, Cephas, the world, life, death, the present and the future—all belongs to you; and you belong to Christ, and Christ to God" (I Cor. 3:21-22 Moffatt). Here Paul says that all religious teachers—Paul, Apollos, Cephas—belong to you, they are a part of your heritage, but you don't belong to them; you belong to Christ. That tipping of the emphasis from good men to the God-Man was decisive. The gazing at Paul, Apollos, Cephas, and glancing at Jesus produced denominationalism and division. The gazing at Jesus and glancing at religious teachers produced Christianity and unity. It also produces maturity. You can never become mature if you make a man and his emphasis the center of your attention. You will exhaust the man and his emphasis in a short time; you will get the kernel of what he presents, and the rest will be husks. Feeding on husks produces stunted, immature Christians— babes in Christ.

The committing of ourselves to a teacher—"I am a Barthian," "I am a Calvinist," "I am a Lutheran," "I am a Wesleyan," "I am Pentecostal," "I am a Neo-orthodox," "I am a Church of England," "I am a This, That, and the Other"—puts blinkers on our eyes, making us see one person and one system, and makes for a starved, stunted, and runted type of Christian faith and Christian living. To be centered in Jesus Christ and in Him alone makes for an eternal expansion and an eternal growth.

O Lord and Savior, save me from the marginal, from half-truths, from anything less than Thee. I want to grow up into Thee in all things till I come to the measure of the stature of the fullness of Thee. Thou art my Everything. Amen.

AFFIRMATION FOR THE DAY: *Centered in half-truths I will become a half-person. I need the Truth to be a whole person.*

"GROW UP IN EVERY WAY"

We look one more day at the possibility of being saved from being babes in Christ. This passage is compelling: "so that we may no longer be children, tossed to and fro and carried about with every wind of doctrine, by the cunning of men. . . . Rather, speaking the truth in love, we are to grow up in every way into him who is the Head, into Christ" (Eph. 4:14-15). "We are to grow up in every way into him . . . into Christ." The only way to grow up is to grow up into Him. You cannot by the very nature of things grow up in every way when you commit yourself to a system of thought organized around one man or a group of men and their emphases. They imperfectly comprehend Him Who is the Truth; so they hold truths about the Truth. You must break out from blinkered systems and "with unveiled face, beholding the glory of the Lord" become "changed into his likeness from one degree of glory to another."

When Jesus Christ is the center of your faith and the center of your quest, then you are upon the Illimitable. Men and their views are exhaustible, but Jesus Christ the Divine is the inexhaustible. The Gospel of Thomas says that Jesus said that the Kingdom "is a movement and a rest." You move toward Him, and you rest in something transforming and satisfying. Then there is a movement again and a rest—and so on, forever. "We are to grow up in every way into him." The "in every way" is significant. It is a total growth—not merely spiritually, but mentally, emotionally, socially, and physically. You become "every whit whole" and "whole" after a pattern of the Son of God—the highest pattern of the universe. This is no lopsided growth—so spiritual you are unfit for material relations, or so material you are unfit for spiritual relations—but an all-round growth—in every way. So it is an eternal growth and a symmetrical growth. Nothing is more beautiful than a truly Christian person.

O Unlimited Christ, Thou art calling me to the Infinite—to partake of Thy Everlastingness, to share Thy Universality, to enter the Boundless. I come. Take my nothingness and make it into Thy Everything—"in every way." In Thy name. Amen.

AFFIRMATION FOR THE DAY: *If I am a Christian in "some" ways, may I shift to being a Christian in "every" way.*

"FATHERS" AND "GUIDES"

We come now to another phase of being "in Christ." "For I became your father in Christ Jesus through the gospel" (I Cor. 4:15). Here Paul contrasts "guides in Christ" and his being a "father in Christ Jesus." He says "you have countless guides in Christ"—people who can guide what has already been created—but you have only one "father in Christ"—the person who created you in Christ. The difference was between those who cannot create, but can only guide the already created, and the person who shares the creatorship of Christ and creates spiritual children. The distinction is important.

Many can tell you how to direct your Christian life, but few can beget that Christian life; yet the latter is the privilege of every Christian. In Christ you can become creative—creating newborn souls, new hopes, new movements, new thinking, new acting, new loving, new health, new everything. To share the creative activity of Jesus and become a center of creation is the glorious and breathtaking privilege of those in Christ.

The pastor is often content to guide his flock—to guide what has already been created. The really surrendered person, however, who lets the creative power of Jesus work through him becomes a spiritual father, creating newborn souls. This is normal. Every Christian should be spiritually creative, or else he sinks into the subnormal, the sub-Christian.

To guide people may be a species of subtle self-assertion— "I'm superior, he's inferior, I must guide him." But to be creative in Christ means a constant surrender of the self to the creative activity of Christ within us. One is self-assertive and the other is self-surrendered. The creative Christian knows that he is only the channel of the creative Spirit of Jesus within him. Only the surrendered are creative. The self-assertive become the guides, the fussy managers of other people.

O Lord Jesus, Thy touch upon life is the touch of creation. Everything Thou didst touch began to have life. Work in and through me this day, with creative power. I want to be the "father" of some new life in Thee today. In Thy name. Amen.

AFFIRMATION FOR THE DAY: *To aspire to be a guide to others may make me a Pharisee; to aspire to be a "father" may make me a Christian.*

"I GOT HER IN"

We pause to look at our passage again: "For I became your father in Christ Jesus through the gospel" (I Cor. 4:15). Note the phrase: "through the gospel." If we preach a philosophy—ideas about life, or a moralism—principles and practices upon which life can be lived, or religious practices—techniques of religious life, we do not become a "father in Christ Jesus"—we do not beget spiritual children. It is only "through the gospel" that we become creative.

To illustrate: A little girl knocked at a popular pastor's door. She was obviously from the slums, and she said, "My mother has sent me to come and ask you to get her in." To "get her in"? The pastor was intrigued, so the little girl took him by the hand into a slum section, they climbed the stairs, and entered the room of a prostitute dying of consumption. He sat down beside her and talked of Jesus as a teacher, but she shook her head and said, "That isn't for the likes of me." Then he told her of Jesus as our example, how He went about doing good, but again she shook her head and said, "That isn't for the likes of me." Then out of desperation he reached back into his past and brought out something he had almost forgotten; he talked of Jesus dying on the cross for sinners. Her face began to light up, and she nodded her head and said, "Yes, yes, that's for the likes of me." The pastor, telling about it later, said, "We got her in—and I got in too!" As long as he presented a philosophy, a moralism, a religious ritualism, he was ineffectual and spiritually uncreative. The moment he gave her the gospel—the crucified and risen Savior—he became creative, the father of a newborn soul; he "got her in." And got himself in! The gospel is the redemptively creative activity of God. And Jesus Himself is that gospel.

O Master of my heart, I thank Thee that in Thee I too can become creative. All I have to do is to surrender myself fully, wholly, utterly, to Thee and have no blocks to Thy creative love, and I too can be a father of new hopes, new life, newborn souls. Amen.

AFFIRMATION FOR THE DAY: *Only through the gospel can I change others—through other ways I may modify here and there, but only through Christ can I create.*

A KNOWLEDGE OF JESUS

As long as religious education conceives of the Christian faith as a teaching about life—good teaching about life, even the best teaching about life—those who propagate it will remain as guides in Christ, but will never become fathers in Christ. They have reduced the Christian faith to the Word become word—a philosophy or a moralism. Until it becomes the word become flesh it is less than the gospel. In that case Christianity is a philosophy of life, a little more reasonable and better adapted to life than other philosophies. It cannot create life; it can only guide what has been created. If Christianity is a moralism directing life into moral channels, a little more moral and more consistently clear than other religions, then again it is less than the gospel. It takes its place among other moralisms—the highest place, for it is the highest morality, as a guide to life, but it cannot create life; it cannot be a father in Christ.

For this reason our churches are filled with people who have come up through religious education who lack the consciousness of Life. They have not been spiritually recreated, nor can they spiritually re-create. Religious education, on the whole, has been a guide in Christ, but it has failed to be a father in Christ.

Somewhere along the way the knowledge about Jesus must turn to a knowledge of Jesus—a knowledge of Him as personal Savior and Lord. This comes through repentance, through surrender, through receiving Christ into the heart and enthroning Him there as Lord by faith. The moment that is done. Life begins within. Then religious education can become a guide in Christ. Otherwise it becomes salvation by process, instead of salvation by a Person. It will produce those who are wistful, but not witnesses. They are always on the way, but not on the Way.

O Lord and Master of my heart and life, I thank Thee that when I know Thee I know Life Eternal as a present possession and not merely as a future longing. I "enter into Life," for Life has entered into me. I thank Thee, thank Thee. Amen.

AFFIRMATION FOR THE DAY: *My religious education will educate me beyond religion to a saving relationship to Jesus.*

NOT "IN" UNTIL THEY GET "OUT"

Paul follows his saying to the Corinthians that he had become their "father in Christ Jesus through the gospel" by saying, "I urge you, then, be imitators of me" (I Cor. 4:16). He expects his converts to convert, to become creative in Christ. He wanted his converts to be converted in his image; he wanted his spiritual children to be like him—contagious.

The only real proof of being in Christ is that we are getting others into Christ. The only proof of our being alive is that we are creating life. Nothing is ours till we share it. The end of evangelism is to produce evangelists. We really haven't got people "in" unless they immediately begin to bring others in. They are not "in" until they go "out."

New converts make the best evangelists. They cannot preach, so they do what they can do—witness. Witnessing is more effective than preaching in winning others. Witnessing comes from the heart—preaching may come from the head. That which is to reach the heart must come from the heart.

A colonel of the American Army was a broken man; his wife had died and he had no resources to meet life alone. He tried suicide, and it didn't work. He tried Christ, and that did work. He became a changed man. He was taken out as a partner in a visitation evangelism campaign, but he was all shut up within himself and let his companion do the talking. The fourth night his companion said, "You're to take the initiative tonight." He consented on one condition: "If I begin to fumble the ball, you will pick it up and take over." The companion consented. He had scarcely begun the conversation when he became a changed man. He simply poured out his soul to the judge whom they were trying to win. He won the judge and his wife to a decision, and then went on to win the biggest oil man in that section—three the first night. He has been contagious ever since. He was really "in" when he got "out"!

O Father, Thou hast given me life, not to keep it, but to share it. Make me an illustration of "freely have I received, so freely must I give." I would share what has been shared with me. Today make all my contacts spiritually contagious. Amen.

AFFIRMATION FOR THE DAY: *My converts are not converted until they become converted from me to my Savior.*

WHEN YOU BRING ONE PERSON TO CHRIST

Paul went on to say: "Therefore I sent to you Timothy, my beloved and faithful child in the Lord" (I Cor. 4:17). Here he presented Timothy as an illustration of what he meant by becoming a spiritual father. Timothy was an example of Paul's spiritual creativeness—a shining example. He had just said that he was the spiritual father of the Corinthians, and now he presented as an example Timothy, whose father was a Greek and his mother a Jewess. Paul could win Jews and Gentiles, and a mixture of both. He could win persons apart from race and class. He was all things to all men that he might win them.

This convert of mixed blood became a great center of spiritual contagion, so much so that Paul wrote him two important letters. Those letters have been a guide not only to Timothy, but to countless millions around the world in all ages. What he invested in Timothy, one person, became an investment in humanity. You cannot tell what you are starting when you start one person for Christ. You touch him, he touches others, and on and on it goes endlessly. Jesus said the seed falling on good ground brought forth thirty-fold, sixtyfold, a hundredfold. Thirtyfold is 3,000 per cent, sixtyfold is 6,000 per cent, and a hundredfold is 10,000 per cent on the investment. High percentage? Yes, but not exaggerated. The investment in persons is the only bank that will not break.

When Singapore fell to the Japanese, two men met on board a ship which was taking refugees out, one a missionary bishop and the other an oil man. The oil man said to the bishop, "You have invested your life in people in Malaya. These people will bend under the storm of the Japanese invasion, and when the war is over they will straighten up again. Your work will be intact. I have invested my life in oil wells which I had to blow up when I left. My life work has been lost."

O Jesus, Thou hast invested Thy life in us. We are amazed at Thy doing it. We are also amazed at the loyalty in our hearts and the gratitude which we feel for Thy investment in us. We are Thy workmanship. I thank Thee. Amen.

AFFIRMATION FOR THE DAY: *When I invest in people, I invest in an everlasting investment.*

"MY WAYS IN CHRIST"

We pass on to an interesting passage: "Therefore I sent to you Timothy . . . to remind you of my ways in Christ" (I Cor. 4:17). "My ways in Christ"—this brings out an important possibility: Jesus is the Way, but is it possible to have individual ways within the Way? Jesus is the Way, but he is not a blocked-off Way, insisting on each person's losing his identity and individuality in following the Way. There can be the expression of individual ways within the Way.

God has made us different. When He created you He broke the pattern. He has never made any one like you, and never will again. Each is unique and can give a unique contribution to the interpretation of Jesus. He is the universal and cannot be fully expressed by any individual or any group of individuals. It will take the sons of men to express the Son of Man. Each is important. He is needed to bring out some facet of His character and work which no one else can bring out. Be yourself in Christ.

This lets down the strain of trying to be someone else and to do the work of someone else. Be yourself and do your own work in Christ. A man who had burdened himself trying to be a Moody, came to the conclusion: "God got hold of a bigger man when he got hold of Moody." He would be himself in Christ. A tension was let down.

This conception of being oneself in Christ, not only lets down tensions, it awakens possibilities. I can be a unique illustration of the redeeming power of Jesus which no one else can illustrate. Paul speaks of "my gospel." Each can say the same: "my gospel." For "the gospel according to you" is a fresh gospel—the Fifth gospel. As Matthew's portrait is different from Mark's, and Luke's different from both, and John's different from all, so yours will be different, perhaps blessedly different. Accept the commission: a unique illustrator of the unique Christ.

O Lord and Savior, I gaze and gaze at Thee from a standpoint different from that of anyone else, and so I see what no one else sees. Let me show what I see, and show it with joy and gratitude and deep humility. Open my lips, for I see more than I can say. In Thy name. Amen.

AFFIRMATION FOR THE DAY: *Let me be myself in God, for there I am supernaturally natural.*

173

POOLING OUR TRUTHS

There is another phase to this statement of Paul about "my ways in Christ." As the individual can have his unique and individual ways in Christ, so the group can also have their ways in Christ. There can be a unique and beneficial illustration of "ways in Christ." This desire to illustrate forgotten or unemphasized phases of Christ has resulted in denominations. Some think these denominations "were conceived in iniquity, born in sin, and reared in cantankerousness." I do not. I think they are attempts to throw fresh light upon the face of Jesus. They may do so provided it is "our ways in Christ" and not just "our ways." If the emphasis is upon "in Christ" and not "in the denomination," then Christ is constantly redeeming the denomination from itself. It is then Christ-centric and not denomination-centric.

If our ways are not attempts to be the Way, but are simply ways to the Way, then they may be beneficial and beautiful. None of us has the truth; we have only truths about the Truth. Only Jesus is the Truth—"I am the way, and the truth."

These truths about the Truth, these ways to the Way may be helpful if they cease claiming exclusive truth about the Truth and come together and pool their truths, so that together they may more closely approximate the Truth. Then they are justified—and sanctified! If they claim exclusive truth, then they are unjustified—and cranktified! I feel that the putting of all denominations into one system, a merger, would be impoverishing. A Federal Union of the Churches would bring these diversities into union without losing the diversities. It would be a richer union than a monolithic merger. In music it would not be a melody, but harmony; therefore richer. Our ways in Christ brought together would not be the Way, but would be a way to the Way.

O God and Father of us all, forgive our attempts to claim to be the Way. Help us to point beyond ourselves and beyond our group to Him. Only thus can "my ways" and "our ways" be instruments of Thy redemption. In Jesus' name. Amen.

AFFIRMATION FOR THE DAY: *I am "a way" in Christ, pointing to The Way—Christ.*

"SUCH WERE SOME OF YOU"

If there is a question mark in the minds of some: "My ways"? They are "my ways," not "my ways in Christ," therefore they are not unique and are not contributive. They tread the treadmill of egocentric barrenness. If there is that question, then the answer is to be found in our next passage: "Do not be deceived; neither the immoral, nor idolaters, nor adulterers, nor homosexuals, nor thieves, nor the greedy, nor drunkards, nor revilers, nor robbers will inherit the kingdom of God. And such were some of you. But you were washed, you were sanctified, you were justified in the name of the Lord Jesus Christ and in the Spirit of our God" (I Cor. 6:9-11). This is one of the most amazingly redemptive passages in literature. Those on skid row were turned into those who were marching upward—upward to the most amazing destiny conceivable. "And we all, with unveiled face, beholding the glory of the Lord, are being changed into his likeness from one degree of glory to another; for this comes from the Lord who is the Spirit" (II Cor. 3:18). These deeply sin-dyed Corinthians were "being changed into his likeness"—the likeness of the most moral and the most beautiful character that ever lived, or ever will live! What a destiny! Nothing higher can be imagined. Yet it was a fact. "And such were some of you." Paul includes them: "And *we all.*" The most hopeful thing ever written! The worst can become the best and highest.

How was this done? By struggling and trying? No, by surrender to Grace: "But you were washed, you were sanctified, you were justified in the name of the Lord Jesus Christ and in the Spirit of our God." Note the order: washed, sanctified, justified. The order seems theologically wrong; it apparently should read, justified, washed, sanctified. Is the doer wrong, or profoundly right? I believe it is right, and significantly right; justified comes last.

O Christ, Thou dost not merely redeem *from;* Thou dost redeem *to*—to the likeness of Thine own image. We are dumbfounded at the idea, and yet we are filled with unutterable joy and expectation. We thank thee. Amen.

AFFIRMATION FOR THE DAY: *My past is past—buried in His love; my present is His, my future unfolds in Him.*

RIGHTEOUSNESS BEFORE GOD ONLY?

We ended yesterday with the question: Is the order washed, sanctified, justified, the right order? Or should justified come first? For a long time I thought the order was wrong, but I've come to the conclusion that the order is profoundly and significantly right.

If to be justified comes first, theologically speaking, then you might be justified in the sight of God. In His sight you are justified through forgiving Grace. He sees you as no longer a sinner but as righteous. While this may be true in the sight of God, we are not yet justified in the sight of men nor in our own sight—not until we know that we are "washed" and "sanctified." The washing and the sanctifying is the justification before men and before ourselves. Men, and we ourselves see, that we are different—washed and sanctified—and therefore justified. We stand righteous, not only before God but before men and ourselves.

The justification is based not only on a supposed transaction between you and God, but it is also based on the manifest fact of your being washed and sanctified. The all-round facts between you and God, you and man, and you and yourself justify the claim of change—you are changed; the facts say so. Therefore the justification is based on facts—facts that are manifest—you were washed, you were sanctified. It is an all-round justification based on facts.

The justification that is based only on being made righteous before God lacks complete justification if it is not based also on being washed and sanctified. It lacks verification in fact. Therefore the justification that is based only on a transaction between the soul and God lacks the verification in life of being washed and sanctified. This justification, coming last, is a more complete justification.

O God, my Father, I feel reconciled with Thee and therefore justified, but I am doubly assured by the washing and the sanctifying. This is full justification therefore full assurance. My whole being cries gratitude. Amen.

AFFIRMATION FOR THE DAY: *I am washed and sanctified, and therefore justified before God and men and myself.*

"THE NAME" AND "THE SPIRIT"

We spend another day on: "You were washed, you were
sanctified, you were justified in the name of the Lord Jesus
Christ and in the Spirit of our God."

The justification coming after the washing and after the
sanctification puts together the two approaches to life—from
revelation down (the Christian approach) and from the facts up
(the scientific approach). The two approaches put together bring
a wider justification, because wider based. The verification from
revelation down and from the facts up bring a wider verification
and a more convincing one.

These three things come about "in the name of the Lord Jesus
Christ and in the Spirit of our God." The washing, the
sanctifying, and the justifying come "in the name of the Lord
Jesus Christ." Could they not come directly from God without
coming "in the name of the Lord Jesus Christ"? The answer is
no! If they came in any other name, meaning, in any other
character, they would not be true to the facts. When you come
directly to God, you don't, really, for you come in your own
name, through your own conceptions, to God. Your conceptions
are the mediator, and they are false. Only in the name or
character of Jesus Christ is reality revealed. Therefore God can't
give in any other name or character, for if He did so He would be
backing unreality or falsity. "There is no other Name under
heaven given among men whereby we must be saved."

This is done not only in the Name of Jesus, but also "in the
Spirit of our God." The Spirit works and works with complete
abandon when we come in the name or character of our Lord
Jesus Christ. Then he is free to work, for He is working in the
right pattern, with the right goal—to be made like Jesus. There
the Holy Spirit can give without limit and without hesitation.

**O Spirit Divine, I come in the Name of Jesus, I make my
surrender to Him, now give and give abundantly of Thy power,
for we have one aim and goal—Jesus! I know here I can expect
Thee to give with both hands. Amen.**

AFFIRMATION FOR THE DAY: *If I act in the Name of Jesus—in His
character and spirit—then I can depend on the power of the
Spirit.*

CALLINGS IN THE LORD

We now proceed to look at another passage: "Were you a slave when called? Never mind. But if you can gain your freedom, avail yourself of the opportunity. For he who was called in the Lord as a slave is a freedman of the Lord" (I Cor. 7:21-22).

Here the question of one's calling is raised. Paul takes the position that everyone who is in the Lord is a person who has a calling—is "called in the Lord." Even slaves were "called in the Lord." Every Christian is a "called" person. We usually use the word "called" to apply to the ministry—"he was called to the ministry." Here, however, every disciple was an apostle, one set to do a particular and unique work for God, a work which no one else can do. This puts dignity, purpose, and goal into every Christian life. There are no longer sacred and secular callings; all callings which are callings "in the Lord" are sacred. Any legitimate work done in His name and for His sake is sacred work.

This gives something greatly needed in the so-called laymen's work. Now it is looked upon as something second best, a lower level of life. As we have said, the word *laos*, from which the word "laity" is taken, literally means "the chosen people of God." A layman is a chosen person of God—chosen to be a layman and to work out his calling as a layman. This makes his call as sacred as that of a clergyman.

This calling can be worked out in any set of circumstances—even that of a slave. Man has destined himself to be a slave, but within that outer compulsion he is inwardly free—free to carry out his Christian calling. Bound to an assembly line you are inwardly free, for you do it "as unto the Lord." Moreover in your free time you do what you have always been called to do.

O Master of my heart, I am free in Thee. Outer circumstances cannot cramp my calling in Thee. I am free, for Thy will can be wrought out in and through me, no matter what the circumstances may be. I thank Thee. Amen.

AFFIRMATION FOR THE DAY: *Today I shall look on my circumstances as a setting for my calling. My circumstances may color, but not cancel my calling.*

"FREE . . . IN THE LORD"

We now look at the next passage: "A wife is bound to her husband as long as he lives. If the husband dies, she is free to be married to whom she wishes, only in the Lord" (I Cor. 7:39).

This is interesting: "free to be married to whom she wishes, only in the Lord"—"free" as she "wishes," "only in the Lord." The "wishes" are subordinate to "in the Lord." If the marriage is in the Lord she is free to do as she wishes. The "in the Lord" provision saves her from undesirable wishes which may get her into trouble, a life trouble.

Everything in the Lord, including marriage, is safe and secure. Everything outside the Lord is unsafe and insecure. So this "in the Lord" is a hedge put up along the road of life to keep us from falling over the precipice. God's prohibitions are God's protections. The right thing is the right thing to do.

I know a man who prayed about his possible marriage and heard God say, "Go on, I will bless you." God didn't say, "I will make you happy," but "I will bless you." He hasn't been happy in his marriage, but he has been blest. He has done a work in spite of an unsatisfactory marriage. He has worked with a pain in his heart, but he has turned that pain into a paean of victory. He hasn't borne the unsatisfactory marriage, he has used it. His wife too has been very useful. Both have carried out their callings in spite of an unhappy marriage. The "in the Lord" provision saved them both from living primarily on wishes. If you carry out your wishes, apart from being or not being in the Lord, then when your wishes change the marriage goes to pieces, whereas if it is in the Lord it will hold together—in spite of!

O Divine Wisdom, we thank Thee that Thou hast provided for our good. That good may come to us through our circumstances or in spite of them. We thank Thee for this unshakable security. In Thee all things cohere. Amen.

AFFIRMATION FOR THE DAY: *Not my wishes but His will must be the central determining element in my life.*

"SEAL OF MY APOSTLESHIP"

The next passage throws a flood of light on a very controversial subject: "Am I not free? Am I not an apostle? Have I not seen Jesus our Lord? Are not you my workmanship in the Lord? If to others I am not an apostle, at least I am to you; for you are the seal of my apostleship in the Lord" (I Cor. 9:1-2).

There are two ways to try to prove your being in succession to the apostles: one is to trace back, if possible, an unbroken line of succession by the laying on of hands to the original apostles. This is "apostolic succession." It points backward. The other is to point to lives changed by you: "for you are the seal of my apostleship in the Lord." This is apostolic succession based on apostolic success. This points to the present.

The attempt to trace apostolic succession by an unbroken line of laying on of hands is futile. It can't be proved—claimed, yes, but not proved. If it could be proved, it would pervert the very thing it tried to prove. The idea that Jesus, Who got His credentials straight from the Father and was not ordained by any laying on of hands, would establish a rigid system of apostolic authority by the laying on of hands through which grace is mediated is so contradictory to the spirit of Jesus as to be unrecognizable. It is unthinkable. It would insert into the Christian faith another mediator—a system of bishops, mediating grace by the laying on of hands. That would substitute mechanics for morality, for grace is supposedly inherent in the office of bishop and is mediated apart from the character of the person mediating it. This is totally foreign to the Christian faith and a perversion of it. In the Christian faith you get grace immediately and directly through the living Jesus Christ alone. There is one Mediator and only One.

O Savior Divine, I need no one between Thee and me. I have access to thee so immediately and intimately that any other mediation is unthinkable. In Thee I find the Father—and Everything. I thank Thee. Amen.

AFFIRMATION FOR THE DAY: *Anything that comes between Jesus and me and makes itself indispensable is idolatry.*

"THERE IS NO OTHER SEAL"

I am writing this in a land where claims and counterclaims of validities of ordination are being made. I see priests claiming they received the Holy Spirit by the laying on of hands of the bishop at ordination but showing little or no signs of the presence and activity of the Spirit in their lives and ministry. "The proof of the pudding is in the eating," and the eating is insipid.

Paul laid down the only realistic and Christian test of being an apostle or of being in line with the apostles. "You are the seal of my apostleship in the Lord"—you, changed people, are the seal of my apostleship! There is no other seal! Any other seal is a stamp of man and an empty envelope. "You will know them by their fruits" is the only test—the outcome is the criterion!

In the time of Elijah, on the Mount of Test with the priests of Baal, the test was: "The God that answers by fire, let Him be God." Today that is obsolete. There is one test: The God that answers by healed men, let Him be God. The individual or the group that answers by changed people are in line with apostolic Christianity—"you are the seal of apostleship." There is no other seal.

Bishop Pakhenham-Walsh was a saint—a real one. He lived in simplicity, pouring out his love and money to the healing of a division in an ancient church in South India. He built the Ashram from his own resources. A group from this ancient church wanted to celebrate holy communion in his chapel. They regretted they could not give communion to the bishop, for the Anglican Church was not recognized as being in apostolic succession by the body they represented. "All right," he replied, "just let me sit at the back without communion." Christ, I am sure, sat with him and was not in the communion.

O Jesus, Master, we can be in line of succession with Thee only when we show Thy Spirit and manifest Thy love. For in no other way can that succession be manifested. Let me this day show that spirit. Amen.

AFFIRMATION FOR THE DAY: *My credentials must be written in the people, not in the past—in flesh and blood and not in claims.*

FROM LAW TO GRACE

We come now to a very interesting side light on the mind of
Paul: "Nevertheless, in the Lord woman is not independent of
man nor man of woman; for as woman was made from man, so
man is now born of woman. And all things are from God" (I Cor.
11:11). This is an interesting righting of the mind of Paul on a
question which was vacillating in his mind.

He slipped from the Christian position back to the law when
he said in the previous verses: "For man was not made from
woman, but woman from man. Neither was man created for
woman, but woman for man." This definitely put woman in an
inferior position. Each time Paul put woman in an inferior
position he turned back to the Old Testament for authority—as
here! In I Corinthians he says: "The women should keep silence
in the churches. For they are not permitted to speak, but should
be subordinate, as even the law says" (14:34). In that place he
turns back to the law for authority as he turned back to the first
creation for authority for the above subordination of women. He
slipped from grace to law to make women subordinate.

In the passage above he feels the pull of the Christian
position: "Nevertheless, in the Lord woman is not independent
of man nor man of woman; for as woman was made from man, so
man is now born of woman." Note the phrase "in the Lord"—in
the law woman was not equal, but in the Lord a person is a
person—a person for whom Christ died. Paul was here pulled
from "in the law" to "in the Lord"—redeemed from the lower
position of the law to the higher position of Grace. The Christian
faith redeems us not only from sin and evil, but also from lower
forms of good. It redeems us from law to grace.

**O Jesus, make all my law into grace, and all my lower
conceptions into Thy higher, for I'm always being pulled back.
All my half-truths and half-goods must be broken up and
redeemed. I want to be fully redeemed. Amen.**

AFFIRMATION FOR THE DAY: *I am prone to slip from the best to the good
and from the good to the bad. Save me from the first small step
downward.*

"FALLEN ASLEEP IN CHRIST"

The next passage is: "Then those also who have fallen asleep in Christ have perished" (I Cor. 15:18). A new thing had come into being with the conception of being in Christ—the very idea of dying dropped out and the conception of death as falling asleep took its place. They simply could not believe in death any longer, so the vocabulary had to be changed. Death dropped out of the Christian vocabulary because it dropped out of Christian experience. Christians did not die; they fell asleep. Jesus did not die; He "bowed his head and gave up his spirit." Stephen did not die; he prayed: "Lord Jesus, receive my spirit. . . . And when he had said this, he fell asleep" (Acts 7:59-60). Paul speaks of death as "a desire to depart and to be with Christ." And he says when his execution was actually at his doors: "The time of my departure is at hand." Jesus said of the death of Lazarus: "Our friend Lazarus has fallen asleep, but I go to awake him out of sleep" (John 11:11).

In the pages of the New Testament after the death and resurrection of Jesus, no one "in Christ" was ever said to have died—except in the book of Revelation written later, when the Resurrection of Jesus had lost its freshness and death came to life again. Even there it says: "Then Death and Hades were thrown into the lake of fire" (20:14). There was the final death of death. In Jesus Christ there was no death. Everything in Him was alive with eternal life; even death was a sleep, a departure, a giving up to God of the spirit. The vocabulary was changed to fit the facts—there was no death, there was nothing but Life. When we are in Christ death is simply unthinkable—this glorious fact of being in Him is incapable of dying, and that includes the body. The body is "changed," but does not die! Nothing in Him dies—absolutely nothing.

O Jesus, Lord and Master—Lord and Master of life and death—as long as I remain in Thee nothing about me can die, for the moment it comes into Thee it lives and lives forever. I thank Thee, thank Thee. Amen.

AFFIRMATION FOR THE DAY: *In Jesus I cannot die, for life cannot do aught but live.*

"IN CHRIST . . . ALL . . . ALIVE"

We must look at one other passage on this question of everything in Christ being made alive: "For as in Adam all die, so also in Christ shall all be made alive" (I Cor. 15:22). "In Christ shall all be made alive" for they are alive—alive by the very fact of being in Christ. "In him was life"—and everyone and everything which is in Him by surrender has life inherently, by the very fact of being in Him. It is not something added as an extraneous gift; it is something inherent by the very fact of being in Him. That includes the total being—body, mind, spirit, and all the possessions and acts. Nothing in Him dies; everything outside Him dies.

Your money, if kept outside Him and His purposes, dies—dies because it has no soul. Your deeds decay outside Him for they have no eternal purpose and hence have no eternal life. Your relationships, including marriage relationships, die if they are not in Him. They have no eternal meaning and hence no eternal life. So in heaven "they neither marry nor are given in marriage," but those who are married in Him live on married in Him, for the marriage has, like everything else in Him, eternal life. No *new* marriages are made in heaven—"they neither marry nor are given in marriage," but marriages that are in Him when the participants fall asleep awake in a more glorious marriage than ever. All is permanent and secure and safe in Him. Outside of Him nothing is permanent, secure or safe—"in Adam all die."

Pathetic attempts to keep the person and his influence and his memory alive by big monuments, eloquent inscriptions, and expensive burials are all mere rouge on the face of a dead man. Death reigns. In Christ Life reigns, and nothing but Life reigns. "O death, where is thy victory? O death, where is thy sting?" There is no victory, nor sting, for there is no death—not in Him.

We thank Thee, Lord of heaven and earth, for the death of death and for the defeat of defeat. We thank Thee that in Thee everything is alive—alive with meaning, destiny, goal—alive forever more. I am grateful. Amen.

AFFIRMATION FOR THE DAY: *I mingle with life and I therefore tingle with life. Glory be!*

"A HUMBLE PRIDE"

Everything is redeemed in Christ—even pride. "I protest, brethren, by my pride in you which I have in Christ Jesus our Lord" (I Cor. 15:31). Can pride be redeemed when it is "in Christ Jesus our Lord"? Yes.

Pride was said to be Lucifer's downfall. The Scriptures generalize it and say, "Pride goeth before a fall." It does inevitably when it is rooted in the unsurrendered self, for the universe doesn't like the idea of the self being God. Hence the proud unsurrendered self runs afoul of the moral universe and is broken.

Pride can be redeemed and can become constructive, however. Pride is a natural good. Without pride we wouldn't wash our faces, tidy ourselves in any way, take satisfaction in our work, or keep ourselves fit for our highest achievements. We would sag as personalities. Here Paul says he has pride in these Corinthians "in Christ Jesus our Lord." His pride was not in himself, nor in the Corinthians; it was "in Christ Jesus"—that is, he was proud that he was enabled "in Christ Jesus" to help these people into a new life.

It was a humble pride; it was a pride that owned Jesus as Lord—"in Christ Jesus our Lord." At the center of his pride was a deep loyalty to Jesus as Lord. He bent the knee to his Lord and then rose up straight before everything else, proud that he was being used of His Lord for redemptive purposes, proud that he belonged no longer to littleness, but to Greatness, proud that he had sense enough to become great in that Greatness.

The pride was in Christ Jesus our Lord, and therefore was redeemed, for in Him everything is redeemed. I can be proud of my pride when it is in Him, for it is a decent pride—proud of the right things and right achievements. In myself pride goes before a fall; in Jesus pride goes before a rise.

We thank Thee, Jesus Lord and Savior, that in Thee everything is changed for the better and the best. All our possibilities become actualities. Everything tingles with possibility in Thee. I thank Thee. Amen.

AFFIRMATION FOR THE DAY: *My pride is redeemed only when I am humbly proud that He sees fit to use me. In which case I am humbled.*

SUCCESS OR FAILURE, IRRELEVANT

The glorious chapter on the resurrection of the body ends up this way: "Therefore, my beloved brethren, be steadfast, immovable, always abounding in the work of the Lord, knowing that in the Lord your labor is not in vain (I Cor. 15:58).

Today I received a letter from the governor of a state, and in it was this sentence: "But I feel a lonely and lost soul and do not know what to do with myself." He had worked hard for his country and had given devoted service, and yet he felt it was all futile, in vain. Why? His work was not in the Lord. It was therefore vain and futile.

Strange how different I felt about my labor in that same country. Outwardly I had not succeeded as he had, but I wasn't working for success or position, but just for and in the Lord. He felt a failure, and I felt there could be no failure. In the Lord success and failure were irrelevant. The only thing that mattered was being in Him. In Him even failure is success. Out of Him even success is failure.

In Him all you ask for is His smile and His "Well done." Note, not "Well succeeded," but "Well done," for it is "well done" if it is in Him and for His sake. I remember speaking in England on my return to India after my first furlough, and saying: "The romance of missions is over. I know exactly what I'm going back to, much of it drab and seamy. But if the Father were to tell me that I would see no success, only failure the balance of my days, I would reply: 'My business is not to succeed or to fail—my business is to be true to the heavenly vision when He said: "It's India." It's lifted above success and failure—it's in Him.' " That made everything safe and secure. Strange to say, when the eyes are on the Savior and not on success, we are embarrassed with unearned success!

O God, my Father, I thank Thee that Thou canst give us a holy indifference to success or failure, and a holy concern as to whether what we do is wholly in Thee. There everything is wholly safe. Amen.

AFFIRMATION FOR THE DAY: *I have one business in life: To live and work in the Lord. Results are His concern.*

"MY LOVE," EVEN TO ENEMIES

Paul ends the first Epistle to the Corinthians in the lovely words: "My love be with you all in Christ Jesus. Amen" (16:4). They are beautiful words, but do not express the full Christian attitude. This is love "to all in Christ Jesus," which is good, but not good enough. The full Christian attitude is to love also those who are not in Christ Jesus. It extends even to enemies. Jesus said: "If you love those who love you, what credit is that to you? For even sinners love those who love them (Luke 6:32).

This circumscribed and restricted love is less than Christian love, for Christian love is Love, Unlimited. The three greatest characters in the New Testament ended their careers with love and prayers for enemies. Jesus died with the most beautiful prayer ever uttered on His lips: "Father, forgive them; for they know not what they do." That verse has gripped India more than any verse in any Scripture, Hindu or Christian. Hindus, sentenced by a British judge to prison during the noncooperation days, in the struggle for independence, would lift their hands and say, "Father, forgive them, for they know not what they do."

The next greatest man in Scripture was Stephen who died amid a shower of stones with this prayer on his lips: "Lord, do not hold this sin against them." Paul, after saying that the time for his departure was at hand, wrote: "At my first defense no one took my part; all deserted me. May it not be charged against them" (II Tim. 4:16). These three greatest characters, one Divine and the other two human, were at their greatest when they showed Love Unlimited. There is no expression of greatness except the expression of a great love. We are great only as we are great in love. There is no other greatness. Without love greatness is littleness. Love alone is great.

O God, our Father, as I go forth into this day make all my contacts love contacts, all my attitudes love attitudes, all my reactions love reactions. Then I will give out love and only love. Then I shall be like Thee. Amen.

AFFIRMATION FOR THE DAY: *If my love is restricted it is constricted—less than Christian love.*

IN HIM IT IS ALWAYS YES

We pass from I Corinthians to II Corinthians in our meditation on "In Christ" passages and come across this great one: "For the Son of God, Jesus Christ, whom we preached among you . . . was not Yes and No; but in him it is always Yes. For all the promises of God find their Yes in him" (II Cor. 1:19-20).

There are those who believe that Christianity is a negative attitude toward life—you can't do this and you can't do that—that it is a denial of the will to live. It is a will to die, the fulfillment of the death wish, described by Freud. It is a no to human living. Solomon Richter says, "Christianity is a set of scruples imposed on the ordinary framework of humanity to keep it from functioning naturally and normally." If so, we can't take it, for we must live by affirmation, not negation.

This verse says the opposite—"in him it is always Yes. For all the promises of God find their Yes in him." As Moffatt's translation puts it: "the divine (yes) has at last sounded in him." He so expresses this affirmative attitude toward life that He is called the "Yes." Everything outside Him is the no. Experience verifies that. When Judas went away from Jesus he went and hanged himself. Does life commit suicide when it goes away from Jesus—sudden or slow? Life says yes. I think a thought, take an attitude, do a deed which departs from Jesus, and around that thought, attitude, or deed is a sense of sadness, a sense of defeat. Everything within us cries, "This is not the way." But the moment you begin to think His thoughts, take His attitudes, do His deeds, everything within you cries, "This is the Way." At that moment all life is affirmed, is verified, and begins to sing and glow with joy divine. Jesus is the Yes—the yes to human joy, to human development, to life itself. He is the Yes!

O Jesus, my Lord, I'm so grateful for this wonderful "Yesness" in Thee. I am affirmed—the real I—when I affirm Thy Lordship. I live when I live in Thee—live to my fingertips. I thank Thee, thank Thee. Amen.

AFFIRMATION FOR THE DAY: *Jesus is the Yes; everything outside Him is the no. I will live in the yes.*

"AFTER"

We spend another day on "For all the promises of God find their Yes in him." All the promises God makes in nature, in Scripture, in history, and in the longings of personal experience find their yes in Him. The New Testament speaks of "the upward call of God in Christ Jesus." Jesus is the upward call of God—calling us from the lower to the higher, the incomplete to the complete, the imperfect to the perfect. Everything in Jesus is upward. Everything outside Jesus is downward. An African after he was converted renamed himself "After." Everything to him was "After"—after death, after sin, after sorrow, after frustration, after alienation. Now everything had promise in it—had a future. In sin there is no future—it is the way to decay and death.

Jesus is the Yes to all the promises of God made everywhere. There are thirty-three thousand promises in the Scriptures, and Jesus is the Yes to every one of them. He writes "Yes" in His own blood on every promise. If you come in His name, you can have them cashed in experience.

I visited a home for the poor—the dream of a young teacher. When he told his dream of such a home to the elders they were full of Noes. There was no money, no one to take charge of it. The young teacher said he would resign his teacher's job and take care of it personally, and he would raise the money. Out of that yes has come a wonderful home for the poor and a thriving hospital for the general public. When that young man died of overwork the community gave him a funeral no bishop ever received. His sister, a saint, died of cholera, infected from a poor patient. In both the divine Yes sounded.

O Lord God, all our Noes becomes Yeses in Thee. We can do anything and be anything we ought to do and be when we are in Thee. The Yes of creation works in us. We feel "the upward call." I thank Thee. Amen.

AFFIRMATION FOR THE DAY: *If I am a yes and no person, hence a blur, from today I become a yes to His yes—affirmative in Him.*

"ESTABLISHES US . . . IN CHRIST"

The next verse: "But it is God who establishes us with you in Christ, and has commissioned us; he has put his seal upon us and given us his Spirit in our hearts as a guarantee" (II Cor. 1:21-22). Here we find four things in Christ: "establishes us," "commissioned us," "put his seal upon us," "given us His Spirit."

There is only one place where we can be established—in Christ. If we are primarily centered in doctrinal belief we will be swayed, "tossed to and fro by every wind of doctrine." If we are primarily centered in some favorite preacher we will not be established; we will go up and down with our likes and dislikes. If we are primarily centered in religious services and observances we will blow hot and cold according to the perfection or imperfection of those services. Only in Christ are we established:

> On Christ, the solid rock, I stand;
> All other ground is sinking sand.

I've seen a church of 200,000 members rocked to its depths over a controversy concerning the nature of communion. In Christ they were one; in doctrine they were divided. The whole controversy was off-center.

"And has commissioned us"—"established" and "commissioned"—these are the alternate beats of the Christian heart—established and commissioned, fixed and furthered, anchored and aggressive. Outside Christ you wear out your emphases—baptism, apostolic succession, tongues, gifts—all these wear thin. But Jesus never wears out or wears thin; He is always fresh, always vital, always to the point, always redemptive. We are "commissioned" to preach Jesus; nothing else is worth preaching, absolutely nothing.

O Jesus, Thou art my Savior and my Lord, but Thou art also my message. Help me not to be drawn off to the margin when the center is calling. Thou art the center of my life and the center of my message. I thank Thee. Amen.

AFFIRMATION FOR THE DAY: *I am commissioned to surrender, to obey, to live, to practice, and to preach Jesus—nothing else! But this is Everything!*

"HIS SPIRIT . . . AS A GUARANTEE"

We consider the rest of the verse: "he has put his seal upon us
and given us his Spirit in our hearts as a guarantee." Those who
are "established" and "commissioned" are also sealed. What
does this sealing mean? It means security and it means
authority. When a document or letter is sealed it is secure.
People hesitate to open a letter which has the seal of a high
official on it. The seal renders the letter sacrosanct and puts the
authority of the sender behind it.

If you go with His seal upon you, you are secure and you are
authoritative. You go with the sense of the authority of Another
beyond you. I was introduced by a Negro minister to a large
audience in these words: "I'm introducing the speaker by
quoting from one of his books. He said that the significance of
Mahatma Gandhi was not in Gandhi the person, but in the
significance of the cause with which he was identified—the
cause of India's freedom. When he speaks, the cause of India's
freedom speaks through him. The significance of the speaker
tonight is not in the person, but in the Cause with which he is
identified—the Kingdom of God." I trembled—and rejoiced at
the implication.

"And given us his Spirit in our hearts as a guarantee." The
guarantee is not a verbal, but a vital assurance; the Spirit in our
hearts is the guarantee of security and authority. The guarantee
is not a promise; it is a performance. The Spirit within is the
guarantee that the promises are being fulfilled. They are being
fulfilled by the operation and power of the Holy Spirit. The
guarantee is a working fact—working within us and through us.

O Holy Spirit, Thou art our guarantee. Thou dost guarantee
the realization of all the promises of God. Thou art the applied
edge of redemption. In Thee everything becomes actuality. I
thank Thee, thank Thee. Amen.

AFFIRMATION FOR THE DAY: *I am sealed with the authority of the King
of kings and Lord of lords.*

IS THERE ALWAYS AN OPEN DOOR?

Our next passage: "When I came to Troas to preach the gospel of Christ, a door was opened for me in the Lord" (II Cor. 2:12). "A door was opened for me in the Lord." Is there always a door opened for us if we stay in the Lord, and provided we "preach the gospel of Christ"? We close doors if we get off the gospel of Christ and if we get off of being in the Lord. It is the devil's own strategy to get us out of the Lord and to get us preaching everything except the gospel of Christ. A passage says: "The Pharisees began to press him hard, and to provoke him to speak of many things" (Luke 11:53). If the Adversary can get us as ministers to "speak of many things" then he has us off of the One Thing—Christ—and he has us rendered innocuous. He doesn't mind how many things we speak about provided he can get us to lay off of Christ. We lay off of Christ if we put Him on the margin and something else at the center.

I have just come from a great church—great in passion and vision of evangelizing India. They are not entering that great "open door," however, for they are tied up in a controversy over whether the communion is a symbol only or whether there is a "real presence in the communion." The devil's own strategy to keep them preoccupied there! I know of an evangelist who could have swept India if he had remained in the Lord and had preached the gospel of Christ; but instead he left the cross and took the judgment seat and began to tell who is going where. He became "an accuser of the brethren"—a name given to Satan in Revelation! His influence is circumscribed—there is no great open door.

I was in another section of India where the church has a great spiritual heritage, but this great church was cancelled out by an inner tension over caste. Which people, from which caste, will be in the ascendency? Both parties have sunk—there was no great open door before them.

O Jesus, my Lord, save me from speaking of many things and missing the One Thing. Forgive me if my heart is preoccupied with championing marginal things so I become spent when it comes to Thee. In Thy Name. Amen.

AFFIRMATION FOR THE DAY: *When I remain in Christ there is always an open door—if I can't do this, I can do that—with and in Him.*

"ALWAYS LEADS US IN TRIUMPH"

We now turn to the very peak of triumphancy in the "in Christ" passages: "But thanks be to God, who in Christ always leads us in triumph, and through us spreads the fragrance of the knowledge of him everywhere (II Cor. 2:14). This passage implies that God always leads us in triumph provided we stay in Christ. This raises questions: Aren't Christians often defeated? Do they not often go down in disaster? The answer is no, not if they stay "in Christ," for staying in Christ is the victory. When you stay in Him you manifest a spirit which cannot be defeated, for the manifestation of that spirit is the victory.

Jesus went down in defeat at the cross, but at the very moment of defeat he manifested a spirit which was the victory: "Father, forgive them; for they know not what they do." That spirit was the victory amid defeat. So if you manifest His spirit amid your defeat, you are led in triumph—for that spirit is the victory, the victory that overcomes the world! When a Roman persecutor said to a Christian who was in the tyrant's grip, "What can your Master do for you now?" the man replied, "He can help me to forgive you." That forgiveness was the victory!

I am in a section of the country in India where Hindus burned the ripened fields of a Christian. When the Christian ran to save his fields, they cut off both his hands. The YMCA secretary, incensed at this outrage, took up a collection to pay the cost of a court case against the perpetrators of this crime. They were known. When the bag of money was placed before their victim he replied, "You have been my teacher. You have taught me the Christian gospel and that gospel says I should love my enemies and forgive them. I can't take the money. I will forgive them." That spirit was the victory—a greater victory than if he had won the court case and sent those men to jail. You're always in triumph when you are in Christ.

Jesus, my Lord, if I remain in Thee, and Thy Spirit remains in me, then I cannot fail though everything tumbles to pieces around me. My spirit is intact when it is in touch with Thee! Evermore give me Thy Spirit. Amen.

AFFIRMATION FOR THE DAY: *"Always leads us in triumph"—today shall be an illustration of that verse.*

"THE FRAGRANCE OF THE KNOWLEDGE OF HIM"

There is another side to this verse: "But thanks be to God, who in Christ always leads us in triumph, and through us spreads the fragrance of the knowledge of him everywhere" (II Cor. 2:14). The illustration I gave yesterday seems passive, and the victory seems to be within the person concerned. The victory is within, but not only within: "God . . . in Christ . . . through us spreads the fragrance of the knowledge of him everywhere." The victory is within, but it spreads the fragrance of the knowledge of Him everywhere. It is positive and expansive and compelling to others. It is power, and it is converting power.

It is a "fragrance"; it smells good. You are converted by it and love to be converted by it, for the conversion is done so lovingly. He breaks down your opposition and does it so graciously, and you love to have Him do it, for you know your opposition is an opposition to yourself as well as to Him. A friend, gloriously converted, changed the usual words into: "I came, I saw, and I was conquered—and loved it so."

The fragrance which comes from a spirit wholly in Christ is the most beautiful thing on our planet. Paul stood before King Agrippa and the royal court and said: "I would to God that not only you but also all who hear me this day might become such as I am—except for these chains" (Acts 26:29). The phrase "except for these chains" is so tenderly beautiful and Christlike that the "fragrance" of that touch floats across the centuries and fills our souls with a sense of unutterable sweetness. The gracious power of it! Anyone with that spirit is irresistible. Someone said of a truly converted friend, "She can go anywhere, to anybody, for she works by love." Love gets behind all defenses and is as all-pervasive as perfume—and as irresistible. We welcome love, for love is the thing for which we are made.

O Jesus, my Lord, lead me in triumph this day, for I would go forth armed with nothing save Thy love. May I meet all hate with love, all indifference with Thy interest, all ignorance with Thy compassion. Amen.

AFFIRMATION FOR THE DAY: *All my deeds and attitudes will have the aroma of Thy love upon them this day.*

"PEDDLERS OF GOD'S WORD"

We move on to another appealing passage: "For we are not, like so many, peddlers of God's word; but as men of sincerity, as commissioned by God, in the sight of God we speak in Christ" (II Cor. 2:17). This phrase is arresting: "peddlers of God's word." Peddlers peddle their wares in order to make a living by them. People were peddling God's Word for their own ends—to make a living out of God's Word.

This is a searching passage, for it cuts deep. How many preachers and lay speakers peddle God's Word to gain attention, to put themselves in the limelight, to satisfy their ego. An opponent of Christianity said to a group of professional Christians, "Jesus died on the cross, but you are living by it." There is just enough truth in it to make it sting. I saw a bird make the cross at the top of a chapel its basis of operation. He would sit on the cross until an insect came near, and then would dart out and gobble it and return to the cross. It was a base for foraging. We use the cross very often for our own selfish purposes. We hold up the cross to win battles in debate, for our own self-glorification. We preach sermons to get compliments at their close. We become missionaries to satisfy our desire for attention. We are peddlers of God's Word.

In contrast to that Paul says: "as men of sincerity, as commissioned by God, in the sight of God we speak in Christ." The difference was in the last phrase: "We speak in Christ." When we speak in ourselves, from ourselves, and for ourselves we are peddlers of God's Word. When we speak in Christ, however, we are "men of sincerity," "commissioned by God," and "in the sight of God." We are not peddlers but prophets. Then we do not air good views; we proclaim good news. Then we take our stand at the cross, not to forage, but to tell forth the good news.

O Lord God, my Father, give me deep sincerity, a sense of commission, and a knowledge that I'm speaking every moment in Thy sight and with Thy approval. Then I shall stand as the illustration and proclaimer of Thy Son. Amen.

AFFIRMATION FOR THE DAY: *Not a peddler of ecclesiastical wares, but a proclaimer of good news—Jesus!*

"INTO HIS LIKENESS"

I am departing from the "in Christ" passages to put in an "into" passage. "And we all, with unveiled face, beholding the glory of the Lord, are being changed into his likeness from one degree of glory to another; for this comes from the Lord who is the Spirit" (II Cor. 3:18). It is important that we pause and see what the "in Christ" emphasis leads us "into." This passage makes it clear that to be in Christ means we "are being changed into his likeness." This unfolds the goal, the place we are heading, the purpose of the whole. The purpose of the whole is nothing less than being changed into His likeness. How tawdry this goal makes the ordinary goals seem—to get to heaven, to escape hell, to be happy, to be healthy, to be successful.

This gives a goal worthy of the great divine redemption—a goal in harmony with its nature. We are to be made into nothing less than his likeness. There is nothing greater, nor conceivably greater than that.

If God were other than the God I see in the face of Jesus Christ He would hold up a goal other than this. He would want to remain unique, different, and apart. He would not want to create beings in His own likeness.

This is seen in mission work where a people like the Syrian Christians will build churches for the outcastes, will educate them, and will do social service for them, but they will not make them into their own likeness—they will not make them Syrians. Missionaries in Africa are often horrified when the African wants to be made into their likeness—to adopt their customs and mode of life. "No, we will do everything for them—except to put them on our own level, make them into our likeness"!

Christ our Redeemer offers to share not only His redemption, but a redemption into His own likeness. That is Love that not only stoops to share, but lifts to share—His own likeness.

Thou Who art the image of the Father, Thou art striving to make us into that same image. Wonderful generosity, wonderful goal! It puts back my shoulders. I am to be like Thee. Let nothing stop me. I'm on the Way. Amen.

AFFIRMATION FOR THE DAY: *"Into His likeness"—my destiny is so great that I must say, Begone all littleness, all slights and hurts and all low aims.*

"HE IS A NEW CREATION"

This passage is very clear and luminous in unfolding the meaning of the new creation which happens when one is in Christ: "Therefore, if anyone is in Christ, he is a new creation; the old has passed away, behold, the new has come" (II Cor. 5:17). "He is a new creation."

There have been three stark miracles in our world. The first was when life was introduced into dead matter and creation came into being. Scientists can produce life from life, but they cannot produce life. The second miracle was the introduction of Jesus Christ into our history. He didn't just perform miracles; He was a miracle—a miracle of being. He rose in sinless grandeur above saint and sinner—a miracle of being. Then being a miracle would He perform miracles? The answer is that being a miracle it would be a miracle if He didn't perform miracles. The third miracle is the miracle of the new birth. "He is a new creation." The new birth is a miracle; it cannot be accounted for except by the intervention of divine power, creating a new type of being as different from the ordinary man as the ordinary man is different from the animal.

In the first creation the account says that "the earth was without form and void, and darkness was upon the face of the deep" (Gen. 1:2). That is the picture of the inner life of the unregenerate: (1) "without form"—no purpose running through it, no goal before it, chaos. (2) "and void"—empty. The life of the modern man seems so full. He is preoccupied with many things, but down underneath these outer things there is a growing emptiness. The life of the modern man could be described as outer revival, inner decay. This inner vacuum is intolerable, for nature and human nature abhor a vacuum. "Void" could be written across the soul of modern man.

O Spirit of Creation, move across the face of this formless void in the hearts of dullness-afflicted men. May a new creation come into being—the creation of a new type of person, and may it begin in me. In Jesus' name. Amen.

AFFIRMATION FOR THE DAY: *My life must be a continuing miracle, an example of the third miracle—the miracle of the new creation.*

"THE OLD HAVE BECOME NEW"

We left off yesterday saying that the unregenerate were "without form" and "void." The last item is: (3) "and darkness was upon the face of the deep." The unregenerate are living in darkness and stumbling from event to event in darkness.

Then the miracle takes place: the Holy Spirit moves upon the face of this dark, empty purposelessness, and lo, out of the chaos comes cosmos, a new personality emerges, with purpose, with fullness, with light. He has a goal and power to move on to that goal.

"The old has passed away, behold, the new has come" (II Cor. 5:17). The basic human nature remains, but this false world of sin and evil passes away. The basic human nature which had attached itself to this false world of sin and evil is cleansed and comes back new. The self which had attached itself to selfishness, trying to make itself God, is cleansed of selfishness and comes back no longer dominant but subservient. Sex is cleansed of sexuality and comes back as creative activity; within the home it is procreation and fellowship, outside the home, creative activity on another level, creating new hopes, newborn souls, new movements. The sex urge has passed away as sexuality; it has come back as creative activity. The herd urge is cleansed of subservience to the herd and becomes fastened on the kingdom of God, and then it comes back as concern for society and its redemption.

The false nature of sin and evil passes away; the basic human nature remains—now dedicated to other purposes and other goals. They are new because they are dedicated to new goals with new motives and drives. This new creation is a miracle; it cannot be accounted for by psychological factors, for it takes a miracle to produce those psychological factors, directed as they are now, to a regenerated person. This can happen to any man.

O Miracle-working Redeemer, may I be a miracle of Thy redeeming grace every moment of my life. May I not frustrate this saving grace, but give it perfect freedom in every part of my being. Amen.

AFFIRMATION FOR THE DAY: *The invasion of newness into the old habits, attitudes, drives—this is redemption.*

"GOD WAS IN CHRIST RECONCILING"

Now we look into the very heart of redemption: "All this is from God, who through Christ reconciled us to himself and gave us the ministry of reconciliation; that is, God was in Christ reconciling the world to himself" (II Cor. 5:18-19). That is one of the most important verses in Scripture, for it makes God and Christ One—in redemption. "I hate God," said a little girl, "but I love Jesus. God wanted to destroy the world, but Jesus wouldn't let Him." She picked that up from Christian teaching, but it is false. A Hindu lady lost her husband by an accident. She said to a Christian friend, "If he had only come home alive, I would have fought with God to save his life." Her idea was that you fight with God and overcome His reluctance. That is not the picture of God we see in the face of Jesus Christ. There God and Christ are one—one in their compassion and love and self-sacrifice.

When man sinned God began to suffer, for it is the nature of love to insinuate itself into the sins and sorrows of the loved one and make them its own. God has had an unseen cross upon His heart from the foundation of the world. "The Lamb was slain from the foundation of the world." The outer cross lifted up in history showed us the inner cross on the heart of God. The cross lights up the nature of God as love. "God was in Christ reconciling the world to himself." The sufferings of Jesus were the sufferings of God. An artist pictures the nails going through the hands of Jesus and piercing the hands of God—and rightly. We could never have known that God was wearing the unseen cross on His heart had it not been for the outer cross of Jesus. At the cross we see God—and ourselves—God as suffering love, and ourselves as causing it all. Only at the cross can you see your sins. In the light of law, custom, and history our sins are understandable. In the light of the cross they are intolerable.

O God, our Father, we see Thee and ourselves at the cross, and seeing Thee and ourselves we can never be the same. We see and we seek, and seeking we find, for Thou art the Love that wilt not let us go. We praise Thee, praise Thee. Amen.

AFFIRMATION FOR THE DAY: *If God was in Christ reconciling, may I be in Christ reconciling—reconciling in everything I touch.*

"THE MESSAGE OF RECONCILIATION"

We must spend another day on God's being in Christ, reconciling the world unto Himself. The other side of that verse is: "gave us the ministry of reconciliation . . . entrusting to us the message of reconciliation" (II Cor. 5:18-19). Here we are given both "the ministry of reconciliation" and "the message of reconciliation." "The message of reconciliation" may be verbal; the "ministry of reconciliation" will be vital. We not only give the message, we give ourselves, the messenger—to reconciliation. The word of reconciliation becomes flesh. We take the conflicts, the hates, the resentments of men, and make them our own. We reconcile them in our own bodies by suffering with them and for them.

I usually take my compliments and lay them at the feet of Jesus as fast as they come, for they belong to Him. But one I've cherished in my own heart as something to live up to. The Africans are very shrewd. After studying each newcomer and his characteristics, they give him a name which expresses his dominant trait or characteristic. They gave me the name of "Reconciler." It sent me to my knees. That is what the Christian is supposed to be. He has the message and ministry of reconciliation. The message becomes flesh in the person and the ministry of reconciliation comes out of the person. He suffers with and for both parties and brings them together in His own broken heart. It takes broken hearts to mend the world.

A doctor on board ship said of a certain mentally and emotionally ill young man, a passenger, "I could straighten him out before we get to the end of the voyage, but I'm not going to do it. It would mean too much suffering for me." He let the man suffer it out himself. The hope of the world is for those who will be willing to enter into the pain and sorrow and frustrations of the world and exercise the ministry of reconciliation.

O God, my Father, I'm to be like Thee—to do what Thou dost do. It is challenging and breath-taking, but I come. Take my heart and fill it with Thy pains for others. I share Thy pains and with them Thy joy. Amen.

AFFIRMATION FOR THE DAY: *"The ministry of reconciliation"—to that I am dedicated and to that I will give myself.*

"WHAT IS HONORABLE"

We come to another passage: "for we aim at what is honorable not only in the Lord's sight but also in the sight of men" (II Cor. 8:21). This is an important correction for those who are in Christ. Being in Christ is a high privilege and an honor and may create spiritual pride and indifference to what men may think and say. Emancipated from the herd by being in Christ, we may flaunt the corrective of the herd. This is a great spiritual danger. This verse corrects that; we are to aim at what is honorable not only in the Lord's sight, but also in the sight of men.

A Christian tried to climb past a non-Christian and get a place which really belonged to the latter by right. The Christian replied, when queried by a fellow Christian as to whether this was honorable, "Well, you see I'm a Christian and do this for the Lord's glory." The Lord's glory and his own advantage!

The Communists of Kerala had lived so encased in their own ideology that when they came to power and took over the government they treated with contempt all suggested correction not based on their ideology. That broke them. The people rose up and threw them out.

The Christian wrapped up in his superior ideology and his superior position of being in Christ cannot afford to refuse to listen to a group correction. If he does, he is riding for a fall. The minister cannot afford to let the group control him, but neither can he afford to refuse to let the group correct him. Often the group from its vantage point can see things he cannot see. He needs to hear what they have to say, but he cannot afford to listen too much and thus become herd-centered instead of Christ-centered. Gaze at Jesus, but be sure to glance at the world. Listen to Him, and then don't refuse to listen to them.

O Jesus, my Lord, I see everything in Thee, but some of this everything in Thee comes through others. Help me to take from Thee with both hands and teach me to take from others with at least one hand. In Thy Name. Amen.

AFFIRMATION FOR THE DAY: *Nothing dishonorable before the Lord or before man shall be done by me today.*

"A MAN IN CHRIST"

Another passage: "I must boast; there is nothing to be gained by it, but I will go on to visions and revelations of the Lord. I know a man in Christ who fourteen years ago was caught up to the third heaven" (II Cor. 12:1-2). Paul here hesitated to talk of his visions and revelations. He knew that there was nothing to be gained by it. He knew it was a false emphasis. He knew that Jesus never went off into any visions or dreams, that there was nothing psychopathic about Him, that He got His guidance when in control of all His faculties. He was infinite sanity as well as infinite sanctity. So Paul hesitatingly departed from the emphasis of Jesus and began to go off into signs and wonders. He felt he had been driven to it by his detractors. A dangerous thing to do—to let someone else determine your conduct—he did this, I must do that! He should have worked out from his own principles regardless of what the other person said or did.

He knew he was off-center when talking about his visions and revelations. But God in the midst of it gave a correction: "And to keep me from being too elated by the abundance of revelations, a thorn was given me in the flesh, a messenger of Satan, to harass me, to keep me from being too elated" (II Cor. 12:7).

Just what was this thorn in the flesh? Those who take an absolutist position about physical healing, believing that all diseases should be cured in this life or else there is sin or lack of faith, are driven to queer interpretations to explain away the thorn as a physical infirmity: (1) This thorn was Paul's struggle with sex. (2) Paul really didn't want to be healed; subconsciously he wanted to suffer, so he wouldn't accept the healing. The first has no scriptural basis, and the second leaves Paul an ambivalent person—consciously asking for healing, subconsciously rejecting it.

O Lord Jesus, clear our vision lest visions and revelations cloud our sight. In Thee we see the Father's revelation of Himself, and in Thee we see the vision of what we can be. Keep our eyes fixed on Thee and Thee alone. Amen.

AFFIRMATION FOR THE DAY: *I ask for no vision save the vision of the Crucified.*

PAUL'S THORN?

When we finished yesterday we were considering what Paul's thorn in the flesh really was. He tells us in Galatians 4:13-15: "you know it was because of a bodily ailment that I preached the gospel to you at first; and though my condition was a trial to you, you did not scorn or despise me, but received me as an angel of God . . . For I bear you witness that, if possible, you would have plucked out your eyes and given them to me." This thorn in the flesh was apparently connected with his eyes; he probably had running eyes, a sore trial to a public speaker. Three times he asked God to heal him and received the reply: "My grace is sufficient for you, for my power is made perfect in weakness." Paul replied: "I will all the more gladly boast of my weaknesses that the power of Christ may rest upon me." When his eyesight went bad, his insight grew better.

The revelation left him with a physical infirmity which he was not to bear, but to use until the final cure in the resurrection when he would get his resurrection body. To keep Paul from being swept off his center in Christ a thorn was given him to make him remember, not the vision and the revelation, but the thorn and its purpose. This was a healthy unhealth. Paul could have preached the necessity of visions and revelations and could have blurred his glorious presentation of Jesus Christ had this humiliating corrective not been given. Christianity under his hand could have become a desire to peer behind the curtain—as in Spiritualism—and a desire to make Christianity a religion of signs and wonders—as in a Christian cult in India where you are not Christian if you do not see visions and revelations. All of which would have made Christians into "a congregation of the queer," the description which a theosophist gave of his group. No, being in Christ makes you a person with deepened insight, heightened moral susceptibilities, a broader, purer love, and a growing Christlikeness.

O Jesus, Lord and Savior, save me from bypaths that take me off the Way. Save me from trying to see any vision save the vision of the Face I see in the Scriptures. Cleanse me from the marginal that I may be given to the magnificent. Amen.

AFFIRMATION FOR THE DAY: *May I need no thorn in the flesh as corrective, but if it comes help me to use it!*

"WEAK IN HIM"

The next passage puts together seeming weakness and manifest strength: "For he was crucified in weakness, but lives by the power of God. For we are weak in him, but in dealing with you we shall live with him by the power of God" (II Cor. 15:4). "For we are weak in him"—we have surrendered to Him, abdicated in His favor, and hence seem weak. We are. We are weak, just as He was weak in His crucifixion when He submitted to God and man and let life wreak its vengeance on Him. Amid that apparent weakness, however, there was a terrible strength—He was the Terrible Meek. "Pilate . . . was the more afraid"—the ruler afraid of his prisoner! "The centurion smote his breast" the crucifier afraid of the Crucified! "The keepers were like dead men"—afraid of this new power, that trampled on death.

The surrendered become the assertive; the weak turn into the meek, and the meek turn into the terrible meek. There is nothing so terrible as a person wholly surrendered to God but who will surrender to nothing else. You cannot bribe, browbeat, or bend such persons.

A boy's lunch was stolen. The principal went down the line and asked each boy whether he had stolen the lunch. No one acknowledged having done it. A hunchbacked boy arose and said he had done it. The principal called him out: "You know the rules. Take off your coat." "Oh no," said the hunchback, "not that." He was poor and had on no shirt, and his deformed back would be exposed to all. The big boy, whose lunch had been stolen, arose and said, "Is there any rule against my taking his punishment?" He took the punishment. It so impressed the hunchback that he was changed and is now preaching the gospel.

You become everybody's door mat and everybody's temple of refuge. You possess nothing—and everything! It turns out to be the only strength.

O Jesus, my Lord and Savior, I want to know Thy weakness that I may know Thy power. I want to be crucified that I may rise into life. I want to empty my hands that I may take everything. In Thy name. Amen.

AFFIRMATION FOR THE DAY: *Let me be weak in the surrender of my rights, and strong in the assertion of my influence.*

"SPEAKING IN CHRIST"

This verse pulls Paul back to the Center: "It is in the sight of God that we have been speaking in Christ, and all for your upbuilding, beloved" (II Cor. 12:19). This is important—very. He writes of "speaking in Christ." To be in Christ is to speak in Christ—to speak with His emphasis and with His spirit.

"With His emphasis." If we are to speak with His emphasis we must saturate ourselves with the New Testament, for here we find the clearest exposition of His emphases. Get your eyes off Him and you sink. In a plane which was tossed about in a wind of eighty miles an hour over mountains, a lady opposite me was reading a book on faith healing and forthwith got sick. I was reading the New Testament and I rode the waves—as He did—with joy!

"With His emphasis." Some of our emphases may be verbal. His were vital. The emphasis of His words and of His acts were the same. The Prime Minister of the Union of South Africa, as he was about to make a speech, loosed a white dove which was the symbol that he would make peace in South Africa. The dove refused to fly, however, and hit the ground with a thud! A very dramatic symbol that you cannot have peace by slogans and symbols. He had one emphasis with his drama and another with his deed. There was no power in it. Jesus' words had power, for His words were deeds and His deeds were words.

"With His spirit"—His emphasis and His spirit. The latter is important. We can say the right thing with the wrong spirit. To speak in Christ is to speak both with His emphasis and with His spirit. A dog knows the difference—throw him a bone and he'll go away without a wag of his tail. Call him to you, pat his head, and give him the bone, and he'll go away with wagging tail. In both cases it is the same act; you gave the bone. The latter was different because it was done in a different spirit.

O Jesus, Savior Divine, may I give Thy gifts with Thy spirit. Then the gifts will be gifts—plus. There will be an aroma about them—the aroma of Thy spirit. All will be upbuilt, for Thou art life. Amen.

AFFIRMATION FOR THE DAY: *Speaking in Christ, thinking in Christ, loving in Christ, living in Christ—may this be my occupation today.*

"CHRIST AND . . ."

We turn now to Galatians for its "in Christ" passages. The first one we find strikes the keynote of the Epistle: "our freedom which we have in Christ Jesus" (Gal. 2:4). There were those who felt that Christ was not enough. They wanted "Christ and"—Christ and circumcision. Without the "and" salvation was not complete.

We try to do the same; we try to piece out the redemption in Christ by adding to Him—Christ and baptism, baptism according to our special formula; Christ and our holy communion; Christ and our apostolic succession; Christ and becoming a member of our church; Christ and the gift of tongues; Christ and our interpretation of Him; Christ and our doctrinal slogans; Christ and our forms of worship. Endlessly we say, "Christ and." Paul refused any "and" added to Christ.

This was the freedom in Christ—a freedom from endless "ands." Christ and Christ alone is necessary to salvation! I went through a famous temple in Madurai, where Brahmins go through burdensome details in meticulously doing this, that, and the other in order to perform their ritual. It literally takes up half the day. As I walked among these ritualists I kept saying to myself, "Christ alone for salvation." I was free from this religious red-tape. "If the Son shall make you free you are free indeed." This was an "indeed" freedom. All else is pseudo freedom. It is freedom to walk amid the 3,600 commandments of the Law and say to yourself, "Thou shalt love God, thou shalt love man." You are freed from complexity to simplicity, from the marginal to the central, from the trivial to the great. No wonder Paul fought the Judaizers; he was fighting for freedom—for himself and us.

O Jesus my Lord, I thank Thee for this "indeed" freedom. I am loosed from a thousand inner and outer bondages. I'm free to love Thee and through Thee to love others. I'm free to be at my best through Thee. Amen.

AFFIRMATION FOR THE DAY: *I am free to love Him alone, and when I love Him alone I am free—free indeed.*

"SOMEONE WHO IS MAD AFTER JESUS"

There is another side of this freedom we wrote about yesterday. It is an indeed freedom that leads you to an indeed bondage. A Mohammedan said to me one day, "You Christians are too free. We have to pray five times a day, but you don't have to. You are too free." I replied, "But after you pray your five times you are off duty. I'm never off duty, for I pray without ceasing. And interestingly enough, I want to pray without ceasing. This is a sweet bondage.

This "freedom in Christ" is a freedom to choose a deeper and deeper bondage. Love is never off duty. There are no moral holidays in being a Christian. You surrender your all to Christ and then look for more to surrender to Him. "I want to see someone who is mad after Jesus," said a Hindu to me one day. Well, the real Christian is possessed of a divine madness which is true sanity; he is mad after the Highest.

Amy Wilson Carmichael was a true saint of South India. For about twenty years before her release she was wracked with pain. She sent a message, "Tell them I'm in Nero's prison, but I'm not Nero's prisoner." She was in the prison house of pain and invalidism, but she was not the prisoner of pain and invalidism; her spirit was free—free to rejoice, even to exult.

Paul, in Nero's prison, was not Nero's prisoner. He, though shut up behind bars, was free to roam the earth and the centuries and to bless and guide through his immortal letters written in prison. Christ, not Nero, had the last word and that last word was Freedom. It is freedom and more freedom: "For freedom Christ has set us free" (Gal. 5:1). He frees us to give us more freedom. God says, "All I ask is that you ask more." And Jesus says: "I give you this freedom so you'll have the freedom to ask for more freedom." This is indeed freedom!

O God, my Father and my Redeemer, save me from subtle bondages that promise me freedom and give me bonds. I want nothing more and nothing less than Thee. In Thee I walk the earth free. I thank Thee. Amen.

AFFIRMATION FOR THE DAY: *Bound to Him, I walk the earth free—free to live.*

ARE WE SAVED BY WHAT WE DO?

We come now to a passage which is the crux of Paul's teaching: "who know that a man is not justified by works of the law but through faith in Jesus Christ, even we have believed in Christ Jesus, in order to be justified by faith in Christ, and not by works of the law, because by works of the law shall no one be justified" (Gal. 2:16). This passage cuts straight to the heart of the problem of salvation in East and West: Are we saved by what we do, or by what God has done in Jesus Christ? Is salvation an attainment or an obtainment? Do we get salvation by climbing the ladder to God rung by rung until we reach the topmost rung of worthiness where we meet God? Or does God come down the ladder to us in incarnation, in the Person of Jesus, and does He meet us at the bottom rung as sinners? Is salvation man's attainment, or is it God's gift?

That is the question that divides all others from the Christian way—not only the Jews, but the Hindus, the Mohammedans, the Buddhists, Confucianists, and what not. They all try to climb the ladder to God. It is an egocentric attempt at salvation. When God comes down the ladder to us it is God-centric salvation. In one case we earn it, in the other we receive it as a gift.

Those who try the first way are always on the way: they never arrive. Salvation is always beyond their fingertips. They are wistful, but never witnesses. They are always uncertain, never sure if they have done enough. But those who are humble enough to empty their hands of all self-righteousness and self-striving do receive, and they do become glad witnesses— glad witnesses of the grace of God. "By grace are we saved through faith, and that not of ourselves; it is the gift of God." The one way leads to a dead end of question marks and the other to the open road of exclamation points!

O God, we could not get to Thee—our sins forbade it—so Thou didst come to us. Thy love impelled Thee. Thou didst come bearing our sins in Thine own body on a tree. We cannot but spread abroad the good news. Amen.

AFFIRMATION FOR THE DAY: *If salvation is by grace through faith, that puts a great humility at the heart of my salvation—I'm humble enough to receive.*

"HOW DO WE RECEIVE THE SPIRIT?"

We find a good many within the Christian churches still trying to climb the ladder of worthiness and ending in barren frustration, trying a little harder, doing a little better, being more disciplined and careful, always whipping up the will, tired with self-effort. A leading layman said to me, "For fifty years I've been trying to climb that ladder, and now I see salvation is the gift of God. I've not been humble enough to receive.

Many are puzzled as to how the Holy Spirit is received. Someone has said, "The biggest question in theology is this: How do we receive the Holy Spirit?" Paul is clear. "Let me ask you only this: Did you receive the Spirit by works of the law, or by hearing with faith? . . . Does he who supplies the Spirit to you and works miracles among you do so by works of the law, or by hearing with faith?" (Gal. 3:2, 5).

Salvation and the gift of the Spirit are both by the hearing of faith, by receptivity, or faith-filled receptivity. There are some still among us who believe that you can get the Holy Spirit by stepping into a long line of apostolic succession and having a bishop's hands laid on you. You may receive Him because you receive Him by faith in the living Christ, but if you have faith that only because you are in this line of succession you will thereby receive the Holy Spirit, the certainty is that you won't receive Him. You are trying to receive Him by a mechanical contrivance—by a so-called unbroken line of laid-on hands, and that is trying to receive Him by the works of the law, by a carefully guarded pipeline. That Jesus should commit His most precious gift, the gift of the Holy Spirit, to that mechanical contrivance is unthinkable. The open heart, surrender, and receptivity upwards and not a leaky line backwards, is the way to receive the Holy Spirit.

Dear Father, we thank Thee that the promise of the Holy Spirit is to those who ask, that this is for everyone who is called, and that Thy grace calls all. I stand under open heavens and receive Thy gift and am grateful to my fingertips. Amen.

AFFIRMATION FOR THE DAY: *The highest gift of God, the Holy Spirit, is free for the asking—if I ask with my life in the asking.*

"CRUCIFIED WITH CHRIST"

Out of the Galatian controversy over whether "Christ and . . ." or just "Christ" is required for salvation came this spark of deathless testimony: "I have been crucified with Christ; it is no longer I who live, but Christ who lives in me; and the life I now live in the flesh I live by faith in the Son of God, who loved me and gave Himself for me" (Gal. 2:20). The old version said, "I live by the faith of the Son of God"—His faith in me! This kindles my faith in Him. He believes in me when I can't believe in myself, so I have to live up to His faith. So the verse, "We love because he first loved us," could also read, "We believe because He first believed in us." He is on a faith-producing offensive as well as a love-producing offensive!

"I am crucified with Christ." The emphasis is on "with Christ," for if you are not crucified voluntarily with Christ you are crucified involuntarily with yourself—crucified on the cross of your own inner conflicts. Many writhe on the cross of their own making where they hang alone, nothing redemptive in it. The chosen crucifixion with Christ, when we offer up the "I" in self-surrender, is redemptive: "nevertheless I live." And how! To the degree that I fully surrender to the cross to be crucified with Him, to that degree do I live and live by the resurrected power of Him, for His cross and resurrection were one. So they become one with me; I am a Calvary and an Easter Morning at one and the same time. The risen Christ lives in me. So I live by resurrection, not crucifixion—by life, not death. All this has its feet on the ground: "the life I now live in the flesh"—"in the flesh"—it is working out in actual practice in life, and life "in the flesh."

The alternatives are these: Be crucified with Christ, or be crucified with myself—one redemptive and issuing in life, the other nonredemptive and issuing in fruitless self-inflicted pain.

O Crucified Redeemer, I consent to be crucified with Thee. I hear Thy reply: "And I consent for you to be risen with Me. You share My cross, now share My conquest over death." Blessed exchange! I thank Thee. Amen.

AFFIRMATION FOR THE DAY: *I am crucified with Christ or I am crucified on the cross of my own conflicts.*

"THE SECRET: PRAY ABOUT IT"

Another blessed passage: "that in Christ Jesus the blessing of Abraham might come upon the Gentiles, that we might receive the promise of the Spirit through faith" (Gal. 3:14). "That in Christ Jesus the blessing of Abraham might come upon the Gentiles"—what was that blessing of Abraham? As I went up by train through Mesopotamia, now Iraq, after the First World War, the guard called out, "Next station Ur-of-the-Chaldees." When I got out and looked at the barren wastes and mounds of rubble, I said to an Englishman, "Well, this is the place Abraham got out of." He replied, "Well, no wonder." When Abraham got out of it, however, it was the center of a thriving civilization. He walked out of that thriving civilization in answer to an inner creative urge—an urge which eventuated in the founding of a great people, the Jewish people.

The spirit within him was the creative Spirit. Paul said that the promise of the creative Spirit, received by faith, is what we receive in Christ Jesus. That creative Spirit works on small and on large scales. In a YMCA in Madras, a beehive of young life, someone told of how George Williams, the founder of the YMCA, was asked, "What is the secret of your success?" He replied, "There is no secret. It is all open. We see a need, pray about it, and then do something about it." Very simple and very effective. The secret was in the second step—"Pray about it." Prayer has been defined as self-surrender—self-surrender to the creative Spirit. Faith is betting your life on the creative Spirit. When this happens you desert, like Abraham, outer brilliance with no soul in it, to found creative movements. You do it by faith. Faith doesn't do it; it's not faith in faith, but faith which is pure receptivity that lets you receive the promised Spirit—the Spirit of Creation and Recreation. You become a creative person because possessed by the Creative Spirit.

O Creative Spirit, I receive Thee by faith. Take all my powers and put a plus to them. Think through my mind, love through my emotions, act through my will, and be through my being. Make every part creative. Amen.

AFFIRMATION FOR THE DAY: *The Spirit within me—the center of creative power in the universe within me—wonder of wonders!*

NOT FAITH IN FAITH, BUT FAITH IN JESUS

Another important verse: "But the scripture consigned all things to sin, that what was promised to faith in Jesus Christ might be given to those who believe" (Gal. 3:22). "The scripture consigned all things to sin"—"consigned all things to sin"—an amazing statement. Does it mean that a new standard of goodness—the life and character of Jesus—has come into the world? He is Goodness. Everything that departs from His life and character is un-goodness, or evil, or sin. Everything outside Christ is sin. Does this mean that all that non-Christians do and are is sin? No, for non-Christians can and often do show His life and character without naming Him, and many Christians can and do depart from His character and life while naming Him. The division is not there; it is in the nature of the act itself, whether performed by a Christian or a non-Christian. If the act is un-Christlike, it is sin. There is no other sin, for there is no other Goodness. Every thought, every act, every attitude, that is un-Christlike, by whomsoever performed, is sin.

We pass from a state of sin to a state of goodness by faith, but not by bare faith—a faith in faith—rather by faith in Jesus Christ. In that act of faith you commit yourself to the object of your faith, to Jesus Christ, not only as an object of belief, but as an object of Lordship. He possesses you; He is Lord—Lord of you and all you have.

Result? Then "what was promised to faith in Jesus Christ might be given to those who believe." We inherit everything He has and is! Faith is answering yes to His offer of His Everything. Faith takes with both hands—the hands of surrender and receptivity, both of them empty enough to take His fullness. "That which is promised" is limitless, so the taking is limitless—and forever. There is no bottom and no end!

O Divine Fullness, I stand before Thee empty but eager—eager to take what is promised in Thee. It is all mine, for I am all Thine. It is my all for Thy all—blessed exchange. I gratefully receive. Amen.

AFFIRMATION FOR THE DAY: *Faith is humility, open and receptive and willing to depend on the dependable.*

JESUS IMMEDIATELY AVAILABLE

"But now that faith has come, we are no longer under a custodian; for in Christ Jesus you are all sons of God, through faith" (Gal. 3:25-26). In the verse preceding we read, "So that the law was our custodian until Christ came, that we might be justified by faith." The transition was from "custodian" to sons of God. In being sons of God there was immediate contact with the Father—the go-betweens were no more. In Christ Jesus you are in immediate contact with God.

In the Reformation, what was the central discovery? It is often said: "The just shall live by faith." That discovery, while good, was not good enough. The central discovery I believe was the immediate availability of Christ. He had been imprisoned in a system. You couldn't get to Him except as you went through the priest, through the church, through Mary, to Jesus and to God. There were three custodians before you got to Jesus. The Reformation made Jesus immediately available to faith. That made Him available anywhere and everywhere, freed us from custodians.

The greatest Hindu philosopher of India was approached by a brilliant student who said, "I believe in your philosophy, I'm a student of your books. Make me your disciple. Be my Guru (Teacher, Master)." The philosopher replied, "I'm not worthy to be your Guru." The student asked, "Then who is?" And the philosopher replied, "There is only one who is worthy—Jesus Christ." "But I thought He was a dead Jew." "No, His followers believe Him to be alive." "Where can I get to Him?" "Get a New Testament. There you can find Him." He did; he became a Christian and now is on fire, winning others. The immediate availability of Jesus to human need is the most precious fact in life. There are no custodians, no gurus, no go-betweens; he is immediately available! This opens infinite possibilities.

O Jesus, my Lord, I do not have to have Thee clouded by custodians or go-betweens. I can stand face to face with Thee. Thy utmost resources are open to my utmost need. Then no reason to be poor. Amen.

AFFIRMATION FOR THE DAY: *Jesus, immediately available—any time, anywhere, in any condition—then there is no room for poverty, weakness, or loneliness.*

WHAT WAS THE "ONE BAPTISM"?

We come to a passage which is intriguing: "For as many of you as were baptized into Christ have put on Christ" (Gal. 3:27). Just what is this baptism which brings you into Christ and makes you "put on Christ"? The answer usually given is baptism with water. Many are baptized with water, however, some in infancy and some in adult years, and they have not put on Christ. Simon Magus had been baptized with water, and yet Peter had to say to him: "For I see that you are in the gall of bitterness and in the bond of iniquity" (Acts 8:23).

The baptism which brings us into Christ and helps us to put on Christ is the baptism of the Spirit. This verse makes it clear: "For by one Spirit we were all baptized into one body—Jews or Greeks, slaves or free—and were all made to drink of one Spirit" (I Cor. 12:13). "Baptized into" by "one Spirit"—so it is the Spirit's baptism. The passage "One Lord, one faith, one baptism" (Eph. 4:5) is usually used as depicting baptism with water as the one baptism. The Lord is the Lord Jesus (Jesus is Lord!); the faith is faith in the one Lord, and the baptism is the baptism which the one Lord gave. What baptism was that?

John said: "I came baptizing with water . . . this is He who baptizes with the Holy Spirit" (John 1:31, 33). Jesus did not baptize with water—"although Jesus himself did not baptize, but only His disciples" (John 4:2). Jesus did not baptize with water, for He saved Himself to give the "one baptism"—the baptism of the Spirit. "Being therefore exalted at the right hand of God, and having received from the Father the promise of the Holy Spirit, he has poured out this which you see and hear" (Acts 2:33). The baptism of the Spirit brings us into Christ and then we put on Christ. The baptism of water brings us into the church fellowship.

O Spirit of God, only Thy cleansing and enabling can bring me into Christ. I open every pore of my being to Thy coming. For Thou dost bring Him. Everything within me cries out for Him. Come, Holy Spirit, come. Amen.

AFFIRMATION FOR THE DAY: *To receive the Spirit—that is deliverance, direction, and dynamic.*

IN CHRIST DISTINCTIONS OBLITERATED

The next passage is rich beyond words: "There [in Christ] is neither Jew nor Greek [race distinction], there is neither slave nor free [social and economic distinction], there is neither male nor female [sex distinction], for you are all one in Christ Jesus" (Gal. 3:28). Another pair of distinctions are added in Col. 3:11: "Here there cannot be Greek and Jew, circumcised and uncircumcised, barbarian, Scythian, slave, free man, but Christ is all, and in all." "Circumcised and uncircumcised" [outer religious distinction], "barbarian, Scythian" [cultural distinction]—in Christ there "cannot be" race, social and economic, sex, outer religious signs or cultural distinctions. Note the "cannot"—if there are these distinctions Christ is absent. All things that divide men are gone. A new society has arisen, where a person is a person—a person for whom Christ died.

Had that blinding vision been kept, a new world would have arisen instead of the mess we are now in. This blinding vision is not based on sentimentality; it is based on hard fact. There are no permanently inferior or superior races. There are underdeveloped races and developed races, but none permanently inferior or superior. Given the same stimulus and the same incentive, the brain of humanity will come out about the same. In Nairobi, Kenya, at an African school run by six missions, there have been, since 1947, only two failures in the Cambridge examinations, the percentage being about 99.9 per cent of passes. The white schools taking the same examinations pass 80 per cent. The Indian schools pass 30 per cent. The Indian young people have no economic, political, or religious incentive, hence they sag; the Africans have the incentive to show they are not inferior, hence they overcompensate and surpass. The Christian vision has its feet on very solid ground—there are infinite possibilities in everybody, everywhere.

O Jesus, Thou art called the Son of Man, as if all mankind were in travail to bring Thee forth. We bow at Thy feet and find in Thee our brother wrapped in many colors, but our brother still. We are all one in Thee. Amen.

AFFIRMATION FOR THE DAY: *In Jesus I am a man of one book and one humanity, because I am a man of one Person.*

"FAITH WORKING THROUGH LOVE"

This verse is very important: "For in Christ Jesus neither circumcision nor uncircumcision is of any avail, but faith working through love" (Gal. 5:6). There are three passages around this thought of "circumcision and uncircumcision." The other two are these: "For neither circumcision counts for anything nor uncircumcision, but keeping the commandments of God" (I Cor. 7:19). "For neither circumcision counts for anything, nor uncircumcision, but a new creation" (Gal. 6:15).

These three are important in an ascending importance: (1) "keeping the commandments of God"; (2) "a new creation"; and (3) "faith working through love."

Circumcision was the dividing sign between Jew and Gentile. Baptism has now taken its place as the dividing sign between Christian and non-Christian. You are a Christian if you have been baptized, you are not a Christian if you have not been baptized. This is a division that does not divide, for many are baptized who are not Christians, and many are Christians who are not baptized—Quakers and the Salvation Army groups do not baptize. So Paul, writing today, would probably say: "For neither baptism counts for anything nor unbaptism, but a new creation." He would throw the emphasis on the "new creation," being born again, as the dividing line.

This phrase "faith working through love" is of the utmost importance. There are four levels of life: (1) The level of instinct; (2) The level of duty; (3) The level of receiving grace through faith; (4) The level of "faith working through love." The faith that works through combat, through criticism, through proving others wrong, is less than a Christian faith. Only the faith which makes all its contacts love contacts, which makes love its working force, is the Christian faith.

O Jesus, Lord, all Thy contacts were love contacts. Love was and is Thy working force. Make it mine. May I love the loveless with Thy love. My love breaks down. Give me Thy love as my working force. Amen.

AFFIRMATION FOR THE DAY: *My faith will work by love and only by love, for if it works by anything else it is not the Christian faith.*

"WE HAVE BEEN ON THE WRONG TRACK"

"Faith working through love"—we must spend another day on this. Faith working through love can be and is the most beautiful thing in the world. Faith working without love can be and is the ugliest thing in the world. It has caused more havoc in the world than possibly any other one thing.

The Mohammedan faith is a very definite and strong faith, but for the most part it works without love and in doing so works havoc. "It finds a desert or makes one."

A man in Africa, just back from tearing down the house of a member of a rival tribe, said breathlessly to a missionary, "God is with me. While tearing down the house the roof caved in and fell on me, but I wasn't hurt. God is with me." He had faith, but it wasn't a faith working by love; it worked ruin.

Francis Xavier, the great missionary to India, wrote to the Portuguese king that he was convinced the only way to Christianize these lands was to instruct the governors sent out that it was their chief business to convert the people and to punish them if they didn't produce adequate converts. The king agreed, and it was done. It was faith, but it wasn't faith working by love, and it worked havoc—to the Christian faith first of all.

A prominent pastor sent a telegram on every Sunday morning to another prominent pastor denouncing him for his lack of the true faith. His wife, before dying, said to her husband, "We have been on the wrong track." Telling about this, the man rolled on the floor of a pastor's study in an agony of remorse. He had faith and had tried to defend the faith, but it wasn't faith working through love.

O blessed loving Savior, help me not to use my faith in the service of my egotism. Help me to have a faith that works by love and by nothing but love. Then and then only will I be a Christian. Let me love with Thy love. Amen.

AFFIRMATION FOR THE DAY: *My faith will work by love or it won't work at all.*

OUR VIEWS MAY BE OUR VIEWS, NOT HIS

"I have confidence in the Lord that you will take no other view than mine" (Gal. 5:10). This is one of those passages that has an invitation and a warning in it. It contains an invitation to be so identified with the Lord that our views are His views. Paul apparently felt that, and in this matter he was right, profoundly right. We see that the requirement of circumcision along with the Christian faith would have been a tragic blunder. It would have crippled the Christian faith through the ages.

This statement also has a warning in it, however, a warning not to assume that our views are necessarily in the Lord. Our views may be reflected customs or a manifestation of our egoism turned religious. They may be leftover prejudices from the years; they may be not in the Lord, but "in my class," "in my denomination," "in me." We may project our subconscious desires into views which we then believe are in the Lord. Or our "views" may be rooted in ignorance, and we may believe them to be in the Lord.

For instance, in my morning mail I found a letter from a disturbed pastor taking me to task for my reply to the question, "What do you think of the idea of the assumption of the Virgin Mary?" I had replied, "It is an assumption." This pastor asked, "Does this mean that you do not believe in the Virgin Birth?" He was sure he was in the Lord when he asked that question, but he was only in a misconception, for the assumption of Mary refers to her being taken up to heaven without death!

This is flagrant, but many of our assumptions of being in the Lord may be subtle and hidden, and therefore more dangerous. Even identification with Him in full surrender may not mean that all our views are in the Lord. Our views are made up of information plus judgment, and both may be wrong and yet we are still in the Lord.

Dear God, cleanse me from the secret fault of assuming I'm right in my views when only my heart is right in Thee. May the Spirit of Truth constantly correct my views and may I be humble enough to heed. Amen.

AFFIRMATION FOR THE DAY: *Today I shall distinguish where necessary between my views and the good news.*

SAINTS IN EPHESUS?

We come to our next passage, passing over to Ephesians, the
richest of all the Epistles in the "in Christ" passages: "Paul, an
apostle of Christ Jesus by the will of God, to the saints who are
also faithful in Christ Jesus" (Eph. 1:1). The marginal reading
says, "who are at Ephesus and faithful." This marginal reading is
significant. It seems to express wonder that these saints are at
Ephesus and yet are faithful. Ephesus with its profligacy and
idolatry—"Great is Diana of the Ephesians!"—was hard on
saintliness.

Being in Christ Jesus may also mean that we are in
Ephesus—in our Ephesus, which translated into modern terms
would mean in a factory, a university, a fraternity, a home, a
lodge, a set, or sometimes most difficult of all, in a church. If
being in Christ were just being in Christ, full stop, it would be
comparatively simple, but being in Him also means being in
them. "There's the rub"!

The "rub" of our environment may be a rub into irritation, or
into irradiation, however. It can be burnishing powder to make
us shine. There can be saints who are also in Ephesus, and there
can be saints who are in hell, living in heaven and hell at the
same time with heaven predominating! Ephesus may not have
the final word in our lives—Christ does. That means we are
saints in Christ Jesus in Ephesus. Not the circumstances, but
the "innerstances" determine us.

O Spirit of God, dwell in me. Then wherever I dwell, I shall
dwell in heaven, for Thou art heaven. No outer hell can touch
this deep-down heaven. I am immune to my environment. In
Jesus' Name. Amen.

AFFIRMATION FOR THE DAY: *I may live environed by Ephesus, but I
really live environed by the Kingdom of God.*

"WITH EVERY SPIRITUAL BLESSING"

This verse is beautiful: "Blessed be the God and Father of our Lord Jesus Christ, who has blessed us in Christ with every spiritual blessing in the heavenly places" (Eph. 1:3). Here it is said that God "has blessed us in Christ with every spiritual blessing." Does this mean that in Christ we have everything which the human personality needs for its fulfillment, growth, and development, and that we need not go outside of Him for anything? Yes. We need not go outside of Christ for anything that is good for us. We have it all in Him. I have a friend who once believed that Jesus is the Way. He now believes that Jesus is a way. He has gone over to a Hindu cult to piece out Jesus—to get something larger and more comprehensive. Result? His wife drew a long breath when asked how they were getting along in their quest and said, "We have a long way to go." The bypaths were dead ends. Their weary feet will wander and wander until they put their feet upon the Way. Now they worship before the tomb of a dead guru instead of walking the open road with the resurrected Jesus. In the meantime their photos tell us by their sad faces that they "have a long way to go" to get to every spiritual blessing.

This doesn't mean that I believe that every denominational expression of Christ is synonymous with "every spiritual blessing." Often the denomination is built upon a phase of truth in Christ, and emphasizing that phase they miss the fullness of life in Christ . Christ is so defined that He is confined. They have a crescent moon instead of a full moon—a quarter Christ instead of the full Christ. Full surrender to the full Christ brings "every spiritual blessing." It is "in heavenly places"—you feel you are in heaven while getting heavenly blessings. And you are! You can't miss heaven, for you've got it—here and now.

O Jesus, my Lord, I am in touch with Thee, and I'm in touch with all I need now and hereafter. Anything outside Thee is emptiness, everything inside Thee is fullness. In Thee all my needs are met—plus. I am grateful. Amen.

AFFIRMATION FOR THE DAY: *Everything outside Jesus does not complete me; it only depletes me.*

"PREDESTINED TO BE HIS"

Another part of yesterday's verse reads: "even as he chose us in him before the foundation of the world, that we should be holy and blameless before him" (Eph. 1:4). This verse says that God "chose us in Him before the foundation of the world." Are we predestined to be His? Is that destiny written into our bodies, minds, and spirits—and our relationships? Yes. I believe by the very constitution of my being that I am predestined to be a Christian. All my organs, my blood, my nerves, my tissues, my brain—everything within me—work well when they work in His way, and they work badly when they work in some other way. I am predestined by my make-up to be His, but I can live against that destiny. If I do, I get hurt—inevitably. His way is my way, and when I do not take His way I'm beside myself, less than myself, against myself. I cannot revolt against Him without revolting against myself.

A commanding officer at an air base said, "If the men on this base would adopt what you said this morning in the chapel, there would be no problems. The problems on the air base are in these persons. If they would be Christians the problems would drop away." The problems of life arise out of our not being Christians, for the moment you are not a Christian, you are a problem to yourself and others. Haydon Edwards said to an officer commanding the United States Army in Korea, "What is the function of the armed forces as you see it?" His reply was, "Our function is to hold things together, if we can, until you people can take over. I am not sure we can, but that's our function." No one but the Christians can hold things together. Everything is made in its inner structure to work in the Christian way. When it does, it works well; when it works some other way, it works its own ruin. We are predestined to be Christian; that destiny is written in us, and hence inescapable.

Jesus, Lord and Savior, I'm grateful that I'm destined to be Thine. That is the highest destiny I can conceive of. I put my shoulders back when I think of it. I, a child of the dust, destined to be like Thee! Glory! Amen.

AFFIRMATION FOR THE DAY: *My destiny is the highest conceivable. I shall not lower it, nor diminish it—I shall fulfill it.*

"HOLY AND BLAMELESS BEFORE HIM IN LOVE"

The marginal reading of the next verse reads this way: "that we should be holy and blameless 'before him in love, having destined us' to be his sons through Jesus Christ, according to the purpose of his will, to the praise of his glorious grace which he freely bestowed on us in the Beloved" (Eph. 1:4-6). The state of being "holy and blameless" is "before him"—not before men. We cannot be holy and blameless before men, for men don't see all, so they misjudge us. We can be holy and blameless before Him, for He sees all and understands all. Even before Him it is "holy and blameless before him in love." Our love may be perfect, but our performance imperfect. We cannot be perfect in character and action—only perfect in intention, in love. When Jesus said, "Be ye therefore perfect as your heavenly Father is perfect," He did not mean perfect in character as God is perfect. The word "therefore" points back and refers to loving enemies and praying for those who persecute you, loving those who do not love you—that is what God does—He makes the sun to rise on the evil and the good. You are to love as God loves—to be perfect in love as God is perfect in love.

The manifestation of this perfect love may be imperfect and yet the love be perfect.

This grace He "freely bestowed on us in the Beloved." This is the only place where Jesus is called "the Beloved," but it is significant. In all other places the emphasis is on the love of Jesus for others. Here is the fruit: the One Who loved becomes "the Beloved." That always happens—if you wish to be beloved, then love. Don't ask for it; give it. Then being beloved will come as fruit and root.

"He freely bestowed on us in the Beloved"—when we are in Christ, "the Beloved," God can give with both hands. He freely bestows at that place, for it is safe to give to us when we are in the Beloved. Outside of the Beloved He gives with a token giving—a token of what He would give if we were in the Beloved.

O Father, help me to remain always, and with all I have, in the Beloved. There Thou art free to give and I'm free to receive. Since Thou dost give with both hands, I take with both hands. I thank Thee, thank Thee. Amen.

AFFIRMATION FOR THE DAY: *Since He freely bestows, I freely receive.*

"IN HIM WE HAVE REDEMPTION"

Our next verse: "In him we have redemption through his blood, the forgiveness of our trespasses, according to the riches of his grace which he lavished upon us" (Eph. 1:7-8). "In him we have redemption through his blood"—can we not have redemption in some other way; is there no other way except through His blood?

The answer is that there are two ways we may get redemption: either through our making atonement for our sins or through God's making atonement. It must be from the side of the human or from the side of the Divine. Can we atone for our sins? By our sufferings, by our good deeds, by our thinking? The answer is No! The guilt comes from a relationship with God which has been broken. That relationship can be mended only by God's initiative, and God can mend the relationship only if He bears our sins in His own body. He has. The cross is the outer sign of that inward bearing of our sins.

Now God can forgive, for the forgiveness He offers is no longer a cheap forgiveness. It costs God to forgive. The cross is the price God pays to get to us in spite of our sins.

"According to the riches of his grace which he lavished upon us." The last verse said "freely bestowed"; this verse says "lavished." The wonder and surprise of being forgiven could only be described by the grateful heart in terms such as "freely bestowed," or "lavished." It seemed incredible! To everyone who receives it, Divine forgiveness is a surprise. "How could He be so generous?" "He took me—even me!" It all seems so incredible, so undeserved. Of course it is! I find myself saying to myself after fifty-seven years, "This is too good for a ransomed sinner." I received a lovely garland in a public meeting, and I whispered to myself, "Too good for a ransomed sinner." All this and forgiveness and heaven too—it seems too good to be true!

Jesus, Lord and Redeemer, how could you be so gracious to the ungracious, so good to the not good, so loving to the unlovely? Thy generosity breaks my heart and there remakes it—remakes it on a higher level. I'm grateful. Amen.

AFFIRMATION FOR THE DAY: *I am not only redeemed* from, *I am redeemed to—redeemed to His glorious Everything! I follow.*

"MYSTERY OF HIS WILL"

Another Ephesians verse: "For He has made known to us in all wisdom and insight the mystery of his will, according to his purpose which he set forth in Christ" (Eph. 1:9). This verse is important in that it shows how God makes known the mystery of His will. He makes it "known to us in all wisdom and insight." In vs. 17 Paul linked "a spirit of wisdom and of revelation in the knowledge of him." Here instead of "revelation" he put "insight." The revelation is there in the latter portion of the verse: "which He set forth in Christ." The revelation is seen in the face of Jesus Christ.

Jesus Christ is God's will become legible. The will of God became flesh and walked and talked, lived and died, and rose again. Jesus is God's will, not spelled out, but lived out. And God's will looked at through Jesus spells out, "God is love."

Now how do we have this "mystery of his will" unfolded to us? By dictation? By special revelation? No, it is by studying and brooding over the New Testament as it unfolds Jesus Christ. As we do, we get wisdom. All knowledge apart from Jesus is foolishness, unless it is used in His way. Jesus is knowledge turned wise; it is "in all wisdom." It is not merely religious wisdom; it is *all* wisdom. It is the wisdom that knows how to live, how to think, how to feel, how to act, how to be! It is wisdom that is wise and only wise.

Then this wisdom is gained through insight. In Jesus the Incarnate we have "the sight." In thinking about Him and meditating and acting according to that sight we have insight—insight into its meaning. Its wonder unfolds. The sight is exciting, but the insight is just as exciting; it is a growing wonder as deeper meanings unfold, larger vistas are seen, and the eternal sweep of it is revealed. The will of God unfolded in Jesus is the most beautiful thing in this universe.

O God, I stand lost in wonder, love, and praise as I see Thy will unfold in Thy blessed Son. That will means well, and it means to make me well. It is not only good, it is redemptive. I love that Will, for it is Love. Amen.

AFFIRMATION FOR THE DAY: *The will of God is my highest interest, always, in everything and everywhere—no exception!*

"A PLAN TO UNITE ALL THINGS IN HIM"

Now: "as a plan for the fullness of time, to unite all things in him, things in heaven and things on earth" (Eph. 1:10). This verse is all-important.

The church is seeking a basis for unity and a plan for unity on that basis. Some would approach it by saying that we should understand each others' position about baptism, about orders, about sacraments, about bishops, about doctrinal emphases, and about church polity and organization. It all ends in futile discussion, raising more questions than it answers, for it is all off-center. These things were never intended to be the basis of our unity. God has a plan and this verse states it: "as a plan for the fullness of time, to unite all things in him"—in Jesus Christ. God's plan is to unite all things, and to unite all things *in Him.*

Jesus Christ is the center of our unity. Nothing else is. We cannot get together around baptism, and should not, for it is no center for our faith. We cannot get together around bishops, and should not, for bishops are not the center of our faith. We can and should get together at one place, and only one place, and that one place is Jesus Christ. He and He alone is the Center of our faith. I wrote, "Everyone who belongs to Jesus Christ belongs to everyone who belongs to Jesus Christ. He may betray that oneness, but he cannot deny it, for it is inherent." Someone replied: "That seems too good to be true." It is too good not to be true.

This is God's plan: "as a plan . . . to unite all things in him." So all other plans based upon this, that, and the other break themselves upon God's Plan. A church united around anything but Jesus Christ alone is a rickety structure and must fall, for its foundation is not the "one foundation." God's purpose is to unite all things, and that purpose has become a plan, and that plan is to unite all things around Jesus Christ and Him alone. All other plans are plans of futility. This is God's plan and is not subject to amendment—Christ and baptism, Christ and bishops. It is Christ alone.

O God, how grateful I am for Thy holding us to this one plan. There is no other possible plan. All other centers for plans are so marginal they are ridiculous. Thy center is our center— Jesus, the center of our faith, hence of our unity. Amen.

AFFIRMATION FOR THE DAY: *Christ alone is, and forever shall be the center of my unity with all those who belong to Him.*

UNITED AROUND CHRIST

We must spend another day upon this blessedly luminous verse: "as a plan for the fullness of time, to unite all things in him, things in heaven and things on earth" (Eph. 1:10).

We have seen that it is God's plan to unite all things in Jesus Christ, and that this plan is "for the fullness of time." Did Paul see that it would have to come "in the fullness of time," the time must be ripe for it? Time will be ripe for it only when, after having rejected God's plan, we have tried our own plans and they have failed. Then will we turn in our futility to God's plan? Is this "the fullness of time"? Have we tried through the ages to unite the church on this, that, and the other, and have all these attempts resulted in further division? Yes! The time is now ripe to turn to God's plan. All other plans have failed and will fail. This is "the fullness of time."

This plan is breath-taking in its sweep; it is to unite all things in Him—"things in heaven and things on earth." The basis of unity is to be the same in heaven and on earth. Then it is obvious that the only basis of unity in heaven is Jesus Christ. Could we get together in heaven around baptism, around bishops, around church government? To raise the question is to answer it. It would be ridiculous. If it is ridiculous there, it is ridiculous here. It is ridiculous anywhere.

Someone introduced me by saying, "Stanley Jones said that if Jawaharlal Nehru is not in heaven he did not want to go there"; which, of course, I didn't say. I don't want to go to heaven for this, that, or the other, nor to see this, that, or the other; I want to get to heaven to see my Redeemer, to lay the tribute of my gratitude at His feet, and to be united at His feet with all others who love Him. He will be the center of unity in heaven, and He will have to be the center of unity on earth—or there will be no unity.

O Jesus, the center of my love and unity. I give Thee my heart, and I give my hand in brotherhood to all those who make Thee the center of their love. Here we are bound together in unbreakable ties. I thank Thee. Amen.

AFFIRMATION FOR THE DAY: *In heaven I shall glance at golden streets and even the faces of my loved ones, but I shall gaze at the face of my Redeemer.*

MORAL UNIVERSE IS ONE

This verse points to an important truth about predestination: "In him, according to the purpose of him who accomplishes all things according to the counsel of his will" (Eph. 1:11). The truth to which it points is this: God's will is limited to whatever is consistent with being in Him—in Jesus! That is breath-taking. God will not do anything that is un-Christlike! If God asks us to be in Him, He Himself does the same thing—He too is in Him. He cannot and does not act in any way inconsistent with being in Him. He limits His acts, His attitudes, His will, to the framework of being in Him.

This means that the moral universe is one—the same for God and for man. That God obeys the moral laws He lays down for us. That Christlikeness is the standard of conduct of God and man.

> By all that God requires of me,
> I know what He Himself must be.

That means that there is not one standard for God and one for man. God is a consistent God. A ruler in India made a law making polygamy illegal, but he married a second wife. When a furor arose he calmly replied, "I make laws; I don't obey them." He was above law. So the people arose and dethroned him. Humanity is slowly but surely dethroning the gods who do not obey the laws they make. That process of dethroning will leave God the Father of our Lord Jesus Christ on the throne of men's hearts, for He and He alone acts in Christ as He asks us to act in Christ. What a God!

Jesus is God's will for God, and God's will for man. Jesus is the way to act for everybody, everywhere. God could not do an unChristlike thing and still be God. He would violate His own nature. Jesus is the human life of God—God in action under human conditions. When we act in Christ we act universally; we act as God acts and manifest the spirit which God manifests.

O God, my heavenly Father, I see in Jesus Thy wisdom for life and my wisdom for life. I see how to live. What a life I see! I'm breathless with expectancy, for this is Life itself unfolding. I am grateful. Thank Thee. Amen.

AFFIRMATION FOR THE DAY: *Since Jesus is my wisdom for life, I shall work out my life by His wisdom.*

"DESTINED AND APPOINTED"

The following verse reads: "we who first hoped in Christ have been destined and appointed to live for the praise of his glory" (Eph. 1:12). "We who first hoped in Christ"—the phrase may mean that we were among the first in time to hope in Christ, or it may mean that we had no hope until we found it for the first time in Christ. Probably the latter meaning is the true one. Hope is born out of contact with Christ, and to be in Christ is to be in hope. To be out of Christ is to be out of hope.

Hope is a Christian virtue, but not a non-Christian virtue. It was looked on as illusion. The non-Christian position is: "Life will keep the word of promise to your ear and break it to your hope." The Christian position is: "May the God of hope fill you with all joy and peace in believing, so that by the power of the Holy Spirit you may abound in hope" (Rom. 15:13). "Abound in hope"—that is the picture of a Christian. He never knows when he is defeated, for he begins with defeat—the defeat of the cross. You cannot defeat Defeat, for the Christian turns the defeat of the cross into the victory of Easter morning. He sees a sunrise in every sunset, an oak tree in every decaying seed. He sees a saint in every Magdalene, a rock in every wobbly Simon, a new beginning in every sad ending.

"We . . . have been destined and appointed to live for the praise of his glory." We are destined to live in His way, for His way is stamped within our blood, our tissues, our nerves, our make-up. We can live against that destiny, but if we do we get hurt—automatically.

We are appointed to live according to that for which we are destined. Suppose the appointed and the destined were in conflict—destined for one thing, appointed to another. Then we would be hopeless conflicts. But to be destined and appointed to the same thing is to be in hopeful concord. Destined—appointed—alternate beats of the same heart!

O God, my Father, how grateful I am that I'm destined and appointed to be in Christ, to think in Him, to act in Him, to love in Him. When I am in Him I am in Life, abundant, overflowing, eternal, now and hereafter. Amen.

AFFIRMATION FOR THE DAY: *Since His appointment for me is my inherent destiny, I shall accept them as one.*

"SEALED WITH THE PROMISED HOLY SPIRIT"

We go on: "In him you also, who have heard the word of truth, the gospel of your salvation, and have believed in him, were sealed with the promised Holy Spirit, which is the guarantee of our inheritance until we acquire possession of it, to the praise of his glory" (Eph. 1:13-14). "In him you . . . were sealed with the promised Holy Spirit." Why only in Him is the Holy Spirit given? Is this narrow and exclusive? No, it is no more narrow than it is narrow that two and two make four. Two and two make four fits the facts—two and two make five doesn't fit the facts. The Holy Spirit can be given only in Him, for He is the only mold that fits the facts. The Holy Spirit is a Christlike spirit, and if He were given in any other mold except in Christ He would be an un-Christlike spirit. So God is shut up to the necessity of giving the Holy Spirit to those in Christ, for any other mold would be a mold for un-Christlikeness. This would make God the author of untruth, for Christ is Truth.

"Now this he said about the Spirit, which those who believed in him were to receive; for as yet the Spirit had not been given, because Jesus was not yet glorified" (John 7:39). "Because Jesus was not yet glorified"—Jesus had to live, teach, die, rise again, and go to the right hand of the Father before the mold was ready—the mold of the meaning of Christlikeness. Then and only then could God lavish upon us the gift of the Holy Spirit. The power could be safely entrusted to this pattern.

A newspaper clipping read: "Incarnation of Durga," (Kali) "An eight-year-old girl is attracting large crowds. The girl is often seized with spasms when her tongue protrudes out by about six inches and her eyes shine strangely." She is an "incarnation" of the blood-thirsty goddess Kali. Could God give the Holy Spirit if that type of strange weird power were the pattern? No, the pattern had to be Jesus.

O Father, Thou couldst not back Kali-ism or any other ism, for in Jesus we have seen "the express image" of Thy person. What an "image"! That image doesn't misrepresent Thee—it represents Thee. So we wait for the Holy Spirit—wait in Him. Amen.

AFFIRMATION FOR THE DAY: *I wait for the Spirit in Him. I am bound to find, for the Spirit is in Him, therefore in me.*

"THE GUARANTEE OF OUR INHERITANCE"

We must spend another day on: "In him you also, who have heard the word of truth, the gospel of your salvation, and have believed in him, were sealed with the promised Holy Spirit, which is the guarantee of our inheritance until we acquire possession of it, to the praise of his glory" (Eph. 1:13-14).

This sealing by the Holy Spirit is given to those who have "heard the word of truth," "the gospel of [their] salvation," and "have believed in him"—so this gift is a believer's gift, not to be identified with conversion, but something in addition to and subsequent to conversion. It is a sealing of the letter of pardon and reconciliation.

After conversion the unsealed letter is open to influences from the uncleansed subconscious. The Holy Spirit cleanses and consecrates the subconscious drives, co-ordinates the subconscious and the conscious, puts them both under one control and redemption, and produces a unified personality. So the personality is sealed off from inner intrusion. The enemies are now largely from without. The inner citadel is safe—safe in the Holy Spirit's keeping.

This sealing by the Holy Spirit is "the guarantee of our inheritance" until we take possession of it. This is a strange statement—the Holy Spirit the guarantee of the inheritance of heaven. Does He bring an inner unity and consequent joy which is a precursor of our heavenly inheritance? Is heaven unity and joy? Yes. It is a unity and joy around the person of Christ; we are united in Him and we joy in Him. Anyone who has the Holy Spirit has a preview of heaven within. The Holy Spirit is the guarantee of heaven, for His presence within brings heaven. We have heaven to go to heaven in. The Holy Spirit brings a miniature heaven within.

O Blessed Spirit, how grateful I am for this glorious heaven of purity and unity and joy which Thou dost bring within. The absence of it is hell; the presence of it is heaven. So I walk the heavenly way to heaven, with heaven within. I thank Thee.

AFFIRMATION FOR THE DAY: *I am a "guaranteed" person—guaranteed as to goal, direction, and quality.*

"I REFUSE TO ACCEPT MY LIMITATIONS"

Ephesians continues to unfold: "For this reason, because I have heard of your faith in the Lord Jesus and your love toward all the saints" (Eph. 1:15). Here faith and love are connected. They are connected time after time: "Timothy . . . has brought us the good news of your faith and love" (I Thess. 3:6). "Your faith is growing abundantly, and the love of every one of you . . . is increasing" (II Thess. 1:3). Why are they connected—by chance? No, as cause and effect. The love comes out of the faith. To urge people to love without faith results in futility. Love must have its roots in faith.

It is not faith in faith. That makes you strain to have more faith, which makes you have less. It is "faith in the Lord Jesus." When you center your attention on Him, faith grows with the attention. "Whatever gets your attention gets you." Your attention centered on Jesus, you begin to love what He loves and you begin to love with His love.

Dr. Massie, pastor of Tremont Baptist Temple, Boston, past ninety and vigorous, said to the writer, "I will pass on to you my philosophy of life: In view of the resources of God, I refuse to accept my limitations." He did not look at his own limitations; he looked at the resources of God, and as he did so his faith grew.

A Belgian Government official said to the Rev. Mr. Gonjola, head of the amazing Belgian Congo revival, "We've been beating these people to make them clean up, and nothing happens. You make them clean up of their own accord." They looked at Jesus and wanted to clean up—from within. You look at Jesus and your faith grows and out of your faith love grows and out of the process you grow—effortlessly. The Rev. Mr. Gonjola said: "Before the Holy Spirit came I was so proud I wouldn't greet anyone. Now I love everyone." The Holy Spirit got his attention fixed on Jesus, and out of that attention love sprang—love for the very unlovable.

O Holy Spirit, shed abroad in my heart the love of God, so that I can love what I can't love, and believe in people I can't believe in. Then I shall be a constant miracle to myself and others. In Jesus' name. Amen.

AFFIRMATION FOR THE DAY: *Faith and love shall be the alternate beats of my heart this day in everything.*

"SPIRIT OF WISDOM AND REVELATION"

This verse is revealing: "that the God of our Lord Jesus Christ . . . may give you a spirit of wisdom and of revelation in the knowledge of him" (Eph. 1:17). This verse tells how we grow in the knowledge of Him: it comes through "a spirit of wisdom and of revelation."

Wisdom is the heightening of our faculties so that we think better, more accurately, and more deeply. It is the sharpening of the person's thinking and reasoning powers. It is man's search upward. Some would say that that method of research is the only method of knowledge. John Dewey took that position—there is no knowledge except that which comes from man's thinking and discovery.

On the other hand, there are those who depend on revelation entirely. They sit with a blank sheet of paper and write down what is "given" to them. It is all and only revelation.

Both of these "either or" methods are incomplete. It is "both and." Wisdom is to be used and can lead us far, but there come times when wisdom is not enough. We need revelation. God steps in and gives us light and insight not our own. So it is a double process; we reach up with our wisdom, and God reaches down with His revelation. These are the alternate beats of the Christian heart: wisdom—revelation; revelation—wisdom. It is a co-operative enterprise.

This co-operative enterprise saves us from pride and self-sufficiency, and from mental laziness and spiritual dependence. This verse puts the two together: "Think over what I say, for the Lord will grant you understanding in everything" (II Tim. 2:7). "Think . . . the Lord will grant you understanding." So Christianity is muscle and miracle—not too much muscle lest we be strained; not too much miracle lest we be drained. We work as if the whole thing depended on us, and trust as if it depended on God.

O Lord Jesus, we put our minds at Thy disposal. Think through them and then inspire them to think more deeply and to aspire more reverently. Set me afire with a divine curiosity and illuminate me with Thy mind. Amen.

AFFIRMATION FOR THE DAY: *I am being invaded from above by Thy revelation, and pervaded from around me by Thy wisdom. How rich I am!*

"HIS GLORIOUS INHERITANCE IN THE SAINTS"

We must spend another day on "a spirit of wisdom and of revelation in the knowledge of him, having the eyes of your hearts enlightened, that you may know what is the hope to which he has called you, what are the riches of his glorious inheritance in the saints" (Eph. 1:17-18). This verse says that "the eyes of your heart" being enlightened you may know. One would have thought that Paul would have said "the eyes of your mind," for he had just talked about wisdom and revelation. Do we see with the heart? Yes, perhaps the only real seeing is with the heart. A loveless knowledge is blind.

Atomic energy scientists saw only with the mind and produced the horrible monster, the atomic bomb. It was loveless knowledge and has led us to the edge of a precipice. Only as we see with the heart the possibility that atomic energy might be used for the raising of the level of life for everybody will this knowledge become wisdom.

Two things come out of this heart knowledge—"you may know what is the hope to which he has called you." You know the amazing sweep of this redemption—you see what is being done in and for us, and it gives us a great hope. This is what we get out of it all. The other thing is what God gets out of it—"what are the riches of his glorious inheritance in the saints." "His glorious inheritance in the saints." Of all things! I thought God was getting trouble and more trouble out of this process of redemption. Look what He has to put up with—even in the saints! But here it says that God is getting a glorious inheritance in the saints! Is that exaggeration? No! A mother and father think when a child is growing up that they didn't get much in a child except trouble and more trouble. The years come and go, however, and that troublesome boy becomes a great man and a great servant of humanity. The riches of their inheritance is that boy! God will look at us some day and say, "Well, I took a lot of trouble with him, but look at him now. I'm rich in such an inheritance."

O God, my Father, is it possible that Thou canst be rich in me, that I can bring Thee something Thou didst not have before? This humbles me and sends me to the highest heaven. "Glorious inheritance"? Then fill me with Thy glory. Amen.

AFFIRMATION FOR THE DAY: *I shall not be God's problem—I shall be His person.*

"IMMEASURABLE GREATNESS OF HIS POWER"

We continue this glorious study of Ephesians: "what is the immeasurable greatness of his power in us who believe, according to the working of his great might which he accomplished in Christ when he raised him from the dead and made him to sit at His right hand in the heavenly places" (Eph. 1:19-20). Here Paul says that "his great might which he accomplished in Christ when he raised him from the dead"—that same "immeasurable greatness" of power is at work in us who believe. The power that raised Jesus from the dead is working redemptively in us to raise us with Him to sit in the heavenly places—the place of final authority.

The resurrection of Jesus is not something in history to be looked at and admired and rejoiced in; it is something to be appropriated and lived by—something that works in us. The same power, which turned the most abject defeat in history—the defeat of the cross—into the most glorious victory in history—the victory of the Resurrection—is available in Christ now. If I am in Christ I'm not in a defeated Christ; I'm in a Christ Who wrought out the greatest victory ever seen on our planet, and wrought it out not as a sole, unique victory, but as a victory available to all who remain in Him and accept this Victory, not only as a concept, but as something you receive as your working way of life. You are living on the greatest power that was ever manifested on this planet—the power that raised Jesus from the dead.

That means that you walk out of a dead past; the past is behind you. You are living on the Living Christ. "It is no weak Christ with which we have to do, but a Christ of power"—that power manifested in the Resurrection. So you plug in at the highest point—at the point of Resurrection—and live by that kind of power. So we live not by the Babe of Bethlehem, or by the dead Christ on a cross; we live by the Resurrected Christ on the Throne.

O Lord, my God, I live by the most glorious Fact in history—Thy Resurrection. And more—I live by that Fact now on the Throne, and alive forevermore. What more can I ask? I do not ask, I take—take with both hands. Amen.

AFFIRMATION FOR THE DAY: *"It is no weak Christ with which we have to do, but a Christ of power."* (Moffatt)

SADNESS—A CHRISTIAN VIRTUE!

Yesterday's verse is supplemented with this next verse: "even when we were dead through our trespasses, made us alive together with Christ (by grace you have been saved), and raised us up with him and made us sit with him in the heavenly places in Christ Jesus" (Eph. 2;5-6). This verse uses prepositions of identification—"made us alive together *with* Christ" . . . "raised us up *with* Him" . . . "made us sit *with* Him." This is breath-takingly wonderful, but it is "with" —three times "with." The "with" was not enough—it had to be "in"—"in Christ"—"in the heavenly places in Christ Jesus." This verse begins with dead men and ends with those same dead men alive, and alive in the heavenly places—alive "in the heavenly places in Christ Jesus." This is redemption.

The life in Christ is a life in heavenly places. Paul wrote that from prison! In heavenly places and yet in prison! Of the early Christians it was said, "They were completely fearless, absurdly happy, and in constant trouble."

Yet how we have changed that. Aphrates, a converted Persian noble, expounding the Nestorian faith, emphasized "fasting, prayer, love, humility, virginity, continence, wisdom, hospitality, simplicity, patience, gentleness, sadness, purity." Note "sadness" was a Christian virtue! I said to Rufus Moseley: "If I were to preach your funeral service, do you know what I would do? I'd call attention to the miracle of your spirit. You were happy when you were well, and you are happy when you are ill, wracked with pain—that is a greater miracle than your healing." He replied, "Well, I think I'd rather have you preach my funeral service than some of the rest of these. They would be wringing their hands and saying, 'Why did Rufus die?' And you would be singing the Hallelujah Chorus." The person who is in Christ is in heavenly places come sickness, come health, come life, come death.

O Jesus, just to be in Thee is to be in heaven. Thou art heaven—the heaven of reconciliation, the heaven of joy in spite of, the heaven of a song while living in an outer hell. O Jesus, Thou art heaven, and I am in Thee and hence in heaven. Amen.

AFFIRMATION FOR THE DAY: *I may be in a hovel or a house, but in Thee I am "in heavenly places."*

"IMMEASURABLE RICHES OF HIS GRACE"

The next verse is illuminating: "that in the coming ages he might show the immeasurable riches of his grace in kindness toward us in Christ Jesus" (Eph. 2:7). The central thing in Christ Jesus is grace. "Grace and truth came through Jesus Christ." He was full of grace and truth. Others brought truth but no grace. Others still brought grace but no truth. The two came together in Him—His grace was truthful; His truth was gracious. Grace can be defined verbally as unmerited favor, but vitally grace can only be defined as Jesus. There we see grace—the Word of grace become flesh. Looking at Him as grace we see the most beautiful thing ever seen on our planet.

Nothing more beautiful will evolve upon this planet: "in the coming ages he might show the immeasurable riches of his grace." In the unfolding drama of the meaning of creation neither wisdom, nor knowledge, nor power, nor authority, nor goodness will seem to be the thing most precious and wondered at—that thing will be grace. Grace is love applied to the loveless, applied to the least deserving, applied to the positively sinful, applied to the prodigal. Grace is love with open arms. Grace is love with tears upon its cheeks saying, "Come home."

This grace is "immeasurable." All our love is measurable; we love the lovable, the deserving, those who love us in return. But here grace shows Love as immeasurable. There are no limits; no matter what you have done, or have been, no matter what you are, grace has open arms, gives you a new start, opens the door to boundless development. God will have nothing more beautiful to show in the ages to come than the products of His grace. God, Who owns everything, will have nothing richer to show the ages than to show us—the immeasurable riches of His grace. We will be the showpiece of God's riches. He will have nothing more precious to show, and there is nothing God will have more satisfaction in showing.

O Father, we begin to see the meaning of the unfolding purpose of creation—it is re-creation. The redeeming of us who spoiled Thy first creation. Thou hast put together the shattered pieces and art building a temple to grace. We thank Thee. Amen.

AFFIRMATION FOR THE DAY: *Across all my accomplishments "grace" shall be written.*

"CREATED IN CHRIST JESUS FOR GOOD WORKS"

The drama unfolds: "For we are his workmanship, created in Christ Jesus for good works, which God prepared beforehand, that we should walk in them" (Eph. 2:10). This verse is the corrective of the preceding verses: "For by grace you have been saved through faith; and this is not your own doing, it is the gift of God—not because of works, lest any man should boast" (Eph. 2:8-9). One verse says: "you have been saved . . . not because of works," and the next one says: "created in Christ Jesus for good works." This gives the Christian position regarding good works—we are not saved *because of* good works, but we are saved *for* good works. Good works do not come out as salvation, they are the outcome of salvation. Salvation is by grace through faith—it is the gift of God. You cannot retain it, however, unless you show this grace at work by good works.

The good works come out of His good "workmanship." He doesn't begin by changing our deeds; He begins by changing us. The good deeds naturally and supernaturally come out of the good person. "The good man out of his good store brings forth good." The fountain is cleansed, and the stream flows pure.

We are destined to bring forth these good works—"good works, which God prepared beforehand." Are we destined to do certain things? Yes, and that destiny is written into the constitution of our being—written into our nerves, our organs, our blood, our tissues. Some things throw sand in the machinery of human living. What are they? Hate, fear, self-centeredness, guilt. We are destined by our make-up not to feel these things. On the other hand, other things put oil in the machinery of human living. What are they? Love, faith, self-giving, joy of forgiveness. Then we are destined to love, to have faith, to give ourselves, to enjoy forgiveness, and to give it. That destiny is written in us, hence inescapable. We can live against that destiny, but if we do we get hurt automatically.

O Father, when we walk in Thy ways we walk; when we try to walk in some other way we stumble and fall. When we take Thy way we take our own. Thy way is our freedom. Help me to take Thy way, for then I shall be free. Amen.

AFFIRMATION FOR THE DAY: *I am predestined by the very structure of my being to love, to be like Him.*

"HE IS OUR PEACE"

Our next verse is growingly important: "But now in Christ Jesus you who were once far off have been brought near in the blood of Christ. For he is our peace, who has made us both one" (Eph. 2:13-14). We often hear of dividing the word "atonement" into "at-one-ment"—atonement is an at-one-ment with God. Here Paul says that the atonement is an at-one-ment with each other—"you . . . have been brought near in the blood of Christ."

Is the blood of Christ some magic wand that is waved over us and makes us one? No. If you are humble enough to cease trying to make atonement for your sins by self-effort and humbly accept the atonement Jesus has made by His blood, then you will automatically become one with everyone who is humble enough to accept the same gift. Humility toward Christ produces humility toward each other. We automatically join the Society of the Receivers. If you belong to those who try to climb the ladder to God to find Him at the topmost rung of the ladder of worthiness, you strive to attain salvation. There is nothing to bind together the attainers—they are covertly competitive, for they are self-assertive. If, however, you belong to those who believe that God meets us at the bottom-most rung of the ladder as sinners, where you do not attain but obtain salvation as the gift of God, then you melt into each others' arms as you talk joyfully about His grace. Grace is by its very nature co-operative around the redeeming Person of Jesus.

"He is our peace, who has made us both one." You do not have to find unity in Christ. You have it inherently. All you have to do is to express the unity which is ours in Him. You may betray that oneness, but you cannot deny it, for it is inherent. A three-hour meeting was held by bitterly opposed parties—opposed in their views of the sacrament. At the close of three hours of inconclusive debate one said, "Well, we can come together at the place of Christ." They could.

O Jesus, Thou art our peace. Around everything else we divide; around Thee we unite. Thou hast made us both one, inseparable as long as we belong inseparably to Thee. When we step out of Thee we step out of each other. Keep us close. Amen.

AFFIRMATION FOR THE DAY: *"He is our peace"—when I am in Him I'm in peace—with myself, my brother, and God—I'm in peace.*

"A NEW MAN OUT OF BOTH PARTIES"

A very informative verse now comes: "that he might create in himself one man in place of two, so making peace" (Eph. 2:15). This verse arose out of the Scriptures during World War II and became my guiding star during the war and has been since. How do we find peace? Paul lifts up out of reality a universal method of finding peace: Get each party to change and come to a third position—a new man out of both parties. There is no other way to peace, from the simplest relationship to the most complex.

For example, take the relationship between a husband and a wife. If the husband conquers the wife and suppresses her there will be no peace—she will plan revenge. Or vice versa. Both must change and come to a third position—the union. Neither one conquers the other, but the union conquers them both. That brings peace.

If the white race attempts to conquer the colored race, as is being attempted in South Africa and in some parts of the United States, there will be no peace. There will be nothing but planned revenge and insecurity. It is said that every white man in South Africa has to have, not one dog, but two—a little dog to wake up the big dog! Why this insecurity and fear? When I was there several years ago, the South African parliament put through thirty-seven restrictive bills taking away the last bit of franchise from the native African. A white legislator said, "Now that we have clipped the native's wings we must be kind to him and be an example to the rest of the world as to how we treat the native." "Kind to him"—while the African is "under" be kind to him, but not just. This underlying philosophy is at the basis of conditions in that unhappiest and most insecure land of the world. If the white man would change and be willing to make a new man out of both parties, peace would automatically come. Now there is only hate and insecurity and war.

O Lord Jesus, Thou art creating in Thyself the new man—the new man who will rule in righteousness and justice and hence in peace. Help me to be that new man in every situation this day, laying hands of peace on everything. Amen.

AFFIRMATION FOR THE DAY: *"Gave us the ministry of reconciliation"—may I exercise the ministry of reconciliation in every situation today.*

"NO OTHER FOUNDATION"

This passage points in the same direction as the previous passages: "built upon the foundation of the apostles and prophets, Christ Jesus himself being the chief cornerstone, in whom the whole structure is joined together and grows into a holy temple in the Lord" (Eph. 2:20-21). These verses raise two questions: Upon what does the Christian Church rest? This verse says, "upon the foundation of the apostles and prophets." Another passage of Paul says: "For no other foundation can anyone lay than that which is laid, which is Jesus Christ" (I Cor. 3:11). Here in this Ephesians passage he says "the apostles and the prophets" are the foundation. Which is right? There is no doubt that the Corinthian passage represents the real view of Paul, and that in the Ephesians passage he was telling the Gentiles that they were now in the line of the Hebrew heritage of the apostles and the prophets.

The attempt to found the church on the apostles, thus trying to prove that the claimant has an "apostolic church," has created more confusion and disruption in the Christian Church than any other one thing. There is no such thing as an "apostolic church," and there ought to be none. The apostles were not the terminus of our faith—it does not rest on them. It rests on Jesus Christ. We are not an "apostolic church"—we are a Christian Church. Jesus Christ is the terminus of our faith. Our faith, and consequently our church, does not rest on wobbly apostles, but on the unchanging Lord!

Besides, this passage doesn't say that the apostles were the foundation—it says "the apostles and the prophets." As "the prophets" was a generic term, meaning the forthtellers of the good news, so "the apostles" must have been generic too, meaning "those sent," and it certainly included Paul who called himself an apostle. The prophets and apostles were "like living stones . . . built into a spiritual house" (I Pet. 2:5), but certainly not the foundation.

O Jesus Christ, Thou and thou alone art the foundation of our faith and our church. A structure built on wobbly human beings would be a wobbly structure. Only Thou art the foundation; we rest our souls and our destiny on Thee. Amen.

AFFIRMATION FOR THE DAY:

> On Christ, the solid rock, I stand;
> All other ground is sinking sand.

"A DWELLING PLACE OF GOD IN THE SPIRIT"

We must put together part of yesterday's verse and a new one: "in whom the whole structure is joined together and grows into a holy temple in the Lord; in whom you also are built into it for a dwelling place of God in the Spirit" (Eph. 2:21-22). This portion makes clear who the center of the Christian faith is; it is not the apostles nor the prophets—"in whom [Christ] the whole structure is joined together"—in Christ, not in them. He holds together the whole structure—the Church. When built on the apostles it is divisive; when built on Jesus Christ it is uniting—the whole structure is joined together. Out of Him it flies apart, the ages being witness. "The whole structure . . . grows into a holy temple in the Lord"—"in the Lord," note. Out of Him—"in the apostles"—it grows into a holy tempest about "apostolic succession."

Again "in whom [not in them] you also are built into it for a dwelling place of God in the Spirit." When you are in Christ, you "are built into it"—the church. If you are not in Christ, but in yourself, then you are not in the church. *The church is the society of those who are in Christ.* Being in the apostles would not make you in the church. One would have to ask, Which apostle? When? "They all forsook Him and fled."

In Christ you are in God and the Spirit is in you—"a dwelling place of God in the Spirit." The "dwelling place of God in the Spirit" gives the sense of permanency—a dwelling place, not a temporary inn where guests come and go. The Spirit does not come and go with our emotions. "He shall abide with you forever." When He comes in, He comes in to stay. The only way we can get Him out is to sin Him out. To sin Him out does not mean a temporary lapse—it means a permanent sin set of the will. This possibility of being a permanent dwelling place of God in the Spirit, individually and collectively, is the most beautiful thing imaginable.

O Jesus, when I have Thee I have God and I have the Spirit. What more can I have? When I have Thee I have Everything—plus. I am rich—immeasurably rich. Help me to want nothing besides, for there is nothing besides. Amen.

AFFIRMATION FOR THE DAY: *I am the "dwelling place of God in the Spirit"—let that humble, embolden, and empower me.*

"GENTILES . . . PARTAKERS OF THE PROMISE IN CHRIST JESUS"

"You can perceive my insight into the mystery of Christ, which was not made known to the sons of men in other generations as it has now been revealed to his holy apostles and prophets by the Spirit; that is, how the Gentiles are fellow heirs, members of the same body, and partakers of the promise in Christ Jesus through the gospel" (Eph. 3:4-6). When Paul wrote that he wrote a very radical thing, for the pious Jew thanked God every day that he was "not born a woman, a leper, or a Gentile." Here Paul said that Gentiles were members "of the same body," "fellow heirs," "partakers of the promise in Christ Jesus." A new concept of society had emerged, and that new concept put its arms around everybody and made them one Family of God in Christ.

Two thousand years have gone by since then, and we are still struggling with this conception. This conception is knocking at the gates of exclusion and so-called superiorities demanding entrance. Behind walled barricades the voice comes: "You're inferior. Not allowed." Upon those walls of exclusion, however, there is a hand writing, "There are no permanently inferior or permanently superior races—only developed and underdeveloped races. Given the same stimulus and the same incentive, the brain of humanity will come out about the same." The facts are with that writing. So "superiorities" are crumbling—crumbling before the facts. I have asked principals of high schools in the Northern section of America where there has been integration for many years whether there is any difference in the examination results between the races. They have one reply, "No difference. There are very bright white and very bright black, and very dull white and very dull black and all shades between, modified slightly by the cultural background out of which they come." The African, looked on as inferior, feels he must prove himself superior—and often does! In the new world everybody must be fellow heirs.

Dear Father, we thank Thee for this social revolution. Thy "little children" are on the march out of suppression and poverty into fuller life. Guide them to the feet of Thy Son. There everyone is a person for whom Christ died. Amen.

AFFIRMATION FOR THE DAY: *I shall look on people not as problems, but as possibilities.*

"THE ETERNAL PURPOSE"

This vital passage follows: "This was according to the eternal purpose which he has realized in Christ Jesus our Lord" (Eph. 3:11). "The eternal purpose . . . realized in Christ Jesus our Lord." In Jesus purpose became performance; the idea became fact; the Word became flesh. In all other religions it is the word become word—a philosophy or a moralism. In Jesus, and in Jesus alone, the Word became flesh.

Through the ages men have purposed and have come short of that purpose. Once God purposed to redeem man through Jesus, and at the close of the fulfillment of that purpose Jesus could say, "It is finished." It was! "Realized in Christ Jesus"—that is the most decisive verse in religious literature. In all faiths, except in Jesus Christ, there is verbal anticipation; only in Jesus is there realization. I have said to seekers in India, "If you can find God in some other way, then find and come back and tell me about it." I've never had anyone to return to tell me he had found. A Hindu once said to Canon Holland, "You Christians find God in Christ; we Hindus find Him in ourselves. It is all the same." "With this difference," replied Holland, "real conversions do take place through Christ. I can take you to many in this city who will tell you they have found God through Christ." The Hindu replied, "There you win. I have found none who have found God in themselves."

There is only one issue left to modern man: it is increasingly Christ or nothing. All the other alternatives are being eliminated. A non-Christian conducted a radio interview with a pastor in Japan. When the minister said he regretted the comparative smallness of the number of Christians in Japan, the interviewer replied, "Your influence has gone beyond your numbers. Take me—I'm no longer a Buddhist. If I'm to be anything, I've got to be a Christian. So don't be discouraged—you'll get me and those like me, sooner or later. There is no alternative." There really is none!

O Jesus, my Lord, since God's purposes were realized in Thee, let my purposes be realized in Thee. Out of Thee there is nothing but barren futility. In Thee there is nothing but realized fulfillment. In Thee I am I—plus. I thank Thee. Amen.

AFFIRMATION FOR THE DAY: *The eternal purpose of God will be realized concretely in me today and always.*

"CONFIDENCE OF ACCESS"

This verse reveals much: "in whom we have boldness and confidence of access through our faith in him" (Eph. 3:12). We are so used to the possibility of access contained in the above that we take it for granted. Outside of Jesus Christ, however, there is no feeling of access to anything except our own resources.

Eric Fromm gives us the verdict of modern pagan psychiatry about the dilemma of modern man:

There is only one solution to his problem: to face the truth, to acknowledge his fundamental aloneness and solitude in a universe indifferent to his fate, to recognize that there is no power transcending him which can solve his problem for him. If he faces the truth without panic he will recognize that there is no meaning to life except the meaning man gives his life by the unfolding of his powers, by living productively.

Albert C. Outler sums up Fromm's position: "Man is alone in a morally neutral universe. Man is, finally, his own and only moral referent" (*Psychotherapy and the Christian Message*, pps. 124, 126). Man has no "access" to God or nature—he is shut up to himself. Bleak prospect!

Nothing could be further from the Christian position, for in it "we have boldness and confidence of access"—access to the highest—to God—and access to that highest in its most available form—Jesus. In Jesus everything is open. The Way is open out of prison into freedom, out of defeat into victory, out of loneliness into fellowship, out of sin into forgiveness and reconciliation, out of determinism into open freedom, out of misery into mastery, out of oneself into God. In Jesus you are out of nothingness and into Everything. No wonder Fromm speaks of "panic" and no wonder Paul speaks of "boldness and confidence"! One ends in panic and the other in possibility. One points to an Open Door and the other points to an open door into the bleak dungeon of yourself where you are locked in forever.

O Jesus, how can I thank Thee enough for this access—access to Thy Everything. It turns my panic into Thy possibilities. I can be more than I can be—in Thee. My hell becomes Thy heaven—and only a step out of one into the other. Amen.

AFFIRMATION FOR THE DAY: *I belong not to panic, but to possibility—I have full access to God and His resources.*

THE MEANING OF "ACCESS"

We pause another day on "access"—access to what? These verses try to tell us: "that according to the riches of his glory he may grant you to be strengthened with might through his Spirit in the inner man, and that Christ may dwell in your hearts through faith; that you, being rooted and grounded in love, may have power to comprehend with all the saints what is the breadth and length and height and depth, and to know the love of Christ which surpasses knowledge, that you may be filled with all the fullness of God" (Eph. 3:16-19).

Here words break down under the weight of new meaning—this not only surpasses knowledge, but surpasses description! It is "the unspeakable gift." Look at the things to which we have access when in Christ: (1) We have access to "the riches of his glory." The riches of His humiliation—His earthly life—are wonderful, but the riches of His glory! What they are I can only imagine. (2) Access to being "strengthened with might through his Spirit in the inner man"—the Holy Spirit, Who is applied redemption, working redemptively in the inner man. (3) Access to Christ dwelling in our hearts through faith. The Holy Spirit and Christ both dwell in the heart—the living Christ is the Holy Spirit with a face—personalized. (4) Access to the life that is rooted and grounded in love. (5) Access to being able to comprehend with all saints, in the words of a Roman Catholic saint, that the love of Christ "is as wide as the limits of the universe, long as the ages of eternity, deep as the abyss from which He redeemed us, and as high as the throne of God itself." (6) Access to being able to know the love of Christ which passes knowledge. (7) Access to being filled with the fullness of God. These accesses to seven wonderful phases of Reality make cheap and shallow the psychiatrist's access to one's own resources and only to one's resources. The comment of George Carver to me concerning a scientific atheist: "The poor man, the poor man," is apropos.

O Jesus, Lord, Thou dost open everything to those who are in Thee. To be in Thee is to be in everything good that is in this universe. I am rich beyond calculation or imagination. I am rich with all the riches of God. Amen.

AFFIRMATION FOR THE DAY: *I am rich in potentiality—I shall be rich in actuality by my receptivity.*

THE CLIMAX!

The climax: "Now to him who by the power at work within us is able to do far more abundantly than all that we ask or think, to him be glory in the church and in Christ Jesus to all generations forever and ever" (Eph. 3:20-21). After this climax there was nothing for Paul to say but Amen! He had said all there was to say regarding redemption. The rest could only be commentary.

He started off this final paragraph by saying: "Now to him who by the power at work within us"—the power at work *within us*. God's power to work *on us* is limited—limited by the extent of our cooperation, but His power to work *within* us is unlimited, for if it is within us it presupposes our co-operation. If there is full co-operation within us God's hands are untied; He is free—free to give—and how!

Paul tells us how! He is able to do what we ask and our asking seems unlimited. Paul said, "all that we ask." The "all" applies to not only all we ask but all that "we ask or think"—you can think beyond your asking. And then "more" than we ask or think; and then "far more" than we ask or think; and then the last "far more abundantly." Adjectives and adverbs fail. The rest is worship. This is "the unspeakable gift." We are lost in wonder, love and praise!

The final ascription is: "to him be glory in the church and in Christ Jesus to all generations for ever and ever." "Glory in the church"—this is the glory limited—limited to this world, the period of existence of the church. Glory in Christ Jesus, however, is beyond this world and endless—"for ever and ever." As long as we are in Christ Jesus God is glorified. You do not have to step out of Jesus and concentrate on God to glorify God. Stay in Jesus Christ and you glorify God, for Jesus is God glorified because He is God as self-giving.

O God, my Father, Thou canst do everything for us if only we live and move and have our being in Jesus. In Jesus we find Thee simplified, approachable, lovable. So we have one duty and aim—to stay in Jesus Christ. Amen.

AFFIRMATION FOR THE DAY: *My one and only duty and obligation is to abide in Jesus. All else follows.*

"GROW UP IN EVERY WAY"

Another climax is reached: "Rather, speaking the truth in love, we are to grow up in every way into him who is the head, into Christ, from Whom the whole body, joined and knit together by every joint with which it is supplied, when each part is working properly, makes bodily growth and upbuilds itself in love" (Eph. 4:15-16).

This verse emphasizes a truth that you become what you habitually give out: "speaking the truth in love . . . upbuilds itself in love." You give out love, and you become a loving person. You are born of the qualities which you habitually give out. Give out criticism, and you become critical. The person is the payoff. So give out love and only love, and you are the payoff—a loving person.

You are to speak the truth in love. You can speak the truth without love and it will not produce redemption, but rebellion. Truth without love can produce a philosophy or a moralism, but bare truth can never redeem. That is why God had to wrap His Truth in Love and call His name Jesus. In Jesus love speaks, acts, and thinks in every word, every syllable, every deed. He is love in action.

When we are in Jesus and speak the truth in love, then we grow up in every way into Him. Note the "in every way"—mentally, emotionally, volitionally, physically, socially. You don't have to wither any of these in order to grow up into Him. An Indian student said he wanted to surrender to Christ, but since he was a good basketball player he found it difficult to desert the game. I told him not to desert it, but to dedicate it. Fully surrendered to Christ he would probably be a better basketball player. Everything good will be better. Love turns all our bad into good, our good into better, our better into best, our best into His Best. This contributes to the whole: "when each part is working properly . . . upbuilds itself in love." "Each part is working properly"—what a responsibility for oneself and others!

O Jesus, I would grow up into Thee in every way. Save me from growing up into Thee lopsidedly—my emotions overdeveloped and my mind underdeveloped, my will not keeping up with my mind. I would be growing up in every way in Thee. Amen.

AFFIRMATION FOR THE DAY: *Trim me, O God, where I'm overgrown, and stimulate me where I'm underdeveloped.*

"FUTILITY OF THEIR MINDS"

Again Ephesians becomes luminous: "Now this I affirm and testify in the Lord, that you must no longer live as the Gentiles do, in the futility of their minds" (Eph. 4:17). This verse is instructive: "Now this I affirm and testify in the Lord"—"in the Lord" all our affirmations become testimonies. Outside the Lord you can affirm but you cannot testify. Outside Jesus all our affirmations are affirmations—the Word becomes word, but in Jesus all my affirmations become testimonies—the Word becomes flesh.

Affirmation says "that"—something outside me, but testimony says "this"—something inside me. Christianity has its "that"—the Jesus of history, but the Jesus of history becomes the Christ of experience—the "that" becomes "this." The two are put together in the words of Peter on the day of Pentecost. "This is that"—this which they had found in the Holy Spirit was that which was spoken of by the prophet Joel.

In the Epistle of I John the word "this" is found twenty-eight times. This Epistle was the last Epistle written, and it was filled with "this"—filled with the fact of Christianity as experience. Historical? Yes. Experiential? Yes. Both.

There are two kinds of reality—the reality of history and the reality of experience. Each can be proved to a very high degree of certainty. The highest degree of certainty, however, is where the reality of history becomes the reality of experience, where they both say the same thing, corroborate each other. When we are in Jesus Christ we have the highest certainty possible—the two kinds of reality dovetail and speak the same thing—in Jesus, the historical reality; in Christ, the experiential reality; in Jesus Christ, the glorious combination of the two.

So in preaching Jesus Christ we affirm the gospel as it was in Jesus and we testify to the gospel as it is in us. Affirmation and testimony are two sides of one Reality.

O Jesus Christ, Thou art my message and my experience. Everything historically promised is experimentally verified. What certainty, what fire, what joy! I could find nothing more sure and more secure. I thank Thee. Amen.

AFFIRMATION FOR THE DAY: *I shall affirm only that which I have experienced—my preaching will be testimony.*

"AS THE TRUTH IS IN JESUS"

This verse follows from the last: "You did not so learn Christ!—assuming that you have heard about him and were taught in him, as the truth is in Jesus" (Eph. 4:20-21). This verse shows how, when you lose the correction of the Jesus of history and concentrate on the Christ of experience, you can run into all sorts of futility.

The Christian faith is static and dynamic. It is static in that something happened in history two thousand years ago that can never happen again—God's self-revelation of Himself in Jesus. That is fixed and final. We are given in Jesus a standard for God and for man. We see what God is like and what we can be like. God is Christlike; we can be Christlike. The idea of periodic and continuing incarnations runs us into all kinds of absurdities.

I sat in a train in India and watched people at every station come into the compartment and fall at the feet of a sadhu—a holy man. I asked his disciple who he was, and he replied, "He is God." I could see he was a spastic unable to coordinate his speech properly. The weird was to be worshiped. Had he been normal the people would not have glanced at him twice. Another case of the so-called messiahship is that of Krishnamurti, whom I have interviewed and whom I have heard swear in good round English.

No, the Christian faith is static—it is fixed once and for all in history. It is dynamic, however; it goes beyond history and enters into experience. We remember Jesus Christ, and we realize Jesus Christ. His revelation is fixed and unfolding—forever ahead of us in history. Jesus stands on the further side of our twenty centuries, forever beckoning us on. This unfolding revelation is according to a pattern—"as the truth is in Jesus." The Holy Spirit guides us into all the truth for "He will take what is Mine and declare it to you." Jesus is the Textbook in the school of the Spirit. You are taught not merely about Him, you are taught in Him. To be taught about Him is verbal theology; to be taught in Him is vital Christianity.

O Jesus, my Lord, I want to be taught in Thee, for then I shall not merely listen, I shall live what I hear. I shall be the informed and the illustration. The Word will become flesh in me. I am in a school of Life. I thank Thee. Amen.

AFFIRMATION FOR THE DAY: *Since I can only be taught in Him, I shall be in Him every moment lest I miss the highest.*

"AS GOD IN CHRIST FORGAVE YOU"

Now this penetrating verse: "and be kind to one another, tenderhearted, forgiving one another, as God in Christ forgave you" (Eph. 4:32).

Here Paul reaches one of those periodic climaxes. He told them what they were to put off: (1) "Put off your old nature . . . and be renewed in the spirit of your minds" (vss. 22-23). (2) "Put on the new nature, created after the likeness of God" (vs. 24). (3) "Therefore putting away falsehood . . ." (vs. 25). (4) "Let all bitterness and wrath and anger and clamor and slander be put away from you, with all malice" (vs. 31). These were the things to let go, and this to let come: "be kind to one another, tenderhearted, forgiving one another, as God in Christ forgave you." That last phrase is the high watermark of morality in the universe: "Treat one another as God treats you in Christ."

How does God forgive in Christ? Lightly? "Oh, well, you're only human. I can't expect too much from you. I'm God, I have the authority, so I'm letting you off." Nothing could be further from God's forgiveness in Christ. In Christ it costs God to forgive. The cross is the price that God pays in order to forgive sins. He offers forgiveness in a nail-pierced hand.

We are to forgive through a costly forgiveness. We must bear the sins of the one forgiven in our very bodies and souls. We too must offer forgiveness in nail-pierced hands—and hearts.

But God not only forgives with a costly forgiveness—He forgives with a generous forgiveness. He forgives with no conditions attached. He blots it out of the book of His remembrance. We stand before Him as though we had never sinned. We must forgive as God forgives—generously, completely, finally. If we do not forgive we break down the bridge over which we must cross—the bridge of forgiveness. The forgiveness which we get and give in Christ is the most beautiful and blessed thing this planet knows.

O Blessed, Forgiving God, make my forgiveness as tender and loving as Thy forgiveness. Let me hold no corners of unforgiveness in my heart. Let me bury anything in the sea of Thy forgetfulness—this to everybody, everywhere. Amen.

AFFIRMATION FOR THE DAY: *Unforgiveness is a cancer—I cannot afford to live with a cancer.*

"IN THE KINGDOM OF CHRIST"

A further step: "Be sure of this, that no immoral or impure man, nor one who is covetous (that is, an idolator), has any inheritance in the kingdom of Christ and of God" (Eph. 5:5). Here Paul said, that neither sins of the flesh ("immoral or impure man"), nor the sins of the disposition ("covetous [that is an idolator]") has any inheritance "in the kingdom of Christ."

This is the first time in the New Testament we have come across the truth that being in Christ means being in the Kingdom of Christ. It is the first time, too, we have come across the fact that being in the kingdom of Christ is the same as being in the kingdom of God.

Now the idea of being in Christ needs the emphasis of the fact that being in Christ means being in the kingdom of Christ. Otherwise being in Him may come to mean a private matter, very personal, but with no social or corporate meanings. It cannot be emphasized too strongly that the entrance into the kingdom of Christ is personal and by a new birth, but the nature of that kingdom is social. When you come into Christ you come into a universal Order, the Kingdom, which embraces all relationships, personal, and social. To be in Christ is to be in the Kingdom which controls your total conduct. All compartmentalisms are down, life is one under one control, the Kingdom.

A woman didn't like the teaching of a theological professor of a certain seminary, and she said, "My mother prayed one man out of this world. And if that professor doesn't change his teaching I'll pray him out of the world." Here was a Christian who used prayer as a means of paying off private grudges! This is private religion, with unsocial application.

In Bombay there is a sign over a liquor shop, "If God be for us, who can be against us?" The kingdom as an all-controlling and all-redeeming Order would save from a disastrous bifurcation of life. To be in Christ is to be in a Kingdom which embraces all and redeems all. If it doesn't redeem all it redeems none.

O Christ, my Lord and my God, I thank Thee that when I come into Thee I come into a Kingdom—a Kingdom which demands a total obedience in the total life. I am made for total obedience so I give it totally. And I'm free! Amen.

AFFIRMATION FOR THE DAY: *A personal religion that isn't social, isn't personal—it is nothing.*

"LIGHT IN THE LORD"

This verse is luminous: "for once you were darkness, but now you are light in the Lord; walk as children of light" (Eph. 5:8). This verse is penetratingly true—"once you were darkness"—not *in* darkness, but darkness itself. It is possible to live in darkness until the darkness penetrates you and you become darkness. The payoff is the person. You become what you habitually think and act upon. That is the punishment. It is automatic.

It is also true the other way round: "now you are light in the Lord." You are not merely *in* the light—you are light as long as you stay in the Lord. That is one of the most important facts of being in Christ—you become what He is. Imperfectly, of course, and always finite, but as you live in the Light you become light. You speak and think the Truth so that you become truth. You think and act upon His purity until you become purity—a center of contagious purity. You live in His Love until you become love. When people think of you they think of love—automatically.

If you step out of Christ into yourself you become darkness—sometimes gradually. There was a good man who gradually gathered ten thousand disciples around him. Then his ego instead of Christ became the center. He had visions and dreams and communications which told that he was greater than Luther, which sent him into assumed abasement but in secret pride. He was not to die; he was to be translated into heaven. He died. He was not to decay. His followers kept the body until they were compelled to bury it. It all turned into darkness and left his followers groping in disappointment and darkness. In the Lord he was light—in himself he was darkness.

"A saint is one who lets the light through." He lets it through and becomes light.

O Jesus, Lord, let me stand in Thy Light until I become luminous with Thee. Let me walk as a child of light until I shall not only give the Light, I shall be the light. In Thee I am light, in myself darkness. Amen.

AFFIRMATION FOR THE DAY: *As a son of light I will admit no dark spots in my character.*

"ALWAYS AND FOR EVERYTHING"

This verse lifts us: "always and for everything giving thanks in the name of our Lord Jesus Christ to God the Father" (Eph. 5:20). This verse gives the spiritual climate of being in Christ. In His Name we give thanks always for everything. The climate is thanksgiving. Is this rhetoric or reality? It is reality.

In Christ you are in One Who made something out of everything that happened. He could and did give thanks always for everything, for everything was opportunity to Him. He turned his interruptions into interpretations. His oppositions into opportunities, His Calvary into an Easter Morning. He didn't bear trouble, He used it. Everything furthered Him.

I walked in meditation under a great banyan tree in an Indian garden. I paused to examine a root reaching down from one of the branches, reaching toward its mother, the earth. Someone had facetiously tied the end of the root into a knot and tucked in the end so it could not reach further toward the earth. It was blocked in its progress. No, the root put out three smaller roots from the knotted root and they were on their way down below the knot. Circumstances may tie you in knots, but the life of Christ in you will put forth fresh roots even from your knots. Strangely enough, your very knots untie you—give you a fresh start.

Amy Wilson Carmichael, a saintly missionary who suffered for eighteen long years, had as her life text: "Blessed is he who is offended by nothing in Me"—one who takes no offense with any of My dealings with him. This is beautiful, but this verse goes further—it says positively that we are to give thanks always for everything. The secret of doing this is the portion which says, "in the Name of our Lord Jesus Christ." We give thanks in His Name, for His dear sake. That makes everything not only bearable, but usable. He redeems everything and makes it contribute.

O Jesus my Lord, Thou art Lord of everything that happens. In Thy hands everything is fruitful—pain, frustration, failure. Thou dost turn everything into Everything. So give me the dancing, thankful heart. In Thy name. Amen.

AFFIRMATION FOR THE DAY: *All my thanksgivings turn into thanksliv-ings—I become what I'm thankful for.*

"TAKE THAT FOR JESUS' SAKE"

This is a commonplace but very important verse: "Children, obey your parents in the Lord, for this is right" (Eph. 6:1). This verse is important for it raises the question of obedience to authority other than the authority of being in the Lord. The tendency may be, "Well, I'm in Christ, I therefore obey no one but Him." This verse answers that: You are to obey others, but you are to do it in the Lord. Just what does that mean?

A verse in the previous chapter is luminous in this connection: "Be subject to one another out of reverence for Christ" (Eph. 5:21). "To be is to be in relations." Sometimes those relations mean that we have to be subject to others. What is the right attitude to take? Some would answer, "Submit for duty's sake." Good, but not good enough. You may submit outwardly, but with inner reservations or rebellion. "Do everything out of reverence for life," said Schweitzer—again good, but not good enough. Much of life, human and subhuman, is not worthy of reverence. The Christian answer: "be subject to one another out of reverence for Christ." That means that you surrender to Christ, primarily and absolutely, then having submitted to Him you can submit to others out of reverence for Him; you do it for His dear sake. Then you can save your inner self-respect: "I have submitted to Him, now I can submit to you for His sake." That saves the relationship and saves your self-respect. You can do it with joy. Even submitting to tyranny and wrong can be bearable—with joy. A man threw a stone at a Quaker and said, "Take that for Jesus' sake." The Quaker replied, "I do." Everything can be not merely borne, but can be accepted as an opportunity to accept it for Jesus' sake. That brings you out on top—not under. Nothing can hurt you, for the balm of doing everything for His sake heals everything. It tends to heal the relationship, for it gets at the heart of the wrongdoer—appeals to him.

O Jesus, I submit to Thee, fully and absolutely. Now for Thy dear Name's sake I can submit to others. That makes me free from tyranny and oppression. In submitting to Thee all the wrongs done to me become rights. I thank Thee. Amen.

AFFIRMATION FOR THE DAY: *Everything for His sake turns out as everything for my good.*

"STRONG IN THE LORD"

Now this glorious passage: "Finally, be strong in the Lord and in the strength of his might" (Eph. 6:10). This verse answers a query in some minds: Doesn't this submission to Jesus and others produce weak, submissive types of character?

It does the very opposite. A Swedish artist has painted a picture illustrating the text: "Except a grain of wheat fall into the ground and die it abides by itself alone." One portion depicts the abiding by itself alone—a person tied up with himself and confined to a narrow shell—the self-centered. Another depicts the herd-centered as in Communism—the shell is larger, really a bag, where the inmates are tied to one another, and around the edge of the bag is a rope held at the mouth by a hand—the hand of Stalin. The third portion depicts those who have surrendered themselves to Christ and are rising out of their shells into a free, full, voluntary fellowship. They are the strong and free in the Lord.

Moreover, you become a strong person inherently by being in the Lord. It is a truism to say that an organism can expend as much as it takes in and no more. Its capacity to grow and give is determined by its capacity to receive. Receptivity is the law of life. The humanists say that we are environed by a physical environment only. We take in what we can from that environment, but nothing more. The Christian, however, believes in and experiences a higher environment—the environment of being in the Lord. He receives from that environment. Which will produce the stronger type of person—the one who lives by a physical environment only, or the one who lives "strong in the Lord and in the strength of His might"? The one who is strong in the Lord is strong in himself. A friend wrote, "Don't tax your strength." I replied, "I don't tax my strength. I take His strength and live by the strength of Another." I expend what I take in—from Him!

O Jesus, my Lord, I am strong in strength not my own, I love by love not my own, I live by life not my own. I am a little child—receiving, receiving. But oh, how strong—giving, giving—and never exhausted; always full! I thank Thee. Amen.

AFFIRMATION FOR THE DAY: *I take from God with both hands so I can give to others with both hands.*

DOES BEING IN CHRIST
MAKE YOU INDEPENDENT OF OTHERS?

Now the human element comes in: "Now that you may know how I am and what I am doing, Tychicus the beloved brother and faithful minister in the Lord will tell you everything" (Eph. 6:21). When we are in Christ are we shut off from relationships with others and their ministrations to us? When we are in Christ are we isolated and insulated from human help and fellowship? Do we become antisocial or unsocial? This verse answers that. Tychicus was "a beloved brother" as well as "a faithful minister." Being in the Lord made them more deeply one in the Brotherhood.

To the description in Ephesians of Tychicus as "a beloved brother and faithful minister," Colossians adds, "a beloved brother and faithful minister and fellow servant in the Lord (Col. 4:7). The last—"fellow servant"—is important. In fact, the combination of all three is most important—beloved brother, faithful minister, and fellow servant. Some are faithful ministers; they are devoted to their work, driving and earnest, but they could not be described as beloved brothers. They are too absorbed in being faithful ministers to be beloved brothers. They have little time for brotherliness. Then some are beloved brothers, hail-fellows well met, but not faithful ministers. They cultivate friends, but do not convert people. They are so kindly they cannot convert.

Then there are those who are faithful ministers but not good fellow servants. They cannot work with others; they are lone wolves. Tychicus was all three, and, most important of all, he was in the Lord. When you are in the Lord, a faithful minister, a beloved brother, and a fellow servant, then you are a strong person indeed—and indispensable. God and man can send you on errands for the Kingdom. Being in the Lord means to be in a brotherhood in the Lord. In the Lord means to be very social.

O Father, I thank Thee that to be in Thee and in Thy Son means to be in fellowship with Thy sons. When we belong to Thee we belong to each other, and anything that takes us out of fellowship with one another takes us out of fellowship with Thee. Amen.

AFFIRMATION FOR THE DAY: *It may be that I have such drive that I drive past human need.*

BISHOPS, NOT SAINTS?

We now begin in Philippians: "To all the saints in Christ Jesus who are at Philippi, with the bishops and deacons" (Phil. 1:1). Taken literally, this verse has embarrassing implications—the bishops and the deacons were classed separately from the saints! Is this an unintentional slip, or was there a basis for this division into saints, bishops, and deacons? There was and is a basis of fact that those who are put in professional position over others are handicapped in the business of being a saint. The position influences the person. I signed an autograph album after a bishop, and I noted that he had signed his name followed by "Bp." and then followed by "Bishop," spelled out. He apparently wanted to be sure that everybody would know that "Bp." meant "Bishop" and "Bishop" meant something of importance! To be self-consciously self-important is a handicap in being a saint.

I was being interpreted into the Tamil language and I said, "To be an evangelist and a Christian is difficult." Then since there were missionaries there I continued, "Yes, and to be a missionary and a Christian is difficult." Since there was a bishop there I turned and said, "Yes, and I suppose to be a bishop and a Christian is difficult." My interpreter put it, "To be an evangelist and a Christian is difficult, but to be a missionary or a bishop and a Christian is impossible!" The bishop arose and bowed gravely! To be any professionally religious person and a Christian is difficult. The marginal reading for "bishop" is "overseer." When one is an "overseer"—one who oversees the work of others—it is not easy for him to be a seer—a prophet, or one who sees and tells what he sees. He gives reports from his overseeing the work of others, but he doesn't report what he sees directly and immediately. There are exceptions of course. Some become saints in spite of being bishops—seldom on account of! Saints are grown in simpler soil.

O Jesus, save me from professionalism, from the smooth phrase and the slick word. Make me real—real in motive, word, and deed. Give me the humble heart and the receptive faith. Then I shall live by Thy simplicities. Amen.

AFFIRMATION FOR THE DAY: *Let all my professionalism be shot through and through with personal simplicity.*

"CONFIDENT . . . BECAUSE OF MY IMPRISONMENT"

This verse throws light on the life in Christ: "and most of the brethren have been made confident in the Lord because of my imprisonment, and are much more bold to speak the Word of God without fear" (Phil. 1:14). This reverses what we would usually expect. The Christians were more confident in the Lord and more free to speak the Word of God without fear through Paul's imprisonment. The usual Christian attitude is that confidence and boldness would come if Paul had been delivered from the hands of his enemies and had been freed from imprisonment. Here it was reversed. The underlying assumptions were different in the minds of the early Christians—different from the usual run of thinking today. We expect the good to be exempt from suffering and pain; God is good if He saves us from trouble and calamity. But Paul had instilled into the early Christians the faith that the Christian isn't exempt from trouble—he uses it. He takes hold of whatever comes, good, bad, or indifferent, and takes it up into the purpose of his life and transmutes it into achievement and victory.

They saw Paul in prison turn imprisonment into fruitfulness. Had he been free to preach we would in all probability have lost his sermons. Shut up in prison, however, unable to preach, he wrote those deathless letters which have enriched the world. He really did more behind bars than free. The Christians got the clue: "What does it matter if we are put in prison? We will preach to prisoners. Dammed up, we will break out in a new direction. So if the worst happens we can turn it into the best. Here goes; we are free, for we can stand anything that happens to us—stand it for we can use it!" Out of that possibility confidence and boldness grew. You cannot get confidence and boldness by whipping up the will; you get them only by knowing that you have cosmic backing, no matter what happens, and that "God works with us in everything for good."

O Lord, my God, I am free, for I'm free to use everything. Banished on Patmos, I will see visions of the Victory. Laid on a bed of sickness, I will make pain my partner and my teacher. Then and only then am I confident and bold in the Lord. Amen.

AFFIRMATION FOR THE DAY: *I do not expect to be exempt from the ordinary sorrows of life—I expect only to be adequate for them.*

"YOU CAME HERE TO INTRODUCE ME"

This verse is searching: "so that in me you may have ample cause to glory in Christ Jesus, because of my coming to you again" (Phil. 1:26). "So that in me you may have ample cause to glory in Christ Jesus." It could have read, "so that in me you may have ample cause to glory." In other words, Paul could have been using Christ for his own glory, instead of Christ using Paul for His glory.

We see tablets on buildings: "To the glory of God and in memory of _____, who gave the money for this building." Then follows a long list of his virtues and benefactions. "To the glory of God" is the setting for personal glorification.

In many pulpits at the back is an inscription to be read by the preacher: "Sir, we would see Jesus." A gentle reminder that the congregation wants to gaze at Jesus and glance at the preacher. Instead of the other way around—glance at Jesus and gaze at the preacher.

When I ask the organist to play a hymn softly as people come to the altar, nothing rubs me more than to hear him throw in all sorts of fancy notes, calling attention to his performance, instead of calling attention to Jesus.

When you hear some preachers, you go away saying, "What a wonderful preacher," instead of saying, "What a wonderful Savior." When Mary was waiting for someone to introduce her to an audience Jesus said to her, "Mary, what are you waiting for? Why do you want someone to introduce you? I thought you came here to introduce me. Go ahead." She did—and how!

"I'm not here to show my clothes or to talk of myself, but to talk of Jesus," said an African pastor. But he did manage to get a plug in for himself and his clothes in introducing Jesus. Paul presented his Master and forgot himself, so we cannot forget Paul. He forgot himself into immortality. Many of us remember ourselves into oblivion.

O Jesus, Master, Thou, not I, art the Desire of the Ages. Forgive my intrusions into the picture. May I see no man save Jesus only, and may I know nothing before men save Jesus Christ and Him crucified. In Thy name. Amen.

AFFIRMATION FOR THE DAY: *To seek to call attention to myself in every situation is to lose myself.*

"GRANTED TO SUFFER"—HIGH PRIVILEGE!

"For it has been granted to you that for the sake of Christ you should not only believe in him but also suffer for his sake, engaged in the same conflict which you saw and now hear to be mine" (Phil. 1:29-30). One would have thought this passage would read: "For it has been laid on you as an obligatory duty not only to believe in Him but also to suffer for His sake." Instead the word "granted" is used, implying that it was a privilege, an honor, to suffer for His sake. Instead of whining, complaining, and asking: "Why should this happen to me?" we are told to look on suffering for Christ as our highest privilege and honor. It is!

When Moses and Elijah talked with Jesus on the Mount of Transfiguration the account says they "appeared in glory and spoke of his departure, which he was to accomplish at Jerusalem" (Luke 9:31). He was "to accomplish" His departure, His death at Jerusalem. Usually death is looked on as an acquiescence, submission to the inevitable. Here it was an accomplishment! Jesus accomplished more in the few hours on the cross than He did in all the rest of His lifetime. He opened His heart to the world's sin and sorrow and allowed it all to be forced through the channel—the single channel of His own broken heart. That broken heart was the healing of the world. It was "granted" to Him to suffer, and that granted suffering became His chief glory.

Whether the suffering be a pinprick or a stab, it is granted to us to take it and do what Jesus did with His departure—"accomplish" something through it. An invalid, blind and paralyzed for years, organized "Courage, Inc.," with 250 members. When asked about his conclusions he said, "I wouldn't trade all the insights I have gained through my years of suffering, for my health back again." He accepted his suffering as granted by God to accomplish "Courage, Inc."

O God our Father, when life gives me a pinprick or a stab, give me the insight to see in this an opportunity to be grateful for Thy grant. If we handle them together we can make them both into accomplishments. Amen.

AFFIRMATION FOR THE DAY: *Everything that happens—good, bad, or indifferent—is an opportunity for accomplishment.*

"BY ALL THE STIMULUS OF CHRIST"

Here is a meaningful verse: "So if there is any encouragement in Christ, any incentive of love, any participation in the Spirit, any affection and sympathy, complete my joy by being of the same mind, having the same love, being in full accord and of one mind" (Phil. 2:1-2). Five things Paul mentioned as being in Christ—encouragement, incentive of love, participation in the Spirit, affection, and sympathy. All of these are outgoing qualities. So being in Christ means that you do not stay in Christ as a closed spiritual corporation, but are in Him as electricity is in a generator—in to go out, yet always "in."

"Any encouragement in Christ"—in Him there is always the positive encouragement. "The bruised reed will he not break, and the smoking flax will he not quench." Barnabas was called "son of encouragement." He took Paul when no one else would take him, and he took John Mark when Paul wouldn't take him. Out of rejected materials he built his temples of God.

This portion, "if there is any encouragement in Christ," is translated by Moffatt, "By all the stimulus of Christ." Christ is the Savior, the Sanctifier, and the Stimulator. Many fail to take Him as Stimulator—Stimulator of mind, spirit, emotions, body. Everything in Christ is at its best, for it is at His best.

A woman confronted with many diseases said to her doctor, "With all the germs and diseases around us everywhere, I don't see how we can ever be well." The wise doctor replied, "Knowing the human body as I do, I wonder why anyone should ever be sick." The resources of health are laid up in the body. In view of the stimulus of Christ I refuse to accept my tiredness, my age, my retirement, my slow-down. In Him I am well and whole. I am as strong as my strength to receive, as able as my ability to appropriate, as alive as my receptivity to His stimulus. Note it says *all* the stimulus of Christ—His "all" is sufficient for my all—and then some!

O Jesus, stimulate my mind to think Thy thoughts after Thee, my feelings to feel Thy feelings after Thee, my will to do Thy deeds after Thee, and my being to become Thy Being after Thee. I open my being to the stimulus of Thy love—I would love after Thee. Amen.

AFFIRMATION FOR THE DAY: *The stimulus around me is not to be compared with the stimulus within me—His stimulus.*

"THE MIND . . . IN CHRIST JESUS"

We repeat a verse already looked at which perhaps is the most important verse in our quest: "have this mind among ourselves, which you have in Christ Jesus" (Phil. 2:5). Then follows the seven steps down which Jesus went: (1) Did not count equality with God a thing to be grasped. (2) But emptied himself. (3) Taking the form of a servant. (4) Being born in the likeness of men. (5) Being found in human form he humbled himself. (6) Became obedient unto death. (7) Even death on a cross (Phil. 2:6-8). He went from equality with the Father to equality with a thief—from the highest to the lowest. Then the seven steps up: (1) Therefore God has highly exalted him. (2) Bestowed on Him the name. (3) Above every name. (4) At the name of Jesus every knee should bow. (5) In heaven and on earth and under the earth. (6) Every tongue confess that Jesus Christ is Lord. (7) To the glory of God the Father.

The mind in Christ Jesus was a mind that lost itself in the deepest renunciation possible and found itself in the highest annunciation possible—"Jesus Christ is Lord." He fulfilled the deepest law of life—lose yourself, and you find yourself. Self-realization is found by self-renunciation.

When we are in Christ we go down with Him—down with Him even to the cross. Then we go up with Him and share His victory. So the self in Christ is not lost. It is affirmed—affirmed with the mightiest affirmation possible—we share His rulership. "They shall sit on My throne." Humanism with all its vaunted emphasis on the dignity of man and his self-affirmation is puny and earth-bound compared to the mighty sweep of this affirmation of man. Humanism breaks itself upon the moral law; it saves its life and loses it—loses it in final despair about its own meaning and survival. It has no horizons. The Christian has meaning both now and forever—the highest meaning. He is identified with the highest life lived on this planet. Humanism is identified with itself alone. It seems cheap and tawdry compared to being in Him.

O Jesus, Lord, when I am identified with Thee in self-surrender and obedience, I'm identified with the name that is above every name. What matters it what my name is? Amen.

AFFIRMATION FOR THE DAY: *If I hit bottom with Him, I also hit the throne with Him.*

"HOPE . . . IN THE LORD JESUS"

This last passage introduces us to another: "I hope in the Lord Jesus to send Timothy to you soon, so that I may be cheered by news of you" (Phil. 2:19). This verse introduces us to the word "hope"—a word which the ancients distrusted and repudiated. The Hindus have built up this distrust of hope into the philosophy of Maya—Illusion. Everything earthly is Maya.

The Christian faith redeemed the word "hope." "So faith, hope, love abide . . ." "May the God of hope fill you with all joy and peace in believing, so that by the power of the Holy Spirit you may abound in hope" (Rom. 15:13). "And endurance produces character, and character produces hope, and hope does not disappoint us, because God's love has been poured into our hearts through the Holy Spirit which has been given to us" (Rom. 5:4-5).

Hope has been redeemed because the earthly life has been redeemed. It is not Maya—it is meaningful. The earthly life for the Christian "produces character"—this life is "a vale of character-making." Every event has destiny in it. The world process and the world itself are to be redeemed. "Thy Kingdom come . . . on earth"—the earth is to be the subject and scene of redemption. It has a future. It is to be added back to heaven from which it broke off because of sin. It is to be redeemed by the blood of the Son of God—His blood stains have rendered sacred forever the soil of the world.

The Christian never knows when he is beaten. He begins with defeat—the defeat of the cross. You cannot defeat defeat. It starts with defeat and turns that defeat into victory—the cross into an Easter Morning. The Christian is incorrigibly hopeful. When he cannot sing of what is, he sings of that which is to be. When that which is to be looks hopeless, he still sings—on general principles! In spite of! A Christian leper had only two fingers left. He used them to grasp a violin and play it—in spite of! That is the Christian hope. It is incorrigible.

Dear Lord Jesus, Thou Who didst say while standing in the shadow of the cross, "Be of good cheer, I have overcome the world," help me this day to live on Thy victory and hope in Thy hope. Thou art the sole ground of our hope. Amen.

AFFIRMATION FOR THE DAY:

> *My hope is built on nothing less*
> *Than Jesus' blood and righteousness.*

"TRUST IN THE LORD"

A passage akin to the last one: "And I trust in the Lord that shortly I myself shall come also" (Phil. 2:24). This trust that he would shortly come to them was never fulfilled. Was it then an illusion? No, for the phrase "trust in the Lord" saves it from all possible nonfulfillment and consequent illusion. If he had left out the phrase "in the Lord" and made it a bare affirmation of faith, then it would have let him down. "In the Lord" gives a new dimension to the trust, for if we trust in the Lord, then He will give us the thing we hope to get, or something better. "Ask and it shall be given you"—not necessarily the thing we ask. He will give us that or something better. Paul was not released from prison, but the Lord let him come to the Philippians through his letters, and the world has come to the Philippians through those letters. So his "trust in the Lord" was bigger in its fulfillment than he could ever have dreamed.

The chief priests with the scribes and elders cried, as Jesus hung on the cross, "He trusts in God; let God deliver him now." God didn't deliver Him, however. Did His trust fail? No, for His trust was in God. God did something more through that trust—He delivered the world through Him—redeemed it. God answers all our prayers. He will give the thing asked for, or else He will give something better.

I saw a number of women with shaved heads. Their hair had been offered to a god: "If you do this for me, I'll give you my hair." This is a strict bargain. The Christian doesn't bargain with God. He trusts in the Lord—knowing that the Lord will give the thing he asks for, or something better. Therefore "he who believes in Him will not be put to shame"—for the believer in Him gets what he asks, or he gets something better. Therefore he who trusts in the Lord always wins. If he trusts only he often loses, but if he trusts in the Lord he cannot lose. He always comes out on top.

Dear Lord, even when I come out underneath, I am on top when I am in Thee. In Thee everything that happens is for my best. It may have started with the devil, but by the time it gets to me in Thee, it is from Thee. Amen.

AFFIRMATION FOR THE DAY: *I do not bargain with God, I trust His goodness and His love.*

"RECEIVE HIM IN THE LORD"

This verse has important implications: "So receive him in the Lord with all joy; and honor such men, for he nearly died for the work of Christ, risking his life to complete your service to me" (Phil. 2:29-30). "So receive him in the Lord with all joy"—we are to receive our fellow Christians in the Lord. The center of our unity is the Lord—the Lord Jesus. Anyone who is in Christ must be in my heart, or Christ isn't there. To exclude the brother in Christ is to exclude Christ!

A Pentecostal leader came to India to try to unify the Pentecostals. In one city there were eleven different Pentecostal groups. He couldn't get them together, not even for prayer and fellowship. Why? Because the center of all the groups was Pentecost, and you can't get together around Pentecost. You can get together only around the Lord—the Lord of Pentecost and very much more. They differed on what happened at Pentecost, and therefore they couldn't have fellowship. In Jesus they were one—if they only had known it! If you say, "What do you believe?" you are divided. If you say, "Whom do you trust?" you are one—one Name upon your lips, one loyalty in your heart. If the emphasis is upon the "whats" it will be divisive; if upon the "Whom" it will be uniting.

When a little girl was asked by another little girl to go to a meeting she replied, "I'm sorry I can't go with you for I belong to another abomination." Sometimes denominations are abominations, if they separate us from fellow Christians. Christians are at once the most divided and the most united body on earth—united at the center—Christ—and divided at the margin in marginal things. Such minute differences divide us! The ironic thing is that we all belong to each other, for we all belong to Christ. "Receive him in the Lord" would settle everything. It would be "with all joy." Outside the Lord it is all controversy and all scowls. In Christ is our one meeting place.

O Jesus Christ, Thou art the Pole Star of my loyalty and my brotherhood. In Thee I find everyone in Thee. In my group I find my group—and only my group. Thus I shut myself from the wider fellowship in Thee. Amen.

AFFIRMATION FOR THE DAY: *I will receive every man in the Lord, in spite of minor differences.*

"REJOICE IN THE LORD"

"Finally, my brethren, rejoice in the Lord" (Phil. 3:1). This was sound, for very, very often you cannot rejoice in anything save in the Lord. You cannot squeeze a drop of rejoicing out of your circumstances, your prospects, your past, but you can always rejoice in the Lord. Habakkuk found that out:

> Though the fig trees do not blossom
> nor fruit be on the vines,
> the produce of the olive fail,
> and the fields yield no food,
> the flock be cut off from the fold
> and there be no herd in the stalls,
> yet I will rejoice in the Lord,
> I will joy in the God of my salvation.
>
> (Hab. 3:17-18)

There are two strains of thought running through the Old Testament in regard to pain and suffering—one is the answer of Job and the other of Habakkuk. The answer of the Book of Job is that you get back twice your losses—he rejoices on account of. The answer of Habakkuk is that you rejoice in spite of. The latter is closer to the New Testament. There you joy in the God of our salvation when you cannot joy in what happens to you.

Jesus said: "These things I have spoken to you, that my joy may be in you, and that your joy may be full" (John 15:11). Note, "My joy may be in you . . . your joy may be full." His joy then is not alien to our joy; they are affinities. Our joy in Him is supernaturally natural.

Many Christians are lacking in joy. Yet "how unbefitting it is to follow your own hearse around." It was said in Luke 10 that the seventy returned with joy and said: "Lord, even the demons are subject to us in your name!" Jesus replied: "Rejoice that your names are written in heaven." Don't rejoice over success or be downcast by failure, but rejoice over your names' being written in heaven—a permanent relationship. "In that same hour [Jesus] rejoiced in the Holy Spirit"—the highest joy.

O Jesus, my Lord, let Thy joy be in me. Then my joy will be full. Then I can rejoice in Thee when there is nothing else to rejoice in. When I rejoice in Thee I rejoice in everything, for Thou art my Everything. Amen.

AFFIRMATION FOR THE DAY: *The joy of the Lord is my strength—the joy of circumstances is my weakness.*

"GLORY IN CHRIST JESUS"

A step further: "For we are the true circumcision, who worship God in spirit, and glory in Christ Jesus, and put no confidence in the flesh. . . . But whatever gain I had, I counted as loss for the sake of Christ. Indeed I count everything as loss because of the surpassing worth of knowing Christ Jesus my Lord" (Phil. 3:3, 7-8).

Yesterday, we meditated on, "rejoice in the Lord." Here we take a step further and "glory in Christ Jesus." To rejoice in the Lord is largely emotional; to glory in Christ Jesus is emotional and intellectual. You see in Him the eternal fitness, the rightness, the altogether satisfactory, just what you longed and sought for. You glory in Him with mind and emotion.

The point of glory here was that Jesus Christ had saved Paul from leaning on any outer prop to bolster his faith. These outer props which people leaned on—rites and ceremonies, sacrifices, circumcision, fasting, mutilating the body, discrimination between clean and unclean foods—all those were gone and Jesus Christ alone was the center of his glorying. Faith and life were reduced to simplicity.

"Indeed I count everything as loss because of the surpassing worth of knowing Christ Jesus my Lord." "The surpassing worth of knowing Christ Jesus"—that sentence makes the Christian faith so different in degree that it becomes different in kind. When you know Him you know all that everybody else knows—plus!

Note "the surpassing worth of *knowing* Christ"—not of knowing about Him, or belonging to a system built up around Him—these are not necessarily transforming. In Latin America, where I have recently been, Christ is imprisoned within a system built up around Him, not immediately available, hence the people are not transformed. If they had an immediately available Christ whom they could know, they would know transformation.

O Lord Jesus, I gaze on Thy surpassing worth and my heart and I are melted with gratitude and praise. And I say "No" to everything else. Thou hast me and hast me forever. I need nothing else. I want nothing else. Amen.

AFFIRMATION FOR THE DAY: *If I glory in my possessions or in my person, my glory is precarious; if I glory in Jesus it is permanent.*

ALL THE CLINGING ACCESSORIES

"For his sake I have suffered the loss of all things, and count them as refuse, in order that I may gain Christ and be found in him, not having a righteousness of my own" (Phil. 3:8-9). The wonder of self-surrender to Christ is this: You not only surrender your troublesome ego, you also surrender all the accessories that cling to the ego to bolster it. It is pathetic how some people lean on some dead ancestor to sustain their present importance. I read a memorial tablet in a church saying that So and So was the son of So and So, and the grandson of So and So, M.P. (Member of Parliament). That M.P. was obviously put in to bolster his importance.

When Paul was crucified with Christ, all the accessories that clung to his old ego were crucified too. He swept the decks of them. From henceforth he would have no righteousness of his own, nor would he depend on the righteousness of any other thing or person. It was Christ and Christ alone.

He not only let these accessories go, he let them go with contempt—counted them as refuse (literally "dung"). He used extreme language for he felt extreme feelings as he saw people trying to add to Christ's sufficiency, piecing Him out by adding this, that, and the other. He saw they were canceling the grace of God by these additions. Paul could say, "I do not nullify the grace of God" (Gal. 2:21). He did not nullify that grace by substitution (the Law), or by addition (the magnifying of a Christian rite or ceremony and making it overshadow the Center, Jesus Christ). It was Jesus only. Paul would have counted all these attempts at piecing out the sufficiency of Christ as "refuse."

Paul wanted to be found in Him—not in this, that, or the other. He could say, "This one thing I do," and "This one Person I know." His impress is upon the ages.

O Jesus, my Lord and Savior and my All, I would have this same simplicity of faith and life and love. Prune me from all that saps my energy, my love, and my loyalty. I would have a single-minded and single-hearted devotion to Thee and Thee alone. Amen.

AFFIRMATION FOR THE DAY: *"Jesus Only" is not merely a slogan—it is a profound reality.*

"MAKE IT MY OWN . . . MAKE ME HIS OWN"

"Not having a righteousness of my own, based on law, but that which is through faith in Christ, the righteousness from God that depends on faith; that I may know him and the power of his resurrection . . . Not that I have already obtained this or am already perfect; but I press on to make it my own, because Christ Jesus has made me his own" (Phil. 3:9-10, 12).

When Paul repudiated his own righteousness and the so-called righteousness of the accessories, he did it to gain the righteousness of God. What was the righteousness of God? It was the righteousness that was manifested in raising Jesus from the dead. It was the positive righteousness that tackled sin in the cross and death in the resurrection. It conquered both. It was not the righteousness of taboo—you can't do this, you can't do that. It was the righteousness that walked up to the worst and conquered it by positive righteousness and love.

To know Jesus was to know Him and the power of His resurrection. This was not knowing about Jesus—a dead Jew. This was knowing the alive and universal Savior. To be in Him was to have resurrection power working in you. In the Belgian Congo in a village which had Roman Catholic Christians in it, there was always a shrine of the Virgin and Child in front of the village. The figure was a baby Christ. No baby Christ is sufficient to redeem the world. Only the Resurrected Christ is sufficient for that.

"I press on to make it my own, because Christ Jesus has made me his own." "Make it my own . . . made me his own." When He makes me His own, then I make all the "its" my own. When I surrender to Him, things surrender to me. I don't struggle to get "it"—I surrender to become His, then "it" becomes subservient to Him—and to me in Him. Everything belongs to me because I belong to Him. I possess nothing—and Everything. Glory be!

O Resurrected and Living Lord, I would know Thee and the power of Thy resurrection in every thought, every word, every attitude, every moment of the day and night. Then I will live in final power and final glory. I do now, but I want more. Amen.

AFFIRMATION FOR THE DAY: *All the "its" of life are under my feet, for I am at His feet.*

"UPWARD CALL OF GOD IN CHRIST JESUS"

These verses go from climax to climax: "I press on toward the goal for the prize of the upward call of God in Christ Jesus" (Phil. 3:14). "The upward call of God in Christ Jesus"—was anything more beautiful ever written? It expresses the heart of the Christian faith—a heart that is under an upward call and pull of God in Christ Jesus.

This verse is the antedote to the complacency that says, "I'm in Christ, therefore safe and secure. All I have to do is to stay here." Being in Christ can be the refuge of static virtues, a fixed character, and an undeveloping personality—a mausoleum for a dead Christianity. A Indian Christian was asked to go to one of my meetings for non-Christians, and he replied: "No, I'm satisfied with my faith. The non-Christians might ask questions of Stanley Jones which might upset my faith." His faith was a fear, and his fear froze him into a stale goodness.

We need to be upset on one level to be set up on a higher level. God breaks our outworn patterns to give us newer and better ones. The little daughter of a missionary in Africa asked her mother, "Mother, how old is Stanley Jones?" When her mother replied, "Seventy-six," she thought a moment and said, "How can that be? He acts as though he were just getting started." The Christian is always just getting started. In Jesus every ending is a fresh beginning. He satisfies you and unsatisfies you by that very satisfaction. You want more—and yet more—and the more you have the more you want. He appeases your appetite and then the appeasement becomes an appetite. You are not dissatisfied, but forever unsatisfied. "The upward call of God in Christ Jesus"—that is the divine dissatisfaction with things as they are in behalf of things as they ought to be. I have seen Him and shall never be satisfied until I shall wake in His likeness. He has set me afire to be like Him.

O God, I feel Thy upward call in Christ Jesus, and I'm on this restful road to more. I rest in Thee and feel the restful restlessness for more of Thee. I am full and pray for enlarged capacity. I shall want Thee forever. Amen.

AFFIRMATION FOR THE DAY: *Everything in Jesus is a beginning—there are no endings, for our endings are only beginnings.*

THE CROSS—TOUCHSTONE OF BEING IN CHRIST

A steadying passage: "Therefore, my brethren, whom I love and long for, my joy and crown, stand firm thus in the Lord, my beloved" (Phil. 4:1). Paul, after having talked of the upward call of God in Christ, here talked about holding steady: "stand firm thus in the Lord." He pointed to the cross as the place to hold steady: "For many, of whom I have often told you and now tell you even with tears, live as enemies of the cross of Christ" (Phil. 3:18). Evidently there were those who claimed to be in Christ, but in Christ without the cross. Stand fast at the place of the cross, he pleads, even with tears.

Was Paul right? Is the cross the touchstone of being in Christ? Yes. Just as self-surrender is the touchstone on our part of being in Christ—no being in Christ without it—so the Divine Self-surrender in the cross is the touchstone of the real Gospel from the side of God. God cannot save without a cross. The cross is the price God must pay to get to us in spite of our sin.

Self-giving on the part of God and man is the crux of the Christian faith. Put one point of the compass there, then let the other point go as far into truth as you will. You are fixed and free!

Paul saw that he had slipped away from the center at Athens. He preached some important truths—God has made of one blood all nations; in Him we live and move and have our being—but he brought in the Gospel as a postscript. A dim postscript: "Because He has fixed a day on which He will judge the world by a Man Whom He has appointed, and of this He has given assurance to all men by raising Him from the dead." There was no cross in it; not confronting men with the real message of the Gospel. He failed at Athens—no church, no letter written. When he came to Corinth he had learned his lesson: "I determined not to know anything among you save Jesus Christ and Him crucified." Out of this emphasis came the Corinthian church and the Corinthian letters!

O God, my Father, I pray Thee help me to stand fast at the cross. There Thou didst reveal Thy heart, didst show us our hearts, and didst redeem them. Not to emphasize that would leave out the very heart from the body. I love Thy cross. Amen.

AFFIRMATION FOR THE DAY: *The cross shall be not merely on my church, it shall be in my consciousness—my working way to live.*

"AGREE IN THE LORD"

"I entreat Euodia and I entreat Syntyche to agree in the Lord" (Phil. 4:2). Evidently the women were good women, devoted, sacrificial, and hard-working. They "labored side by side" with Paul "in the gospel." When there was a third person [Paul] present to be a shock absorber they worked side by side—got along beautifully. When Paul was taken away, however, the side-by-sideness left, and these women began to confront each other. Their views on many things differed. Paul called their attention to the one place where they did agree—in the Lord—they both belonged to Him and therefore fundamentally to each other. Wesley was wise when he said, "If your heart is as my heart, give me your hand." He didn't say, "If your head is as my head give me your hand." When there is heart agreement in loyalty to Christ, we can put up with a lot of lesser disagreements. These lesser disagreements must be expected and provided for—and overlooked.

Paul didn't de-Christianize these women because they disagreed. He said they were both in the Lord and that their names were "in the book of life" (vs. 3). Being in the Lord does not mean mental and emotional agreement. There must be a great capacity in the Lord to absorb shocks of disagreement. This verse, "Let all men know your forbearance (vs. 5) has been translated, "Let your yieldingness be known to all men"—a willingness to yield on minor issues, uniting on the great central allegiance to Christ.

The Japanese love three trees—the pine because it stands up straight against the storms, the plum because it bravely puts out its blossoms while winter lingers still, the bamboo because it bends, but doesn't break. Many are like the pine—they stand straight on everything, they never bend. A combination of the stiffness of the pine and the bendingness of the bamboo is the strongest combination. Some say: "Be reasonable, take my way"—they remain the lone pine.

O Christ, teach me when to stand straight and when to bend. Let me not be afraid to bend lest I be considered weak. The bending bamboo is stronger than the unbending pine. Teach me to be both, for I want to get along with others in Thee. Amen.

AFFIRMATION FOR THE DAY: *My yieldedness shall be known to all men except when it comes to principle.*

"REJOICE IN THE LORD ALWAYS"

"Rejoice in the Lord always; again, I will say, Rejoice" (Phil. 4:4). This word "rejoice," or "joy," occurs thirteen times in this letter to the Philippians—a letter written from jail! Thirteen lotus blossoms of joy come to the surface of this letter, rooted in the muck and mire of injustice. It is a joy "in spite of."

The Christian faith is the most joyous faith in the world. It is not a Pollyanna type of religion that sees no evil, however. It is rooted in pessimism—the pessimism of the cross. It wins its optimism out of pessimism. So it is at once the most pessimistic and the most optimistic of religions. Buddhism says, "Life is suffering." Christianity says, "Life is suffering—Glory, hallelujah, Easter is here!" Some stop at the first half, and they "follow their own hearse around." They have an Easter in their calendar, but not in their character.

Psychology is stressing the health of joyfulness. The joyless person is on the skid—physically. Nothing tones up the system as much as a constant flow of joy. Nothing tones down the system as much as a constant flow of depression and sadness.

In Christ life is joy. Outside Christ life is pure sadness. On a plane everybody got air sick except the stewardess and one passenger, for the plane was tossing violently. This passenger helped many. After the storm had died down, the passenger began to sing to himself. This irked a lady passenger behind him who said bitterly, "No one has a right to be as happy as you are." He went back and sat with her and told her of the source of his happiness—Jesus Christ. She listened intently, and before the journey was finished she had accepted Christ and was rejoicing too. This movie star had been on the top of the world on the outside and down in the dumps on the inside. Now she moved from the cellar to the sky parlor. J-O-Y—Jesus Over You. Jesus and joy are one and inseparable.

O Jesus, Thou art joy—joy with no hangover. Thou art pure, unalloyed joy. I do not have to seek for joy when I have Thee. To have Thee is to have joy. My soul sings its way down the joyous years. I thank Thee, thank Thee. Amen.

AFFIRMATION FOR THE DAY: *My springs of joy are in the everlasting hills—they never run dry.*

"PEACE . . . WILL KEEP . . . YOUR HEARTS"

"Have no anxiety about anything, but in everything by prayer and supplication with thanksgiving let our requests be made known to God. And the peace of God, which passes all understanding, will keep your hearts and minds in Christ Jesus" (Phil. 4:6-7). "Have no anxiety about anything"—does this mean we are to have no forethought about anything? No, Jesus taught forethought in providing for the future in the parable of the unjust steward. Forethought means getting all the information about a thing, praying over it, and then surrendering it into the hands of God to await His guidance. Anxiety is holding things in your hands and trying nervously to hold things together with your own resources. Forethought is essentially God-centered; anxiety is essentially self-centered.

The next portion is the remedy for anxiety: "but in everything by prayer and supplication with thanksgiving let your requests be made known to God." "Prayer . . . with thanksgiving." The thanksgiving is the element that saves prayer from anxiety prayer. Prayer, without surrender and thanksgiving, can be and often is a species of anxiety. It is anxiety turned toward God, instead of faith, confidence, and surrender turned toward Him.

The result of this prayer surrender is: "And the peace of God, which passes all understanding [and all misunderstanding!], will keep your hearts and minds in Christ Jesus. The peace of God is tapped by prayer and thanksgiving and surrender and flows into the surrendered heart and mind. Note "heart" first. You can accept the peace of God with the heart when the mind doesn't see the way clear. This is a heart-foremost acceptance instead of a head-foremost knowing. The result of that peace of God is that you are kept in Jesus Christ. In Him there are no insolvable problems; out of Him there are no solvable problems.

O Peace of God, which passes understanding, take possession of me and keep my heart and mind in Jesus Christ. In Him I have no problems. They are all possibilities. So possess me, Peace of God, possess me. Amen.

AFFIRMATION FOR THE DAY: *I have a heart that is "kept"—kept by the peace of God.*

"HE GIVES ME PENNIES EVERY DAY"

"I rejoice in the Lord greatly that now at length you have revived your concern for me" (Phil. 4:10). Here is a rejoicing in the Lord which is different from the other rejoicing we have found in this Epistle. The other rejoicings were general rejoicings over permanent relationships in the Lord. This rejoicing is over a specific thing that had happened—their concern for him had revived.

Are these rejoicings on the same level and of the same importance? No. The rejoicing mentioned in this verse is more akin to happiness than to joy. Happiness is dependent on happenings, and is therefore occasional; joy is dependent on relationships with Christ, and therefore permanent. We should let our weight down on joy, but not on happiness. Happenings bringing happiness very often don't happen. Yet many reiterate happenings to prove the goodness of God to them instead of reiterating the permanent joy which comes from living in union with Christ. This is a well of joy; the other is a shower-dependent stream which may dry up.

"I love my Daddy—he gives me pennies every day," said a little fellow. That was penny love. Later he will probably say, "I love my Daddy"—that is personality love.

If Paul had depended too much on people's concern for him he would have been disillusioned and frustrated. In the end people let him down: "At my first defense no one took my part; all deserted me. May it not be charged against them! But the Lord stood by me and gave me strength to proclaim the word fully. . . . The Lord will rescue me from every evil and save me for his heavenly kingdom. To him be the glory for ever and ever" (II Tim. 4:16-18). Here the concern of people for him had collapsed. But Paul didn't collapse. His joy was in two things: his life work was being fulfilled, and he belonged to an eternal Kingdom. His joy was intact and flowing—in spite of!

O Jesus, I thank Thee for the happenings along the way. But I thank Thee most of all for the Way. It leads Home! I'm at Home in Thee, going Home. "In Thee" counts, all else is marginal. I thank Thee, thank Thee. Amen.

AFFIRMATION FOR THE DAY: *My happiness does not depend on happenings, but upon Him Who is above happenings.*

"OFFERING ME SECURITY"

This great passage: "Not that I complain of want; for I have learned, in whatever state I am, to be content. I know how to be abased, and I know how to abound; in any and all circumstances I have learned the secret of facing plenty and hunger, abundance and want. I can do all things in him who strengthens me" (Phil. 4:11-13).

This is indeed a great passage—an insight into the soul of the world's greatest Christian, and an insight into the secret of his greatness. He had learned to take what came and make something out of it. If plenty came he could use it! Some people are afraid of plenty. They are wedded to poverty. "Sister Lila," the Greek saint who is an expert masseuse, massaged lepers, made them well, and loved everybody, everywhere. I offered her a modest allowance so she could be free to serve everybody. She said in horror: "It is a temptation of the devil. Brother Stanley is offering me security." She could stand poverty, but couldn't stand a very modest plenty! I think Paul would have taken it and used it! On the other hand, there are others who can stand plenty, but not poverty. I spoke in a previous reference of the silk manufacturer who lost all—all but his dignity and joy. He had a faith. A manufacturer in Japan lost all and in similar calamity paid his promised pledge to charity and committed suicide. He had no faith. He couldn't stand poverty.

A French philosopher has said, "No man is strong unless he bears within his character antitheses strongly marked." Paul was strong because he was humble and self-assertive, passive and militant, world-renouncing and world-realizing, tender and terrible, meek and masterful; he could take poverty and plenty in his stride! Everything was grist to his mill. He made the grain of everyday happenings into the bread of the Kingdom. The secret was this: "I can do all things in him who strengthens me." "In Him" was the secret. Out of Him, he was weak; in Him, strong for anything.

O Jesus, Lord, in Thee there isn't anything that comes except for my good. I can, by Thy grace, rescue good out of it. It may be bad in its origin and intenion, but it becomes good in its destination—it contributes to me. I thank Thee. Amen.

AFFIRMATION FOR THE DAY: *My security is found in adventure with Him.*

PROBLEM CONSCIOUS OR POWER CONSCIOUS?

We must spend another day on: "I can do all things in him who strengthens me" (Phil. 4:13). I prefer this translation from Moffatt: "in Him who strengthens me, I am able for anything." This verse has sung its way through my mind and heart for years, until it has become a part of me. I have passed it onto many a troubled, seeking soul. I ask them to repeat it just before they drop off to sleep so that it will work in the subconscious mind as they sleep, replacing the old negative thinking. Then I urge them to say it the first thing when they open their eyes in the morning—their salutation to the dawn. I ask them to keep saying it to themselves again and again throughout the day. It creates a climate of peace and victory around the soul.

An Indian woman spoke to me of "those who are problem conscious and those who are power conscious." You could see the difference in her face. She was power conscious—adequate for anything.

Trying to analyze this verse is like picking a rose to pieces to find its beauty. It is beautiful and perfect as it is. Note the following, however: (1) "In Him"—not through Him, an outside Helper, but in Him. Since I am in Him, and He possesses me, then I possess all His resources. (2) *"Who* strengthens me"—note the "who." He directly and immediately strengthens me. There is nothing between—Soul upon soul, Life upon life. (3) "Who *strengthens* me"—this is present continuous. "As thy days"—and hours and minutes—"so shall thy strength be." (4) "Who strengthens *me*"—the total me, body, mind, and spirit. He doesn't do everything, weakening my personality. He, the Strong, makes a strong me. (5) "I am able for anything." Healed at the heart, I can say, "Let the world come on." Let anything come, for I can use everything; not bear it, use it!

O Jesus, my Lord, not my responsibility, but my response to Thy ability makes the difference. And what a difference! Now I am power conscious, not problem conscious. In Thee all problems are possibilities. I thank Thee. Amen.

AFFIRMATION FOR THE DAY: *I shall whisper to myself this verse all day:* "In Him who strengthens me, I am able for anything."

"SUPPLY EVERY NEED OF YOURS"

This blessed, blessed passage: "And my God will supply every need of yours according to his riches in glory in Christ Jesus" (Phil. 4:19). "My God will supply every need of yours." This is no chance saying; it is the summing up of a Divine intention as revealed in the Scriptures. He intends to supply our needs—not our greeds, but our needs. "He will rise and give him whatever he needs" (Luke 11:8). "Your heavenly Father knows that you need them all. But seek first his kingdom and his righteousness, and all these things shall be yours as well" (Matt. 6:32-33). " 'Why are you untying the colt?' And they said, 'The Lord has need of it.' And they brought it to Jesus" (Luke 19:33-35). "They sold their possessions and goods and distributed them to all, as any had need" (Acts 2:45). Now this verse sums up the whole Divine Intention—to "supply every need of yours."

Before we were brought into the world the Father provided for our needs. The child on being born needs air to breathe; it is there for the taking—taking by a cry. It needs milk; it is there in the mother's breast. It needs love, and love is there in the parents' hearts ready to be poured out as needed. As God has provided for our physical and emotional needs, so He has provided for all our spiritual needs—provided for them on a lavish scale: "according to his riches in glory in Christ Jesus." We plug in to have our needs met, not at the place of His poverty—His earthly wanderings—but at the place of His riches in glory. We plug in at the very highest place—His riches *in glory*. This is "glory" giving, and not from the ordinary possession of glory, but "according to his *riches* in glory." To be poor in the face of that is to be poor in receiving. The giving end is rich, the receiving end is poor in receiving. Stay in Him and your needs—every need of yours—is supplied! I could dance—I do, at least in my heart! Who wouldn't?

O my Father, I am overwhelmed at the lavish provision Thou hast made to supply every need I have. I am also overwhelmed with shame that I take so little. Thou art offering by handfuls and I take with thimblefuls. Forgive me. Amen.

AFFIRMATION FOR THE DAY: *As long as I stay in Jesus God underwrites the supply of all my needs.*

SAINTS IN CAESAR'S HOUSEHOLD!

The next verse is illuminating: "Greet every saint in Christ Jesus. The brethren who are with me greet you. All the saints greet you, especially those of Caesar's household" (Phil. 4:21). Someone has defined a saint as "one who tries a little harder." That is a false notion of a saint—a person who struggles hard to be good, who whips up the will. The New Testament type of saint is different; the saint is not one who tries hard to be good, but one who surrenders to Goodness, to Jesus; not one who whips up the will, but who surrenders the will, not one who resists primarily, but who receives primarily. New Testament prescription: "Live in union with Christ," and the sainthood takes care of itself, automatically. "In union with Christ," His goodness is your goodness, His saintliness is your saintliness—unconsciously so. A conscious saintliness is less than saintly. Like Moses, we do not know that our face shines. But it does!

Note the environment of this saintliness: "Caesar's household." Of all places! Caesar's household—a place of intrigue, of lust of the flesh, and of lust of the spirit for power; no one was safe from whispering tongues. Comparable to this is the situation in the Nizam's palace in Hyderabad, where no two of his numerous wives are allowed to speak to each other; three guards watch each one night and day! Saintliness out of that? It happened in Caesar's household! Paul knew, for he was a prisoner in one of Caesar's household prisons. If by remaining in union with Christ the members of Caesar's household became saints, living as they did in two worlds at once, then it is possible to be a saint anywhere. A friend of mine, high up in India's government, is called "A sadhu (holy man) in Government." He lives in a sticky environment, but none of it sticks to him. He simply lives in union with Christ day by day, hour by hour, moment by moment, and he emerges an unconscious saint.

O God, if I have to live in a little Caesar's household, where I am daily subjected to temptation to respond in kind, let me remember that I belong to Thy household even when my body has to live in Caesar's. Let me absorb Thy goodness amid this badness. Amen.

AFFIRMATION FOR THE DAY: *I live the heavenly life amid a very hellish environment.*

FAITH AND LOVE LINKED

This verse links two important factors: "because we have heard of your faith in Christ Jesus and of the love which you have for all the saints" (Col. 1:4). Here faith and love in Christ Jesus are linked, as they are many times in the New Testament. They are Siamese twins; cut them apart and both die. If you are going to have love for man, you will have to have faith in God, and in the kind of God revealed in Jesus Christ. Jesus joined these two in the two great commandments: "Thou shalt love the Lord Thy God," and "Thou shalt love thy neighbor." Really there were three commandments: Love God; love thy neighbor; love thyself. The last is important, for self-hate and self-rejection are as bad as other-hate and other-rejection.

Pagan psychology teaches the last two: self-love and other-love, but severs them from love to God. It won't work, for some supreme love must lift you out of eros self-love, cleanse it, and give it back to you as agape love. That supreme love will make it possible for you to love your neighbor, however unlovable he may be, for he becomes "a brother for whom Christ died." The supreme love redeems the lesser loves.

The Indian government set aside millions of rupees to lift the tribal people of Orissa. They had been living in grass huts on the mountainsides. The government built them brick houses at the foot of the mountains. They lived in them a few days, and then went back to their mountain grass huts. A Christian layman asked a non-Christian government official in charge, "Why?" He replied, "We can give them money, but only you Christian workers can give them love. And love is what they need. You can lift them, we can't." Another tribe of 150,000 has the largest murder rate of the world, and there is no Christian work among them. Of them a non-Christian government official said, "They are this way because they have no one to love them."

Dear Lord, teach me the secret of faith and love, the alternate beats of the Christian heart. My faith draws love from Thee, and my love expresses that faith in love to everybody, including myself. May my life this day be an expression of faith and love. Amen.

AFFIRMATION FOR THE DAY: *Love shall be the manifestation of my faith.*

"THE KINGDOM OF HIS BELOVED SON"

"He has delivered us from the dominion of darkness and transferred us to the kingdom of his beloved Son, in whom we have redemption, the forgiveness of sins" (Col. 1:13-14). Note: "In whom we have redemption," not merely "through Whom." If you do not pass from the "through Whom" to the "in Whom," there is no redemption. The "through" is outside us in history, but the "in" is inside us in experience. The historical must become the experiential or it isn't redemption, except in potentiality—not in actuality. I can accept the "through Whom" without personal self-surrender; but I cannot accept the "in Whom" without personal self-surrender.

The unsurrendered self, acting as God, creates a "dominion of darkness." The self-centered live, move, and have their being in a dominion of darkness. They are fumbling and stumbling in the dark with this business of living. The universe doesn't back their being God, so none of their sums add up to sense—only nonsense.

Then comes the great self-renunciation, self-surrender. We renounce self, and we receive God. Then He, and He only, delivers us from the dominion of darkness. He who made our selves can deliver us from the tyranny of making our selves God. The deliverer is God. We cannot pummel and beat and murder ourselves. We let go and let God. He delivers and He transfers us to the Kingdom of His beloved Son. There everything is light and everything adds up to sense.

The center of that transference is "the forgiveness of sins." Many want redemption without forgiveness of sins. They would like to add virtue to virtue and thus be redeemed. It can't be done. That is trying to get blood out of a turnip—virtue out of an unsurrendered, hence unforgiven, self. The unsurrendered self invades all the added virtues and turns them into vices. The self and its sin must be surrendered. Then forgiveness, reconciliation, redemption, and the kingdom of His Beloved Son can be ours!

O Beloved Son, to be in Thee is to be in Thy Kingdom, and to be in Thy Kingdom is to be in Life, in Freedom, in Everything. Here I sing and dance and rejoice as a little child. Here I am calm with the wisdom of God. I thank Thee. Amen.

AFFIRMATION FOR THE DAY: *The Kingdom of His beloved Son—this is my environment, my homeland.*

"IN HIM ALL THINGS WERE CREATED"

The next passage is a passage indeed: "He is the image of the invisible God, the first-born of all creation; for in him all things were created, in heaven and on earth, visible and invisible, whether thrones or dominions or principalities or authorities— all things were created through him and for him" (Col. 1:15-16). Jesus is "the image of the invisible God"—He takes the place of idols for us. Idols misrepresent God; Jesus represents God. Jesus is the express image of God's person; God is a Christlike God.

"He is . . . the first-born of all creation"—we not only see the person of God in Jesus, we see the purpose of creation in Him. In Him we see the purpose and meaning of creation—creation reveals Him, or creation perishes.

"For in him all things were created, in heaven and on earth, visible and invisible . . . all things were created through him and for him." The Christian world has not taken this passage seriously—has treated it as a rhetorical flourish. Nothing in Scripture, or outside, is more important. What does this strange passage mean? That God created all things through Him and for Him? Does it mean that the touch of Christ is upon all creation, and deeper, that all things are intrinsically made to work in His way and that if they do, they work well, harmoniously? Do they find the purpose of their being when they work in His way? Do they work their own ruin automatically if they try to work in some other way? I can give a wholehearted and categorical yes to those questions.

The way of Christ is written in the Bible and in our blood, our nerves, our tissues. The discovery of that fact is going to be the greatest adventure of the future. If we are created by Him and for Him, then He is inescapable. You cannot jump out of your own skin. If you revolt against Christ, you revolt against yourself. God has us hooked. We may run away in short excursions of freedom, but He reels us in. The facts are against us.

O Jesus, Lord, we stand in awe before the wonder of Thy redemption. It is not imposed on us, but exposed out of it. Thy laws are our freedom. When we do Thy will we do the thing for which we are made. We bless Thee, bless Thee. Amen.

AFFIRMATION FOR THE DAY: *Like the watermark in paper, Christ is written into the very texture of my being.*

"IN HIM ALL THINGS HOLD TOGETHER"

This verse clinches everything: "He is before all things, and in him all things hold together" (Col. 1:17). "In him all things hold together"—out of Him all things fly apart, go to pieces. One translation says "cohere"—in Him all things are coherent, they make sense; out of Him everything is incoherent, makes nonsense.

The climate of being in Him is love. This same epistle says: "And above all these put on love, which binds everything together in perfect harmony" (Col. 3:14). Everything in Christ is bound together in perfect harmony by love. Everything outside Him is centrifugal, goes to pieces. "He that gathereth not with Me scattereth." Everything outside Christ scatters. This is not merely theological opinion. It is working fact.

I have come from a section of India where Lal Mohan Patnaik became a Christian. He was disinherited by his Hindu family. Then the family began to quarrel over his portion of the inheritance. Lal Mohan was called in to arbitrate the distribution of his portion, for he was the only one everybody could trust. And he did! The family got his portion—plus the tensions. He was deprived of his inheritance, but had peace within. He rose to be the Speaker in the Assembly of Orissa State and was the most influential layman in Cuttack and the leading spirit in founding Christ College. By his love he held the family together, held the Assembly together, held the college together—because he was held together within by being in Christ.

In a group of Christians say "Christ" and you are together. Say "baptism" or "bishops" or "church custom" and you are apart. The one fact in Christianity which holds us together is Christ. Show His spirit in any situation and it is healing. Show some other spirit and it is disruptive. By trial and error we will have to come together around Him—nothing else will work.

O Jesus, Thou art my center and my circumference. In Thee I am bound and in Thee I am free. In Thee I am free to love, and thus feel one with all. Give me the sense to stay in Thee every moment in every situation. Amen.

AFFIRMATION FOR THE DAY: *Soul of mine, listen to this: In Him all things hold together; out of Him all things fall to pieces.*

"IN HIM ALL THE FULLNESS OF GOD"

"For in him all the fullness of God was pleased to dwell, and through him to reconcile to himself all things, whether on earth or in heaven, making peace by the blood of his cross" (Col. 1:19-20). This passage is bursting with meaning: "For in Him all the fullness of God was pleased to dwell." "Pleased to dwell"? In most of us He dwells, but sufferingly dwells. We give Him much pain; he stays, but with many a pang. Here, however, was one place God was pleased to dwell—in Jesus. He was at home in Jesus. He was the perfect vehicle through which God could express Himself.

There is no record or hint that Jesus went from a once-broken life through conversion into wholeness. All of us have to go through that—Jesus didn't. He was natural in His relations with women, but there is no hint that He was battling with sex. He hesitated about the self urge, only to find the will of God for it. Once found, He never hesitated even to take it to the cross. All His virtues were balanced by opposite virtues, all held in a living blend. Perfect manhood and perfect Godhood flowered in Him.

Someone has said that "the attempt to impose divine qualities upon the framework of human nature has always resulted in a monstrosity—always, except in the case of Jesus." Here the supernatural was natural. No wonder it is said that all the fullness of God was pleased to dwell in Him. "This is My beloved Son in Whom I am well pleased." No wonder, for He was such a Son! After two thousand years we have not found it possible to add to or subtract from Him to make Him more perfect. When we attempt to make Him more perfect, we go away smiting our breasts and saying, "God have mercy on me a sinner." As everything was reconciled in Jesus—material and spiritual, manly and womanly, passive and aggressive—so Jesus becomes the center of reconciliation of things in heaven and things on earth. Everything and everyone is reconciled in Him.

Dear Son of God and Son of Man, by dwelling in Thee may I too become a center of reconciliation. May I absorb all differences, all conflicts within myself and through my suffering bring reconciliation. In Thy name. Amen.

AFFIRMATION FOR THE DAY: *In Jesus "all the fullness of God"; in others, portions of God.*

THE CONTINUING CROSS

"Now I rejoice in my sufferings for your sake, and in my flesh I complete what is lacking in Christ's afflictions for the sake of his body, that is the church" (Col. 1:24). "In Christ's afflictions for the sake of . . . the church"—just what does that mean? Does it mean Christ is afflicted in the afflictions and persecutions of His church? Yes, I'm sure it does. Does it also mean that Christ suffers on account of the church—on account of its being such a poor representative of Him in the world? Yes, I'm sure it does. It means both.

We stress the cross as the suffering of Christ for the world—and rightly. That was once and for all. But what about this continuous suffering He undergoes from those who say they love and bear His Name, and yet in that very Name do such ugly things? I've mentioned a situation where a whole church is divided over the nature of the communion—is it a symbol, or is there a real Presence? The communion is blessedness, but out of this blessedness has come bitterness. Christ bleeds again. The blood drops of Jesus are upon this whole controversy.

In another place there is a court case over the possession of church property. Again He bleeds. Casting lots for His garments and gambling over court decisions for the possession of His property—is there any difference? Little or none! Again He bleeds!

Paul said: "I enter this daily crucifixion of Christ and take my share of His sufferings and bleed for Him. Every nail that goes into His hands goes into mine. I am in Christ and therefore I'm in His sufferings for the church." Then both Paul and Christ are in a constant state of misery? Oh, no, for there is nothing so absolutely blessed as suffering for and in behalf of others. The heart sings with a strange, wild joy. We put strings across the bars of the cross and make a harp of it. And the music of God is heard.

O Jesus, my Lord, Thou hast given me the privilege not only of being in Thee, but of being in Thy blessed sufferings. My sufferings shall sing. I shall steady the cross with one hand and play my cross-harp with the other. I thank Thee. Amen.

AFFIRMATION FOR THE DAY: *If I have to bear a cross because of some people in the church, I will remember He bears the cross of all the people in the church.*

"CHRIST IN YOU, THE HOPE OF GLORY"

This glorious verse: "the riches of the glory of this mystery, which is Christ in you, the hope of glory" (Col. 1:27). We have called attention to the double and reciprocal "in's"—you in Christ and Christ in you. The pervading idea in India is that if you find God your personality is virtually wiped out; you are a raindrop lost in the ocean of Being. But the Christian concept of "Christ in you" preserves the personality, heightens it, and makes it the "glory" point for God and you. "Christ in you, the hope of glory"—the hope of glory for God.

The glory of God in heaven will not be that He is seated on a rainbow throne. I've seen maharajahs seated on golden thrones especially set up for them in my meetings, but they are gone and their glitter with them. God's glory will not be in golden streets. The Nizam of Hyderabad, dressed in a towel around his waist and seated in a wheel chair, periodically surveys his dust-laden chests of gold, looking for disturbed dust as a sign of tampering—dust reviewing dust!

The glory of God is not the glory of adoring multitudes chanting His praises. The glory of God is the redeemed. The only glory that God would want is the glory of a grace that redeemed sinners and made them into the astonishingly beautiful persons they are as they bear Christ within themselves. That is the only hope of glory God has—"Christ in you." When He sees what grace has made out of nothing, and worse—"that will be glory for Me," says God.

In the Lee Memorial Home in Calcutta, an emaciated little girl of five came up the steps carrying her sick brother of a year and a half. She had been rescued from a locked room in which the mother lay dead. The years went by, and the girl, having passed the B.A. and her teacher training, B.Ed., and having taught her first day at school, stood before her father-in-God (a missionary) without a word. She had arrived. Neither spoke. The glory of this redeemed girl was enough for "father" and "daughter."

O God, we know Thee through Jesus. We know through Him that the real joy in heaven is over repenting sinners and redeemed lives. So Thy glory can only be the glory of those who have Christ in them—the one hope of Glory. I love Thee. Amen.

AFFIRMATION FOR THE DAY: *My only glory is Christ, and the people He transforms through me.*

"MATURE IN CHRIST"

This meaningful passage: "Him we proclaim, warning every man and teaching every man in all wisdom, that we may present every man mature in Christ. For this I toil, striving with all the energy which he mightily inspires within me" (Col. 1:28-29). Here we come to the goal of being in Christ. The goal is not a reward in heaven—being in Him now in order to be with Him then. The goal is maturity in character and life—a maturity of a certain type—maturity in Christ. This is a goal which is the highest conceivable. Being in Christ means, not the mysticism which lets God do everything, nor the humanism which makes man everything and God nothing; it means that you are in Christ. He is supreme; He is Lord. Yet it also means that the very being "in Christ" brings the person to maturity as a person. Both the Divine and the human are affirmed.

This maturity is far more than the usual psychological maturity—you are "mature" when you can function well in your environment. This might be a very immature maturity—making man a cog in a social and economic machine.

The center of being mature in Christ is being mature in love. That will make a person function well in his environment without being an echo of that environment. Love is creative.

"For this I toil" sounds strained and tense until we see the next portion: "striving with all the energy which he mightily inspires within me." His toiling and striving was not in the energy of the flesh, but in the power of the Spirit. He lived by all the energy which Christ mightily inspired within him. Christ was breathing into [the meaning of "inspire"] him the energy which he expended. He worked with effortless activity—pouring out what was poured in—and this in no meagre bits, but with *all* the energy which He *mightily* inspired. What a goal! What a means to that goal!

O Lord Jesus, to be mature in Thee is to be mature indeed. Make me this day mature in all my contacts with everybody. That means I will give out love and only love to everybody at all times. I yield my all to Thy maturity. Amen.

AFFIRMATION FOR THE DAY: *I strive with all the energy He inspires—this is effortless striving.*

"IN WHOM ARE HID ALL THE TREASURES"

Then this: "that their hearts may be encouraged as they are knit together in love, to have all the riches of assured understanding and the knowledge of God's mystery, of Christ, in whom are hid all the treasures of wisdom and knowledge" (Col. 2:2-3). "Hearts may be encouraged as they are knit together in love." The contrary is true—hearts are discouraged if the attempt is made to knit them together in anything but love. This works automatically.

"To have all the riches of assured understanding"—some understanding is not assured understanding. Pagan psychiatry is based on understanding, but it has no assured understanding, since the understanding is not grounded in God. Assured understanding comes when you feel that the sum total of reality is behind you, backing you—you have cosmic support.

You get this by having "the knowledge of God's mystery, of Christ." This is interesting; Christ unfolds the mystery of God, and God unfolds the mystery of Christ—a double unfolding. In both directions, the more you know, the more you know you don't know. What you know sets you on fire to know more. It is therefore not static, but dynamic.

"In whom are hid all the treasures of wisdom and knowledge." Jesus Christ is the Revelation of God and man and life, but He is a hidden revelation—He reveals and He conceals. You know, and you don't know; you see, and you don't see. What you don't know and don't see stirs you to perpetual discovery. This perpetual discovery becomes the most exciting thing in life. It keeps you on your toes, for you feel there is something big just ahead. This unfolding revelation of Christ puts a surprise around every corner, makes life pop with novelty and discovery, makes life living and worth living. The life in Christ is perpetual discovery and perpetual development.

O Lord Jesus, I know Thee, and what I know of Thee sets me on fire to know more and more and more of Thee. This perpetual discovery of Thee will go on forever, for Thou art inexhaustible. We will never go beyond Thee. I thank Thee. Amen.

AFFIRMATION FOR THE DAY: *I'm on the most exciting treasure hunt in the world—the treasures hid in Him.*

LIFE HOLDS TOGETHER IN CHRIST'S WAY

"For though I am absent in body, yet I am with you in spirit, rejoicing to see your good order and the firmness of your faith in Christ" (Col. 2:5). These two things go together: good order and the firmness of faith in Christ. It works the other way; where there is no firmness of faith in Christ there is no order—there is disorder.

This disorder extends to the body, mind, spirit, and relationships. Some time ago I met an evangelist who had been a very disordered person a few years before. His eyesight was awry; he tried seven different types of glasses. He was allergic to this, that, and the other. The reason? He had taken his eyes off Jesus and put them on a guru, a spiritual master. He found that his idol had feet of clay and the shock was shattering. I pointed out to him that the upset in his eyesight was probably the conversion of a spiritual symptom to a physical symptom—he couldn't see spiritually, so he couldn't see physically. He couldn't digest this spiritual disappointment, so he couldn't digest his food. He got his eyes back on Christ again, and now he sees perfectly without glasses and digests everything. Incidentally, the ten thousand disciples of this guru pathetically held to the belief that he would be "translated" and not die, so they held the body for two days after his death, expecting a miracle. The result was disorder, spiritually and socially. Anything outside Christ will let you down if you let your full weight down on it. Life holds together in Christ's way and goes to pieces in any other way. Firmness of faith in Christ and good order are root and fruit. Loss of faith in Christ and disorder are also root and fruit. Both of them work with an almost mathematical precision. Life works that way; to try to make it work some other way is to face disillusionment. Life works in God's way or it doesn't work.

O Lord God, my Father, I thank Thee that life holds together at the center when we are firmly fixed in Thy Son. When we are in Him we are in Thee. We have Everything behind us. We are in good order when we are under Thy orders. Amen.

AFFIRMATION FOR THE DAY: *In Him I am in "good order"; out of Him I am in disorder.*

SURRENDER AND RECEPTIVITY

"As therefore you received Christ Jesus the Lord, so live in him" (Col. 2:6). This verse points to the attitude and the atmosphere of living in Christ—the very way you received Him, live in Him. How did they receive Christ Jesus? By surrender and receptivity. They gave to Him; they took from Him. Give and take—this is the relationship reduced to its simplest terms. The giving means the giving of the one thing and the only thing we own—ourselves. When He has that He has all.

When this is done, the way is cleared to receive. The end is the receiving. God asks that we give all in order to make it possible for Him to give all. Among the things He gives is ourselves! He cleanses the self from a thousand contradictions and conflicts and then gives it back to us. We are at home with ourselves because we are at home in God, for God is our home.

From birth to death we live by surrender and receptivity. The child before birth surrenders to its environment and receives everything from its mother. This is a life process; we live as we receive. The kneeling calf sucking its mother's milk is a vivid symbol of that humble, surrendered receptivity which must characterize the growing Christian.

The unsurrendered Christian is inhibited by his unsurrender from taking the grace of God. He feels timid, ashamed to take, for he knows he hasn't given. The moment he gives all, however, a holy boldness takes possession of him—he can now take all. He takes with both hands, for he gives with both hands.

Note that it says, "As therefore you received Christ Jesus the Lord." He is "Lord"—not merely example, doer, teacher—He is Lord. You cannot call Him Savior unless you call Him Lord. He saves those whom He owns—no others. If you make something else Lord, you are cut off from His giving.

O Lord, I cannot even think of any other as Lord, for any other lord is lord of a ruin. Thou art the Lord of the redeemed and the being redeemed. We are on the Way—the way to the best. To take anything else is to lose ourselves. Amen.

AFFIRMATION FOR THE DAY: *I have received the Lord by surrender, receptivity, and faith, so I shall live in Him by the same three things.*

"ROOTED AND BUILT UP IN HIM"

"Rooted and built up in him and established in the faith, just as you were taught, abounding in thanksgiving" (Col. 2:7). This phrase "rooted and built up in him" emphasizes two sides of our being in Christ. The "rooted" emphasizes the receptive side, and "built up" emphasizes the activity side.

We are rooted in Christ. This presupposes an affinity between the soil and the plant. They are made for each other. The plant assimilates from the soil elements akin to its own nature. The New Testament teaching is that we are made by Christ and for Christ. When we put the roots of our life into Him we come to our very own—the thing for which we were made. We have been made alien to Him through sin, but now that we are being redeemed from sin we are at home in Him. When we think His thoughts, feel His feelings, will His purposes, and become His being, we are fulfilling ourselves. This is the Divine intention. We were made in His image, unmade by our sin, and now were being remade into that image of God as seen in Christ.

If the "rooted" expresses the receptive side, the "built up" expresses the active side. This saves being in Christ from becoming a quietism, and the "rooted" saves it from being a mere activism. The "built up" puts emphasis on the disciplined life. After all, a fruit tree may be of the best stock, planted in the best of soils, and watered well, but if it is not pruned and sprayed it will be comparatively fruitless. You do not find the new life in Christ through disciplines, but you cannot keep it without it. The daily quiet time spent in reading the Bible and prayer, the reading of the best books, the sharing with others—all these are a part of the process of being built up. We trust as if the whole thing depended on God, but we work as if the whole thing depended on us.

Dear Father, I would take, take, take. I would build, build, build. I would be rooted and built. Let all that I take from Thee simply fit me to give more. I would be the best person I can be in Thee. Amen.

AFFIRMATION FOR THE DAY: *The materials to put into my building come from Him, how I build comes from me.*

"IN HIM THE WHOLE FULNESS OF DEITY"

Now this most astonishing passage: "For in him the whole fulness of deity dwells bodily" (Col. 2:9). The preceding verse gives the background out of which this verse comes. It was the background of Gnosticism with its belief in matter as evil and spirit as good. This brought forth the amazing statement of Paul: "For in him the whole fulness of deity dwells bodily." The emphasis was on the "bodily." God came into matter in incarnation and thus redeemed matter as evil, making it the vehicle of the divine revelation and redemption. Nothing could be more important for our existence on earth, environed as we are with matter.

The material was not alien; it was an ally. The spiritual would cease to try to manifest itself apart from the material and would manifest itself in material forms and in material relationships. "A body hast thou prepared for me . . . Lo, I have come to do thy will" (Heb. 10:5, 7). The will was to be done in and through the body.

The Greeks said, "Matter is evil"; the Hindus say, "Matter is illusion" (Maya); the Christian says, "Matter is God-made, God-approved (God saw it was good) and will be used by God and man for redemptive purposes." The kingdom is to come on earth. The earth has a future and a goal. It has meaning.

To stop up all holes, such as saying that God may have come into matter temporarily and partially, Paul says, "In Him the *whole fulness of deity* dwells." There is nothing in God that isn't in Jesus Christ—at least in character and essence. Jesus is God accommodated to human form. This did not happen only once; it still happens—"dwells (present tense) bodily." The body was taken up into Deity, transformed and transfigured, as in the Mount of Transformation, and will probably bear the glorified nail-prints forever. So body and spirit were reconciled in Him, and now "beat out music vaster than before."

O Lord Jesus Christ, the meeting place of God and man, matter and spirit, and the reconciling place of all, I come to Thee. Make all my conflicts into concords and all my cross currents into one current of love for Thee. Amen.

AFFIRMATION FOR THE DAY: *As the Word becomes flesh in me, so my body becomes word.*

"FULNESS OF LIFE IN HIM"

Now the application of the previous verse: "And you have come to fulness of life in him" (Col. 2:10). The Gnostics had bypassed the Incarnation saying it was beneath God's dignity to come into matter and that you could attain fullness of life in knowing God directly and immediately, without the revelation of the Incarnation. Hence they were called the Gnostics or Knowers. Anything that attempts to bypass the Incarnation perishes, as Gnosticism, and as the Unitarianism, which tries to bypass Jesus, is now doing.

We come to fullness of life in Jesus Christ or we don't come to fullness of life. Apart from Jesus we know little or nothing about God, and what we do know is wrong. He is life, and apart from life we cannot and do not come to fullness of life.

There are those who in the interests of universality take Christ and something else, to piece Him out. The attempt to piece Him out by adding other ways reduces the universality, for He is the Universal. "In him all the fulness of deity dwells bodily." To be in Him is to be in everything that is of reality in the universe. The more Christian you are, the more universal you are. A Jewish shopgirl said, "It is good to see a real Christian—they are so gracious and kindly. All I've seen have been Christmas shoppers."

"And you have come to fulness of life in him"—fullness of life for mind, spirit, and body. There is a renewing of the mind, a unifying of the spirit, and not only a face lifting but a total body lifting— a rejuvenation. You will have the best mind, the best spirit, and the best body you are capable of having if you live wholly in Him, all the time, with all you have. Live wholly in Him and you live wholly. It is as simple as that—and as profound! "All great discoveries are a reduction from complexity to simplicity." This is the greatest discovery of living: Live fully in Him and you come to fullness of life.

O Jesus, my Lord and my Life, I bring everything to Thee to be transformed from existence to life. In Thee everything lives and out of Thee everything perishes. I see and know the secret. Help me to act on it, beginning now. Amen.

AFFIRMATION FOR THE DAY: *"Fulness of life in him"; emptiness of life outside of Him—this is the verdict of all life.*

NATURAL AND SUPERNATURAL NOT AT WAR

"In him also you were circumcised with a circumcision made without hands, by putting off the body of the flesh in the circumcision of Christ (Col. 2:11). Paul had been saying that "neither circumcision counts for anything, nor uncircumcision, but a new creation." The dependence upon circumcision and the rights and privileges it brought in a Jewish society should die. In its dying, however, something good comes out of it; it pointed to the circumcision in Christ in the cutting away of the body of the flesh. What does that mean? Certainly not the body (soma); it was looked on as good in Christianity. It must mean the flesh (sarx), the false nature built up by sin, the dissolution of "sentiments" organized around wrong centers.

When that false nature is dissolved and replaced by the new nature in Christ, we are truly natural—supernaturally natural. We have put out the Trojan horse filled with enemies and are now no longer allergic to ourselves. We are at home with ourselves because we are at home with God.

The bodily urges are still there and must be kept in control by the new life, for the leftover drives from the presence of the flesh still linger as hang-over. The natural urges soon learn their Master's voice and soon learn that the good is good for us and the bad is bad for us, that the natural and the supernatural are not at war—they are both at war with the unnatural sin. They are allies and not aliens.

If this physical circumcision was of no avail, then the physical baptism mentioned ("buried with him in baptism") would be of no avail. Only a spiritual circumcision and a spiritual baptism would be of avail. "By one Spirit we are baptized into the body of Christ." It is the baptism of the Spirit that brings life and renewal. The baptism of the Spirit may occur during physical baptism, or it may not.

O Jesus, Thou didst come to baptize us with the Holy Spirit and with fire. May the alien flesh be cut away in Thy circumcision and may the baptism of the Spirit bring me into union with Thee alone. In Thy Name. Amen.

AFFIRMATION FOR THE DAY: *The false nature dies; the real nature lives—in Him.*

"TRIUMPHING OVER THEM IN HIM"

"He disarmed the principalities and the powers and made a public example of them, triumphing over them in him" (Col. 2:15). The marginal reading says, "in it" (the cross). Whether it was "in Him" or "in the cross," it is the same—He triumphed over these powers in the cross. These principalities and powers represented the heirarchies of beings in Hebrew and Gnostic thought. He stripped them of their powers, disarmed them at the cross.

Two great powers joined in crucifying Jesus—the power of religion, represented by the high priests, and the power of the state, represented by Pilate and his Roman officers and soldiers. He disarmed them both, made a public showing of them. "By our Law He ought to die." Jesus replied by abolishing the law. "If you let this Man go, you are no friend of Caesar's." Jesus replied by abolishing Caesar—made Himself Lord and King.

He did this masterfully and simply. They asserted themselves; He surrendered Himself. They offered sacrifice to God and to Caesar; he abolished both by Himself becoming the sacrifice. Then that Sacrifice became final Power—"the keepers were like dead men"—He rose before their eyes and left them disarmed.

A dramatist puts it this way, saying through the centurion to Mary at the cross: "Woman, I tell you this dead Son of yours, shamed, spit upon, has built a Kingdom this day that will shake into dust the kingdoms founded on blood and fear. Something has happened on this hilltop this day that will never die. The Meek, the terrible Meek, the fierce, agonizing Meek are about to enter their inheritance." He was right. The Cross towers o'er the wrecks of time. The wrecks are stripped—He stands girded to control the future. There is no alternative; it is Christ or chaos. He rules or we ruin. If love will not rule us, hate will rubble us. He lives—all else dies!

O Jesus, Lord and Conqueror, we thank Thee that Thy conquest is our conversion. We are put into the dust to rise to the highest heaven. We are beneath Thy feet and beside Thee on Thy throne. We are conquered and we conquer—in Thee. Amen.

AFFIRMATION FOR THE DAY: *"Triumphing over them in him"—today I determine the content of "them"—may it be all.*

"CHRIST IS ALL AND IN ALL"

"Here there cannot be Greek and Jew, circumcised and uncircumcised, barbarian, Scythian, slave, free man, but Christ is all, and in all" (Col. 3:11). This is one of the most important verses in the Scripture depicting the life in Christ. In an age seeking equality of opportunity for all, this is the charter of equality. Nothing in all literature can compare with this.

A dramatic scene took place in the Indian Parliament when a bill to prohibit conversions to Christianity among the outcastes was being debated. A member of Parliament, himself an outcaste, arose and said, "You want to protect us? From Christians? What about this?" He read a passage from the Hindu lawgiver Manu: "If an outcaste should listen to the words of the Vedas he should be beheaded." He tore the page out of the book and threw it away. A commotion ensued. The bill was thrown out—by government. That commotion in Parliament was a tempest in a teapot compared to the world commotion caused by this verse. It bumped into the whole structure of society and shattered it — and it is still shattering it and will continue to shatter it until man is free—and equal.

Listen: "Here [in the new man in Christ] there cannot be Greek and Jew [race distinction], circumcised and uncircumcised [religious rite distinction], barbarian, Scythian [cultural distinction], slave, free man [social, economic distinction]." Gal. 3:28 adds: male or female [sex distinction]. "Christ is all and in all." This abolishes race, religious rite, cultural, economic, social, and sex distinctions. It sweeps the field. Note: "cannot be." If there are these distinctions, then you are not in Christ. You are in something else. The equality is not artificial or paper—"Christ is all and in all." Note the "in all"—if we reject them, we reject Him. Nothing could be more thorough-going.

O Jesus Lord, Thou hast inspired Thy servant to sweep the decks of all artificialities and snobberies and to set men free. Thou art pressing upon the citadels of privilege. They too shall fall. Thou wilt be King over all men, and all men will be free. Amen.

AFFIRMATION FOR THE DAY: *The Jews let the Gentiles into the outer court of the temple; I let everybody everywhere into the shrine of my heart.*

RECEPTIVITY TURNS INTO ACTIVITY

"And whatever you do, in word or deed, do everything in the name of the Lord Jesus, giving thanks to God the Father through him" (Col. 3:17). This adds an important touch to our being in Christ. We have emphasized the receptive side of being in Christ — and that is right for you are primarily receptive. But the receptivity turns into activity. "And whatever you do"—you are to do as well as to receive and be. The being can only be manifested by the doing, and here the doing has a definite characteristic: you "do everything in the name of the Lord Jesus." You do everything as representing Him; you do it in His name, in His stead, in His spirit.

In Christ your actions not only manifest you, they manifest Christ. People judge Him by you. Years ago in India I was going along a country road on a bicycle. A cowherd boy in a field called to another, "Yisu Masih ka admi ja raha hai"—"the Jesus Christ man is going along." I was startled; I felt like getting down from my bicycle and dropping on my knees in prayer that I might not be unfaithful to the village boys who saw in me a "Jesus Christ man." We are all just that; we do everything in His name if we are professedly His. His name goes up or down with our representation. We are the only Bible some people read.

This doing everything in the name of Jesus is not a point of terror and tension, lest we misrepresent Him. It is a point of confidence and assurance. I do this, not in my name and my power, but in His name and therefore with His power. "In the name of Jesus Christ rise up and walk." In His name there is power, final power. If we go forth humbly in His name we can expect His power to attend that name. When we come in His name we represent His power at work in the world. We belong to the name before which every knee shall bow. Then we go not as cringers, but as conquerors.

Dear Father, we do give thanks to Thee through Him. We go representing Him as He came representing Thee. Keep our words and our deeds as clear instruments of His glory. When we speak, may He speak too. In His name. Amen.

AFFIRMATION FOR THE DAY: *Unless my receptivity becomes activity, it ceases to be receptivity—the inflow stops when there is no outflow.*

"BELOVED BROTHER," "FAITHFUL MINISTER," "FELLOW SERVANT"

Personal: "Tychicus will tell you about my affairs; he is a beloved brother and faithful minister and fellow servant in the Lord" (Col. 4:7). These personal references to people in the Lord have their universal significance, for they tell us what we must be in the Lord.

The central thing in Tychicus was that he was a "faithful minister"—that was the center of his life call. He had a call and was faithful to that call. That call gave him drive and direction. He was single-pointed. But that central drive and direction in the fulfillment of his call subjected him to the temptation of not being a "beloved brother" and a "fellow servant." He did not fall into that temptation—as many of us do. He was so brotherly that he was "beloved," and he was able to work with others, so he was called a "fellow servant."

This temptation of not being a brother and not being able to work with others as a fellow servant is the temptation of the strong, devoted, driving type of Christian worker. He is so busy and so absorbed in fulfilling his mission that he neglects to be brotherly; he is so absorbed in his own affairs that he cannot work with others. In the end he is isolated. He hasn't been brotherly along the way and hasn't worked with others, so he is a victim of his own drive. He has driven himself apart from others in successful loneliness. He has succeeded in being a lonely soul.

Tychicus was a well-rounded person—faithful in his ministry, brotherly in the midst of his ministerial drive, and capable of working with others as a fellow servant, instead of being a lone wolf. If we are to stay in the Lord and function at our best, we must be driving, brotherly, and cooperative. Then we are strong; otherwise our strength is weakness.

O Lord Jesus, Thy drive to fulfill Thy ministry and Thy mission was all-absorbing. Thou didst set Thy face to go to Jerusalem, and yet how tender and brotherly and how concerned about the brotherhood. Make me like Thee. Amen.

AFFIRMATION FOR THE DAY: *Search me. Am I a beloved brother, a faithful minister, and a fellow servant?*

"HE COULD NOT SAY NO"

Personal again: "And say to Archippus, 'See that you fulfill the ministry which you have received in the Lord' " (Col. 4:17). This exhortation differs from what we found in Tychicus. He was a faithful minister and had drive and direction, but Archippus was probably weak at the center. He was probably a man who lacked central drive. He was probably a person who could not say no to relatively unimportant things. He let himself be absorbed in the marginal and had little drive left for the central call of his life—the ministry.

Many a minister is called to be a minister of souls—to save them, develop them, and mature them—but he finds himself doing everything but that. Paul said, "This one thing I do," and this minister can say, "These forty things I dabble in." One leaves a mark, the other leaves a blur.

In dealing with many ministers in personal counseling, I find this frustration regarding the fulfillment of the central call of their lives is their most important problem. The pull of the marginal against the center divides a man's time—and divides the man.

This temptation to take the easier and unimportant plagues us all. I find that sometimes when I have real decisions to make concerning important things, I wash my nylon shirt! It is easier! And if I succumb to it—deadly.

This fulfillment of the ministry applies not only to professional ministers, but to laymen as well. Everyone in the Lord has a ministry. Being in the Lord means not only being in the Lord, but also being in the Lord's plan for us. That plan can be worked out as a full-time minister, or as a full-time layman. Being in the Lord means being in a creative plan of action for and with the Lord. Everybody in the Lord is in service and in the ministry whether it is the preaching ministry or the lay serving ministry.

O Lord Jesus, no hands were laid on Thee in ordination, and yet the choice of the Father was upon Thee. Thou didst fulfill that ministry. With or without hands of men upon me, help me to fulfill my ministry. In Thy name. Amen.

AFFIRMATION FOR THE DAY: *May no unimportant weeds choke the fine wheat of the Kingdom.*

BOTH EMPHASES MAINTAINED

We come now to an important emphasis: "Paul, Silvanus, and Timothy, to the church of the Thessalonians in God the Father and the Lord Jesus Christ" (I Thess. 1:1). The greetings in I Thessalonians and II Thessalonians are the same—and unique. The greetings to the churches in Paul's Epistles are varied and revealing: Romans: "To all God's beloved in Rome, who are called to be saints." I Corinthians: "To the church of God which is at Corinth, to those sanctified in Christ Jesus." II Corinthians: "To the church of God which is at Corinth, with all the saints who are in the whole of Achaia." Galatians: "To the churches of Galatia." Ephesians: "To the saints who are also faithful in Christ Jesus." Philippians: "To all the saints in Christ Jesus who are at Philippi, with the bishops and deacons." Colossians: "To the saints and faithful brethren in Christ at Colossae." The greetings to Timothy and Titus are personal.

It is obvious from the above that Paul never intended to give a name to the churches—a name which should be used for all, everywhere—for he varied the name and the greeting. The attempt to get one scriptural name for a church is doomed to disappointment. If, however, one name is selected which covers the widest range of fact, then this one to the Thessalonians probably is that one: "To the church [universal] of the Thessalonians [particular] in God the Father [the Ultimate Ground] and [in] the Lord Jesus Christ" (the revelation of the kind of fellowship—a Christlike fellowship).

If it is "The Church of God," the emphasis on Christ is dimmed; if it is "The Church of Christ," the emphasis on God is dimmed. In this greeting the emphasis on both God and Christ is maintained. Both have to be maintained, for God without Christ is a question mark and Christ without God is a question mark. The two together make an exclamation point. When we are in Christ we are in God, and when we are in God we are in Christ.

O God, in Thee I see Christ, and O Christ, in Thee I see God. The vision I see is so satisfying that I go no further. This is It. There is nothing further. Thou art the real God; Thou art the real Christ. Thou art both reality. I thank Thee. Amen.

AFFIRMATION FOR THE DAY: *Jesus puts a face on God and I need a God with a face, for God as energy and power leaves me cold.*

"LIFE ON BROKEN SPRINGS"

"Remembering before our God and Father your work of faith and labor of love and steadfastness of hope in our Lord Jesus Christ" (I Thess. 1:3). These Epistles are a miracle of fresh variety. It is an amazing fact that Paul, writing to the different churches on the same subject, rarely repeated himself. The man's mind was under the creative impact of the mind of Christ. Here he picks out three things he had used before—faith, hope, love: "So faith, hope, love abide, these three; but the greatest of these is love" (I Cor. 13:13). Here he speaks of their "work of faith," their "labor of love," their "steadfastness of hope." All three are "in our Lord Jesus Christ." Outside of the Lord you can have work and labor and steadfastness, but all three lack a soul. There is no faith in the work, no love in the labor, and no hope in the steadfastness. In the end it means irksome work, laborious labor, and hopeless steadfastness—what Bertrand Russell calls "an unyielding despair."

Being in Christ puts taste into everything. It puts faith in our work, for we are doing it for Him; love into our labor, for we labor for Him Whom we love; and steadfastness into our hope, for we hope in Him.

A prominent Hindu official came to our Ashram at Sat Tal. As he left he said to the group: "I came here without faith or hope or love. I am afraid I am going away without faith or hope, but here I have found love. I am taking that with me." Without being in Christ that is what happens—life bumps along on broken springs. In Christ work is worship, labor is love, and steadfastness is full of abounding hope. Life is living. The years are not tears. An Indian official said to a Christian, when the Christian suggested that the basis of a certain project be broadened to take in non-Christians: "You Christians began this, didn't you? Well, you'd better keep it. For what you begin you complete. You never get discouraged."

O Jesus Lord, Thou art working a work of faith, laboring a labor of love, steadfastly hoping—give me Thy persisting, creative love. Thou dost not fail nor art Thou discouraged. Make me like that. In Thy Name. Amen.

AFFIRMATION FOR THE DAY: *I shall not fail nor be discouraged until I have set love in my situation.*

IN CHRIST CAN WE IMITATE OTHERS?

"For you, brethren, became imitators of the churches of God in Christ Jesus which are in Judea; for you suffered the same things from your own countrymen as they did from the Jews" (I Thess. 2:14). Previously, in the same letter, Paul had said: "And you became imitators of us and of the Lord, for you received the word in much affliction, with joy inspired by the Holy Spirit" (I Thess. 1:6). Here the question of imitation of others is raised—both individual and collective. "And you became imitators of us and of the Lord." Here is an individual imitation of Paul and a collective imitation of the churches in Judea. Is there a place for imitation of others if we are in Christ? Does not being in Him make us separate and unique—a new creation?

The answer is that one portion of the passage, "imitators . . . of the Lord," makes possible the imitation of others without loss of self-respect and individuality. When we are primarily imitators of the Lord, we can be secondarily imitators of others without losing our unique personality. The core of the personality is being shaped by being in Christ, and by being imitators of the Lord. This holds the citadel firm. Without this central loyalty and imitation one becomes a mere echo, but with the citadel firm, one is a voice.

Sure of oneself in Christ and sure of the primary imitation, one can afford to take any good from others he may deem useful. He is not afraid of taking from others since he takes so deeply and primarily from Christ. Imitation can become initiation when it goes through the creative activity of being in Christ. While we are in Him we take from everything and everybody, and then putting it all through the new creation we turn these things into something new.

O Lord Jesus, I thank Thee that in Thee I am bound and free. I'm free to take any good I see in anything or anybody, for I see good in Thee. Everything serves me, now that I serve Thee. I have the wealth of Thee and of all good people. Amen.

AFFIRMATION FOR THE DAY: *I am primarily an "imitator of the Lord," so now I can be an imitator of any good man.*

TO BE IN CHRIST IS TO BE IN THE KOINONIA

"We sent Timothy, our brother and God's servant in the gospel of Christ, to establish you in your faith and to exhort you, that no one be moved by these afflictions. You yourselves know that this is to be our lot" (I Thess. 3:2-3). We finished yesterday by stressing the possibility of being imitators of others, provided we are primarily imitators of Christ. This verse stresses the possibility of being helped by others, even though we are primarily in Christ.

To be in Christ is to be in the fellowship, the *koinonia*, of fellow believers. This new life in Christ cannot be cultivated in solitary aloneness. The Hindu ascetics try it and end in vacuity. Christian ascetics tried it and ended in the same vacuity—and ultimate extinction. A high-court judge left the bench and sat, clothed in ashes, on the banks of the Ganges in solitary meditation. When I began a conversation with him he politely said, "Please leave me alone. You are disturbing my meditation." He was of far more use to the world as a judge than as an ascetic. As the latter he was withering.

Those who inwardly withdraw from fellowship while remaining in society undergo that same sterile degeneration. We need our Timothys to establish us in the faith, for that faith is by its very nature corporate.

The point of help that Timothy brought was that Christians should not be moved by afflictions, that it is our very lot as Christians. This cuts across the thinking of many present-day Christians, for they think the special favor of God is shown by their exemption from afflictions. They are in the success mentality of modern life instead of in Christ. To be in Christ is to be different, therefore persecuted. Society demands conformity; if you fall beneath its standards it will punish you; if you rise above its standards it will persecute you. Hence this is our lot.

O Jesus, Lord, I do not ask to be exempt from suffering. I only ask power to use whatever comes, good, bad, or indifferent. In Thee I am able for anything. So I am safe, since I can use all. In Thy blessed name. Amen.

AFFIRMATION FOR THE DAY: *If afflictions are my lot, then I choose to turn afflictions into opportunities.*

"I AM IF YOU ARE"

"For now we live, if you stand fast in the Lord" (I Thess. 3:8). This is a beautiful illustration of the identification that Paul had with his converts and fellow Christians. He lived when they lived spiritually; he died when they died spiritually. This was beyond sympathy ("suffering with")—it was empathy ("suffering in"). As a missionary and an evangelist I have felt that I was alive in the life of a convert, and I've inwardly died as he died. The African has a reply when you ask him if he is well: "I am if you are."

This statement of Paul's is a rose to be smelled; it is not to be picked to pieces as a botanist would do. If you pick it to pieces its beauty is gone. Paul did not live with the life of his converts, nor did he die when they died. He was primarily in Christ, and not in them. The real Paul came out in this passage: "At my first defense no one took my part; all deserted me. May it not be charged against them! But the Lord stood by me and gave me strength to proclaim the word fully, that all the Gentiles might hear it. So I was rescued from the lion's mouth" (II Tim. 4:16-17).

Paul didn't die in their desertion of him, for he didn't live in them—he lived in Him. Whether they went up or down he did not go up and down. He was in Jesus Christ Who is "the same yesterday, today, and forever."

Again and again when we ask, "Lord, and what shall this man do?" Jesus has to say to us, "What is that to thee? Follow thou Me." We must gaze at Jesus and glance at people, for if we gaze at people and glance at Jesus we will be in trouble.

I have had to say to many a troubled soul, their gaze out of focus, "If you look within you'll be discouraged; if you look around you'll be distracted; if you look back you'll be paralyzed; but if you look at Jesus you'll have peace." We live if people stand fast in the Lord, but if they don't we live anyway! We live in Him.

O my Lord, give me an empathy with those around me, but a limited empathy. My final and unlimited empathy is with Thee. In Thee "I live and move and have my being"—in others I live and move. I thank Thee. Amen.

AFFIRMATION FOR THE DAY: *I am unconditionally committed to Christ; I am conditionally committed to His followers.*

"DO SO MORE AND MORE"

"Finally, brethren, we beseech and exhort you in the Lord Jesus, that as you learned from us how you ought to live and to please God, just as you are doing, you do so more and more" (I Thess. 4:1). Paul was in Christ, but he knew how to be in people. He knew how to make them and to make them grow. He complimented them for what they were, and then told them what they needed! He complimented them, and then complemented them. Listen to this: "For what thanksgiving can we render to God for you, for all the joy which we feel for your sake before our God, praying earnestly night and day that we may see you face to face and supply what is lacking in your faith" (I Thess. 3:9-10). "What thanksgiving can we render to God for you . . . supply that which is lacking in your faith." He patted them on the back with one hand and pointed his finger with the other to what they were going to get and going to be. That was spiritual genius. If we have that we know how to make men.

Paul repeats the same attitude: "just as you are doing, you do so more and more." You are doing fine, now do more and more! These converts were subjected to "all the stimulus of Christ" and to all the stimulus of Paul! And rightly. The life in Christ is a growing life or it is not in Christ. As Christ is the eternally creative, so He is eternally creating us anew. The eternal cry of the Christian is, "More." His attitude is, "I've seen so much I want to see more"; "I've tasted so much I want to taste more"; "I've become so much I want to become more." This "more and more" will stretch beyond the grave and forever, for the finite will forever approach the Infinite, but will never arrive. That growth will be our eternal joy, and there is no joy greater than the joy of creative growth. There is room for infinite growth in Christ.

My Lord and my God, I feel I have taken hold of the Inexhaustible, the Unexplorable. Yet how intimate and satisfying! Yet how inspiringly unsatisfying! I am on the stretch and yet I rest. I have Everything and want more. Amen.

AFFIRMATION FOR THE DAY: *"More and more"—this is my life's motto and my life's movement.*

"IN HIM IS THE DEATH OF DEATH"

This passage is intriguing: "And the dead in Christ will rise first; then we who are alive, who are left, shall be caught up together with them in the clouds to meet the Lord in the air; and so we shall always be with the Lord" (I Thess. 4:16-17). "The dead in Christ." In many ways this phrase is a contradiction in terms—there are no dead in Christ. Everything in Christ is alive and alive forever more.

Paul tried to use a more accurate phrase: "those who are asleep" (vs. 13); "those who have fallen asleep" (vs. 14, 15). Then he drops the "asleep" metaphor and adopts the "dead in Christ" metaphor. Both of them are metaphors and therefore cannot fully express the reality. The reality is in these verses: "My desire is to depart and to be with Christ." "To be absent from the body is to be present with the Lord." "I am the resurrection and the life; he who believes in Me, though he die, yet shall he live, and whoever lives and believes in Me shall never die."

These verses tell us that to be in Christ is to be in life whether it be this side or the other side of the thing we call death. In Him is the death of death.

We must revise many of our viewpoints in regard to death. We can easily adopt the pagan viewpoint and vocabulary, neither of which fits the Christian facts. In Christ there is no death—there is only entrance to a larger life. The authentic view of death by one in Christ was seen in a very intelligent and saintly woman's so-called death. It was an amazing experience as I saw her clapping her hands in joy at the approach of death, her face the face of an angel. "They tell me this is death—it is life. They tell me that to be tickled to death is a hyperbole, but I'm being literally tickled to death. O death, throw open the gates." As I knelt beside her bed she put her hands on my head, ordaining me to preach this gospel of life!

O Jesus, my Lord, when I am in Thee, death seems impossible and absurd. It is swallowed up in life. Thy life possesses my life, and therefore I am deathless too. Help me to clap my hands in the face of death. Amen.

AFFIRMATION FOR THE DAY: *When I toss aside an outworn body on the way to life, I shall be more alive after it is gone.*

"OVER YOU IN THE LORD"

"But we beseech you, brethren, to respect those who labor among you and are over you in the Lord and admonish you, and to esteem them very highly in love because of their work. Be at peace among yourselves" (I Thess. 5:12-13). "Over you in the Lord." Isn't this a contradiction? Can there be anyone over you in the Lord? Isn't the earliest Christian creed decisive: "Jesus is Lord"? "There is one Lord." Are there underlings?

Yes. It would be simple if we had to obey Christ and Him alone. He is so trustable. I said to a lady missionary at conference time who was troubled over her proposed appointment, "Well, surrender it to Christ and trust Him." "Yes," she snapped, "I can trust Christ, but I can't trust the bishop and the district superintendent." It is the underlings who are often the rub. The answer?

We must turn again to that decisive verse: "Be subject to one another out of reverence for Christ" (Eph. 5:21). You submit to Christ primarily and fully, and then out of reverence for Him you can submit to others for His sake. When you do it for His sake, you save your self-respect. You are not now submitting to injustice—you are submitting to injustice for His sake. That wrings out of the whole procedure a victory. You are on top even when you are underneath, for you are morally and spiritually superior. This is one side.

The other side: "esteem them very highly in love because of their work." Look at them in love, not in rebellion. If you look at them in love you can see the good qualities and not merely the point that rubs you. Don't magnify the point of irritation until the good is blotted out. "Be at peace among yourselves." Don't give him a piece of your mind, for you will lose your own peace of mind. Peace within is better than position without. Choose peace—it passes understanding!

Dear Father, I thank Thee for those who are over me in the Lord. Their burdens are heavy. Help me not to add to them. Make me easy to get along with according to Jesus Christ. I'll need grace. I thank Thee. Amen.

AFFIRMATION FOR THE DAY: *Those who are over me in the Lord are working for His sake, so I shall obey for His sake.*

THE CHRISTIAN TEN COMMANDMENTS

This sentence is illuminating: "Rejoice always, pray constantly, give thanks in all circumstances; for this is the will of God in Christ Jesus for you" (I Thess. 5:16-18). This portion is taken from what might be considered Paul's ten commandments: (1) "Admonish the idle, encourage the faint-hearted, help the weak, be patient with them all." (2) "See that none of you repays evil for evil, but always seek to do good to one another and to all." (3) "Rejoice always." (4) "Pray constantly." (5) "Give thanks in all circumstances." (6) "Do not quench the Spirit." (7) "Do not despise prophesying." (8) "Test everything." (9) "Hold fast what is good." (10) "Abstain from every from of evil" (I Thess. 5:14-17). These ten commandments are vital and Christian. They can be applied to all in Christ since it is stated in one set of them: "this is the will of God in Christ Jesus for you." It must apply to all. So they could be called "the ten commandments for those in Christ."

Paul adds something to save it from being a legalism: "May the God of peace himself sanctify you wholly; and may your spirit and soul and body be kept sound and blameless at the coming of our Lord Jesus Christ. He who calls you is faithful, and he will do it" (I Thess. 5:23-24). Without these two verses these ten commandments would lay an impossible burden on the will and would be a counsel of perfection. If these commandments are a demand, however, the two additional verses are an offer: "May the God of peace himself sanctify you wholly"—you do not have to struggle to fulfill these high commands; God Himself will sanctify you wholly and will keep you sound and blameless in spirit, mind, and body. Then comes the clincher: "He who calls you is faithful and he will do it." These ten commandments turn from a legalism to a life—a life offered by grace—He Himself will sanctify and keep you, and "he will do it." Don't struggle to fulfill these—be receptive of grace.

O Lord God, Thy commandments are Thy enablings. Nothing is laid on our wills without Thy adequate reinforcements. Thy commandments are Thy call to take grace and more grace. I thank Thee, thank Thee. Amen.

AFFIRMATION FOR THE DAY: *"His commandments are not burdensome," for He commands only the good and the good is good for me.*

"DOES NOT DEPEND ON OUR RESOLUTION"

"To this end we always pray for you, that our God may make you worthy of his call, and may fulfill every good resolve and work of faith by his power, so that the name of our Lord Jesus may be glorified in you, and you in him, according to the grace of our God and the Lord Jesus Christ" (II Thess. 1:11-12).

This follows from the call of yesterday—He will make you worthy of His call. Further, He will fulfill every good resolve. It does not depend upon our resolution, but upon His revolution in us. Besides the good resolve, He undertakes to fulfill every "work of faith" which you have already started. By prayer you may tap resources adequate for anything that should be done.

The result of all this interplay between His power and our need is this: "so that the name of our Lord Jesus may be glorified in you, and you in him." This is amazing, for it is a double glorifying: the name of our Lord Jesus glorified in you and you glorified in Him. To glorify the name of the Lord Jesus would be enough for any ransomed sinner, but to be told that in the very glorifying of Jesus he himself would be glorified in Him—well, that is just too overwhelmingly good! But that is grace—grace overwhelms us with its graciousness. But this reveals the intention of redemption—it is not the glorifying of the Redeemer, but the glorifying of the redeemed. In the glorifying of the Redeemed the Redeemer is thereby glorified. Each saves his life and finds it. Each thinks only of glorifying the other, and each ends in being glorified! All this is "according to the grace of our God and the Lord Jesus Christ." Hail to grace!

O Jesus, our Redeemer, we thank Thee for a grace which not only redeems us and regenerates us, but also glorifies us. We shrink from glory, but we cannot escape it if we are in Thee. Thy grace is glory. We thank Thee. Amen.

AFFIRMATION FOR THE DAY: *My working faith: A faith that He will "fulfill every good resolve and every work of faith by his power."*

"CONFIDENCE IN THE LORD ABOUT YOU"

"And we have confidence in the Lord about you, that you are doing and will do the things which we command. May the Lord direct your hearts to the love of God and to the steadfastness of Christ" (II Thess. 3:4-5). This passage again links command and grace. Paul tells the Thessalonians that he has "confidence in the Lord" that they "are doing and will do the things" which he commands. Apart from Jesus Christ, that would have been another Law of Moses, only this time it would have been the Law of Paul. The next verse, however, directs their hearts "to the love of God and to the steadfastness of Christ." In doing this Paul not only saved these disciples from a legalism in fulfilling his commands, but he also saved himself from being a lawgiver. He took them beyond himself and pointed them to the love of God and the steadfastness of Christ. It was no longer between Paul and the Thessalonians, but between the grace of God and the Thessalonians, with Paul on the sidelines urging them to that grace and that steadfastness. He was never greater than in that hour. The heart of the man is revealed. As he steps out of the picture he steps into it—the greater for having stepped out.

Another thing emerges: he had confidence in the Lord about them. If he had not introduced them to the grace of God and to the steadfastness of Christ, then he would have had to say, "I have confidence in my power over you that you are doing and will do the things I command." That would have left Paul tense and anxious, as every dictator must be, wondering whether he can put things across. Instead he was confident and assured in the Lord. He stood off and watched God and the Thessalonians work it out together. Everybody and everything was fulfilled.

Our confidence wavers and fades unless it is a confidence in the Lord. That confidence in the Lord is fed by the grace of God and the steadfastness of Christ. It is confidence well-grounded.

O Grace of God, and O Steadfastness of Christ, my confidence is buttressed by Thee. My anchor holds, held by these two prongs. I believe in people because I believe in Thee. I keep on believing, sometimes in spite of. I thank Thee. Amen.

AFFIRMATION FOR THE DAY: *Confidence in the Lord about people, that is the secret of making people.* —

"IN THE LORD" NO IDLENESS

A striking passage: "Now we command you, brethren, in the name of our Lord Jesus Christ, that you keep away from any brother who is living in idleness and not according to the tradition that you received from us. . . . We gave you this command: If any one will not work, let him not eat" (II Thess. 3:6, 10). When Paul wrote that last sentence, little did he dream that it would find its way into the Soviet Constitution. I think the Soviets think it came from Lenin!

This sentence is finding its way not merely into the Soviet Constitution, but we are discovering that it is written into the constitutions of our beings and into the constitution of society. It is written into the nature of God: "My Father is working still and I am working." It is written everywhere. The creative urge is written into creation. If we violate it we get hurt. We have made the goal of life to get to the place where we don't have to work. The result? People get so jumpy and jittery and frustrated they are sent to a sanitarium where they are put to work at occupational therapy to regain their shattered health. A Divine joke! If people do not work they get stiff and old and die, and then they can't eat. Or if they linger on they are on diets—then they can't eat.

Two things regarding economic matters emerged out of the New Testament, and they live on with greater and greater power: (1) Distribution according to need—"distribution was made to each as any had need" (Acts 4:35). (2) Contribution according to ability—"If anyone will not work, let him not eat." These two principles—distribution according to need and contribution according to ability—are being more and more adopted throughout the world. They are ruling the development. Communism as the method of realizing these goals failed in the Acts, and it is failing in society now wherever tried, but these two principles live on. They are in the Lord, hence permanent.

O Son of God, Thy wisdom is written in the Word and in us. Thy laws are the laws of our being, hence inescapable. Thou art pressing us to just distribution and to just contribution. Thy will is our freedom. Help us to follow. Amen.

AFFIRMATION FOR THE DAY: *Wesley's motto is mine: "Never unemployed, and never triflingly employed."*

"DON'T RETIRE; CHANGE YOUR OCCUPATION"

Paul now turns to the idle: "Now such persons we command and exhort in the Lord Jesus Christ to do their work in quietness and to earn their own living. Brethren, do not be weary in well-doing" (II Thess. 3:12). If this last verse had stood alone—"Brethren, do not be weary in well-doing"—we would have thought it meant works of charity and service of others. Here Paul equates well-doing with earning your own living and working with your hands. Is that well-doing? Yes.

India is finding it so. Hundreds of thousands of "holy men" have lived in holy idleness, seated in ashes, in meditation. Now that is changing. I received an invitation to speak to a center established by the government for the rehabilitation of these holy men, teaching them to work and contribute to society instead of being parasites. Brahma was the actionless God, hence the devotees of Brahma were to be actionless. But Brahma, the actionless, is being replaced in the minds of men by the conception of the Father Who works hitherto and is now working. The God who does not work, does not eat. This works for God and man. It is basic to life; if you don't work you don't live.

That happens to the idle rich who live on the earnings of their parents. They degenerate. "Three generations from shirt sleeves to shirt sleeves" is a saying packed with observation and wisdom.

A woman upset and distracted said to me: "My husband and I got along as long as he was working. But now that he is retired with nothing to do he is unhappy and grumpy and he is under my feet all day and we are in conflict." Don't retire—change your occupation. You are happy only when you are creative. You are created by the Creator for creation, and if you are not creative you are cranky and unhappy, because you are unfulfilled. Life says, Create or perish.

O Creative Spirit, live within me and make me a creative being. It may be that my creations are tiny, but they will be creations. I will be in line with the will and purpose of the Creator—hence adjusted, hence happy. In Jesus' Name. Amen.

AFFIRMATION FOR THE DAY: *When I fulfill the creative will of God, I fulfill myself, for I am made for creation.*

"THE GRACE OF OUR LORD OVERFLOWED"

We turn now from the Epistles written to churches to Epistles written to individuals. When Paul told the churches that they were in Christ he thought of Christ as a corporate Person; to be in Him was to be in a Divine Society. He is also a personal Person, however, and one can be in Him as an individual. The letters known as the Pastoral Epistles emphasize this. Paul gives his personal testimony to a person, Timothy. "Though I formerly blasphemed and persecuted and insulted him; but I received mercy because I had acted ignorantly in unbelief, and the grace of our Lord overflowed for me with the faith and love that are in Christ Jesus" (I Tim. 1:13-14). "The grace of our Lord overflowed." It couldn't be kept within the bounds of legality—Paul was guilty before the law—nor could it be confined to the good—it overflowed to him though his hands were stained with blood. It overflowed and found him. He never got over the wonder and surprise of it. The most beautiful introduction I've ever heard was by a Negro bishop when he called out his wife: "Here is the lovely lady. Thirty-five years ago I looked into the limpid depths of her eyes and I've never gotten over the spell of it." Paul felt that way. He looked into the limpid depths of the eyes of Jesus and saw faith and love there—faith in him in spite of what he was, and love for him in spite of what he had done. And he never got over the spell of it!

Nor have I! Fifty-nine years ago I looked into His eyes and saw forgiveness there, and I've never gotten over the spell of it. And never will! Faith in me—think of it! Love for me—think of it! It's incredible. Yet looking at Him it becomes the most credible thing in the world. He being what He is could not do other than just that. The incredible, credible thing is the Person. His grace overflows all boundaries and barriers of unworthiness and reaches us redemptively.

O Jesus, Lord and Master, Thou art the miracle—the miracle of grace. Others claim signs and wonders, but in Thee the sign and wonder is Thy grace that overflows me and overwhelms with the deepest gratitude imaginable. I thank Thee. Amen.

AFFIRMATION FOR THE DAY: *"The grace of our Lord overflowed"—let that be said of every day of my life.*

"WE BEAT THEM, NO RESULT"

"The saying is sure and worthy of full acceptance, that Christ Jesus came into the world to save sinners. And I am the foremost of sinners; but I received mercy for this reason, that in me, as the foremost, Jesus Christ might display his perfect patience for an example to those who were to believe in him for eternal life" (I Tim. 1:15-16). We have heard the saying that Jesus Christ came into the world to save sinners so often that it has lost its punch. That is the most startling thing that could ever happen or ever be imagined.

The Hindus are a deeply religious people and have speculated concerning God as no other people ever have done; yet the highest they could reach in their speculation concerning the redemptive purpose of God was this: "Whenever there is a decline of righteousness and unrighteousness is in ascendance, then I body myself forth. For the protection of the righteous, for the destruction of evil doers, and for the establishment of righteousness I am born from age to age." Note: For the destruction of evil doers! The difference between destruction of evil doers and "Jesus Christ came into the world to save sinners" is so vast that they are not in the same world of ideas and attitudes. Some time ago a government official in the Congo said to one of our pastors: "You are cleaning up whole villages and tribes and sections in this amazing revival—cleaning them up from evils of crime and superstition, even cannibalism. And you do it so gently and easily. We beat them to get them to change with no result. It is a miracle." And it is! The miracle is wrought on cannibals and on a Pharisee like Paul—it is the same miracle. A part of the miracle was that Paul's past was made redemptive. It was to be used as an example to help others. He not only redeems from the past, but He redeems the past and makes even that redemptive. We help others through it.

"To believe in him for eternal life"—when you really believe in Him you have eternal life now. Eternity simply unfolds it.

O Blessed Lord and Savior, Thou dost save me and save my past. Thou dost pick up the pieces of a broken past and put them together in a new and glorious pattern. Thy touch upon everything is redemptive and always redemptive. I thank Thee. Amen.

AFFIRMATION FOR THE DAY: *Jesus Christ can display me as an example of His saving power.*

PLACE FOR AMBITIOUS PERSONS "IN CHRIST"?

"For those who serve well as deacons gain a good standing for themselves and also great confidence in the faith which is in Christ Jesus" (I Tim. 3:13). "A good standing for themselves"— is there a place for an ambitious person in Christ? At the close of an address to a civic club a member arose and said, "There seems to be no place for an ambitious person in Christianity." He was right if by an ambitious person we mean an egoistic place and power seeker. The first thing Christianity demands is self-surrender. The ego, trying to be God, must be renounced and surrendered. Once that surrender is made, however, there is a place in Christianity for the ambitious. The ambition now has a new motive and goal—we are ambitious to serve. The word "deacon" comes from *"dia,"* through, and *"konos,"* the dust. This calls up the figure of the camel driver going through the dust leading the camel while someone else sits on the camel. The deacon is the humble server, going through the dust.

An amazing thing happens, however. The servant of all becomes the greatest of all. Jesus said that "whoever would be great among you must be your servant, and whoever would be first among you must be your slave" (Matt. 20:26-27). If you would be great be a servant; if first, be a slave. Degrees of self-giving determine the heights to which you rise. The deacon who forgets himself in self-giving service gets, as a by-product, a good standing for himself. He wants nothing except to serve, and gets everything. Moreover, there is another by-product: he gains "great confidence in the faith which is in Christ Jesus." He gains great confidence in the faith; he sees that it works; it is self-verifying. He feels he has the sum total of reality behind him. The egoistic feel inwardly insecure. The self-giving, serving type feel confidence and security. They feel they are on the right track.

O Lord Jesus, when we take Thy way we know that it is the Way. When we are obedient to Thy will we know it is the Will. When we live Thy life we know it is the Life. This great confidence possesses us. Glory be! Amen.

AFFIRMATION FOR THE DAY: *I have "great confidence in the faith" because I have great confidence in the center of that faith, Christ.*

LIFE AND PROMISE OF LIFE

"Paul, an apostle of Christ Jesus by the will of God according to the promise of the life which is in Christ Jesus" (II Tim. 1:1). This adds a touch to the life that is in Christ. When we are in Christ we have life. "In him was life." We also have the promise of life; there is more life to follow. "I came that they may have life, and have it abundantly." If you love life there is attached to it a ticket which says this is the first installment of more abundant life.

One of the things that kills the inner spirit is the feeling that there is no future in what one is doing. It leads to a dead end. I paused in writing one day to listen to an Indian father, our gardener, tell of his frustration concerning his son, who is in a job which has no present—and more important, no future. There is no "promise" in it. In Jesus everything is promising. There is at the heart of every possession a promise. There is more—and yet more, for the taking.

This sense that in Jesus there are no dead ends, that everything is open, is the most exciting thing about it. Even the grave has an open end—an open end into eternal life. Sorrow has no dead end; we can use it and make it into song. As I sit each evening in meditation and prayer beneath a pine tree, I can hear the sharp pop of a pod on a tree, like a mild pistol shot, as it breaks open. With this pop it scatters its seed far from the tree. The breaking of your heart with sorrow may scatter the seeds of your victory into other lives. Everything in Jesus has promise. If I stub my toe I fall into His arms. If I fall, I fall on my knees and get up stronger and wiser. If I lose the skirmish, it helps me win the battle. I am "a child of promise"—nothing static do I receive—it is just a promise of the "to be." All His promises are life.

Dear Lord, there is a tingle of expectancy in being in Thee. Every little thing is big with destiny. Every gift is but a promise. I feel the outreach. The future beckons. It is filled with Thee, and in Thee is Life. I thank Thee. Amen.

AFFIRMATION FOR THE DAY: *There is the promise of life in everything if I know how to find it and use it.*

"MADE EVERYTHING TO WORK IN JESUS' WAY"

"Who saved us and called us with a holy calling, not in virtue of our works but in virtue of his own purpose and the grace which he gave us in Christ Jesus ages ago, and now has manifested through the appearing of our Savior Christ Jesus, who abolished death and brought life and immortality to light through the gospel" (II Tim. 1:9-10).

We saw yesterday how there was promise of life in Christ Jesus—it stretches out into the future forever. Here we see that it stretches back "ages ago." This redemption in Christ is not an afterthought of God, brought on by man's sin. Jesus was not heaven's trouble-shooter sent down to get us out of a jam. He was God's own purpose—the purpose wrought into creation. God knew if He made man free, man would sin, but He decided to create. Jesus was the redemptive answer. He made everything to work in Jesus' way. That was redemptive. If man still sinned, Jesus would take all the penalties and sins upon Himself at a cross. "The Lamb slain from the foundation of the world"—the cross was inherent in creation.

Now it has been "manifested through the appearing of our Savior Jesus Christ." In Him we see the purpose of creation. One of His purposes was to abolish death. He "abolished death and brought life and immortality to light through the gospel"—in Him there is no death. In Him, and in Him alone, there is "life and immortality." There is no life and there is no immortality apart from Him "who alone has immortality" (I Tim. 6:16). Therefore those who are in Him alone have immortality. The immortality of the soul is not a natural endowment; it is a supernatural gift of God in Christ. The grace that does not give immortality to those outside Christ is grace indeed. It is the kindest thing possible, for being outside Christ is hell.

O Jesus, Savior and Redeemer, I am grateful that Thou hast come to abolish death and to bring life and immortality to light. May it not be brought to light merely, but brought to life in me. May I live nothing but life. Amen.

AFFIRMATION FOR THE DAY: *Soul of mine, you are made to work in Christ's way; if you work in some other way, you work your own ruin.*

"THE FAITH AND LOVE . . . IN CHRIST JESUS"

"Follow the pattern of the sound words which you have heard from me, in the faith and love which are in Christ Jesus; guard the truth that has been entrusted to you by the Holy Spirit who dwells within us" (II Tim. 1:13-14). Here we find Paul's prescription for being sound in the faith: (1) "Follow the pattern of sound words which you have heard from me"; (2) "Guard the truth that has been entrusted to you by the Holy Spirit who dwells within us"; (3) In both cases, whether from me or from the Holy Spirit within, test it all in the light of "the faith and love which are in Christ Jesus." This last named is the touchstone—whether it comes from Paul or from the Holy Spirit within, it must be tested by "the faith and the love . . . in Christ Jesus." If it rings true to Him, it is true; if it doesn't, it is not true. Put up your question marks.

The center of the gospel is Jesus Christ, not Paul's teaching or the teaching of the Holy Spirit within. Both have to be brought to the judgment bar of Christ. We follow Paul as Paul follows Christ. We follow the Holy Spirit within if the Holy Spirit within points toward Jesus. If it points some other way it is some other spirit—not the Holy Spirit. "When the Spirit of truth comes, he will guide you into all truth; for he will not speak on his own authority. . . . He will glorify me, for he will take what is mine and declare it to you" (John 16:13-14). "I was in the Spirit, and lo, a throne stood in heaven, with one seated on the throne!" (Rev. 4:2). When we are in the Spirit we are not free to act and think and go where we will; there is a throne to which we must be subservient and obedient.

We follow good people and we follow the inner guidance of the Holy Spirit, but only as they follow "the faith and love which are in Christ Jesus." Note: "faith and love"—both, for we may hold the "faith" unlovingly.

O Spirit of God, teach me to discern between Thy voice and the voice of my subconscious desires. May I be so attuned to Jesus that the discernment may be easy and immediate. This is my growing point. In Jesus' name. Amen.

AFFIRMATION FOR THE DAY: *I follow the guidance of the spirit only as the guidance of the Spirit follows the mind and spirit of Christ.*

"STRONG IN THE GRACE . . . IN CHRIST JESUS"

"You then, my son, be strong in the grace that is in Christ Jesus, and what you have heard from me before many witnesses entrust to faithful men who will be able to teach others also" (II Tim. 2:1). This is vitally important: "be strong in the grace that is in Christ Jesus." Many think that a doctrine of grace does not produce strong men, that it produces weak and dependent men. Some doctrines of grace do produce weak men, but this is not "the grace that is in Christ Jesus." It produces strong men, like Paul, the greatest advocate of grace. His impress is upon the ages. He could say, "I am what I am by the grace of God." He was the greatest human who ever lived, and yet he lived by grace.

Jesus is a strong man creating strong men around Him. That is what Paul advocated in Timothy: "Be strong in the grace that is in Christ Jesus, and what you have heard from me before many witnesses entrust to faithful men who will be able to teach others also." In other words, the strong man is the one who is creating strong men around him; he is creating creators. The weakness of some so-called strong men is that they cannot create strong men to take over when they pass out. Then all their work collapses, and the strong man is shown by results to be a weak man. "It is better to get ten men to work than to do the work of ten men."

The strength of the visitation evangelism campaign was that it taught laymen to teach others—and won them to winning. The strength of the revival in the Central Congo was that the converts at the end of the week stood before the altar and pledged themselves out of gratitude to go back to win their families, their villages, their tribes, and then the neighboring tribes. And they did it! People right out of the bush became flaming evangelists of the good news. The grace that trusted the leaders makes the leaders make leaders out of their followers.

O Lord Christ, make me strong in the grace that entrusts to others what has been entrusted to me. Create in me a strong faith in Thee and in others. Make me to be a maker of men. Then and then only I shall be strong. Amen.

AFFIRMATION FOR THE DAY: *Grace makes me strong because grace makes me humble enough to receive.*

"GLORY NOW"

"Remember Jesus Christ . . . the gospel for which I am suffering and wearing fetters, like a criminal. But the word of God is not fettered. Therefore I endure everything for the sake of the elect, that they also may obtain the salvation which in Christ Jesus goes with eternal glory" (II Tim. 2:8-10). "The salvation which . . . goes with eternal glory"—how could he talk about salvation and eternal glory when he lay undelivered in prison chains! Yes, how could he? In only one way: "Remember Jesus Christ"! He was doing just that—he was remembering Jesus Christ. Had he put his attention on the injustice of his situation, on the hardships he was going through, on the biting of the iron in his flesh, he could not have talked about a salvation that went with eternal glory. He would have chewed on his resentments, would have curled his lips and said, "My God, why?" Instead, he talked of eternal glory, and the eternal glory stretched into the now. It was glory now.

He used the word "glory" not as a future anticipation, but as a present experience. Remembering and looking at Jesus, everything was glory, not as an exclamation, but as an experience. This happens today in similar circumstances when the eyes are on Christ instead of on the self. A Canadian missionary contracted leprosy while tearing down a leper house. The disease came out in England when he was on his way home on furlough. Arriving in Canada, he was isolated in a log cabin in a wilderness. A missionary friend from India went to see him, and as they talked of the old days in India pity and compassion crept into the missionary's voice. The leper stopped him: "You are feeling sorry for me. You shouldn't. These walls are filled with the glory of the Lord. I have never been so happy in my life. It is glory." The glory world invades this world of suffering and pain, and makes it heaven now.

O Jesus, my Lord, I remember Thee, and remembering Thee all my pinpricks are naught beside Thy nailprints and all my injustices are nothing compared to putting the Redeemer to death. May my littleness be lost in Thy greatness. Amen.

AFFIRMATION FOR THE DAY: *The Eternal Glory reaches back into the Now—reaches back into me. I walk in it!*

HIS CHAINS WERE ONLY PHYSICAL

"Now you have observed my teaching, my conduct, my aim in life, my faith, my patience, my love, my steadfastness, my persecutions, my sufferings, what befell me at Antioch, at Iconium, and at Lystra, what persecutions I endured; yet from them all the Lord rescued me. Indeed all who desire to live a godly life in Christ Jesus will be persecuted" (II Tim. 3:10-12). There is a strange portion in that passage: "Yet from them all the Lord rescued me." He was then in prison! He called himself "an ambassador in chains" (Eph. 6:20). He was in chains, but an ambassador still, and never more an ambassador of the Kingdom than when in chains. From that prison his influence extended to the ends of the earth and to the ages.

All Paul's chains were only physical. Inwardly he was free—as free as the birds that fly. His spirit roamed all thought, all history, all conditions, and he spoke through his letters as though he were master of that outside world. And he was! The ages have proved it.

Many are ambassadors in chains, and all their chains are inward. They are bound by fears, resentments, self-preoccupation, unresolved guilt. They are infinitely worse off than Paul, who was in nothing but outer chains. I paused to talk to a couple who had come to see me. We had been giving a pension to a woman whose deceased husband had worked for us for many years, but had to stop it because she was living with her stepson and had children by him. Both of them were in chains, and all their tears could not wash out a line of that record. Worse, they had tied God's hands, and mine. We were in chains too, helpless to help them, for there was only denial of guilt. There is no bondage but sin.

My Lord and my God, when we throw ourselves upon Thy redeeming mercy our bondage is at an end. Until then we are fettered with our self-wrought fetters. Make us free inwardly, and we shall walk the earth conquerors. Amen.

AFFIRMATION FOR THE DAY: *If I have to have bondages, let them all be outward, none inward.*

THE SCRIPTURES AND "IN CHRIST"

"And now from childhood you have been acquainted with the sacred writings which are able to instruct you for salvation through faith in Christ Jesus. All scripture is inspired by God and profitable for teaching, for reproof, for correction, and for training in righteousness, that the man of God may be complete, equipped for very good work" (II Tim. 3:15-17). "The sacred writings which are able to instruct you for salvation through faith in Christ Jesus." What part has the Scriptures in the life of those in Christ?

The temptation—and it is a real one—is to say: "I am 'in Christ'; He will guide me from within; I need no other guidance." In that direction lies disaster. First of all, we know little or nothing about Jesus Christ except through the Scriptures. If you depend on your inner light solely, or mostly, you will probably wander off into vagaries. You will probably go off into visions and dreams and voices, many of them from the subconscious. Anything from within needs correction from the Scriptures. Here it is said the Scriptures give four things: (1) Teaching—"profitable for teaching." It corrects ignorance of the mind. (2) Reproof—"for reproof." It corrects sin of the soul. (3) Correction—"for correction." It corrects errors of emotion, conscience, and judgment. (4) Discipline—"training in righteousness." It corrects undisciplined living. The Scriptures give corrections to the total person—the mind, the will, the emotions, and disciplines them all into maturity.

One trying to live without the guidance of the Scriptures would be like a captain of a ship who would brush aside chart and compass and stars and would say, "I will be guided by my intuitions." No person can be spiritual who is not scriptural. If there is dust on your Bible, there is dust on your experience of Christ. As I sat in a train reading my Bible a woman remarked, "You must love Him." I do, for I love His Word.

O Jesus, these words of the Scripture take me by the hand and take me beyond the words to the Word, to Thee. Therefore I love them, for I love Thee. New light is breaking out from Thy Word all the time. I thank Thee. Amen.

AFFIRMATION FOR THE DAY: *The Scriptures have been close to the Savior, and if I am to keep close to the Savior I must keep close to the Scriptures.*

A RELATIONSHIP OF RESPONSIBILITY

"I charge you in the presence of God and of Christ Jesus who is to judge the living and the dead, and by his appearing and his kingdom: preach the word, be urgent in season and out of season, convince, rebuke, and exhort, be unfailing in patience and in teaching" (II Tim. 4:1-2). "I charge you in the presence . . . of Christ Jesus." To be in Christ is to be in the presence of Christ Jesus—the judge. It is not an amiable relationship of mystic sweetness alone; it is a relationship of responsibility to Jesus as Lord and Judge.

That responsibility is sevenfold: (1) "preach the word"—preach Jesus, for He is the Word. "Great indeed, we confess, is the mystery of our religion: He was manifested in the flesh" (I Tim. 3:16). One would have thought Paul would say, "Great indeed is the mystery of our religion: It . . . ." No, it is not an "it"; it is a "He." (2) "Be urgent in season and out of season"—preach for a verdict, a choice, a decision; "in season"—in the pulpit, "out of season"—everywhere. It was said of "Brother Bryan" of Birmingham, Alabama, that he sometimes held up the traffic on a sidewalk, and even in the street, while he prayed for a man in need. The city loved him for it and put up a monument to him in the center of the city, a man kneeling with hands outstretched to God in prayer. (3) "Convince"—be a convinced Christian and a convincing Christian. (4) "Rebuke"—love a person enough to rebuke him, but rebuke him in love. (5) "Exhort"—exhort for decision. In the old days of Methodism "exhorters" got up after a sermon and exhorted the people to decision. Now the exhorters have dropped out and so have the decisions! (6) "Be unfailing in patience"—don't give anyone up. "We never give them up in Waterstreet" was the motto of that mission. (7) "And in teaching"—Paul's own example: "teaching you in public and from house to house."

O God, our Father, Thy Word has been and is a lamp unto our feet and a light unto our pathway. Help us to hide it within our hearts that we may not sin against Thee. Thy Word leads me to Thy Son. Amen.

AFFIRMATION FOR THE DAY: *His judgments are my salvation, for He judges me for my good and only for my good.*

"ALL THE GOOD THAT IS OURS IN CHRIST"

"And I pray that the sharing of your faith may promote the knowledge of all the good that is ours in Christ" (Philem. 6). This very touching and beautiful letter of Paul to Philemon, the owner of a runaway slave converted through Paul while in prison, reveals the heart of a man in Christ. Here Paul urges Philemon to share his faith by taking Onesimus back, forgiving him, and receiving him as a brother. A real strain on a slaveowner's faith!

To be in Christ is to share one's faith, for you cannot have a share in Christ unless you share Him with others. Nothing is ours till we share it. The sharing of the faith makes it possible to share in the faith. Otherwise not—if you are not winning others, Christ has not really won you.

When you share your faith, then you "promote the knowledge of all the good that is ours in Christ." "All the good that is ours in Christ"! That is what sharing your faith means—it means telling people around all the good that you have found in Christ. It doesn't mean that you have to win people by argument; it means that you invite people to share a "good"—all the good which is yours in Christ. That is the easiest and most natural thing in the world.

"All the good that is ours in Christ"! Christ is the good, and that good turns out to be good for us—good for the mind. The mind in Christ feels it is no longer biting on futility, but on reality. Good for the soul—the soul, after wandering through futile and disappointing allegiances fastens itself on Jesus Christ and says, "This is it." The body, now freed from the conflicts of mind and soul, bounced back with health and says, "This is good." The relationships, now unsnarled by love, say, "This is the way to live—it is good." It is good and only good!

O Savior Divine, Thy way is good and only good, unsullied by any evil. In everything else I have to pick and choose—in this I have to accept, and accept completely. Thou art good and Thy good is good for me. I thank Thee. Amen.

AFFIRMATION FOR THE DAY: *"All the good that is ours in Christ" has its opposite: "All the bad that is ours outside Christ."*

"FOR LOVE'S SAKE"

"Accordingly, though I am bold enough in Christ to command you to do what is required, yet for love's sake I prefer to appeal to you" (Philem. 8-9). This adds a very beautiful phase of being in Christ. To be in Christ is to be bold, for you feel secure and unafraid with the sum total of reality behind you. In society you are not bold, for you look around to see what effect your actions will have on others. That makes you an echo. If you are in you, you are not bold, for there is nothing behind you but you. If you are in Christ, however, everything is behind you. You can be bold, for when you speak He speaks through and in you. You are bold with His boldness.

In Christ timidity is gone. "For God did not give us a spirit of timidity but a spirit of power and love and self-control" (II Tim. 1:7). Feeling the sense of boldness—a boldness which was able to command—Paul turned and said, "yet for love's sake I prefer to appeal to you." The consciousness of strength is the secret of humility. "Jesus, knowing that the Father had given all things into his hands . . . rose from supper, laid aside his garments, and girded himself with a towel . . . and began to wash the disciples' feet." Jesus, knowing that He had all things in His hands, used those hands, not to wield a scepter, but to wash His disciples' feet. The little, the empty cannot afford to be humble. They must keep up their precarious position; so they sit stiff. To bend would crack their brittle show-off. For self's sake they refuse to bend. But Paul "for love's sake" bent and stood tall in the bending. Jesus in washing the disciples' feet washed from our hearts silly prides. Our Lord bent, and we too can bend for His love's sake and can be great in the bending. Bold, but appealing instead—that is what it means to be in Christ.

O Christ Jesus, make me bold enough to face any man in any situation and yet make me humble enough to win them rather than browbeat them. The end is to win. Help me to be winsome, like Thee. In Thy Name. Amen.

AFFIRMATION FOR THE DAY: *My boldness in Christ shall not be cocky self-assertion, but a manifestation of "for love's sake."*

"NO LONGER AS A SLAVE"

"Perhaps this is why he was parted from you for a while, that you might have him back for ever, no longer as a slave but more than a slave, as a beloved brother, especially to me but how much more to you, both in the flesh and in the Lord" (Philem. 15-16). This portion is filled with beauty and dynamite: "no longer as a slave but more than a slave, as a beloved brother." There is enough dynamite packed in that simple statement to blow every form of slavery to pieces. Someone has said, "There is no method of reform so powerful as this, that alongside a corrupt custom you lay an incompatible principle." That incompatible principle will work, like the tiny roots that creep into a crack of granite, and will break in pieces the greatest monuments of man's pride. That is how slavery was killed. The incompatible principle of every person's equality before God killed the custom of man's inequality before man, slavery. It silently worked its overthrow.

"More than a slave."—Africa, once the land where potential slaves dwelt, is now the land of potential possibility. The leaven of freedom is working. Over a dozen nations have received their freedom and others are slated to follow. An African pastor put it this way: "Before a baby is born it begins to kick. Africa is kicking, for Africa wants to be born." Another African put it thus, "We are tired of being 'under.' " The worm is turning, and nations and the world are shaking. The ideas at the heart of the gospel are responsible for this uprising of man. We will all be richer when Africa is free, and when the Negro is free in America. We are poor in their poverty, degraded in their degradation. We rise when they rise, and rise only when they rise. "More than a slave, a beloved brother" is the watchword of that rising.

O Lord God, the leaven of Thy love is at work. We feel its stirring everywhere. We rejoice in it, for I'm free only in every man's freedom; I'm bound in every man's bondage. Help me to give full rein to this freeing love. Amen.

AFFIRMATION FOR THE DAY: *"No longer as a slave" can mean to me: No longer what I've been.*

"REFRESH MY HEART IN THE LORD"

"So if you consider me your partner, receive him as you would receive me. If he has wronged you at all, or owes you anything, charge that to my account. . . . I will repay it—to say nothing of your owing me even your own self. Yes, brother, I want some benefit from you in the Lord. Refresh my heart in Christ" (Philem. 17-20).

This was the summing up of the appeal. This is the beginning: "I, Paul, an ambassador and now a prisoner also for Jesus Christ—I appeal to you for my child, Onesimus, whose father I have become in my imprisonment. (Formerly he was useless to you, but now he is indeed useful to you and to me.) I am sending him back to you, sending my very heart" (Philem. 9-12). Here Paul puns—a comfort to punsters! "Onesimus" means "useful"—formerly "he was useless," now "useful."

Another note in passing: Paul calls himself an "ambassador"—the marginal reading, "an old man." Are the old to be ambassadors? Yes, of gentleness, of goodwill, of thoughtfulness, of examples of being easy to get along with, of real service.

The real point is this: "Refresh my heart in Christ." Paul was being refreshed from within—was refreshed by being in Christ—but he asked for this refreshment from without. Do we get refreshment from both directions—from within and from without? Yes. The within is primary and all-important, however. If we depend on refreshment from without, it will let us down again and again. We must not be self-contained, we must be Christ-contained. We must depend on Him for our primary refreshment. Then if anything comes from without it is all something thrown in, a plus. Glance at the refreshments from without, gaze at the refreshment in Christ. We must give refreshment to others if we are to keep it in Him.

O Blessed Redeemer, refresh me so blessedly that whether I get refreshment from without or not, I will be safe and satisfied. Then I can take joyously anything that comes from others. I do not depend on it. I thank Thee for this freedom. Amen.

AFFIRMATION FOR THE DAY: *I shall receive gratefully refreshments of spirit from without, knowing I have inexhaustible inner springs.*

327

HUMAN DEPENDABILITY

"Epaphras, my fellow prisoner in Christ Jesus, sends greetings to you, and so do Mark, Aristarchus, Demas, and Luke, my fellow workers" (Philem. 23-24). These five men represent what we shall probably meet in the way of human dependability when we are in Christ. First, Epaphras was pure joy. Paul writes of him in Colossians: "as you learned it from Epaphras our beloved fellow servant. He is a faithful minister of Christ on our behalf, and has made known to us your love in the Spirit" (1:7-8). Again: "Epaphras . . . remembering you earnestly in his prayers, that you may stand mature and fully assured in all the will of God" (4:12). That last phrase—"stand mature and fully assured in all the will of God"—shows the type of endeavor Epaphras was putting forth. A high type, he was so positive that he got into jail over it. In Colossians he was free, in Philemon he was in prison with Paul. So his high spirituality could stand low and heavy chains.

Second, Mark—he was a disappointment and a joy. After he turned back from the work in Pamphilia Paul refused to take him on another journey, and he and Barnabas "parted in irritation" over Mark. He came back, however, made good, became a fellow worker of Paul, was "profitable for the ministry," and wrote a gospel! He is the example of the man who lost a skirmish and won the battle.

Third, Aristarchus was faithful and a joy. In Colossians he was called a fellow prisoner (4:10), here a fellow worker. Whether in prison or free, he was faithful. Fourth, Demas was a deep disappointment. "For Demas, in love with this present world, has deserted me" (II Tim. 4:10). His name now stands for the worldly-minded. Fifth, Luke, who was more than continuous pure joy, wrote a gospel and the Acts. In Christ you may find three continuously faithful, one who wobbled but who got his feet again, and one who was nothing but disappointment. Christ remains steady.

O Lord Christ, amid the joys and disappointments of men, I find Thee the same yesterday, today, and forever. I am glad my Center holds. I lean lightly on others, wholly on Thee. So I sing amid my disappointments. I thank Thee. Amen.

AFFIRMATION FOR THE DAY: *I will not go up with the faithfulness of others, nor down with their unfaithfulness—I remain steady in Him.*

"SHARE IN CHRIST"

We turn now to Hebrews where the "in Christ" passages are scarce; there are only two. One of them says: "For we share in Christ, if only we hold our first confidence firm to the end" (3:14). This one is important—"we share in Christ." To be in Christ is to share in Christ. It is thinkable that we might be in Christ and not share in Christ, as it is thinkable to be in a rich man's home and not share in his riches. But here we are told that to be in Christ is to share in everything in Him. All He has is yours.

When you go into a rich man's house in India he will politely say, "It is all yours," but it is a pleasant politeness. It may be like a man who promised his god that if he had a bumper crop he would give half to the idol. His wife pulled his sleeve and said, "It's too much." The man wiggled his tongue—the sign among the Tamils of South India that you are saying something you do not really mean!

In Jesus Christ there is neither pleasant politeness nor the wiggling of the tongue; promises are meant. All Christ has is yours if you are in Him—yours for the taking. The rub is in the last—yours for the taking. The motto of a movement, "God gives, man refuses to take," is true here. Many are in Christ but are comparatively poor. Here is Christ's Everything—His strength for our weakness; His wisdom for our ignorance; His holiness for our sin; His guidance for our confusion; His companionship for our loneliness; His fullness for our emptiness; His love for our lovelessness; His all for our all. It is all there for the taking. I can be strong in His strength, pure in His purity, loving in His love, and mature in His maturity. I share in the highest there is. My emptiness is a crime against this. My littleness is treason against His greatness. Let me share with both hands and a whole heart.

Dear Lord Jesus, the wonder that Thou hast thrown open Thy everything to me puts me in the dust, and yet makes me tingle with expectation. It is all mine, and I refuse to accept my poverty—I take Thy riches. Amen.

AFFIRMATION FOR THE DAY: *I will share in Christ to the limit of my capacity to receive.*

"HE IS PRECIOUS"

"Behold, I am laying in Zion a stone, a cornerstone chosen and precious, and he who believes in him will not be put to shame. To you therefore who believe, he is precious, but for those who do not believe, the very stone which the builders rejected has become the head of the corner" (I Pet. 2:6-7). "He who believes in him will not be put to shame." This is the Magna Carta of our faith. Put your whole weight down on Him and He will never let you down. That has been corroborated by the millions through the ages. I do not know of a single true follower of Christ who has said: "I trusted Christ implicitly, I followed Him sincerely and wholeheartedly; but He let me down. I'm sorry I ever began or continued to follow Him. It is all an illusion. He is a fraud. I've been put to shame." Why has no one ever said that? Because they couldn't.

On the other hand, thousands who have deserted Him have gone away with heavy hearts, burdened consciences, and in confusion and shame. It works with an almost mathematical precision. Nothing in history has been so universally verified as this. It is verified knowledge.

"He who believes in him" may not always have gotten what he believed in Him for, but he has gotten that or something better. He was not put to shame.

May I testify? Threescore years ago I began to walk with this Man—to walk with Him through all lands, under all conditions. I have let Him down again and again, but He has never let me down. Not once! He hasn't merely been faithful, He has been faithfulness itself. Everything outside Him upon which I have depended has let me down. He has never once let me down. I can hear the echo of millions saying, "Amen." The heavenly host takes up the "Amen" and makes it universal—here and there.

O Jesus, in Thee have I trusted, in Thee do I trust, and in Thee will I trust forever. If these lips should ever deny Thee they would be parched and cracked with anguish. Now they sing, for I trust with all I have in Thee. Amen.

AFFIRMATION FOR THE DAY: *"He who believes in Him will not be put to shame"—let me be an illustration of this.*

"IN HIS STEPS"

"Because Christ also suffered for you, leaving you an example, that you should follow in his steps" (I Pet. 2:21). "In his steps" is not quite the same as in Him, but if we are in Him we must follow in His steps. Not that "in his steps" is primary in the Christian gospel. He is not primarily our example. The attempt to follow Him primarily as example ends in tenseness, strain, and disillusionment. We must follow Him primarily as Savior and Lord, then as Example. Following Him as Savior and Lord means self-surrender and acceptance; following Him as example means you give Him your deeds and works, but not necessarily yourself.

Once surrendered to Him, you follow in His steps; not merely the footsteps He left in Palestine two thousand years ago—they are important, for the universal is in those local steps—but also the steps of this Man in the present. He is alive and walks the roads of today, and he who is in Him must be with Him as He walks up the new Calvaries of modern life, where He is being crucified on a cross of gold, a cross of nationalism, a cross of war, a cross of greed, a cross of racialism, a cross of hate.

The slogan, "Don't wrestle, nestle" is good to show that we are to cease our struggling and nestle in His love, but it can become a quietism, an escape. Jesus bids us follow Him in new battles, on new fronts, in new situations. "You preach a very troublesome gospel," said a Reformed minister of South Africa to me. "You preach a Kingdom of God on earth, and that upsets everything. I preach a Kingdom in heaven, and that doesn't upset anything now." No, but it leaves Christ alone crucified on a cross of racialism, and it leaves a situation which is growingly like a hell on earth—a heavenly kingdom and an earthly hell! We must follow in His steps now.

O Christ, our Redeemer, if we are to follow Thee we must hasten our steps, for Thou art out ahead of us, fighting the battle with weapons of love on new fronts. Help us to be sensitive to where the real issues are. In Thy name. Amen.

AFFIRMATION FOR THE DAY: *If I am in Him I must be in His steps on every issue with His attitudes.*

"NOT ON MY BODY"

"He himself bore our sins in his body on the tree" (I Pet. 2:24).
Again to be in Christ and in His body are not exactly the same,
and yet they belong together. You cannot be in Christ and not be
in everything that is in His body. In His body are our sins, which
He bore once and for all on the cross, and yet continuously bears
in His body in the continuing cross of identification with our sins
and sorrows. If we are to be in Him we too must bear in our
bodies what He did and does bear in His.

"It's not on my body" is an old Chinese saying, meaning "It is
not my responsibility." A missionary tried to pay some
fishermen to save a drowning man, but each shrugged his
shoulders and said, "It's not on my body." That saying and that
attitude was the cause of the downfall of the old China. Atheistic
Communism stepped in and said, "The condition of the poor
and the dispossessed is on our bodies, is our responsibility."
They took over, and they will run their course, and then fail for
they are using wrong means, and the means are corrupting and
will corrupt the ends and ruin them sooner or later. Then
someone with right ends and right means will take over—and
that will be the Kingdom.

Last year there was translated to heaven a saint—a rugged,
battling, loving saint, Mrs. Nobu Jo. After three days and nights
in prayer in the mountains around Kobe she came down
convinced that the suicides taking place at a certain bend in the
railway track were on her body, were her responsibility. She put
up a sign at the spot: "Don't. See Mrs. Nobu Jo first. God is
love." I asked her how many she had rescued from suicide, and
she replied: "We have a record of five thousand. And a record of
sixty thousand more who probably would have committed
suicide if we hadn't helped them." The sorrow and despair of
these people were on her body. At the end the Emperor and
Empress came to thank her. We all do.

O Lord Jesus, we see lesser problems around us. Help us to
take them this day on our bodies and make them our own. That
will mean a cross, but it will also mean an Easter morning for
us—and them. In Thy blessed name and spirit. Amen.

AFFIRMATION FOR THE DAY: *If I refuse to take the sins of others on my
body, then I refuse His taking my sins on His body.*

"GOOD BEHAVIOR IN CHRIST"

"Always be prepared to make a defense to any one who calls you to account for the hope that is in you, yet do it with gentleness and reverence; and keep your conscience clear, so that, when you are abused, those who revile your good behavior in Christ may be put to shame" (I Pet. 3:15-16). "Your good behavior in Christ." That is the answer that brings shame. If you answer cleverness with cleverness, that will bring mental arrogance. If you answer overbearing with overbearing, that will bring combat. Your good behavior is your best answer. The answer of Christianity is the Christian.

"Your good behavior in Christ"—just what would that mean? The fact that I cannot define accurately "behavior in Christ" is in its favor. If I could define it, it would be a verbalism, or a big schism, but I know "behavior in Christ" when I see it. So does everyone else. A Christian layman taking over his office as a member of the Railway Board in New Delhi called his staff, mostly non-Christians, together and said: "I am a Christian. I want to be a better one. If you find in me any departure from the highest Christian standards, please call my attention to it. Help me." A few days later some Hindu clerks said to him: "Mr. Venugopal, you seem down and sad today. Didn't you have your quiet time this morning?" These Hindus saw that to be sad and down is not good Christian behavior. When non-Christians said of Keshab Chandu Sen (a man who was not a Christian) that he had "a New Testament face," they knew what a New Testament face was, though they could not define it. "Good behavior in Christ" is the way Christ would behave in a situation.

A Methodist pastor was shot by the Communists in Korea. His daughter knelt beside him as he was dying and said, "I'll avenge this." "No," said the father, "we must love." The daughter did just that. She knew her answer was wrong and her father's answer was right—profoundly right, because profoundly Christian.

Dear Lord Christ, when I am called upon to give an answer to the hope that is within me, wilt Thou fulfill Thy promise that it shall be given in that hour how and what I shall speak, for the Holy Spirit will speak within me. That is my only hope. Amen.

AFFIRMATION FOR THE DAY: *My "good behavior in Christ" will mean that I will be Christian in every situation.*

THE STATE OF GLORY

"And after you have suffered a little while, the God of all grace, who has called you to his eternal glory in Christ, will himself restore, establish, and strengthen you" (I Pet. 5:10). "His eternal glory in Christ"—just what does this "glory" life mean, now and forever? We usually associate it with the eternal glory in heaven. Peter says this glory is in Christ and it must therefore be now as well as hereafter. Again he speaks of "a partaker in the glory that is to be revealed" (I Pet. 5:1). "A partaker" now! Again: "If you are reproached for the name of Christ, you are blessed, because the spirit of glory and of God rests upon you" (I Pet. 4:14). "The spirit of glory and of God rests upon you"—now.

This glory experience in Christ is partly received and seen in the new birth; there is an extension of it in the receiving of the Holy Spirit, but there seems to be a very definite experience of glory which the New Testament writers are trying to express, beyond both of these two mentioned experiences. What it is, I'm out to know. I've felt periods when for days I was in the glory. I've seen it in Rufus Moseley, an authentic saint. He lived in the glory more than any person I've ever seen. The word "glory" was upon his lips constantly, for the state of glory was a constant state within him. This persisted through health and through painful sickness. I have seen it in a Kerala Christian in South India, whom we called "Stotrum"—"Praise." That word "stotrum" was upon his lips for everybody and everything. He said it as a greeting, and he said it as a farewell. I called on him when he was past ninety and on his bed in what proved to be his last illness. He greeted us with "stotrum," and after prayer we left, and his last word was "stotrum." It was not a phrase; it was an experience. His face and his words said the same thing, "stotrum."

Dear Lord Jesus, upon the Mount Thou didst appear in glory and so did Moses and Elijah appear in glory. It must be associated not with place, but with condition. Give me that condition that I may appear in glory now. Amen.

AFFIRMATION FOR THE DAY: *I will name one foot "Glory" and the other "Hallelujah," and I will walk the Glory Road with feet and heart saying "Glory Hallelujah."*

"PEACE . . . IN CHRIST JESUS"

"Peace to all of you that are in Christ" (I Pet. 5:14). This may seem a mere greeting as we say, *"Salaam,"* "Peace" in India. But it may mean more; it may mean that all those who are in Christ have peace. Note the "all." Is being in Christ to be in a state of peace? Is it a special peace, different from anything the world calls peace? Yes. Jesus said: "Peace I leave with you; my peace I give to you; not as the world gives do I give to you. Let not your hearts be troubled, neither let them be afraid" (John 14:27). Is there a peace called "my peace"? Is it different, profoundly different, from the psychological peace called "peace of mind"? Yes.

A friend, deeply disturbed, had an operation in which a portion of the front part of his brain, the troubled part, was severed. He now has peace of mind, but it is the peace of indifference. That is one kind of peace—peace at a price of personality. Another kind of peace is the peace of tranquilizers—a deadening of disturbed centers with drugs. This too is peace—at a price—the price of aliveness. There is the peace of stimulants. A chaplain said he could not preach unless he had a drink of liquor beforehand. This is peace—the peace of a false world of stimulation. Another is the peace of mental assertion that there is nothing to fear. This is peace—the peace of illusion. Another is the peace that comes from remembering that a reward in heaven awaits. This is the peace of "pie in the sky." Then there is the peace of Christ. It is a peace of adequacy, a peace of assurance that you are adequate for anything, for you cannot only bear everything, but can *use* everything that comes—good, bad, or indifferent. This is the peace without illusions. It says pain, sorrow, sickness, and death are real. There is a Reality within that faces this reality without and transforms it into character and achievement—hence peace!

O Jesus, Lord and Master of this business of life, I thank Thee for Thy secret—the secret of Thy peace. Thou didst walk up to the cross and didst make evil contribute; didst make it redemptive. Teach me Thy secret; then I shall know Thy peace. Amen.

AFFIRMATION FOR THE DAY: *I shall have no pseudo peace—it shall be the peace of reality—all else lets me down.*

"A FAITH OF EQUAL STANDING"

"To those who have obtained a faith of equal standing with ours in the righteousness of our God and Savior Jesus Christ" (II Pet. 1:1). "In the righteousness of our God and Savior Jesus Christ" is a phase of being in Christ—the phase of righteousness which we find in Christ. This is important. Grace is primarily in Christ, but underlying that grace is a basic righteousness. This righteousness is seen in the words "a faith of equal standing." Everyone has an equal standing before God and therefore before men.

This is the basis of democracy: equal before God and therefore equal before men. When a faith of equal standing is lacking, then democracy becomes halting or impossible. That is one reason why in purely Roman Catholic countries democracy is not found. There is no faith of equal standing, for pope and cardinals and priests are a hierarchy of privilege before God and man. Hence Roman Catholic countries turn naturally to dictatorships—that is inherent in their faith. That is the reason S. Kurusu, Japanese Special Ambassador to Washington before Pearl Harbor, said to me after the war, "Japan will never become a democracy until Japan becomes Christian." He saw that the Shinto faith provided for difference, not a faith of equal standing. That is why democracy in India is pulling against the undertow of caste and will not really be established until caste goes. That is why there can be no political democracy in Islam, for the God of Islam is an autocrat, doing as his will decides. Pakistan, a Moslem state, is working well under a dictatorship; it worked badly under democracy. That is why atheistic Communism is a dictatorship, for it has no God, therefore no faith of equal standing before God, hence no democracy. The only faith that can sustain a democracy is the Christian faith, and that faith interpreted by evangelical Christianity.

O Gracious Jesus, Thou dost not only offer grace, but basic equal justice as well. Many of us are willing to be kind, but unwilling to be just. Save us from patronizing kindness which refuses basic justice. In Thy blessed Name. Amen.

AFFIRMATION FOR THE DAY: *Starting with the basic attitude of a faith of equal standing I will treat all with equal treatment.*

TO BASIC FAITH ADD SEVEN THINGS

"Become partakers of the divine nature. For this very reason make every effort to supplement your faith with virtue, and virtue with knowledge, and knowledge with self-control, and self-control with steadfastness, and steadfastness with godliness, and godliness with brotherly affection, and brotherly affection with love. For if these things are yours and abound, they keep you from being ineffective or unfruitful in the knowledge of our Lord Jesus Christ." (II Pet. 1:4-8)

It is possible to become "partakers of the divine nature" and yet be "ineffective and unfruitful" in the knowledge of Christ, or in Him. Why? Because while we are rooted in Him, we are not built up in Him. "Rooted" means taking Divine resources, "built up" means human disciplines. Here Peter emphasizes the necessity to *make every effort* to supplement your faith. That is our part. To your basic faith you are to add seven things: virtue, knowledge, self-control, steadfastness, godliness, brotherly affection, and love. Love is the capstone. It begins with faith and ends with love. Faith and love are the two slices of bread of the sandwich; the rest are the middle filling portion. Without faith and love all the Christian virtues fall to pieces. A great faith applied by love—these are the two things which make you fruitful as a Christian.

To be in Him and yet to be ineffective and unfruitful is to be empty amid plenty, to be ignorant amid knowledge, to be weak amid strength, to be lifeless amid Life, to be nothing amid Everything.

These seven things must not only be in us, but must "abound"; there must be an overflow. We must not be half full vessels trying to run over. In Christ there is not only life, but life abundant. To be in Him is to be in Divine abundance, making it possible for us to live abundantly.

O Lord Jesus, Thou dost not give the Spirit by measure. Thy giving is a measureless giving. Yet our life and our love are so measured, calculated, small. I have the cup, give me rivers. Flow in, Divine Love, flow out, human gratitude. Amen.

AFFIRMATION FOR THE DAY: *If I am to be fruitful and effective I must abound in Christ.*

"GROW IN GRACE AND KNOWLEDGE"

"But grow in grace and knowledge of our Lord and Savior Jesus Christ" (II Pet. 3:18). Usually "But grow in grace and knowledge" is quoted and religious education taking that as its text begins to impart religious education in general. Then it becomes a swamp instead of a river. The difference between a swamp and a river is that a river has banks—it confines itself to objectives—a swamp has no banks; it spreads over everything. This verse has banks: "But grow in the grace and knowledge of our Lord and Savior Jesus Christ." The growth was not growth in general, but growth in the grace and knowledge of Jesus Christ. Cancer growth is growth, but a growth toward death. Growth in the grace and knowledge of Jesus Christ is growth in life, and this life becomes Life itself.

How do we grow? The usual answer is by taking in food, air, and exercise; food—assimilating the Word of God; air—breathing in the good and breathing out the bad; exercise—sharing with others. It might be put in another way: growth depends on (1) assimilation, (2) elimination, and (3) dissemination.

First, assimilation—you assimilate through the reading of the word of God and prayer. Cut off either one of these and the soul dies. The quiet time with the Bible and prayer is a *sine qua non* of spiritual growth. The diabolical strategy is to cut off the food supply and then sit back and watch the soul die. Second, elimination—life depends almost as much on elimination as upon assimilation. When the body can no longer eliminate it dies. When the soul is no longer pruning fruitless branches, it too becomes fruitless. Third, dissemination—if a tree doesn't produce its kind, it will die and the species will die with it. The Christian must produce Christians or not remain Christian. We grow as we sow.

Dear Father, Thou dost give seed to the sower—and to no one else. If we do not sow what Thou dost give, Thou dost withhold the giving. Let me be a sower, going forth today to sow beside all waters. In Jesus' dear name. Amen.

AFFIRMATION FOR THE DAY: *These three things in full operation in me today—assimilation, elimination, dissemination—then I will grow.*

"TO WALK IN THE SAME WAY"

"By this we may be sure we are in him: he who says he abides in him ought to walk in the same way in which he walked" (I John 2:5-6). We turn to I John in which the phrase "in Christ" or its equivalent is found twenty times. The word "this" is found twenty-six times, so there is a "thisness" about being in Christ. It is all tied very closely to life. It is not a doctrine, but a doing.

This verse puts the two together: "By this . . . in him." The one thing that brings surety that we are in Him is that we "walk in the same way in which he walked." To walk as He walked is to live as He lived. Can we live as He lived, in the same circumstances? No. On the same principles? Yes. We can apply His principles to our circumstances.

1. He met life as a man, calling on no power for his own moral battle not at your disposal or mine. He expected His Father to give Him power to meet whatever came and to use it for higher purposes. He expected no favored treatment and got none. We can apply that principle: Meet life as it comes and make something out of it.

2. He kept up His disciplines of reading the word of God and praying. "As his custom was . . . he stood up to read." "He went out into the mountains to pray as His custom was." We can apply that principle: Have a disciplined life of praying and reading of the Word.

3. He gave out what He found. "He taught them again as His custom was." We can apply this principle: Share with others what you have found from God.

4. He gave out love and only love to everybody—to enemies as well as friends. We can apply that principle: Love everybody, even enemies.

5. He made a full surrender to God: "Not my will, but thine, be done." We can apply that principle: A full surrender of the will.

6. "He set His face steadfastly to go to Jerusalem." Applied: Face everything, even the hardest, with God.

Dear Son of Man, in Thee Who strengthens me, I am able for anything. I can only walk in Thy ways as I live in Thy life. I can do the impossible—with Thee. So drawing heavily on Thee I walk Thy ways with joy. Amen.

AFFIRMATION FOR THE DAY: *I will walk in His ways with His power.*

"TRUE IN HIM AND IN YOU"

"Yet I am writing you a new commandment, which is true in him and in you" (I John 2:8). Here John rewrites what he recorded in his gospel from Jesus: "A new commandment I give to you, that you love one another; even as I have loved you" (John 13:34). Again: "This is my commandment, that you love one another as I have loved you. Greater love has no man than this, that a man lay down his life for his friends" (John 15:12-13).

This "new commandment" and this "my commandment" is the commandment to love and to love specifically—"as I have loved you." To be in Christ is to love as Christ loved.

This is important: "true in him and in you"—there is not one code of conduct for the Divine and another for the human. The commandment "is true in Him and in you." That is the most breath-taking sentence ever uttered. The Divine acts on the same principles He requires of us! India, the most religious and philosophical nation of the world, never arrived at that. There is always one code of conduct for the gods and another for man. "*Samarthi ko khuch dosh nahin lagta*"—"to the strong there is no blame." They are above the Law of Karma.

Jesus put Himself under the law of love and called it "my commandment"—a commandment which He obeyed and gave.

Interestingly enough, that commandment to love is being discovered as the law of life and not merely the commandment of Jesus. Eric Fromm, a psychiatrist, said that the necessity to love is the most deeply ingrained thing in human nature. You must "love or perish," said Smiley Blanton, another psychiatrist. The commandment which Jesus gave is being found to be the same commandment that life is giving. Is Jesus then the author of that life?

O Jesus, Thou didst lift up the laws underlying our beings, and didst call them "my commandments." They are Thy commandments, for they are Thy creations. Help us to live by Thy Law of Love and we shall find it the law of life. Amen.

AFFIRMATION FOR THE DAY: *"True in him and in you"—that gives me a moral universe and not a moral multiverse.*

ONE BUSINESS: "ABIDE IN ME"

"Let what you heard from the beginning abide in you. If what you heard . . . abides in you, then you will abide in the Son and in the Father" (I John 2:24). Just what does "Let what you heard from the beginning abide in you" signify? One commentator says it refers to the beginning of your Christian life, your conversion. But the context would point to the beginning as the Incarnation. "That which was from the beginning which we have heard, which we have seen with our eyes"—Jesus! The immediate context says: "Who is the liar but he who denies that Jesus is the Christ?" (I John 2:22). The issue is Jesus, the Incarnate, who was the Christ. If you let this fact of the Incarnation abide in you, you will abide in the Son and in the Father. Both Father and Son are found in the Incarnation. If you lose the Incarnation—Jesus—you lose both the Son and the Father. The Gnostics lost Jesus the Incarnate and lost the Son and the Father. So do we if we lose Jesus. The issue is Jesus.

Rufus Moseley began as a Southern Baptist professor of literature, wandered through Christian Science, New Thought, and Pentecostalism and came out finally to Jesus. He saw with deep clarity that the Incarnate Jesus was the issue—not Christ, nor God, nor the Holy Spirit, nor the Kingdom of God, but Jesus. When he came to Jesus his wanderings were over. He had arrived. To hear him say "Jesus" was to hear the music of heaven, and to look into his face was to see his Master. When he found Jesus he found the key to everything—God, Christ, the Holy Spirit, the Kingdom of God, Everything, to Life itself. Lose the Incarnate Jesus and everything tumbles with the loss. Jesus once said to Rufus: "You have one business in life and only one business: Abide in union with Me." When he did that, he had everything.

O Jesus, my Lord, when I deepen my consciousness of Thee everything falls into its place, everything adds up to sense and meaning. All my life becomes Life, and all my joy becomes Joy. I thank Thee for Thee. What else do I need? Amen.

AFFIRMATION FOR THE DAY: *The key to the Christian faith is not the information it imparts, but the Incarnation it presents.*

THE ANOINTING TEACHES YOU
ABOUT EVERYTHING

"But the anointing which you received from him abides in you, and you have no need that any one should teach you; as his anointing teaches you about everything, and is true, and is no lie, just as it has taught you, abide in him" (I John 2:27). Yesterday we saw the emphasis laid upon the revelation of God and life through the Incarnate Jesus. To abide in Christ meant to abide by this revelation in history of the Incarnate Jesus, and not to wander off into vagaries and philosophical myths. Anchor to Jesus was the emphasis.

Here John goes a step further and says that the anointing abides in you and that anointing teaches you everything. This provides for a continuous unfolding revelation. If yesterday we emphasized the static, this emphasizes the dynamic. This goes beyond Jude with his emphasis on "the faith which was once for all delivered to the saints" (vs. 3). There is a truth in this faith once for all delivered, but that truth must be supplemented by a dynamic unfolding through the anointing. Jesus provided for this unfolding: "When the Spirit of truth comes, he will guide you into all the truth . . . He will glorify me, for he will take what is mine and declare it to you" (John 16:13-14). So the Christian faith is "once for all," and yet an unfolding of that which was infolded in Jesus.

This anointing which teaches everything must be the Spirit of Truth, the Holy Spirit dwelling within. He becomes the Counselor, or as one commentator has put it, the Interpreter. The Holy Spirit interprets the teaching, the life, the death, the resurrection, the ascension to the place of final authority, and the return of Jesus. New meanings, new applications, new depths, new heights, new breadths, new lengths—new everything is constantly being revealed through the Spirit, the anointing.

O blessed Holy Spirit, Thou art teaching me according to the Textbook, Jesus. I thirst to know more and more of Him, for He satisfies me and sets me on fire to know more of Him. I thank Thee for Thy unfolding. In Jesus' name. Amen.

AFFIRMATION FOR THE DAY: *The Holy Spirit abiding in me reveals Jesus and ever more of Jesus.*

"NOT AT HOME IN YOUR HOME"

"And now, little children, abide in him, so that when he appears we may have confidence and not shrink from him in shame at his coming" (I John 2:28). Note: "abide in him, so that . . . we may have confidence and not shrink from him." In other words, he tells us to be at home with Him. Is it possible to be in Him and yet lack confidence, to feel a sort of shrinking from Him? Yes, it is possible to be not at home in your Home. Jesus Christ is our home, the soul's homeland, but many have not become truly naturalized in Him. They keep thinking of their own unworthiness—keep looking at themselves. This is a mistake. It is true you are not worthy of being in Him; nobody is. Our confidence is not in ourselves, but in Him. He is worthy—"Worthy is the Lamb"—and we are worthy of His worthiness. Your confidence will grow as you look at Him. When Peter kept his eyes on Jesus he walked on the water, but when he took his eyes off Jesus and thought of the wind and the waves and his own inadequacy, he began to sink. Look at Jesus and you can walk on anything.

When I was small, a big bully had me down and was pummeling me. I was hopeless. But suddenly the tide turned. My big brother turned the corner and took in what was happening, and the bully, seeing him, turned and fled, with my brother in full pursuit. My tears turned to triumph. I sat there and clapped my hands in triumph—triumph in my brother's triumph. I was strong in his strength, victorious in his victory. If you ask me why I have confidence, I point to Christ. I am worthy in His worthiness. "Bold I approach the eternal Throne." I let my full weight down on the fact that He has me; therefore I have Him and all He has. The shrinking is not humility—it is disloyalty, treason.

O Jesus, Master, the sinful, the timid, the shrinking, were at home in Thy presence. Thy forgiving grace covered all their sin and shame and they stood before Thee at home in Thy forgiveness. They weren't what they were. I thank Thee. Amen.

AFFIRMATION FOR THE DAY: *I am at home in Thy grace; I never can be at home in my worthiness.*

"WE SHALL BE LIKE HIM"

"Beloved, we are God's children now; it does not yet appear what we shall be, but we know that when he appears we shall be like him, for we shall see him as he is. And every one who thus hopes in him purifies himself as he is pure" (I John 3:2-3). "And every one who thus hopes in him"—"thus hopes in him"—to what does "thus" refer? The "thus hopes" refers to the hope of being like Him. Because you hope to be like Him, you purify yourself as He is pure—according to His standard and type of purity.

This completely answers the charge of some against Christianity that it is a reward morality. A South American sceptic said to me: "You Christians have to be bribed to be good. You have to have heaven dangled before your eyes before you will be moral and righteous." This is true of some brands of Christianity, but it has nothing to do with New Testament morality. Here the supreme motive is to be like Him, and because we want to be like Him we purify ourselves according to His purity. The reward is a type of being—to be like Him. The payoff is in the person. If we are like Him it would be an insult to offer any outer reward, for if we are like Him we have everything, including heaven. Where He is, there is heaven, and anyone like Him would be in heaven even if he were in hell.

If to be like Him is the goal, then it determines the quality of the motive for morality. We will slough off anything that keeps us from being like Him. No higher motive for morality is possible. Search the motives for morality, and they all fade into insignificance before this one: "I want to be good because He is good and pure, and He is the center and the motive of my morality." To be in Christ is to have a passionate desire to be like Christ in character and life and disposition.

O Lord Jesus, one look at Thee and I renounce everything that comes in the way of my being like Thee. Everything I want I see there. Outside Thee is hell. Inside Thee is the heaven of goodness. Strip me of all that makes me unlike Thee. Amen.

AFFIRMATION FOR THE DAY: *My one and only motive for morality is to be like Him.*

"PURIFIES HIMSELF AS HE IS PURE"

We must spend another day on this verse: "But we know that when he appears we shall be like him, for we shall see him as he is. And every one who thus hopes in him purifies himself as he is pure" (I John 3:2-3). Note: "We know that when he appears we shall be like him, for we shall see him as he is"—the assumption underlying this is tremendous. It is this: If you really see Him as He is, you simply cannot become other than like Him. Everything else will fade out, and this will possess you. He will be so overwhelmingly beautiful and gracious that you cannot do other than fall at His feet and cry out to be like Him. Coercion? No, it is the coercion of reality upon unreality. Unreality collapses in the presence of reality.

Then the reason we are not like Him is that we do not see Him as He is. We see a distorted caricature of Him—a kill-joy, a pale Galilean at Whose breath the earth is turned to ashes, a No, a cosmic policeman with a heavy nightstick raised, the all-seeing eye watching for faults and sins, a dead Jew Who taught a code of love and died of a broken heart, a dead issue in a world of progress. These are only a few of the mistaken views we have of Him.

Some asked, "Why wasn't Gandhi a Christian?" The reply is that he never really saw Jesus through the racialism of South Africa. The fact is that when Gandhi in that next world sees Jesus as He is, he will probably fall at His feet and say, "My Lord and my God."

One of the leading Communists of India came to our Ashram at Sat Tal and spent some days. He said to his companion at the close of his visit: "Why these people really expect to get me sooner or later. That impressed me most." Yes, we expect to get everybody, for if they really see Him as He is, they will want to be like Him. Now they are seeing something else.

O Blessed Lord Jesus, when the scales of misinformation and caricature fall from our eyes and we really see Thee, we cannot but seek Thee and want to be like Thee. If we don't want to be like Thee we will not want to live, and so, perish. Amen.

AFFIRMATION FOR THE DAY: *When I see Jesus as He is, I can't stand seeing myself as I am—I must change.*

"NO ONE WHO ABIDES IN HIM SINS"

"You know that he appeared to take away sins, and in him there is no sin. No one who abides in him sins; no one who sins has either seen him or known him" (I John 3:5-6). This brings us face to face with our chief problem: sin. It is a very unpopular word in some circles, but an all-important problem in all circles everywhere. What is sin? I asked that of a Hindu, and he reached up, broke off a twig of a tree, and said: "That is sin. I have hurt life." His definition of goodness was not to hurt life—an impossible and twisted standard, for in all the water he drank and the food he ate, though he was a vegetarian, he took life in the water, in the grain, and in the plant. What is sin?

It is according to your standard of goodness. My goodness is Jesus Christ. When you ask me what is good, I do not add virtue to virtue; I think of Jesus of Nazareth. He is good incarnate. Therefore sin is any departure from that goodness. Anything that is un-Christlike is sin. The method of keeping from sin is to abide in Him—"No one who abides in him sins." Never sins? The verb "sins" is present continuous—habitually sins. He may sin as an aberration, as a momentary fall, but if he hates it and loathes it and repudiates it and repents of it, it is not what this verse means when it speaks of "sins." This verse means willful and deliberate and continuous sin. In another book I said that one of the differences between a sheep and a pig is that if a sheep falls into a mud hole it bleats to get out, but if a pig falls into the same mud hole it wallows in it and loves it. You can tell to which you belong by your reaction to a fall. If you fall, and fall on your knees, you are still His even though the relationship is upset for the moment. The relationship is still there; you are His. If you stumble, then stumble into His arms, and He will restore and forgive you and teach you a lesson out of the stumble.

O Jesus Savior, if we are not saved from sin we are not saved from anything. Then save us from sin—all sin. When we sin against Thee we sin against ourselves. I consent for Thee to save me from every sin. In Thy name. Amen.

AFFIRMATION FOR THE DAY: *A simple remedy to keep from sinning is to abide in Him.*

"IN HIM THERE IS NO SIN"

We must turn back a verse: "You know that he appeared to take away sins, and in him there is no sin" (I John 3:5). "In him there is no sin"—that sentence could not be used of any being who has existed on this planet except One. "For all have sinned." Jesus was the sinless exception to our common humanity. All human beings on our planet, if they pass on into goodness, have to pass out of a once broken, disrupted life through repentance and a new birth. All except Jesus. He told His disciples to pray: "Our Father . . . forgive us our debts," but He never prayed that prayer. "When you pray . . . pray then like this." It was their prayer, not His. On the cross He did not cry for forgiveness for Himself; He dispensed forgiveness: "Father, forgive them." After two thousand years when we go to the account to pick a flaw in His moral character we go away smiting our breasts and saying: "God have mercy on me a sinner." Into none of His words does there creep a sense of guilt or estrangement. He shares our temptations, minus our falls. He was acutely aware of sin, but not of any in His own life. "Which of you convicteth Me of sin?" He asks, and the ages are silent. There was none.

"And in Him there is no sin." Sin and evil have met their match, His footprint is upon their necks—He has conquered them. He can and does conquer them in us. "He appeared to take away sins." My first sermon in India fifty-three years ago was upon this text: "Thou shalt call His Name Jesus, for He shall save His people from their sins." Not *in* their sins, but *from* their sins. He saves you if He saves you from your sins. If not, He is not your Savior. I call Him a Savior because He saves me from what I don't want to be, to what I want to be. This is verified knowledge.

My Savior, I surrender the sins—You take them away. I consent. You give the power. Sin shall have no dominion over me, because You have dominion over me. I cannot save myself, but I can consent. You are the Savior. Amen.

AFFIRMATION FOR THE DAY: *I am saved from sin if I remain in the Savior from sin.*

GOD'S HIGHEST COMMANDMENT:
BELIEVE IN JESUS!

"And this is his commandment, that we should believe in the name of his Son Jesus Christ and love one another, just as he has commanded us" (I John 3:23). This is very interesting and important, for it seems that God is here pointing us, through the apostle, to two things: That we believe in the name of His Son Jesus Christ, and that we love one another. God is telling us to believe in His Son! In one place Jesus tells us to believe in God: "Let not your hearts be troubled; believe in God, believe also in me." Here God says, "Believe in the Name of Jesus Christ, My Son." The fact is that God could not give a higher commandment than just that. If you believe in the name (character) of Jesus, then everything comes out right concerning God and man and life. If you don't believe in the name of Jesus, if you take some other key for life, then everything comes out wrong concerning God and man and life. Jesus is God's self-disclosure—He is the truth about God. Moreover, He lifts up in His own person and teaching the underlying principles of the moral universe. He summed them up in Himself. He is the revelation of Life; live by Him and you live; if you do not you perish. So literally God could not say anything higher than, "Believe in the Name of Jesus"! Nor can we say anything higher than just that. We call that evangelism. It is just sense—common and uncommon—it is sense.

The second: "Love one another." Those two things—believe and love—put the whole of the Christian faith into simplicity itself. Believe in the kind of God, the kind of man, the kind of life, you see in Jesus. Love each other the way He loved, and nothing more is required or necessary. That is it! It need not be added to or subtracted from.

O Jesus Lord, when our eyes fall on thee in loving trust and surrender and obedience, then we can say to those eyes: "Blessed are our eyes for they see"! They see what the ages have longed to see. We see and are satisfied forever. Amen.

AFFIRMATION FOR THE DAY: *Believe in Jesus and love people—those two things are the alternate beats of the Christian heart.*

THE HIGHEST END RESULT

"All who keep his commandments abide in him, and he in them" (I John 3:24). This follows yesterday's verse and adds something to it. Yesterday's verse said: "this is his commandment, that we should believe in . . . Jesus . . . and love one another." Believe and love! If we do these two things, two results will follow: We will abide in Him and He will abide in us. If the two commandments, believe and love, are the Christian faith reduced to simplicity and profundity, then these two things—We will abide in Him and He will abide in us—reduce that faith to its greatest simplicity and profundity as far as end results go. Nothing can be higher than for us to abide in Him and He in us. I want nothing beyond that and I can have nothing beyond that. If I have those two things I have no problems. I have nothing but possibilities.

We saw that for us to abide in Him means to abide in life, and for Him to abide in us means that life abides in us. God is affirmed as God, and we are affirmed as man. A great God and a great man live together in right relationships.

This is no esoteric, inner-circle business—it is open to all: "All who keep his commandments abide in him, and he in them." That is as widesweeping and all-embracing as "whosoever believes in Him shall not perish." This breaks down the walls and opens the highest to all—all who will believe and love. If the "whosoever" passage is the gospel of invitation, this passage of "all" is the gospel of participation. We can participate in the highest thing for man—he in Christ and Christ in him—and there are no qualifications of age, sex, race, or standing—it is open to all. If we weren't so used to hearing this we would begin to dance and throw our hats in the air. My heart does sing—sing with the deepest joy known to man.

Dear Father, Thou dost ask me to believe and love, and nothing is easier than when I look at Thy Son. Nothing seems to be possible but to do just those two things. Looking at Him they become natural. I am grateful! Amen.

AFFIRMATION FOR THE DAY: *Soul of mine, learn this: Nothing higher in this universe than to abide in Him and He in me—nothing!*

"BY THE SPIRIT WHICH HE HAS GIVEN US"

"And by this we know that he abides in us, by the Spirit which he has given us. . . . By this we know that we abide in him and he in us, because he has given of us his own Spirit" (I John 3:24; 4:13). This emphasizes the method of knowing that we are in Him and He in us—we know by the Spirit which He has given us. We may have questions about the sufficiency and reality of our believing and loving. The Holy Spirit gives assurance. "The Spirit bears witness with our spirit"—not bears witness to, but *with* our spirit. We say, "Yes, I do believe and love," and the Spirit says, "Yes, you do believe and love." Then there is the double witness and the double assurance—God and man witness to the same fact. Then we are sure we are sure and certain we are certain.

A young minister was troubled. He had been brought up to believe that you must experience what you preach. Then he took a course that emphasized that we are to preach the word, and the word is bigger than the bearer. He then would have the assurance of the word whether or not he had any assurance of the Spirit. He could preach the word though he himself was full of conflicts. This gave him comfort, but not assurance. Assurance comes through the Spirit. He was preaching a Holy Spiritless Christianity. It was the Word become word, but not the Word become flesh, therefore less than the Christian belief and less than the Christian Gospel.

Had the disciples after Pentecost gone across that uncertain world preaching the witness of the word, but not the witness of the Spirit, they would have been uncertain men preaching to uncertain men about an uncertain gospel. But they could say: "This is that"—this which we experience is that which is written in the Word. Without the witness of the Spirit they would have had to say, "That is that," not "this is that."

O Holy Spirit, we thank Thee that Thy assurance assures us with a divine assurance. Our questionings drop away and we stand in wonder, love, and praise. We thank Thee for the witness of the Word, we thank Thee for the witness of the Spirit. Amen.

AFFIRMATION FOR THE DAY: *The Spirit cannot witness* through *me unless He witnesses* to *me.*

"FOR HE WHO IS IN YOU IS GREATER"

"Little children, you are of God, and have overcome them; for he who is in you is greater than he who is in the world" (I John 4:4). This verse technically does not belong to the "in Him" passages, but actually it does, for in mentioning "he who is in you" it presupposes you are in Him—for you cannot have Him in you unless you are in Him. That point needs to be re-emphasized as we draw near to the close of our study. He cannot abide in us unless we first abide in Him. To abide in Him means self-surrender—pulling up the roots from a self-centered life and putting them into Christ, making you a Christ-centered person. You cannot ask Christ to walk into an unsurrendered ego. He comes in to take over and not to be alongside of. He is Lord.

"For he who is in you is greater than he who is in the world." Note that it says "in you," and not "for you." The difference is important. A woman said: "God must have been with me in coming to this Ashram. I found exactly forty dollars in my husband's pocket, and since it was the exact amount I needed to come I took it. If it hadn't been the exact amount I wouldn't have taken it." There is no "if" in this: "*For* he who is in you." The other part is certain too: "is greater than he who is in the world." All reality is behind you if you're in Him, and nothing is behind you if you are in the world. "The world passes away, and the lust of it; but he who does the will of God abides forever" (I John 2:17). Outside the will of God everything perishes. Inside the will of God everything is intact. If you would preserve your money or influence, put it into the will of God. Take it out of that will and it perishes like a fish taken out of the water. God's will is the only safe place in the universe.

O Lord God, we are in Thee and thou art in us and therefore we are not afraid of anything in this world. We abide—it passes away, perishes. There is nothing in the world except emptiness. There is nothing in Thee except everything. Amen.

AFFIRMATION FOR THE DAY: *He Who is in me is greater than anything I can meet in this outer world.*

"HIS LOVE IS PERFECTED IN US"

"No man has ever seen God; if we love one another, God abides in us and his love is perfected in us" (I John 4:12). Here we use another verse where we find "God abides in us" instead of "Christ abides in us." The amazing thing is that in the New Testament Christ and God are interchangeable. Jesus is called God: "in the righteousness of our God and Savior Jesus Christ" (II Pet. 1:1). In experience I can't tell where Christ ends and God begins, or where God ends and Christ begins. They blend in experience. This verse says, "No man has ever seen God," and yet Jesus said, "He who has seen me has seen the Father." Contradiction? No, the word "God" is unqualified; no man has seen the unqualified God. In Jesus we see the qualified God—God qualified by Incarnation. Jesus is the human life of God, God simplified, God approachable, God lovable, for He is God loving.

This verse says: "if we love one another, God abides in us and his love is perfected in us." This is an interesting addition: if we love one another, His love is perfected in us. We don't have to perfect our love—that makes us self-conscious and therefore unloving and unlovable. If we simply and sincerely love each other and show it in loving deeds and attitudes, then God's love is perfected in us. Our love is not perfected; God's love is perfected in us. We begin to love with a love not our own. We begin to love impossible things and impossible people. I do not have to perfect my love, I simply let His love be perfected in me. The way it is done is by simply and unself-consciously loving people. That takes the strain out of trying to perfect our love, for where there is straining after being loving, we are not loving. Agape love loves and thus lets the love of God be perfected in us. It is unself-conscious, therefore love, therefore the divine agape.

O Love of God, so pure and changeless, let me love with Thy love. Then it will be simple, genuine, and unpretentious, and as I love, my love will be perfected by Thy love. Oh let me love as Thou dost love. Amen.

AFFIRMATION FOR THE DAY: *I do not have to perfect my love; I have to love people and let the love of God be perfected in me.*

"CONFESSES . . . JESUS"

"Whoever confesses that Jesus is the Son of God, God abides in him and he in God" (I John 4:15). This adds something very important to our being in Christ. Interestingly enough, John now slides almost imperceptibly from being in Christ to being in God. He uses them interchangeably as though they were one. And they are! Nothing is more important than that—to be in Christ is to be in God. Then you can't go beyond Christ, or apart from Christ if you are to be in God. He is an ultimate!

How do you stay in God and in Christ? The text answers: "Confesses . . . Jesus"—confesses Him as the Son of God, not an example, or doer, but as the Son of God, no less.

Why this confession of Jesus? Is it arbitrary?—a potentate who wants to be acknowledged as supreme? Or is there an inherent necessity to confess Christ if you want to share Christ? Can you share Him without confessing Him? The answer is No.

If the outer without the inner is hypocrisy, so the inner without the outer is also hypocrisy. The whole life must be one—inner and outer. You may be a secret believer in Jesus, but you will be in a belief; you will not be "in Jesus," for to be in Him means to confess Him by both word and life.

The law of life is: "There is nothing covered that shall not be revealed"—what is within shall come out for good or ill. If loyalty to Christ is covered, it soon turns to disloyalty and is not there as loyalty, hence there is no "in Christ." It is a law of the mind that that which is not expressed dies. Expression deepens impression. Nothing is ours till we share it. All Christians are confessional Christians or they are not Christians, except in name.

O Jesus my Lord, how can we love Thee without confessing Thee? Shall the sun's rays refuse to confess the sun? The child deny its parent? Sooner shall these happen than that I should refuse to confess thee, my Lord and my God. Amen.

AFFIRMATION FOR THE DAY: *I shall confess Jesus today by thought, deed, and word.*

"HE WHO ABIDES IN LOVE"

"God is love, and he who abides in love abides in God, and God abides in him" (I John 4:16). This brings us to the very culmination of the revelation in Christ. God is identified as love. God is love, and to abide in love is to abide in God and God to abide in us. Nothing higher can be said of God.

When that phrase was about to be written, all heaven bent over in anticipation to see whether John would really write it, for it had never been said before in human history. When John did write it, heaven broke out in applause: "They've got it. They have really seen it—God is love." That was the high-water mark in Revelation—nothing higher, for it revealed the very nature of God. God not only loves, He is Love and couldn't do an unloving thing without violating His own nature. He loves us whether we are good, bad, or indifferent. He loves us. He loves us even though He cannot approve of us.

Then to abide in God and have Him abide in us is to love—to abide in love, not to be in love one moment and in temper the next moment, but to abide in love as our constant home and atmosphere and life attitude. Strangely enough, psychiatry would agree with this verse: "He who does not love remains in death" (I John 3:14). Those who do not love remain in a living death—the hell of conflict and disruption and mental and emotional anguish. That verse about remaining in death if you do not love is the most widely corroborated verse in literature, corroborated from tens of thousands of doctors' offices and psychiatric couches—and more, from the persons who walk around in a living death without love, living corpses. Everything is saying, "Love or perish." Remember who first said it, and fall at His feet in surrender and submission.

Dear Lord, it is all so simple. Help me to abide in love in every situation, all the time. If I do, nothing else matters. This is the solution for everything! Then help me to make it my life rule. Amen.

AFFIRMATION FOR THE DAY: *This is my religion simplified: Abide in love and thus abide in God. Nothing simpler and nothing profounder.*

"HE WHO HAS THE SON HAS LIFE"

"And this is the testimony, that God gave us eternal life, and this life is in his Son. He who has the Son has life; he who has not the Son has not life" (I John 5:11-12). As we come down to about the end of our verses on "in Christ" the search is drawing to a conclusion—and the verdict is a very uncompromising one: "God gave us eternal life, and this life is in his Son. He who has the Son has life; he who has not the Son has not life." No more terrible conclusion can ever be reached. This is the conclusion of conclusions. Is it harsh, arbitrary, and imposed on life, or is this the verdict that life itself is rendering? Did this scripture just record it? I am persuaded that this verse is true, and that it is recording what life itself is deciding: In Christ we have life; outside Christ we have death. Dogmatic? No, verified experience!

Anyone can verify it for himself. Let anyone go out and put it to a test. Let him say the un-Christian thing, think the un-Christian thing, and act in an un-Christian way in every situation for a week. Then let him report on how he got on. I said that once to a hardboiled reporter, and he snorted, "Shucks, you'd be bumped off before the end of the week." If no man bumped you off, then life would bump you off, for life would tie you in knots inevitably. Life won't work in any way but His way. I find the Hindus of India say more than anything else in any discussion of religion: "Well, all religions are the same. All roads lead to the top of the mountain. All lead to God." This statement is a statement, not a testimony. Life says something else, and what it says is exactly what this Scripture says: "He who has the Son has life; he who has not the Son has not life."

O Jesus my Lord, I hear Thee say, "I am the Way," and life echoes back and says, "Thou art the Way." We cannot buck life and not get hurt. Then help me to walk in Thy Way—the Way of love, this day and always. Amen.

AFFIRMATION FOR THE DAY: *The lines are closing in, life is rendering its verdict: "He who has the Son has life."*

HE HIMSELF IS THE ANSWER

"I write this to you who believe in the name of the Son of God, that you may know that you have eternal life. And this is the confidence which we have in him, that if we ask anything according to his will he hears us. And if we know that he hears us in whatever we ask, we know that we have obtained the requests made of him" (I John 5:13-15). Apart from this and another passage in John's Gospel there is almost no mention of prayers being answered in the "in Christ" passages. Why? We would have thought that this would be the main emphasis, for in many minds that is the main desire—to be in Christ so that you will have your prayers answered.

The reason seems to be this: When you are in Christ and Christ is in you, you have the answer. He Himself is the Answer! When you have Him you have everything you need—plus. While you are in Him your needs are automatically supplied. "My God will supply every need of yours according to His riches in glory in Christ Jesus." Anyone who is in Christ Jesus has every need supplied and guaranteed if you are in Him.

This passage takes that for granted and speaks in the next verse about praying for a brother who sins. The account says, "he will ask, and God will give him life for those whose sin is not mortal" (I John 5:16). This verse points to requests made of Him as requests for others who are in mortal danger. It points to intercessory prayer rather than prayer for personal needs. Having those needs guaranteed by the fact of being in Christ you now have a heart "leisured" so you can reach out and take on your soul the needs of others. That is spiritual maturity. And that is a culminating point in being in Christ—you want others to be "in." It is your prayer and your endeavor.

O Father, being in Jesus is heaven and my deepest desire is to bring others in so that they too may taste and know this heaven. My prayer today is that I will find one of those this day and lead him to the heaven of forgiveness and being in Thee. Amen.

AFFIRMATION FOR THE DAY: *Now that I am in Christ my deepest wish is that others may be in too.*

"IN HIM WHO IS TRUE"

"And we know that the Son of God has come and has given us understanding, to know him who is true; and we are in him who is true, in his Son Jesus Christ. This is the true God and eternal life" (I John 5:20). Here the notes are gathered together in one crashing crescendo of conclusion: "The Son of God has come; He has given us understanding in general; He has given us understanding in particular, to know Him Who is true; and we are in Him Who is true; and we are in His Son Jesus Christ; this is the true God and eternal life." No more resounding climax could ever be reached.

These conclusions are cosmic in their sweep and importance: (1) We know that the Son of God has come—not will come, has come. The Hindus are looking for the Nishkalank Awatar—the spotless Incarnation—who will be born in Sambhal, Moradabad District. The Jews are looking for a messiah. "Ours is a religion of frustration," said a Jewish rabbi, "for we are looking for a messiah who has not come, and for a kingdom that is not here." Amid this vast uncertainty of expectation and frustration we stand and say, "The Son of God *has* come." (2) And He has come to give us understanding, to know Him Who is true—not to know about Him, but to know Him personally. (3) And we are in Him Who is true, in His Son Jesus Christ. We not only know Him, we are possessed by Him and we possess Him—we are in Him and He is in us. (4) This is the true God and eternal life. Note the "this," not "that" in history or off in heaven, but "this," here, present, within me. I am no longer seeking God, I've found Him; or rather, He has found me. This, this, this! (5) And eternal life. The eternal life is not merely a future life—a "that" in heaven; it is a "this," a present possession now. Eternal life in heaven is a fruit of this blossom now! Thus John puts on the capstone of revelation. No greater capstone than that. This is it!

O Father God, Thou hast disclosed Thy heart in Thy Son. In Him we see reality and nothing but reality. In Him we see Love and nothing but Love. In Him we see ourselves, growing up in Him in all things. What a destiny! Amen.

AFFIRMATION FOR THE DAY: *"This" that I find in Christ is the true God—all else is unreality.*

THE TRIBULATION, THE KINGDOM,
AND THE PATIENT ENDURANCE

We pass by two verses in II John: "Any one who goes ahead and does not abide in the doctrine of Christ does not have God; he who abides in the doctrine of Christ has both the Father and the Son" (II John 9). Here "in Christ" was transformed into "in the doctrine of Christ," and if you are "in the doctrine of Christ" you have "both the Father and the Son." This is the position of many today—correct doctrine and you are "in," otherwise not. This doesn't necessarily follow. Correct doctrine may point to Christ and surrender and obedience to Him, but it may stop you at itself, in which case it becomes an idol.

We come now to one of two passages in Revelation: "I John, your brother, who share with you in Jesus the tribulation and the kingdom and the patient endurance. . . " (Rev. 1:9). He shared "in Jesus" three things: the tribulation, the kingdom, and the patient endurance. First "the tribulation"—that strikes them first. But "the Kingdom" is beneath their feet; they are steadied, so there is "patient endurance," power to face the tribulation.

This Kingdom element in being in Jesus is important. Apart from the Kingdom element the fact of being in Christ is personal and individual, but lacks corporate and cosmic emphasis. If being in Christ means being in the Kingdom, then that supplies just the needed universal and corporate emphasis.

To be in Jesus is to be in the Kingdom. Jesus is the Kingdom personalized; they are one. He used interchangeably "For my sake" and "for the kingdom's sake." This means that not only divine goodness and love look out of His eyes, but divine power and authority also are in those eyes. "All authority is given unto me in heaven and on earth" is more than an exaggerated saying. It is fact. He is the Alpha—the Christ of the Beginning—and the Omega—the Christ of the final Word.

O Lord of the Kingdom, Thou art the answer to our individual longings, and Thou art the answer to our corporate longings—longings for a total answer, to the total needs. Thou art the Answer—full stop. I thank Thee. Amen.

AFFIRMATION FOR THE DAY: *When I am in Christ I am in the Kingdom—the Person and the Order coincide, thus meeting my personal and social needs.*

"IN THE LAMB'S BOOK OF LIFE"

"But only those who are written in the Lamb's book of life" (Rev. 21:27). "In the Lamb's book of Life"! Names written in the book of Life of the God Who gave Himself as a sacrifice to redeem men!

There are just two books in the universe. They are the only two books that count, and every man's name is in one or the other. The books are "The Lamb's book of life" and "The self's book of death." There are just two groups of people in the world—those who make themselves God, who are centered in themselves as God, who refuse to surrender themselves and insist on asserting themselves and working out from themselves as God. Their names are written in the self's book of death. The verdict has been pronounced: "Whoever would save his life will lose it." The other group are those who are humble enough to renounce themselves as God and surrender themselves to the acceptance of the self-giving of God in the Cross. They are humble enough to receive the gift of God. Their names are written in the Lamb's book of life. They live, for they come under the law: "Whoever loses his life . . . he will save it." They live now and will live eternally. The other group perishes—it perishes now and will perish forever.

The Lamb's book of life! That book is now open for checking up to see if your name is there, and for registration. Your name is there if you are in Christ. You are in Christ if you have surrendered your self to Christ, with all you have—you are His. You are out of Christ if the self is on the throne of your life, no matter how religious you may be. If the self is on the throne, then you are registered in the book of death, for everything out of Christ is subject to decay and death. Everything in Christ is under the law of life—it is written in the Lamb's book of life. This life is spelled with a capital "L"—it is Life.

O Lamb of God, Thou art the God of the great self-giving, and Thy self-giving has broken me down. Thy self-giving has caught on within me. I give myself to Thyself in the deepest self-giving of which I am capable. I thank Thee. Amen.

AFFIRMATION FOR THE DAY: *My name is written in the Lamb's book of life if two words are written across my heart: "In Christ."*

HE STEPPED OUT OF CHRIST

The thesis of this book has been that in Christ there is life and outside Christ there is death. This is not a doctrine imposed on life; it is a fact of observation and experiment. Step into Christ and you step into life; step out of Christ and you step into death. News was brought to me of a man, happy, adjusted, and useful when in Christ. He stepped out of Christ, however, became a different person, took to drink, divorce followed, and then he drove his car over a cliff to his outer death.

Every road that leads away from Christ has a precipice at the end of it. In Christ there is nothing but life and outside Christ there is nothing but death. We see that fact at work now. The question arises, What will happen after death? Does this process of death continue after death until those who live in spiritual death finally become death and perish? What is the future of those who live in Christ, and those who live outside Christ?

Various answers are given. I will give mine in the light of what I conceive to be the Christian gospel, but first we must look at some other answers.

First, the answer of the materialistic secularist. Life is over when this life is over. Man is a chemical combination, and life is no more than a flame which comes from chemical combination and combustion, and when the flame dies we die. This view has the answer in itself—then ultimately *we* are no more important than a combination of chemicals. Life is cheapened while it lives, and it is extinguished when it dies. Anything that cheapens life in this way is a cheap view of life.

Blessed Father, we cannot believe that this life within us is just a chemical combination. We feel that when we hunger for Thee it is a hunger kindled by Thee. We are made by Thee, for Thee, and are restless until we rest in Thee. Amen.

AFFIRMATION FOR THE DAY:
> *"Life is real! Life is earnest!*
> *And the grave is not its goal;*
> *Dust thou art, to dust returnest*
> *was not spoken of the soul."*

THE ANSWERS ABOUT LIFE AFTER DEATH

We are examining the answers about life after death. We know that we are too big to find our final goal in a narrow grave. The next answer is Reincarnation. There are those who believe that since this life is too short and too indeterminate to work out our final destiny we will come back again—be reborn on a higher or lower scale of existence according to our deeds—our karma. India has been the center of belief in reincarnation, except that the Hindus believe in transmigration as well. Reincarnation teaches that you come back in human form, while transmigration teaches that you may go below the level of the human to the level of animals or birds. I reject both reincarnation and transmigration for the following reasons. (1) The Christian Scriptures do not teach either one. The fact that Moses and Elijah came back on the Mount of Transfiguration teaches survival, but not reincarnation. When Jesus said: "If you are willing to accept it, he is Elijah," speaking of John the Baptist, He does not teach reincarnation, but only that John came in the spirit and power of Elijah. He was not Elijah.

(2) Reincarnation would be a very poor remedial system. There is no memory of previous births. Therefore if you are being rewarded or punished for deeds done in a previous birth, it is a poor system that would reward or punish you without any connecting link of memory between reward or punishment. Suppose a judge would punish or reward you and not tell you what for? It is true that some have claimed they have fleeting memories of this, that, and the other regarding a previous birth, but these are precarious and doubtful. Everybody should remember.

O Father God, we need light on the future. The half-lights leave us in confusion. Show us the direction we are going, and the goal. We want to walk into the future with sure and certain tread. In Jesus' name. Amen.

AFFIRMATION FOR THE DAY: *I need not reincarnation, but regeneration in this incarnation.*

VARIOUS ANSWERS

We look at another answer regarding the future: Universalism. Universalism teaches us that everybody will be saved finally, that salvation is universal. Those who hold this doctrine feel that the love of God cannot fail. But it can fail. It failed in the case of Judas, for the will of man is free and can decide for or against the love of God. God cannot save a person against his will, for if He saved that person against his will he wouldn't be saved. Kant said: "There is nothing good but a good will, and there is nothing bad but a bad will." God cannot coerce a bad will, for it wouldn't be a will after it was coerced. Man can continue to refuse to obey God, and he will therefore be lost. Universalism is wishful thinking, and contrary to the facts as we know them at work now.

Another answer is that those outside of Christ will burn in hell forever, literally. This literalism has been responsible for a great deal of heartache and questioning concerning the character of God. If universalism makes the love of God too loose, literalism makes the love of God too rigid and vindictive. There is a view that is more consistent with the love of God and more consistent with the laws we see at work now.

This view would not do away with hell, but would put the responsibility for it where it belongs—on the person who persistently and continuously rebels against God. I don't know where hell ends, but I certainly know where hell begins. Sin is hell begun. It is a state before it is a place. Anyone who is living in sin is living in hell now. You take that state of sin out with you into the next life, and you will get a place corresponding to the inner state. Hell is portable. God doesn't give it to you; you choose it.

O God, when we sin we sin not only against Thee, but also against ourselves. We are trying to live life in a way it was never intended to be lived. So we sin against life—our life—when we sin against Thee. Forgive us that we hurt Thee and ourselves. Amen.

AFFIRMATION FOR THE DAY: *The good is good for us and the bad is bad for us.*

PUNISHMENT IS SELF-INFLICTED

We are considering what happens to those who die outside Christ. One thing we can be sure of is that everybody will have an adequate chance to say yes or no to the love of God. Many have never had such an adequate chance. Will they be denied that chance? Knowing the love of God as seen in Jesus, we can say that that is impossible. Certainly the love of God is not exhausted in this life. When people have not had an adequate chance in this life, they will be given an adequate chance in another.

I do not say they will take it. They often refuse it in this life, and they may refuse it in the next life. They may persistently refuse it. In which case death follows that refusal—spiritual and physical death. If that process is kept up long enough, would the personality decay? Would it finally destroy itself? Would it render itself unfit to survive? From what we see now, the answer would have to be yes. The moment a person steps out of Christ a change takes place—for the worse! Deterioration sets in. If that process is kept up long enough the personality will deteriorate to the point of extinction. The personality will perish. "God so loved the world that he gave his only Son, that whoever believes in him should not perish but have eternal life." The opposite of eternal life is to perish. The punishment is the perishing. That punishment is self-inflicted—God doesn't do it; we do it! We light the fires that are not quenched till we burn up our very persons. We allow the worm that "dieth not" to eat away our personalities until we perish. The life forces are snuffed out and the personality is gone.

O God, our Father, we see that the most serious thing in this sin business is that it separates us from Thee—from Thee Who art life. We embrace death when we embrace sin. Help me this day—and always—to embrace Thee and life. Amen.

AFFIRMATION FOR THE DAY: *As poison is to the blood, as ugliness is to the eye, as hate is to the heart, so sin is to me.*

GOD SAYING "THY WILL BE DONE"

We come now to the crux of the problem: Can the soul sin so that it actually does die? The Scripture says it can: "The soul that sinneth, it shall die." Does that mean what it says? Can it die eternally? Can it render itself unfit to survive? Can the spark go out?

The word for "iniquity" in the Greek is "amartia," "missing the mark." If the soul misses the mark—misses the mark of his life, Jesus his Lord—by deliberate, willful sinning, does he, like a missile, go into "outer darkness" and burn himself out? Would that be the kindest thing the universe could do—to let him do it—since he in willful sinning would be a torment to himself and others? The continuously sinning soul could not be taken to heaven, for it wouldn't be heaven to him; none of his desires could be fulfilled there. It would be hell to him. If he were there long he would turn heaven into hell. There is simply no alternative except to let the rebellious soul burn himself out.

Would grace follow that soul clear to the end? When the last spark would go out would there be a teardrop on the cheek of grace? Yes, and there would be a sigh upon the lips of grace, "You would not."

Someone has said that in heaven the redeemed gladly say to God, "Thy will be done." In hell God sadly says to the unredeemed, "Thy will be done." God doesn't send any man to hell; the soul sends itself, with God blocking the way at every step and reminding it, by the pangs that sin brings, of the ultimate outcome—death.

O God, my Savior and Redeemer, Thy proddings in conscience are not our punishment—they are our redemption. They are Thy love saying, "Don't." So the pangs are Thy redemption in action. Help us to hear and heed. Amen.

AFFIRMATION FOR THE DAY: *God's laws are the thick hedge along the precipice of life to keep us from destroying ourselves.*

"WHO ALONE HAS IMMORTALITY"

Two passages of Scripture throw a flood of light upon this whole question of the ultimate destiny of those who live and die without Christ, and after an adequate chance to change continue to live in unrepentant rebellion against love. We have looked at them; we must look at them again. The first: "who saved us and called us with a holy calling, not in virtue of our works but in virtue of his own purpose and the grace which he gave us in Christ Jesus ages ago, and now has manifested through the appearing of our Saviour Christ Jesus, who abolished death and brought life and immortality to light through the gospel" (II Tim. 1:9-10).

Here it is said that life and immortality were "brought to light through the gospel." If you accept that gospel and live by it, you have life and immortality. If you do not accept that gospel, you have death and mortality. Immortality is not inherent in us. It is a gift of grace. When you are in Christ you have life and immortality; when you are in yourself you have death and mortality. The choice is ours—life or death—and it is real life and real death.

Another passage: "and this will be made manifest at the proper time by the blessed and only Sovereign, the King of kings, and Lord of lords, who alone has immortality" (I Tim. 6:15-16). Here it is said that Jesus Christ alone has immortality. Immortality is not inherent in us; it is inherent in Him—and in Him alone. When we are in Him we have immortality; when we are out of Him we do not have immortality—we perish. Or as another passage puts it, we suffer "eternal destruction"—self-destruction.

O Blessed Redeemer, save us from self-destruction. Help us in every thought, in every word, in every deed to choose Thee. Then we choose life and immortality, and we live in life and immortality now—hence forever. Amen.

AFFIRMATION FOR THE DAY: *In Christ I do not look for eternal life. I have it now—a quality of being.*

SECOND CHANCE OR ADEQUATE CHANCE?

Another question remains to be faced: Is there another chance to accept Christ as our Lord and Savior in the next life? Of course I do not know; I can only surmise. Knowing the character of God as seen in Jesus Christ, I can surmise this: Everybody will be given an adequate chance to decide whether they will be in Christ or in themselves, either in this life or in the life to come. Some have had an adequate chance in this life to be in Christ and have decided against it. They decide to be in themselves. They have chosen death, and if they take death out with them they will have death forever. Whether or not they have had an adequate chance, only a wise and good God knows. He must decide.

Some have not had an adequate chance, however—the vast non-Christian world; those in so-called Christian lands who for one reason or another never have had a real chance to say yes or no to Him. These, I believe, will be given an adequate opportunity to accept or reject Him.

Can we preach the gospel of a second chance in another life? No, for we are not certain whether the person concerned has had his adequate chance. We can only preach the gospel of an adequate chance—here and there. That leaves the responsibility on the individual; here or there he must decide, and the only safe thing is to decide now. This moment may be your adequate chance.

The conclusion: The redemptive love of God is not exhausted in this life or that, but we may exhaust our ability to receive the love of God—and perish.

O Father God, we thank Thee that if we are willing to receive, even the slightest willingness to receive, Thy grace is there with open arms. Nothing, nothing blocks Thy redemptive grace save our wills, and our wills are ours. Save us. Amen.

AFFIRMATION FOR THE DAY: *If any soul is lost, he will only be able to look within and say, "I am responsible."*

ON BEING "A FIRSTHANDER"

This mysticism of being in Christ is the healthiest and most vital mysticism I know, and I've lived in a land of mysticism the best part of my life. I have never liked the term "mysticism," however—it seems too misty! I prefer the term Rufus Moseley used of himself. He said, "I'm not a mystic, I'm just a firsthander." Being a firsthander describes the deepest thing mysticism is trying to describe, a firsthand relationship with God. It describes a nothing-betweenness, an immediate contact with God, and deeper, a union with Him that is somewhere between purpose and essence. It is more than having the same purpose with God, but is this side of the same essence. You do not become that ultimate reality, but everything in that ultimate reality becomes yours by surrender and receptivity. You live in union with Him, but He is He and you are you. There are moments when the union is so deep that you can scarcely tell where He ends and where you begin, and where you end and He begins. You never topple over and become lost in the ocean of being. It is a union of communion, not a oneness of being.

This mysticism, or firsthandedness, of being in Christ and Christ being in us, produces its own particular type. It is different from the God-centered type of union and communion. The God-centered type, not being anchored in history, is liable to wander amid its own states of consciousness, uncorrected by any norm or pattern. It is not more immediate than that which comes through a historical Person, for its own conceptions become the mediator. Uncorrected they are liable to be wrong and give an incorrect view of God.

O God our Father, we cannot come to a false abstraction called God. We must come to Thee. We cannot be satisfied this side of Thee, nor with anything other than Thee. We want to know Thee face to face and heart to heart. In Jesus' Name. Amen.

AFFIRMATION FOR THE DAY: *I cannot trust my surmises about God; I must have God's self-revelation.*

GOD-CENTERED AND
HOLY SPIRIT-CENTERED MYSTICISM

If the Jesus Christ-centered "firsthandedness" differs from
the God-centered type of mysticism, it also differs from the Holy
Spirit-centered type of mysticism. The Holy Spirit-centered
type suffers from the same shortcoming as the God-centered; it
is not anchored in the historical Person, Jesus, so the
movements centering in the Holy Spirit are liable to get off into
"manifestations." These "manifestations" are not those of the
Spirit of Jesus in human relations, but are manifestations of
"signs"—"tongues," "signs and wonders," "revelations," and
tossing off miracles, interfering with human events, stopping
Hitler, and others. Those who manifest these powers become
seven-day spiritual wonders. They are admired and glorified by
their followers. The Spirit-centered movements become in the
end man-centered. Losing the God-Man as the center, they
often make man the center. The shift is often so gradual that it is
seldom noted. Beginning in the Spirit they end up in trying to
be made perfect by the flesh—by following some so-called
Spirit-endowed man.

In Revelation it is said: "I was in the Spirit, and, lo, a throne
stood in heaven, with one seated on the throne!" (4:2). When we
are in the Spirit we are not autonomous, going where the Spirit
guides, for the Spirit's guidance may be our own subconscious
desires. If we are in the Spirit we need "a throne"—some central
Authority to which we are loyal, supremely loyal. To us the one
on the throne is Jesus Christ—"Jesus is Lord." Without that
throne we are liable to wander off into spiritual vagaries.

**O God, our Father, we cannot come to Thee and be sure it is
Thee except through Thy Son. Holy Spirit, we cannot trust Thy
supposed guidance except it be close to the revelation in Jesus.
O Jesus, when we come to Thee we come to all three. Amen.**

AFFIRMATION FOR THE DAY: *If I come to the Father or the Spirit
without the Son, I miss all three. Jesus is the key.*

"THE WORD MYSTICISM"

There is another mysticism which rejects all mysticism—it is "the Word mysticism." Barthianism, afraid of the subjectivism of mysticism, finds the center of authority in the word. But that "word" is not to be identified with the Bible—the written word. It is the word of God's self-revelation, using the Bible, but not being identified with it. God speaks to us the saving word, but that "word" is the Word become word. It is not the Word become flesh. It is spoken to us from God, but because it is spoken it is the Word become word. It is the mysticism of paradoxical phrases. They mystify one with wordy phrases—the more incomprehensible, the more true!

The "firsthandedness" of our being in Christ and Christ in us is the only safe starting point. You begin with God's authentic self-revelation, which begins with Jesus, the Incarnate. The Incarnation is the key to the whole of the Christian faith. There the Word became flesh. God revealed Himself in understandable terms—human terms. There God spoke, but He spoke not in a verbal revelation, but in a vital revelation. The Word did not become a philosophy of life, a morality, or rules of life; the Word became flesh; the Idea became fact. The revelation was realism. "Behold a great wind blew through the Scriptures, and it stood up, and the book was a Man!"

We don't begin with God, and we don't begin with man; we begin with the God-Man, and in Him we find both God and man. In Him we find the Holy Spirit. In Him we find all.

O Son of the Father, we see the Father in Thee, and perfectly only in Thee. Outside Thee our views of the Father are broken lights of Him—in Thee we see light and only light. We thank Thee that the true light is now shining. Help us to walk in it. Amen.

AFFIRMATION FOR THE DAY: *When I begin with Jesus, the Incarnate, the lowly One, I end with "Jesus is Lord"—the absolute One.*

BIBLE MYSTICISM

We have spoken of the God mysticism, the Spirit mysticism, and the Word mysticism. There is one more we must mention—Bible mysticism. There are those who make the Bible the center of their mysticism. They go into mystical states over assertions about the Bible. This book mysticism has been carried to an extreme among the Sikhs in regard to the *Granth Sahib*, the sacred book of the Sikhs of India. They keep it under mosquito nets, to keep insects away, and fan it to keep the heat away. It is attended like a baby. This is extreme. Those in Christianity who have a book mysticism put the emphasis upon the verbal. It becomes in large measure a literalism. It is the Word become words.

The Word in the Bible is not the words—it is the Word become flesh. These words of the Bible take us beyond the words to the Word—the Word become flesh. The gospel lies in His Person. He didn't bring the good news—He was the good news.

When we begin with the Word become flesh then we find the Bible. It becomes alive with Him. These words of the Bible have been so close to the Word that they become alive with His life. They are vibrant with His vitality; they are vital because they lead us beyond themselves to Him. If they had stopped us at themselves they would have saved their lives and lost them, but the words lose themselves in the Word and find themselves again—they are alive with Him. I believe they are inspired because I find them inspiring. They are a revelation, because they reveal Him.

O Blessed Redeemer, Thou dost redeem me from wrong actions and wrong attitudes and from wrong emphases. Be Thou my central emphasis, and all my problems will begin to come out to solutions, for Thou art my solution. Amen.

AFFIRMATION FOR THE DAY: *I have only one Affirmation: Jesus Christ is my affirmation, my divine yes!*

THE JESUS CHRIST EMPHASIS

In Christ we find both the Father and the Holy Spirit. Out of Him, or apart from Him, we lose both.

When Jesus said, "He who has seen me has seen the Father," it was sober truth. Apart from Jesus you may see abstractions about God, more or less true, but to see the Father—the truth about God—you have to come to the Son. Just as you have to come through the sun's rays before you come to the sun, so you have to come to the manifested God before you can get to the unmanifested God.

You cannot come to the Holy Spirit until you come through Jesus Who gives the Holy Spirit. Go to the Holy Spirit apart from Jesus and you go into all sorts of vagaries and extravagances and all sorts of "manifestations." The Holy Spirit is a Christlike Spirit. The Holy Spirit will make us Christlike persons, for Christ is the pattern.

God could not give the Holy Spirit until the pattern was fixed. "Now this he said about the Spirit . . . for as yet the Spirit had not been given, because Jesus was not yet glorified." The Spirit could be given only when it was clear that the Spirit would make us Christlike persons. Then God could give with both hands.

"One Lord, one faith, one baptism." What was the one baptism? The one Lord was Jesus—"Jesus is Lord"—the one faith was faith in the Lord Jesus, and the one baptism was the one baptism which the Lord Jesus gave. What baptism was that? Jesus did not baptize with water, He saved Himself to give the one baptism—the baptism of the Holy Spirit. He went to the Father and gave the one baptism—the baptism of the Spirit.

O Jesus, my Lord, Thou art today giving the one baptism. Help me not to be content with the shadow and miss the substance. Help me to be a "firsthander"—I want the Holy Spirit and Thou dost want to give me the Holy Spirit. Amen.

AFFIRMATION FOR THE DAY: *Affirm all that Thou hast promised by giving me the mighty affirmation—the affirmation of the Holy Spirit.*

IN JESUS YOU FIND THE FATHER
AND THE SPIRIT

John said of Jesus: "I baptize you with water for repentance, but he who is coming after me is mightier than I . . . he will baptize you with the Holy Spirit and with fire." Again Jesus said: "John baptized with water, but you shall be baptized with the Holy Spirit." When the Holy Spirit was given on the day of Pentecost, Peter said: "This Jesus God raised up, and of that we all are witnesses. Being therefore exalted at the right hand of God, and having received from the Father the promise of the Holy Spirit, he has poured out this which you see and hear" (Acts 2:32-33). This was the one baptism which Jesus came to give—the baptism of the Spirit.

If you have the Christ "firsthandedness" you are sure to find the Holy Spirit if you follow through far enough with Him. It is the intention underlying our relationships with Him. "But this spake He of the Spirit which they who believed on Him were to receive." "Were to receive"—it is in the intention of Christ to give the Holy Spirit.

The emphasis on Jesus Christ as the center of the "firsthandedness" brings both the Father and the Spirit. If the emphasis is on either the Father or the Spirit, however, you miss both because the Incarnate is dimmed.

If the Incarnate Jesus is dimmed, the content of the union with the Father or the Holy Spirit is dimmed and uncertain. The Word become flesh puts the highest content conceivable into the union—it is a union based on Christlikeness. The emergence of a Christlike character is the end product. Nothing higher than that for God or man. It is the acme.

O Jesus, my Lord, when Thou art Lord and I'm wholly Thine everything falls into its own place. I know the Father and I have the Holy Spirit. I have Everything. Help me to be a one-centered person—centered in Thee. In Thy name. Amen.

AFFIRMATION FOR THE DAY: *I have hold of the right end of the stick when I begin with the Cross.*

THE CHRIST-CENTERED EMPHASIS
SPECIALIZES IN CHRISTLIKE CHARACTER

In summing up the soundness of emphasizing being in Christ and Christ's being in us, we may add this: If the emphasis is on God, the tendency will be to try to become identified with God in essence—to become God. India in her quest for union with God has missed the union and has also missed the communion. The Christian in seeking for union as communion has found both the communion and the union—this side of identification.

Those who emphasize the Holy Spirit as the center of the mysticism run off into signs and wonders. Their Mecca is this passage: "And these signs will accompany those who believe: In my name they will cast out demons; they will speak in new tongues; they will pick up serpents, and if they drink any deadly thing, it will not hurt them; they will lay hands on the sick; and they will recover" (Mark 16:17-18). This passage is not a part of the original Gospel of Mark. It is so stated in Moffatt and in the Revised Standard Version. It is a later attempt to piece out the Gospel, which was broken off at verse 8.

In any case, it shows the departure in spirit from the Christian gospel. The signs of a believer are casting out demons, speaking in tongues, picking up serpents, drinking deadly things without harm, and laying on hands to heal the sick. The sign of a believer was a sign and wonder—not one of them a moral quality or a Christian virtue. If these are the signs of a Christian, then the Christian faith deals in signs and wonders instead of Christlike character.

A firsthandedness centered in Jesus specializes in the Christlike spirit, manifested in attitudes, actions, and relationships. Its first fruit is love—love to everybody, including enemies.

Blessed Savior and Lord, when centered in Thee I'm centered in Thy Spirit and mind. Thy Spirit and mind is love. Give me Thy love and only Thy love, for Thy love is the greatest thing on this planet. In Thy Name. Amen.

AFFIRMATION FOR THE DAY: *The greatest thing on this planet is the love of Jesus. I shall manifest it in all my relationships today.*

WE DON'T BEGIN WITH SELF-CONTROL

We have been insisting that this Jesus-centered firsthanded-ness is the soundest approach to God and reality. It is under the constant redemptive correction and conversion of the person of Jesus. It has a Savior at its heart, saving not only from sin and guilt, but also from marginal values which creep into the center and become dominant. He saves from the trivial. By His amazing sanity He keeps His movement and His men from going off into the queer. It is healthy-minded goodness. Sanity and sanctity go hand in hand. In Him they are wedded forevermore. The fruit of that union is "love, joy, peace, patience, kindness, goodness, faithfulness, gentleness, self-control." The first-born is love, and the last-born is self-control.

The Christian way doesn't begin with self-control through the usual way of "know thyself." It begins with: "This is eternal life, that they know thee the only true God, and Jesus Christ whom thou hast sent." It begins by knowing God through and in Jesus Christ. Knowing the Redeemer, you know yourself as a redeemed child of God. Knowing yourself as under redemption you can accept yourself in Him, for it is an acceptable self. You can love yourself since He loves you. So all self-hate, self-loathing, and self-rejection drop away—drop away through the expulsive power of a new affection—love for Jesus Christ.

Then there is self-control as a result of Christ-control. Self-control is last of the fruits, not first as in out-of-Christ procedures. If self-control is first it results in tension and strain—a strained goodness. This way of Christ-control is effortless striving, hence unstrained.

O Jesus, my Lord, when I cease striving and surrender to Thee and let Thy power work in and through me, I'm not sitting on a lid. I let nature caper, for that nature is controlled by Thy easy yoke and Thy light burden. I thank Thee. Amen.

AFFIRMATION FOR THE DAY: *My self-control is rooted in Christ-control, therefore relaxed and receptive—and effective.*

ON BINDING THE STRONG MAN

We ended yesterday by insisting that this form of Christ mysticism is rooted in grace and not in strenuous striving. There is discipline in this way, but discipline is not first. If you put discipline first you are disciplining yourself around an unsurrendered self. This discipline is sitting on a lid, keeping an unsurrendered self down. The way that we are advocating says, first self-surrender, not self-discipline. Then, having shifted the basis of life from yourself to Christ, you can discipline yourself around the new center. This discipline then is not imposed from without, but exposed from within, the result of chosen disciplines as the expression of our love to Him. We submit to disciplines because we have already submitted to Him. "Be subject to one another out of reverence for Christ"—we submit to others and to disciplines out of reverence for Christ. Having submitted to Him we can submit to others out of reverence for Him, and now we can do it without loss of self-respect.

This priority of self-surrender before discipline is seen in Jesus' saying: "But no one can enter a strong man's house and plunder his goods, unless he first binds the strong man; then indeed he may plunder his house" (Mark 3:27). You cannot plunder the strong man's goods unless you first bind the strong man; you cannot overcome the deeds of the strong man—the unsurrendered self, deeds such as wrong reactions, resentments, fears, and so on—until you bind the unsurrendered self by surrender to Jesus. In that case we deal with the roots, not with the fruits; the disease, not the symptoms. After binding the strong man by surrender, taking over his goods is easy.

O Jesus, my Lord, I let Thee bind the strong man within me—my very self. Having that Thou hast my all. Now with the center in Thy hands, we can together mop up the areas of continued resistance. The rest is a victory march. I thank Thee. Amen.

AFFIRMATION FOR THE DAY: *Surrender, once and for all, and continuous, is my watchword and my attitude. What He has, He saves.*

"I'M IN HIM AND HE IS IN ME"

Since grace, not attainment, is written across this approach to God and life, then this way is open to all. This is not for the elite, not for the elect, but for the "whoever will." This possibility of firsthand, saving contact with God through and in Christ is open to all, from the dregs of humanity to the highest moralist on the same terms—surrender!

This is what I mean: Robert Jones, a Negro sentenced to electrocution, was converted and filled with the Spirit. The chaplain said that the first night Robert was in prison one of the hardened criminals brought to his cell was converted. The next night three more were converted, and the last night every one the chaplain could get in to Robert's presence was converted. The chaplain expressed the conviction that if the state would permit Robert to live he would be the greatest colored man of his time, greater even than Booker T. Washington. As he took his seat in the electric chair and was asked if there was anything he would like to say, he said he hoped all of those present would repent and go where he was going. Looking around and seeing the sons of the man he had killed, he told them he did not mean to kill their father, that he was sorry he had struck him, and that he wanted them to forgive him. He went on to say that he was not the same man who struck the blow, but that if they wanted to kill him for what that former man had done it was all right with him. After the cap was put over his head and just before the death lever was pulled, Robert was heard saying, "I'm in Him, and He is in me." The law with its retribution could not touch this deathless thing in a dying man: "I'm in Him, and He is in me. The highest was open to the lowest through Grace.

O Jesus, Lord and Savior, I stand amazed at Thy grace that takes a thief from a cross and translates him into Paradise, and a condemned murderer from a cell and makes him calm and in control in an electric chair. What a Savior! I thank Thee. Amen.

AFFIRMATION FOR THE DAY: *I'm in Him, and He is in me—that makes me impervious to any earthly happening.*

HEADACHES THROUGH LASH OF DUTY

This release from any situation through grace is the most open door to man out of his dilemmas and predicaments I know, or anybody knows. It stretches from a man with straps around him in an electric chair to a highly respectable vice president of an insurance company suffering from severe headaches over a period of years. He was a highly moral man, driven by duty to be good. There was a tinge of the perfectionist in him; he wanted to be perfectly good. He was a good moral man, but his striving for goodness would not allow him to get a firsthand contact with God, and it built up a wall between himself and his wife. They couldn't get close to each other. There was a strange barrier. He was in the hands of a psychiatrist for three and a half years, three times a week, at thirty-five dollars a sitting, with little or no result.

Pagan psychiatry could not probe the real reason, and if it had probed it could not have remedied it. It was this, as his wife whispered it to be before I saw him, "It's his wrong view of religion." He was striving to be good under the lash of duty. He was trying to climb the ladder to God to find Him on the topmost rung of worthiness—the egocentric attempt at salvation. I told him of the other Way, in which God comes down the ladder to us in Incarnation, in Jesus, and meets us, not at the topmost rung, but at the bottom-most rung as sinners. There we are humble enough to empty our hands of our self-striving and self-righteousness and take the gift of God. "It's too simple," he exclaimed in incredulity. He took it, and when we rose from our knees his face was a sunrise. He stood up the next day and announced that his headaches were gone.

O Divine Redeemer, whether I have a black cap over my head or a band of aches around my head, it is the same. Thou art the Savior whether I'm in an electric chair or on a psychiatrist's couch. Thou art the Savior—let that suffice me. I thank Thee. Amen.

AFFIRMATION FOR THE DAY: *Anything that makes me tense and anxious is unchristian. The Christian way is the way of surrender and faith and trust.*

"YOU HAVE YOUR CHRISTIANITY"

We have looked at a Negro youth in an electric chair and at a high executive with a perpetual headache. We take another example—at a time when the props of security go out from beneath us. To be in Christ is the ultimate security.

Two Japanese navy officers met the night defeat came to Japan—one a Shintoist and the other a Christian. The Shintoist said bitterly: "It can't be true. How can Divinity go down in defeat? It is a lie." The Christian went to the Navy Headquarters to find out if it were true. He came back and said it was. The Shintoist replied: "Yes, you have your Christianity; I have nothing but loyalty to the Emperor. If he goes down, I go down too. I will end my life." The Christian took away his pistol. The Shintoist officer went away, and two days later they found him disemboweled. The Christian had something within, held steady, made something out of the defeat. He is now a professor of theology in Kwansie Gakwin University, Kobe, Japan. One was out of Christ and the other was in Christ. Does it matter whether you are in or out?

In a sanitarium a woman was screaming as if in great pain. One of the patients said to a colored maid, "She must be in great pain." "No," said the maid, "her inner environment ain't good." When you are out of Jesus your "inner environment" isn't good. The fish out of water is unhappy; its inner environment isn't good—isn't good because the outer environment has been lost. Being in Christ is being in our real environment. He is our homeland. When we are out of Him we are out of the life for which we are made. We feel orphaned, estranged. The sickness of the world is homesickness, homesickness for God.

O my Lord and Savior, I come to Thee as to my very home. All coming to Thee has the feel of a homecoming upon it. Thou art the end of my life quest. When I arrive at Thee I know I have arrived. All else is beside the point. This is it. I thank Thee. Amen.

AFFIRMATION FOR THE DAY: *Outside of Christ I commit suicide—sudden or slow, I do disintegrate, self-destroyed.*

A SONG TO SING AND A CREED TO BELIEVE

Mankind needs two things: a song to sing and a creed to believe. Perhaps they should be reversed—a creed to believe and a song to sing.

In order to sing, the heart and mind must have something to sing about. A missionary in Korea, while making purchases in a bazaar, unconsciously began to sing. The people gathered around him, and when he finished they asked him to sing another song. He said, "I will, if you will sing one for me." A little girl spoke up and said, "But, sir, we have nothing to sing about." "We have nothing to sing about"—that is the deepest revelation of the heart of the majority of mankind. They have nothing to sing about.

To sing you must feel that the sum total of reality is behind your song—that you voice "the music of the spheres," that you are taking up the song that was sung at creation when the morning stars sang together—the song of creation. We must feel that we are singing the song of the new creation. When we are in Christ we can sing that song of the new creation. We are a part of it. It is working in us.

During the persecution of the Christians in Madagascar some of those who were being hunted hid in a cave. They said to their leader, "We must sing." He replied: "I beg you, brethren, not to sing. Our enemies are hunting us and to sing would give away our hiding place." "But," the Christians replied, "we must sing. We will sing in our minds." So they did! When they were finally discovered and thrown over a cliff, they sang as their bodies hurtled through the air. The early Christian martyrs sang as they marched to their death, "This is the day that the Lord hath made; we will be glad and rejoice in it."

O Jesus, my Lord, I do not deserve to sing. I sing through Thy redeeming grace, and when I sing, I know I'm not singing a surface song. I'm singing creation's and re-creation's song. It comes from the depths, for it comes from being in Christ. Amen.

AFFIRMATION FOR THE DAY: *Affirming what Christ affirms, I affirm what reality affirms; everything backs me and blesses me.*

SINGING "IN SPITE OF"

As we come to our last day together we find ourselves singing the song the redeemed sing on Mount Zion: "They sing the song of Moses . . . and the song of the Lamb." We can sing the song of Moses now, for the law is no longer a club held over us; it is a law written in our hearts—we love to fulfill it for we love Him. The law has turned to love. We can sing about the fulfilled law because we believe in and belong to Him Who is the Lamb—the One Who offered Himself to redeem us. We sing, not because we are worthy, but because He is worthy; we sing, not because of what we have done, but because of what He has done. "Worthy is the Lamb" is our theme song.

Because our song is based on His worthiness it is an incorrigible song. It must be sung or the stones would cry out. An illustration of this incorrigible song, in spite of, is Sarah Perkins, a white-haired missionary who spent five years in a Communist prison in China, thirty-seven months in solitary confinement. She summed it up in these luminous words, "I was not a prisoner of the Communists—I was a prisoner of Jesus Christ." Out of that fact she began to sing. The Communists forbade it. Then she whistled, and they forbade that. Then she hummed, and they forbade that. Then she hummed to herself under quilts. She memorized the whole Gospel of John with a light hidden under quilts. That humming under quilts has been heard in all the world, and that light hidden under quilts is lifted up in all the world. The humming has become a hymn of victory, and that smothered light lightens our pathway to victory!

The French have a saying that "no one can sing unless he sings out of a broken heart." We sing because our broken hearts have been mended, our broken lives remade. We sing because we are in Him—the Redeemer.

O Lord Christ, our Redeemer, we sing because there is literally nothing else to do. It is the only appropriate thing to do. If blows fall they beat the glory out. We sing "in spite of" when we cannot sing "on account of." We sing "Jesus is Lord!" Lord of Everything. Amen and Amen.

AFFIRMATION FOR THE DAY: *My creed and my song are one—my creed: "Jesus is Lord"; my song: "Jesus is Lord!" I'm in Him and He is in me. Hallelujah!*